C000138485

CULTURAL HISTORIES OF CINEMA

This new book series examines the relationship between cinema and culture. It will feature interdisciplinary scholarship that focuses on the national and transnational trajectories of cinema as a network of institutions, representations, practices and technologies. Of primary concern is analysing cinema's expansive role in the complex social, economic and political dynamics of the twentieth and twenty-first centuries.

SERIES EDITORS
Lee Grieveson and Haidee Wasson

ALSO PUBLISHED
Arab Cinema Travels: Transnational Syria, Palestine, Dubai and Beyond, *Kay Dickinson*
Cinema Beyond Territory: Inflight Entertainment and
Atmospheres of Globalisation, *Stephen Groening*
Cinema Beyond the City: Small-Town and Rural Film Culture in Europe,
edited by Judith Thissen and Clemens Zimmermann
Empire and Film, *edited by Lee Grieveson and Colin MacCabe*
Film and the End of Empire, *edited by Lee Grieveson and Colin MacCabe*
Global Mexican Cinema: Its Golden Age, *Robert McKee Irwin and Maricruz Castro Ricalde*
(with Mónica Szurmuk, Inmaculada Álvarez and Dubravka Sužnjević)
The Grierson Effect: Tracing Documentary's International Movement,
edited by Zoë Druick and Deane Williams
Making Movies into Art: Picture Craft from the Magic Lantern to Early Hollywood,
Kaveh Askari
Shadow Economies of Cinema: Mapping Informal Film Distribution, *Ramon Lobato*
Spanish Film Cultures: The Making and Unmaking of Spanish Cinema,
Nuria Triana-Toribio

Films That Sell

Moving Pictures and Advertising

Edited by **Bo Florin, Nico de Klerk and Patrick Vonderau**

•

A BFI book published by Palgrave

First published in 2016 by
PALGRAVE

on behalf of the

BRITISH FILM INSTITUTE
21 Stephen Street, London W1T 1LN
www.bfi.org.uk

There's more to discover about film and television through the BFI. Our world-renowned archive,
cinemas, festivals, films, publications and learning resources are here to inspire you.

PALGRAVE in the UK is an imprint of Macmillan Publishers Limited, registered in England,
company number 785998, of 4 Crinan Street, London N1 9XW. Palgrave Macmillan in the US is a
division of St Martin's Press LLC, 175 Fifth Avenue, New York, NY 10010. Palgrave is a global
imprint of the above companies and is represented throughout the world. Palgrave® and
Macmillan® are registered trademarks in the United States, the United Kingdom, Europe and
other countries.

Cover design: Paileen Currie

Set by couch

This book is printed on paper suitable for recycling and made from fully managed and sustained
forest sources. Logging, pulping and manufacturing processes are expected to conform to the
environmental regulations of the country of origin.
British Library Cataloguing-in-Publication Data
A catalogue record for this book is available from the British Library
A catalog record for this book is available from the Library of Congress

ISBN 978–1–84457–891–7 (pb)
ISBN 978–1–84457–892–4 (hb)

Printed in China

Contents

Acknowledgments

The idea for this book first grew from a workshop, Advertising Film: The Images that Changed Your Life, held at the Nederlands Filmmuseum (now: EYE) in Amsterdam in 2009. We would like to thank Julia Noordegraaf (University of Amsterdam) for initiating the dialogue between archivists and scholars that became the starting point for our own collaboration, and also for a subsequent conference held in cooperation with the Swedish Film Institute in Stockholm in May 2012, Exploring Advertising. This was a lively event, and many participants helped us, articulating ideas for the organisation and structure of this book. We would especially like to recognise the contributions of Mats Björkin, Mats Jönsson, Martin Koerber, Charles McGovern, Anke Mebold, Sean Nixon, Jacob Östberg, Floris Paalman, Amy Sargent and Jon Wengström. Thanks are also due to Jörgen Andersson and Jan Nord (Esprit) and Andreas Hellström (SWE Advertising Agency).

We have been fortunate in having editorial assistance during the production of this book. In this respect, we owe much gratitude to Heather Macdougall. As editors of the Cultural Histories of Cinema series, Haidee Wasson and Lee Grieveson provided determined support from beginning to end. We are grateful to our anonymous readers who offered detailed feedback and astute commentary. This book also benefited from assistance supplied by the BFI's/Palgrave's expert editorial and production team, including Jenna Steventon, Sophia Contento and Nicola Cattini.

Financial aid came from the Swedish Foundation for Humanities and Social Sciences (Riksbankens Jubileumsfond) and Stockholm University.

Notes on Contributors

CASSIE BLAKE is a Film Archivist at the Academy of Motion Picture Arts and Sciences. In 2010 she helped establish the world's largest collection of theatrical trailers on film, the Packard Humanities Institute Collection at the Academy Film Archive. She holds a master's degree in Library and Information Science and has presented on the subject of promotional films at various conferences worldwide. Her curated trailer screenings have been staged in several major cities including Los Angeles, Portland and, most recently, New York, at the Museum of Modern Art.

WILLIAM BODDY is Professor in the Department of Communication Studies at Baruch College and in the Certificate Program in Film Studies at the Graduate Center, both of the City University of New York. He is the author of *Fifties Television: The Industry and Its Critics* (1990) and *New Media and Popular Imagination: Launching Radio, Television, and Digital Media in the United States* (2004) and is currently researching the history of electronic screens outside the home.

ROBERT BYRNE is an independent film preservationist and President of the San Francisco Silent Film Festival. He has worked on restoration projects including *Shoes* (1916), *The Spanish Dancer* (1923), *Twin Peaks Tunnel* (1917), *The Half-Breed* (1916), *The Last Edition* (1925) and *The Phantom of the Opera* (1925). He has published articles and reviews in *FIAF Journal of Film Preservation*, *The Moving Image* and *Nisimazine*. In addition to the San Francisco Silent Film Festival, Robert also serves on the board of directors for the Global Film Initiative and the Film Preservation Society.

DYLAN CAVE is a curator at the BFI National Archive, where he develops the archive's fiction collection and leads in the acquisition of contemporary British features, shorts, music videos and trailers. He regularly contributes to *Sight & Sound* and has written for the preservation journals *The Moving Image* and *Journal of Film Preservation*.

LUCY ČESÁLKOVÁ is an Assistant Professor in the Department of Film Studies and AV Culture at Masaryk University Brno, Czech Republic. She also works as a Research Department Head at the National Film Archive, Prague, and is editor-in-chief of the Czech peer-reviewed film journal *Iluminace*. Her research focuses on nonfiction and non-theatrical cinema, mostly on their utility functions (educational, promotional, instructional, etc.). Currently she is working on a book about Czechoslovakian short films.

SEMA COLPAN is a Research Fellow at the University of Applied Arts and the Ludwig Boltzmann Institute for History and Society, Vienna, and a PhD candidate at the Department of Cultural History and Theory at the Humboldt University of Berlin. Her dissertation focuses on advertising films and their relation to socioeconomic modernisation. She co-edited (with Lydia Nsiah and Joachim Schätz) *Sponsored Films: Strategien und Formen für eine modernisierte Gesellschaft* (2014) and *Kulturmanöver. Das k.u.k. Kriegspressequartier und die Mobilisierung von Wort und Bild* (2015, with Amália Kerekes, Siegfried Mattl, Magdolna Orosz and Katalin Teller).

CATHERINE CORMON is Head of the Collections Management Department at EYE Filmmuseum, Amsterdam. After working for a decade as an assistant film editor, she graduated from the Selznick School of Film Preservation at George Eastman House and received the first Haghefilm Fellowship. She subsequently worked for Memoriav in Switzerland before emigrating to the Netherlands. She has occupied several positions in the Film Collections Department of the Nederlands Filmmuseum and worked as an audiovisual archivist for the Heineken Collection Foundation.

MICHAEL COWAN is Reader in Film Studies at St Andrews University. Focusing primarily on the modernist period in the German and French contexts, his research interests include film and the moving image, visual culture, the body and techniques of subjectivity, media technologies and the avant-garde. Recent and forthcoming publications include *Walter Ruttmann and the Cinema of Multiplicity: Avant-Garde, Advertising, Modernity* (2014); a co-edited collection on Hans Richter; and articles on abstract film and dance, silhouette design in print and film, radio and the emergence of 'political' cinema between the wars, Abel Gance's *La Fin du Monde*, the history and epistemology of the 'cross-section' in Weimar visual culture, and the screen cultures of early advertising film.

NICO DE KLERK is a researcher at the Ludwig Boltzmann Institute for History and Society, Vienna. Before this, he was a film researcher, archivist and curator at the Nederlands Filmmuseum, Amsterdam. He has published widely, as editor, researcher and archivist in international books and journals. He is on the editorial board of *The Moving Image: The Journal of the Association of Moving Image Archivists*. He recently completed his PhD at Utrecht University, the Netherlands, on the performance of public accountability by film heritage institutes.

SKIP ELSHEIMER is the founder of A/V Geeks LLC in Raleigh, North Carolina. In the early 1990s, he began collecting 16mm educational films and now has over 23,000 films in an archive. He also acquired telecine equipment, a variety of videotape machines and video digitising equipment. He has digitised several thousand hours of material from his own collection and for clients such as the Internet Archive, Duke University Special Collections, Stanford University and NASA.

BO FLORIN is an Associate Professor in Cinema Studies at the Department for Media Studies, Stockholm University. Publications include: *Moderna motiv, Mauritz Stiller i retrospektiv* (ed., 2001), *Regi: Victor Sjöström/Directed by Victor Sjöström* (2003) and

Transition and Transformation: Victor Sjöström in Hollywood, 1924–1930 (2013). He has contributed several articles to international journals such as *Film History* and *Montage AV*.

CYNTHIA B. MEYERS is Associate Professor in Communication at the College of Mount Saint Vincent, New York City. She is the author of *A Word from Our Sponsor: Admen, Advertising, and the Golden Age of Radio* (2014) and has written about advertising and broadcasting in journals such as the *Historical Journal of Film, Radio and Television* and the *Journal of Radio and Audio Media;* in the collection *Media Industries: History, Theory, and Method* (2009); and on the blog *Antenna: Responses to Media and Culture.*

CHARLES MUSSER is Professor of Film and Media Studies at Yale University, where he teaches courses on documentary and silent cinema. His books include the award-winning *The Emergence of Cinema: The American Screen to 1907* (1990) and *Edison Motion Pictures, 1890–1900: An Annotated Filmography* (1997). His documentaries include *Before the Nickelodeon: The Early Cinema of Edwin S. Porter* (1982) and *Errol Morris: A Lightning Sketch* (2014).

LYDIA NSIAH is an artist and researcher, currently writing her PhD on rhythm in advertising and industrial films at the Institute of Art and Cultural Studies at the Academy of Fine Arts Vienna. She is a Research Associate at the Film Collection of the Austrian Film Museum, and as a Doc-Team scholarship holder (Austrian Academy of Science) was a Project Collaborator at the Ludwig Boltzmann Institute for History and Society, Vienna. She has published, lectured and exhibited on avant-garde and advertising, commemorative culture and audiovisual arts. (www.lydiansiah.net)

DEVIN ORGERON is Associate Professor and Director of Film Studies at North Carolina State University. He is the author of *Road Movies: From Muybridge and Melies to Lynch and Kiarostami* (2007), co-editor of *Learning With the Lights Off: Educational Film in the United States* (2012) and previously co-edited *The Moving Image* (the journal of the Association of Moving Image Archivists, published by Minnesota Press).

LEENKE RIPMEESTER is a collection specialist for animation and a sales manager of the Film Collection at EYE Filmmuseum, Amsterdam. She completed her PhD, *Permitted Performativities: The Construction of Youth in Music Videos*, at the University of Amsterdam in 2006.

JOACHIM SCHÄTZ is a film scholar and critic living in Vienna. Currently, he's working as a researcher in the project Exploring the Interwar World: The Travelogues of Colin Ross (1885–1945) and writing a dissertation on rationalisation and contingency in industrial and advertising film. Publications include *Werner Hochbaum. An den Rändern der Geschichte filmen* (2011, ed. with Elisabeth Büttner); *Sponsored Films* (issue 2/2014 of the journal *Zeitgeschichte,* ed. with Sema Colpan and Lydia Nsiah).

JEZ STEWART has worked at the BFI National Archive since 2001, focusing on the advertising collection for many years, and since 2010 as the Curator of the animation collection. His writing has been published in FIAF's *Journal of Film Preservation*, and he has contributed to the BFI's DVD booklets and online resources, as well as *Sight & Sound* in print and online.

ARIANNA TURCI is Curator at the Cinémathèque de Toulouse. She is responsible for the conservation, cataloguing, restoration, digitising and valorisation of film and non-film – posters, photos, papers, costumes and pre-cinema objects – collections. From 2006–15 she was an archivist at the Archivio Nazionale Cinema d'Impresa (National Italian Industrial Film Archive), where she was in charge of the conservation, cataloguing and restoration of film collections.

ANDY UHRICH is a Film Archivist at the Indiana University Libraries Moving Image Archive. He is also a PhD student at IU working on a history of film collectors and private methods of film preservation. This chapter comes out of his research into the history of non-theatrical films from Chicago, Illinois, with a specific focus on the intersections of amateur, industrial, documentary and educational film production.

WILLIAM URICCHIO is Professor of Comparative Media Studies at MIT and Professor of Comparative Media History at Utrecht University, the Netherlands. He has written widely on old media when they were new (from early cinema and television to games and interactive documentary). He heads MIT's Open Documentary Lab and the MIT Game Lab.

PATRICK VONDERAU is Professor in Cinema Studies at the Department for Media Studies at Stockholm University. His most recent book publications include *Behind the Screen: Inside European Production Cultures* (2013, with P. Szczepanik), *The YouTube Reader* (2009, with P. Snickars) and *Films that Work: Industrial Film and the Productivity of Media* (2009, with V. Hediger). He is a co-editor of *Montage AV* and a co-founder of NECS – European Network for Cinema and Media Studies.

GREGORY A. WALLER teaches in the Cinema and Media Studies programme at Indiana University in Bloomington, Indiana. He is editor-in-chief of the quarterly journal *Film History*. His publications include *Main Street Amusements: Movies and Commercial Entertainment in a Southern City, 1896–1930* (1995), which won the Theatre Library Association award and the Katherine Singer Kovacs award from the Society for Cinema Studies. His most recent publications have focused on the history of non-theatrical cinema.

HAIDEE WASSON is Professor of Cinema at Concordia University, Montreal. She is author of *Museum Movies: The Museum of Modern Art and the Birth of Art Cinema* (2005) and co-editor of *Inventing Film Studies* (2008) and *Useful Cinema* (2011). She also co-edits, with Dr Lee Grieveson, the Cultural Histories of Cinema book series for the BFI. Her current research investigates the history of portable film projectors in the USA.

YVONNE ZIMMERMANN is Professor of Media Studies at Philipps-Universität Marburg, Germany. She holds a PhD from the University of Zurich and was a Guest Professor at the University Sorbonne Nouvelle Paris 3. She is the author of *Bergführer Lorenz:*

Karriere eines missglückten Films (2005) and editor and co-author of *Schaufenster Schweiz: Dokumentarische Gebrauchsfilme 1896–1964* (2011). She has published widely on industrial film, 'useful cinema' and non-theatrical exhibition.

Introduction: On Advertising's Relation to Moving Pictures

Patrick Vonderau[1]

Advertising's present moment is one of 'media chaos', or so stated a New York-based firm in the trade in 2015. Making this assertion in a video on its website, the company conjured up a dystopia of increasing market fragmentation, consumer control, ratings declines and of a steadily growing clutter of 'messages beamed from thousands of sources to millions of people every second every day'.[2] The video appealed to a shared sense among advertisers as to the drawbacks of digitally networked media and the diminishing 'chances of your ad winning the attention lottery', especially among younger consumers understood to be unplugged from conventional television and unlikely to click on ads online. The video then went on to promote the company's ad-space brokering services to national and regional advertisers, introducing a seemingly new solution to the present day's chaos, called cinema:

> Now imagine a place where people are paying attention. And we don't mean a few people. We are talking about a place with both scale and reach. With massive live and engaged audiences. ... When you add cinema to your media mix, you are connecting at that completely rare and elusive moment of uninterrupted awareness, where attention more easily can be turned into action. ... They are literally closer to connecting to your brand, emotionally, and often times physically. We have got the perfect environment, with the perfect audience, at a perfect time.[3]

Somewhat surprisingly to many European moviegoers, who have been accustomed to advertising for decades, US trade circles still regard the theatrical screen as an unusual space for placing ads. Cinema ad-sales revenues in the USA may have increased since 2002, but at around $630 million (US$) they remain a far cry from the approximately $78 billion committed to television in 2014.[4] Accordingly, industry-oriented research in the USA describes the history of cinema-screen advertising as beginning as late as in 1977, when Screenvision was founded, the very ad-space brokering company whose self-promotional video is quoted above.[5] In this widespread yet historically problematic view, cinema's role for advertising is merely a complementary one: it was, and remains, an 'underused medium' that never primarily depended on ad sales, and the only one that audiences have been accustomed to experiencing as largely free from advertising.[6] In a history dominated by powerful American agencies, we learn, advertisers only began to use moving pictures efficiently in the 1960s, when the thirty-second television spot became the 'dominant form of audiovisual advertising'.[7]

Production cultures for advertising, television and film thus appear largely disconnected, despite some occasional stylistic border walks between these spheres.[8] It consequently also looks as if advertising histories would differ markedly between the USA and Europe, where advertising and moving pictures are seen to have been intimately related through cinema's avant-garde networks and a widely shared experience of modernity as early as in the 1920s. Here, advertising seems inextricably linked to art, urban life and new technologies, promoting a visual culture that entirely recast the nature of memory, experience and desire, thus contributing to the creation of cinematic spectatorship in the first place.[9] The contrast to the USA could hardly be more pronounced, given that advertising and moving pictures primarily seem related through broadcasting networks there, with their relationship crystallising into the spot commercial or what Erik Barnouw famously called television's 'inner fortress'.[10] According to this history of multiple disconnects, then, a history apparently marked by both an abundance of old adverts and a lack of properly contextualised paper records,[11] cinema is far from having provided advertisers with the 'perfect environment' and 'perfect audience' at a 'perfect time'. Always caught up in some temporal disjunction with the present, the promotional screen seems to switch from a site for experiments and experiences of the modern to a remedy for DVRs, skip-ad buttons and commercial-free viewing. Film, in short, never seems to have 'sold' anything, at least not in US cinemas.

Challenging such widespread views, this book provides significant evidence to the contrary. Through a detailed examination of the historical period prior to 1970, it demonstrates the degree to which screen advertising by then had come to be characterised by a multitude of moving-picture forms, including pre-show advertising films, lantern slides, promotional tie-ins, sponsored 'educationals', business films shown at trade fairs, outdoor projections at busy street crossings, animated billboards, multimedia illustrated lectures, or small and portable projections. It points not only to occasional overlaps, but also to a dynamic and lasting relationship between print, film, broadcasting and advertising cultures, a dynamics never driven by ad agencies alone. Chapters in this volume also testify to the interlinked, comparable histories of advertising in Europe and the USA, documenting that moving pictures have been well used for promotional purposes since the late nineteenth century. Long before French media advertising company Mediavision established Screenvision as its US subsidiary in the 1970s, for instance, European advertisers strived to make 'artistic' advertising the answer to American models. Brands, laws, markets and theories well known in the USA likewise shaped the professionalisation of advertising in Europe, where it was fully institutionalised as an industry by the 1910s. This book finally also sheds light on the archives and archival epistemologies that have informed advertising history in the past, indicating how a dazzling array of new American and European sources may be used to shape its future. It is with an eye on such future histories of the present that the subsequent chapters have been compiled.

Simply labelling this book a 'history' of moving-picture advertising, however, would fall short of recognising its particular stance on how advertising so far has been historicised. Previous studies have tended to describe advertising as an institution that is both distinct and unique in its capability to shape human consciousness, a monolithic 'black box' which causes either positive or negative effects on culture and society.[12] Often textually fixated on advertis*ements* for establishing its claims, this approach sees advertising constantly evolving in power and sophistication, and thus in its capability to produce consumers required by western capitalist systems. As a consequence, works variously have resulted in broad epochal views and periodisations alongside far-reaching theories of social practice as language, signification and ideology, and in a curious historical split where advertisements today appear as inescapable instruments of surveillance, while earlier ads seem unusual or naive in their 'mirroring' of society.[13] The teleology invoked in such notions of a both distinctively patterned and rationalist development has been accompanied by a widespread distaste for industries and markets as proper objects of analysis, especially in film and cultural studies. As Liz McFall has pointed out, this has led to an 'anti-historical historicisation of advertising in critical literature', culminating in works that broadly identify advertising with processes of modernisation, as having 'dreamed', 'made way for', or 'sold' modernity.[14]

The aim of this book is to revise such arguments, and to differentiate and explore. Borrowing from Foucault's well-known project of genealogy, it approaches history as a 'curative science' for overcoming the fixation on advertising's unbroken, linear continuities, a cure that may allow us to 'laugh at the solemnities of the origin'.[15] Providing specific histories that patiently accumulate details and accidents, sideroads and reversals, jolts, surprises and numberless beginnings, the contributors to this book show the heterogeneity of what so often is understood as consistent with itself. In doing so, much of the work gathered here can be seen as part of a more general trend in research into cinema history. Over the past twenty years, such research has shifted its focus away from the filmic text as its sole or preferred object, to consider questions of circulation, agency, brokerage, utility, exchange and experience. Think, for instance, of Jean Mitry's 1973 project of a film *histoire totale*, or of the structural approaches advocated by the French *Annales* tradition of socio-cultural history, that would inform how later historians would combine the comparative analysis of larger series of films with microhistorical enquiries.[16] Their attempts, in turn, resonate with various others during this period to develop, for instance, a historio-pragmatics of cinema, to analyse broader social discourses about cinema and its patrons, to study cinema's functional integration into other cultural spaces, or to establish anti-positivist counter-narratives for an archaeology of media.[17] Differences between such histories notwithstanding, they all testify to a broader tendency of conceptualising cinema as an 'open system' whose pasts include many dead-ends and a still unwritten 'history of possibilities'.[18]

While scholars have been revising conventional film history for more than a generation, this recent tendency of opening up cinema has taken a more pronounced shape in its turn towards non-theatrical or sponsored films, invoking collaborations between archives and researchers. Prompted by new forms of online access – and by archival or curatorial interests in this specific type of material that challenges established policies of selection, classification and handling – a flurry of research activities has been initiated. These include, among others, the biennial Orphan Film Symposium (since 1999), several special issues of the journal *Film History* (since 2003), the edited volumes *Films that Work: Industrial Film and the Productivity of Media* (2009), *Useful Cinema* (2011) and *Learning with the Lights Off* (2012), filmographies and field guides, and the work of copyright-reform activists and 'first-person archives' such as

Rick Prelinger.[19] A large part of these activities has been devoted to liberating cinema history from its focus on oeuvre and authorship, in order to establish new explanatory frameworks for films that never were meant to be interpreted, let alone preserved.

Such frameworks have been premised on the general observation that industrial, sponsored, or educational films are better explained in terms of use and functionality, rather than meaning or style. Evoking earlier structural approaches that would submit larger series of films to the same kind of questioning in order to formulate hypotheses on permanence, evolutions, or ruptures, scholars have suggested beginning with enquiries about the 'three As' – that is, the *Auftraggeber* (who commissioned the film), *Anlass* (the occasion for which it was made) and *Adressat* (the use to which it was put or the audience to whom it was addressed).[20] Others have described sponsored film as a form that can only be read through the industrial organisation that produced it. These scholars have suggested identifying an industrial film's 'three Rs' or main areas of purpose and asking about its function as *record* (for institutional memory), *rhetoric* (for governance) and *rationalisation* (for optimising processes).[21] Again other researchers have challenged us to not only see sponsored films defined by their individual use, but to also acknowledge that their usefulness is always contingent on socio-historical change and indicative of a broader relationship between culture and power. Emphasising an institutional perspective, these researchers have invited us to map the sites or *topographies* where such media are shown, to focus on their recurring *topoi* and to understand them as ever-changing, *transient* objects, rather than finite artefacts – subject to constant re-versioning and reinterpretation, as they continue to circulate in society.[22]

These combined efforts to come to terms with sponsored materials may have left us with a new acronym, or perhaps a new meaning attributed to the notion of *A-R-T*, but not with a deepened understanding of advertising's relation to moving pictures. Somewhat paradoxically, the most useful, or at least most brazenly instrumental form of sponsored film-making so far has not been explored as such. But what exactly is it that makes moving pictures a cultural form used, or underused, for advertising purposes? Writing the history of this cinema indeed remains, as Gregory A. Waller notes in this book, dependent on 'investigating – so far as is possible – how useful cinema was actually put to use'. Such an investigation, however, will also need to work through some of the categorical dualisms that have informed notions of advertising's utility in the past.

THE USES OF SCREEN ADVERTISING

A basic observation of this book is that moving pictures have been inextricably linked to advertising ever since both gained social momentum in the late nineteenth century. Not only were movement and projection generally pervasive elements of advertising, to be associated with stereopticons, lantern 'slide-vertising', mechanical trade cards, thumb books, moving automata and shop window installations, 'electric spectaculars' (i.e. animated coloured roof-type structures), or projected film.[23] Advertising also formed a pervasive cultural context of useful communication that influenced how films were made, how they were packaged and promoted and how they were understood by audiences.[24] In apparent historical synchronicity, both advertising and cinema developed into institutions of their own, each establishing its own 'cultural paradigm', in the sense of a distinct system of codification and normalisation, while still remaining co-present in the 'cultural series' of the other – that is, in the various forms of signification such paradigms came to produce.[25]

Hence, Charles Musser's apt observation in his chapter that a 'film's amusement value' in the kinetoscope era and beyond might be seen only as the 'necessary pre-condition' for its underlying purpose: to sell goods and services. Focusing on Edison motion pictures and the American motion-picture industry in the 1893–1900 period, Musser gives a detailed account of Edison's (self-)promotional film production, from short kinetoscope demonstration films to more elaborately staged, gimmicky forms of cross-promotion. Advertising film not only became one of the more popular genres of early cinema, but also a mainstay of outdoor advertising, 'attracting the attention nightly of thousands of people', as a trade journal quoted by Musser noted in 1897. Taking this enquiry even a step further in his contribution, William Uricchio explores 'how the motion picture was sold to the public' through the Sears, Roebuck & Company's *Consumers Guide*, a mail-order catalogue mass-distributed in the USA and Canada around 1900. Arguing that more than any other depiction in the period, this one defined the 'horizon of expectations' that greeted the new medium, Uricchio studies how ads in the *Guide* searched to define moving pictures as technology, experience, economic activity and textual system. His contribution points to larger contemporary constellations of media practice and to the interdependencies of new to other media as a key framework for understanding the relation between advertising and moving pictures, while also registering numerous parallels to our present-day media environment.

There is, indeed, ample evidence that American cinema, far from being the natural site for Hollywood product, took shape through a long-lasting struggle over its own institutional belonging, a struggle fought between competing cultural paradigms such as advertising and entertainment. In 1931, for instance, a report commissioned by the then newly formed committee on screen advertising of the American Association of Advertising Agencies found that most of the opposition to this practice over the past twenty years had emanated 'from competing interests in the motion picture business'.[26] Various entertainment trade groups, among them the Motion Picture Patents Company and exhibitor organisations such as the Motion Picture Theatre Owners of America or the Motion Picture Exhibitors League, had reportedly lobbied against screen advertisers since 1911.[27] In response to these attempts to keep control over the screen and to secure a share of advertising profits, screen advertisers began to form their own organisations. Having identified the 'problem of providing circulation for industrial and advertising pictures' as 'the knotty one to be solved' in 1914, these organisations gradually achieved agreements on codes of rules and regulations, exhibitor rates and on merging leading firms into a nationwide screen advertising service in the early 1930s.[28] By 1938, this service had gained a foothold in more than half of the nation's approximately 16,000 motion-picture theatres – prompting action by the Federal Trade Commission in 1942 against a 'conspiracy to suppress competition and create monopoly'.[29] The question of who 'owned' the cinema, in short, came up repeatedly even in Hollywood's classical era.

Advertising, understood as an institutionalised process associated with a set of codified practices and a host of content types or cultural forms designed for promoting consumption, evidently emerged through an intimate relationship with communication technologies that included moving pictures. As Michael Cowan reminds us in his chapter, this concurrence of mass trademark advertising and mass media often has been explained as responding to a crisis in the control of consumption dating back to the early 1880s.[30] According to this view, new machinery enlarged the ratio of output, requiring more capital and a large and predictable demand for products. Cinema thus seems to have formed 'part of a broader technology of economic control' geared towards the capitalist marketplace. Against this background, Cowan investigates the role of animation in German screen advertising from experiments in the 1910s to more codified forms in the late 1920s, showing how an earlier reliance on tricks and phantasmagories gradually came to be replaced by more instrumental images, based on psychological studies. Contemporary advertising theorised animation as a tool for capturing and centring attention on brands, among others. And yet, as Cowan is quick to point out, such theories are not simply to be taken at face value, referring to indications of 'just how tenuous advertising's control strategies might have been in reality'. In a similar vein, Sema Colpan's and Lydia Nsiah's chapter details how cinematic techniques such as sound, colour, or animation were used in crafting the screen appearance of brands in neighbouring Austria during the inter-war period. Describing in minute detail how a shampoo named Sorela emerged through an interplay of animation, Gasparcolor and the Selenophon sound system in the advertising short *Morgenstunde* (1935), Colpan and Nsiah complicate the idea of such techniques being just a means to an end – for both the film and its devices also served to showcase, and codify, screen advertising practice itself.

What, then, to make of the notion of control so persistently attributed to the workings of cinema and advertising, respectively? As obvious as their co-evolution may seem, cinema's utility for advertising clearly requires more than a monocausal explanation. We may begin sketching the contours of such an explanation by pausing at the notion of the trademark to which the idea of control over consumer demand is tightly connected. For how would demand for goods be caused if there was no criterion for distinguishing goods in the first place? Trademarks are signifiers that establish the right of a seller to exclude others from using the seller's reputation for the quality of his goods.[31] Similar to patents or copyrights, trademarks thus facilitate the deployment of informational capital. Although they may have existed since ancient times, their codification into law historically relates to the advent of capitalism. Both in Europe and the USA, trademarks gradually received protection between approximately 1870 and 1905. Despite significant cultural differences in legal practice,[32] the codification of trademark law thus came to introduce a key distinction on both continents, a distinction that not only contributed to the emergence of capitalist markets and market theories, but also incentivised, and established, reputations to begin with. Trademarks are, in other words, a *device* for constructing the very market they supposedly only supply.[33]

The conceptual shift away from advertising as a process that 'matches' products to already existing markets, towards a notion of advertising as a process of market-*making* has some interesting consequences. Not only does it suspend the idea of cinema being a straightforward technology of control for bridging supply and demand.[34] It also prompts the questions of if and how the screen brings trademarks into view. Was screen advertising confined to institutionally sanctioned, legally codified practices for distinguishing and building reputations? Certainly not. During the 1910–40 period, for instance, observers in the USA and Europe consistently pointed to a multitude of *non-institutional*, less formally organised practices that diverged from the norms and codes of paid-for commercial product advertising. Trade discourse abounded with attempts to marginalise 'incompetents' and forms not corresponding to the standards and genres understood to be most efficient for screen advertising.[35] In some European countries, this process even involved state authorities and censorship.[36] A broad variety of promotional genres and the often marginal actors providing them testify to advertising's lasting diversity that even included avant-garde, educational and experimental works.[37]

In addition to non-institutional forms, screen advertising, of course, also included a significant amount of *non-theatrical* films. As several chapters in this book illustrate, even films made by institutionalised screen advertisers to introduce trademarked goods or services were frequently never meant for cinema, or not for cinema alone.[38] Nico de Klerk presents the curious but not uncommon case of an ad for a service that was not yet available – a series of non-theatrical films promoting Pan Am's intercontinental destinations to Dutch viewers between 1960 and 1965, a time when Holland was just coming out of a period of reconstruction after the war. Distributed through International Film Services, a privatised Film Department of the American embassy in The Hague for screenings in schools, businesses, clubs and other venues, the *New Horizons* series neither created nor controlled demand for air travel. Its Dutch screenings can rather be explained as a form of trade advertising devised in the context of post-war recovery programmes, as de Klerk argues. Lucy Česálková, in her chapter, studies a similarly unlikely case, socialist screen advertising, in the context of Czechoslovakia's planned economy in the 1950s and 60s. The rapid increase of such ads after 1955 related to the organisation of state trade. In a system with no competition between brands, theatrical and non-theatrical films were means to direct interest towards goods with a scheduled sales priority, covering other market shortages.

The history of screen advertising is characterised by a diversity of forms and practices which can hardly be subsumed under one universal model. Such diversity is best represented as a spectrum, rather than a binary division between the institutional/non-institutional or theatrical/non-theatrical. Thinking of screen advertising as a continuous line, with differences as variances of degree rather than fundamental oppositions, also is productive in relation to *direct and indirect* appearances of trademarks on screen – that is, forms that link a product to a film with or without overtly calling attention to product qualities or price. In fact, the often-heard claim that moving pictures were merely complementary to advertising before 1970 seems largely due to a narrow focus on institutional, theatrical and direct practices. If a product is not clearly distinguishable in an ad, supporters of this position seem to ask, what function does the ad have and does it qualify as one at all? American motion-picture industry discourse in the classic era indeed drew a clear line between advertising, on the one hand, and publicity and promotion, on the other.[39]

This distinction between a paid, unambiguous announcement in a communications medium and other, partly freely given forms of promotion was related to a then-established division of labour in the industry. In this context, direct and indirect advertising developed as separate professional practices and tactics.[40] At the same time, however, such practices not only overlapped increasingly over time, their forms also often coincided within specific campaigns. In his chapter, Patrick Vonderau invites us to rethink the function of product placements by provocatively declaring the presence of commodities in cinema not as an obstacle to, but rather as a 'key reference point' for aesthetic pleasure. Studying 'tie-ins' as both cultural form and industrial practice, he relates the indirect and direct promotions that accompanied, and permeated, Richard Quine's *Strangers When We Meet* (1960) to the question of how they were viewed and experienced.

Such emphasis on the relevance of indirect forms, however, is not meant to downplay, once more, the significant role of direct product advertisements on theatrical screens in the USA and elsewhere before 1960. In his as-yet-unpublished dissertation, Jeremy W. Groskopf indeed demonstrates that the 'spot' commercial did not originate on television, but had already become a standard of cinema advertising by 1916. Despite their marginal position in the programme (e.g. in the intermission), one-minute 'trailers' or 'playlets', later called 'screen broadcasts' or 'minute movies', were emblematic of a rapidly codifying theory of advertising in moving media, according to Groskopf.[41] In following a similar historical trajectory that saw short ad films emerge out of earlier slide advertising practices during the 1910s, European screen advertisers developed related theories of cinema's role in the marketplace.[42] There are several reasons why such theories did not come to dominate industry practice in the USA or Europe. These include an already noted competition between various screen trade groups, changes in programme structure and also a lack of consistent organisation regarding the placing and auditing of screen ads.[43] Larger agencies, which had integrated creation, strategy and market research into their advertising services early, could have provided a model, but long preferred to remain on the sidelines. When J. Walter Thompson and others finally 'pioneered' in cinema's 'new audience' around 1940, the Hollywood studios were quick to pinpoint that they had 'been in commercial pictures for 28 years' (see opposite).[44]

It is helpful for an initial mapping of screen advertising's historical practices to trace its different forms along these various tensions between institutional and non-institutional processes, commercial and non-commercial circuits, or direct and indirect modes of address. But such an initial mapping of this diverse field does not resolve the issue of why advertisers would choose onscreen moving-picture ads over other forms of advertising. What more could be said about this issue, apart from noting a co-evolution between mass communication and mass trademark advertising, theories of control, the momentum developing between competing industries, the appeal of new media technologies, or agency intervention?[45] Over its long history, advertising seems to have followed a strategy of using multiple media, underlining that it never was medium-specific but always required a *Medienverbund*, or a 'network of competing, but also mutually interdependent and complementary media or media practices', in order to count as effective.[46] Cinema's key competitive advantage, in this context, has early and consistently been identified as delivering a captive audience.[47] Unlike print,

broadcasting, or even digital media, the motion-picture theatre promised 'uninterrupted awareness', and still does, as illustrated by the Screenvision self-promotion above. Yet although comparative discussions of formal properties in the trade press sometimes ended in attempts to identify signs of inferiority in older/other media, screen advertising practices themselves were often modelled on concepts developed elsewhere. Cinema's indirect tactics of product placement, for instance, resemble camouflage advertising in print, a technique of blending ads with editorial features and styles in order to avoid the advertising tone of voice.[48]

Print even inspired broadcasting, as Cynthia B. Meyers argues in her chapter. Focusing on the 1960s as a transitional decade for American commercial television and the advertising industry that sustained it, Meyers shows how a shift from the radio-era business model of single sponsorship to the network-era model followed a 'magazine plan' of advertising: the networks, like magazine editors, came to select the programming, and then sell interstitial airtime to advertisers. As her close examination of debates and institutional changes reveals, these changes emerged out of a 'conflicted evolution of business models, advertising strategies, and aesthetic values'. Relatedly, William Boddy's chapter documents how, during the 1940–60 period, the US broadcasting industry discussed TV commercials in regard to issues such as medium specificity, perception, or psychology. Boddy demonstrates that as mass communication technologies, cinema, radio and television were always embedded in a broader cultural discourse on human nature and the social functions of media, enquiring to which degree these culturally contested relations between advertising and mass communication were specific to the USA. In rounding up the discussion on television, Skip Elsheimer and Devin Orgeron detail the background and workings of a direct commercial product advertising campaign. How does the cultural work of television commercials function in practice? Focusing on Sugar Crisp, an American brand of pre-sweetened breakfast cereal introduced in 1949, the chapter analyses the campaign's use of 'Sugar Bear' as a recurring figure through the 1960s and 70s, illustrating how branded characters and forms of televisual serialisation worked together in constructing a market for teens, while distracting attention from the product's low nutritional value.

PARA-SITED CINEMA: ONE APPROACH, MANY METHODS, COUNTLESS SOURCES

Taken together, then, the chapters in this book testify to the need for an approach that goes beyond the mere study of promotional film (or film promotion, for that matter). Exploring the uses of moving pictures for advertising purposes, they approach 'cinema' as an open system, one whose institutional borders were both clearly defined and often contested. As an instantiation of 'useful cinema', screen advertising prompts questions about clients and addressees, about recurrent rhetorical forms and their re-versioning over time. But it also challenges us to acknowledge the diversity of its practices, spread out across a spectrum of more or less direct, theatrical, or institutional modes. Sketching out the components of such an approach, contributions to this volume situate cinema within a network of competing (and complementary) media, historicising notions of film's specificity. They also suggest seeing screen advertising not only as a means for market-related 'knowledge production',[49] but also as a device for making markets in the first place.

Any exploration of advertising's relation to moving pictures would be baseless without the proper sources, however. All chapters in this volume, therefore, also contribute markedly to reconfiguring the canon of sources. William Uricchio, for instance, by studying a mail-order catalogue, or Nico de Klerk by closely following an archived distribution print. In addition, a separate collection of nine shorter chapters is entirely devoted to making the archive the key entry point for a discussion of screen advertising. Providing the epistemological and practical foundations for future research, these chapters analyse various media and forms of screen advertising both in regard to archival issues and by explaining their historical relevance. Joachim Schätz presents a collection of film-related materials from the archive of Rudolf Mayer Film, a company active in Vienna between 1937 and 1939, demonstrating the insight to be won about contemporary industry practices through a proper contextualisation of such paper records. Catherine Cormon describes general challenges in handling advertising film, emphasising how time, space and resource-intensive it is, not to mention the difficulties of metadata and contextualisation. Leenke Ripmeester explores the vast Geesink collection of advertising films at EYE Filmmuseum, Amsterdam, abstracting from her own years of experiences in working with this collection. Arianna Turci represents the Archivio Nazionale Cinema d'Impresa (ANCI – National Film Archive for Industrial Film) in Ivrea by surveying the collection's history and organisational principles. Robert Byrne introduces lantern-slide advertising as an important subject of enquiry, based on an overview of archival holdings and a sketch of their history. Dylan Cave sheds light on the Rodney Read collection of trailers and teasers in the British Film Institute's National Film and Television Archive, London, while Jez Stewart situates two large collections in the same archive relating to early British television commercials and the role of animation in advertising. Their detailed survey is complemented by Cassie Blake's survey of so-called snipes, or policy trailers, in the Packard Humanities Institute Collection of moving-image promotional materials at the Academy Film Archive, Los Angeles. Andy Uhrich, finally, shows how the commercial works of the Film Group, primarily known for its political documentaries on the Black Panthers and the protest movement, and now accessible in the Chicago Film Archive, may challenge us to rethink, once more, the categorical dualisms on which previous notions of screen advertising were founded.

Do all these various archival sources and research chapters imply, however, that screen advertising's form was fundamentally unstable, constantly changing according to function? And consequently, that research would always need to engage in piecemeal, case-based historicising of how a given screen medium was put to use, working out specificities against larger socio-cultural contexts? Or are there, maybe, further regularities in the relationship between moving pictures and advertising that could be identified in order to generate new templates for questions, enable international comparisons and streamline the book's findings into a still more consistent approach?

A convenient, if somewhat clichéd response to the challenge of developing a clear-cut explanatory framework for advertising's relation to moving pictures has been to describe this relation as parasitic. That 'ads are parasitic upon their surroundings and other genres' has been a commonplace of critical mass communication research at least since the 1980s.[50] The trope of a host–parasite relationship also permeated industry discourse early on, sometimes evoking correspondences to contemporary 'media infection' theories.[51] More recently, media historians have taken up the term, stressing that industrial film is not a genre but a 'strategically weak and parasitic form' adapting to an organisational purpose it aims to fulfil.[52] While thought provoking, this position has been criticised for downplaying the strength or persistence of sponsored arrangements, and for failing to account for the mutuality in the relationship.[53] It also misses the fact that the sponsored arrangements of screen advertising took form in rather stable, clearly labelled and identified content types, some of which – such as the spot commercial – turned out to be surprisingly robust and widespread internationally, in both their key parameters (e.g. length, structure, trademark mention) and perlocutionary functions (i.e. to induce a particular response in viewers). Screen advertisement is not a weak, soft, or malleable form, but designed to persist, especially where 'it seeks us, rather than we it'.[54]

The point here, however, is, of course, to avoid narrowing down the view on advertisement in the first place, because this would again mean to reduce the manifold relations between moving pictures and advertising to a purely discursive or communicative level. If anything, advertising sometimes may appear 'parasitic on existing *institutional forms and routines*'.[55] Rather than always constituting a sealed-off institution in itself, screen advertising has often drawn together actors from other institutions. Historical genre terminology evidences these overlaps and blurred boundaries between 'industrials', 'educationals', or entertainment, and thus forms a viable starting point for interpreting screen advertising as an industrial process, set of codified practices and cultural form. Still needed, though, is at least a concept that allows for a closer examination of what it is that connects or disconnects various institutional actors, while acknowledging that one can't assume their relation is sufficiently explained by using a suggestive, yet derogative term such as the 'parasite'.

Yvonne Zimmermann, in her chapter, prepares the ground for such an approach by suggesting a topological view on screen advertising. Emphasising the question of where, rather than what advertising film is, she demonstrates that a study comparing exhibition, programming and viewer experience in the USA and Europe may productively contribute to conceptualise screen advertising practice. Provoking researchers to 'look at moving images not only before cinema, but also beyond cinema', the chapter is based on an understanding of topography as 'composed of the various cultural series that moving images were and are part of', thus expanding the field beyond cinema in the narrow sense. In a similarly programmatic vein, Haidee Wasson's chapter extends the call for an expansion of the field to encompass what she calls 'exhibitionary cinema', focusing on a space specifically built to promote the ideals of industry and consumption: the World's Fair of 1939 and 1940 held in New York City. At the fair, a family of technologies 'operated in a kind of partial and para-cinematic way', linking still and moving displays, flashing lights, or amplified sound, for instance, in order to create a new interface between corporate and consumer desire. This remaking of cinema as a 'selling machine' at the fair accompanied a larger trend to rearticulate the cinematic apparatus, a trend Wasson suggests exploring with a focus on media ecologies, viewing devices and exhibitionary practices. Gregory A. Waller's contribution furthers the case for methodological clarity by coining the notion of 'multi-sited cinema', inviting us to enquire about the 'varied and historically specific ways that motion pictures have been put to a host of different uses across a wide range of locations well beyond the commercial movie theatre'. Revisiting an alleged point of origin of commercial film-making, Waller studies the Essanay film *Back to the Old Farm* (1911) through the lens of the screen advertising industry's historical self-understanding, providing a detailed account of corporate production practices, distribution infrastructures and exhibition strategies. His research reveals that the movement from commercial to non-commercial (and largely non-theatrical) screenings, often combined with a shift from indirect to more direct trademark mentions, was a regular trajectory for 'business' films in the USA during the 1910s.

Waller's conclusion is that screen advertising, far from being essentially unstable or parasitic, simply often underwent a complicated process of genrification – a 'pragmatically driven, historically grounded, sometimes quite contentious activity of generically identifying individual films and constituting genres'.[56] While not being specific to advertising, the concept of genrification indeed helps to overcome the idea of this cultural form's spineless malleability, refocusing attention on how, and by whom, it was labelled, distributed, presented, or re-versioned. But again, it is not only the discursive dimension of screen advertising that is at stake here. The notion of multi-sited cinema indeed also resonates with both Zimmermann's more general suggestion to look at moving images before and beyond cinema, and Wasson's observation of the 'para-cinematic way' in which various projection technologies came to reconstitute the idea of the apparatus in specific exhibition contexts. In drawing these arguments together, we may propose the study of screen advertising as a *para-sited cinema*.

To briefly sketch out this proposition, let us return once more to the widely stated claim of advertising being rather inconsistently related to cinema. There is certainly some truth in this statement, provided that we identify cinema with its most notorious apparatus, and advertising with its most robust form, the spot commercial. Yet screen advertising often moves considerably beyond this apparatus, while remaining entirely internal to it: it is both, in Wasson's words, its disarticulation and rearticulation, it is, over and above, in and out of cinema, in short: *para-*. It is defined not by being exclusively within this or that social space, but precisely by moving in between, borrowing from the different logics or cultural series that constitute cinema as an open system. At the same time, screen advertising is also *sited* in concrete topological, social and material ways. It is 'sited' in the sense of being marked as advertising primarily through where and how it was actually shown, requiring scholars to trace its circulation and include distribution or exhibition as key parameters of analysis. Speaking of screen advertising as a para-sited cinema in this sense also means to acknowledge advertising's key function for making or localising markets. Moving picture ads not only serve this purpose by being shown in a suitable context, they also work as devices for constellating consumer communities in the first place.[57] Para-sited cinema is a situated, targeted form of address that counts on, and forcefully constructs, a captive audience.

To the informed reader, both 'multi-sited' and 'para-sited' are, of course, terms with a certain resonance in the social sciences, famously coined by anthropologist George E. Marcus for stimulating a methodological rejuvenation of ethnographic fieldwork in the globalised and industrialised world.[58] While multi-sited ethnography aims at the study of phenomena that cannot be accounted for by focusing on a single site, requiring researchers to follow people, connections, associations and relationships across space, the notion of the para-site is meant, in Marcus's account, to mark the kind of 'cultural work that subjects do in the construction of a para-site in relation to some level of major institutional function'. In consequence, studying screen advertising as para-sited cinema could mean, first, to establish its trajectory across space as the actual object of research and, second, to look closer at the ways screen advertisers have nested into institutional forms and routines, not so much in the exploitative sense of a parasite, but in the sense of their labour invested for creating a 'site of alternativity in which anything, or at least something different, could happen'.[59] Although this might be hard to swallow for traditional cinephiles, screen advertising as a para-sited cinema indeed evokes another possibility of cinema, opening a horizon of assumptions about the uses of cinema beyond art or entertainment, often from within established institutions.

Think, for instance, of the ways early screen advertisers regularly attempted to articulate the specificities of their medium through elaborate comparisons between lantern slides, print, or radio, engaging in a 'great experiment' and consistent cultural work not only of defining a given trademark value and its market, but also the future uses of the screen.[60] Advocating for the superiority of the moving picture vis-à-vis 'printed salesmanship', among others, while consequently borrowing from established educational, entertainment or industrial film-making practices, these practitioners disarticulated institutional structures in order to carve out a space for themselves.[61] Envisioning a medium that would combine light, sound, motion, scale, dramatic sequence and the 'lifeness' of a factory tour, they became part of networks that would stretch beyond a single nation and screen advertising's own industrial territories. Following their various connections and relationships, and tracing moving pictures across the contexts and circuits in which they came to function (or not) as advertising, this book is an invitation to explore cinema in a new and different way.

NOTES

1. No introductory chapter is an island. The ideas articulated here have been shaped by discussions with my co-editors, Bo Florin and Nico de Klerk, and with the contributors to this collection, especially Greg Waller, Haidee Wasson and Yvonne Zimmermann. Thanks also to Joel Frykholm and Lee Grieveson for comments on an earlier draft of this chapter.
2. 'Screenvision Upfront', screenvision.com (accessed 11 January 2016).
3. Ibid., emphasis original.
4. 'John Partilla Takes on Cinema Advertising as Screenvision CEO', *Advertising Age*, 1 October 2015, adage.com (accessed 11 January 2016). Cf. Harold L. Vogel, *Entertainment Industry Economics: A Guide for Financial Analysis*, 8th edition (Cambridge: Cambridge University Press, 2011), pp. 51–5.
5. Keith F. Johnson, 'Cinema Advertising', *Journal of Advertising* vol. 10 no. 4 (1981), pp. 11–19; Bruce A. Austin, 'Cinema Screen Advertising: An Old Technology with New Promise for Consumer Marketing', *Journal of Consumer Marketing* vol. 3 no. 1 (1986), pp. 45–56.
6. Kim B. Rotzoll, 'The Captive Audience: The Troubled Odyssee of Cinema Advertising', in Bruce A. Austin (ed.), *Current Research in Film*, Vol. 3 (Norwood, NJ: Ablex, 1987), pp. 72–87.
7. Paul Grainge and Catherine Johnson, *Promotional Screen Industries* (New York and London: Routledge, 2015), p. 28.
8. Ibid.; Lynn Spigel, *TV by Design: Modern Art and the Rise of Network Television* (Chicago and London: Chicago University Press, 2009).
9. Malte Hagener, *Moving Forward, Looking Back: The European Avant-Garde and the Invention of Film Culture, 1919–1939* (Amsterdam: Amsterdam University Press, 2007); Pamela E. Swett, Jonathan Wiesen and Jonathan R. Zaitlin (eds), *Selling Modernity: Advertising in Twentieth-Century Germany* (Durham, NJ: Duke University Press, 2007); Laura Markus, *Dreams of Modernity: Psychoanalysis, Literature, Cinema* (New York: Cambridge University Press, 2014).
10. Erik Barnouw, *The Sponsor: Notes on a Modern Potentate* (New York: Oxford University Press, 1978), pp. 79–99. See also Aeron Davis, *Promotional Cultures: The Rise and Spread of Advertising, Public Relations, Marketing and Branding* (Cambridge: Polity Press, 2013). Film or cinema are hardly ever mentioned in John McDonough and Karen Egolf (eds), *The Advertising Age Encyclopedia of Advertising* (London and New York: Routledge, 2002).
11. Cf. Chris Wharton, *Advertising: Critical Approaches* (London and New York: Routledge, 2015), pp. 20–3.
12. See, for instance, Daniel Boorstin, *The Image: A Guide to Pseudo Events in America* (New York: Harper & Row, 1961); Paul Baran and Paul Sweezy, *Monopoly Capital* (New York: Monthly Review Press, 1966); Stuart Ewen, *Captains of Consciousness: Advertising and the Social Roots of the Consumer Culture* (New York and London: McGraw-Hill, 1976); Stewart Ewen and Elizabeth Ewen, *Channels of Desire: Mass Images and the Shaping of American Consciousness* (New York, St Louis and San Francisco: McGraw-Hill, 1982).

13. Judith Williamson, *Decoding Advertisements* (London: Marion Boyars, 1981); Gillian Dyer, *Advertising as Communication* (London: Methuen, 1982); Stephen Fox, *The Mirror Makers: A History of American Advertising and Its Creators* (New York: William Morrow, 1984); Robert Goldman, *Reading Ads Socially* (London: Routledge, 1992); Guy Cook, *The Discourse of Advertising* (London and New York: Routledge, 1992); Scott Lash and John Urry, *Economies of Signs and Spaces* (Thousand Oaks, CA: Sage, 1994); Charles Forceville, *Pictorial Metaphor in Advertising* (London: Routledge, 1996); Angela Goddard, *The Language of Advertising* (London: Routledge, 1998); Arthur Asa Berger (ed.), *Ads, Fads, and Consumer Culture: Advertising's Impact on American Character and Society* (Lanham, MD: Rowman & Littlefield, 2000); Mark Tungate, *Adland: A Global History of Advertising* (London and Philadelphia: Kogan Page, 2007); Stephane Pincas and Marc Loiseau, *A History of Advertising* (Cologne: Taschen, 2008); Wharton, *Advertising*; and many of the chapters in Joseph Turow and Matthew P. McAllister (eds), *The Advertising and Consumer Culture Reader* (New York and London: Routledge, 2009).

14. Liz McFall, *Advertising: A Cultural Economy* (London: Sage, 2004), p. 189. Cf. Roland Marchand, *Advertising the Amercian Dream: Making Way for Modernity 1920–1940* (Berkeley, Los Angeles and London: University of California Press, 1985); Anne Friedberg, *Window Shopping: Cinema and the Postmodern* (Berkeley, Los Angeles and London: University of California Press, 1993); Leo Charney and Vanessa R. Schwartz (eds), *Cinema and the Invention of Modern Life* (Berkeley, Los Angeles and London: University of California Press, 1995); Thomas Elsaesser, *Weimar Cinema and After: Germany's Historical Imaginary* (New York: Routledge, 2000); Kevin Hetherington, *Capitalism's Eye* (London and New York: Routledge, 2007) and others.

15. Michel Foucault, 'Nietzsche, la généalogie, l'histoire', in S. Bachelard *et al.* (eds), *Hommage à Jean Hyppolite* (Paris: Presses Universitaire de France, 1971), pp. 145–72.

16. Michèle Lagny, 'Film History: or History Expropriated', *Film History* vol. 6 (1994), pp. 26–44; Richard Abel, '"Don't Know Much about History", or the (In)vested Interests of Doing Cinema History', *Film History* vol. 6 no. 1 (1994), pp. 110–15.

17. See, for instance, Roger Odin, 'Sémio-pragmatique du cinéma et de l'audio-visuel: Modes et institutions', in Jürgen E. Müller (ed.), *Towards a Pragmatics of the Audiovisual: Theory and History* (Münster: Nodus Publikationen, 1995), pp. 33–46; Frank Kessler, 'Historische Pragmatik', *Montage AV* vol. 11 no. 2 (2003), pp. 104–12; Charles R. Acland, *Screen Traffic: Movies, Multiplexes, and Global Culture* (Durham, NC, and London: Duke University Press, 2003); Frank Kessler and Nanna Verhoeff (eds), *Networks of Entertainment: Early Film Distribution 1895–1915* (Eastleigh: John Libbey, 2007); Richard Maltby, 'New Cinema Histories', in Richard Maltby, Daniel Biltereyst and Philippe Meers (eds), *Explorations in New Cinema History: Approaches and Case Studies* (Malden, MA: Wiley-Blackwell, 2011), pp. 3–40; Jussi Parikka, *What Is Media Archaeology?* (Cambridge: Polity Press, 2012); *Film History*, special issue *Inquiries, Speculations, Provocations* vol. 25 no. 1–2 (2013); or Carolyn L. Kane, *Chromatic Algorithms: Synthetic Color, Computer Art, and Aesthetics After Code* (Chicago: Chicago University Press, 2014).

18. Leonardo Quaresima, 'Introduction', *Dead Ends/Impasses*, *Cinéma & Cie: International Film Studies Journal* no. 2 (2003), pp. 11–13.

19. *Film History*, special issues *Small-Gauge and Amateur Film* vol. 15 no. 2 (2003), *Nontheatrical Film* vol. 19 (2007) and *Nontheatrical Film* vol. 25 no. 4 (2013); Rick Prelinger, *The Field Guide to Sponsored Film* (San Francisco: National Film Preservation Foundation, 2006);

Vinzenz Hediger and Patrick Vonderau (eds), *Films that Work: Industrial Film and the Productivity of Media* (Amsterdam: Amsterdam University Press, 2009); Charles R. Acland and Haidee Wasson (eds), *Useful Cinema* (Durham, NC, and London: Duke University Press, 2011); Devin Orgeron, Masha Orgeron and Dan Streible (eds), *Learning with the Lights Off: Educational Film in the United States* (Oxford and New York: Oxford University Press, 2012). See also the websites of the Orphans Film Symposium (http://www.nyu.edu/orphanfilm/, last accessed 15 January 2016) and Rick Prelinger (www.prelinger.com, last accessed 15 January 2016).

20. Thomas Elsaesser, 'The Place of Non-Fiction Film in Contemporary Media', in Hediger and Vonderau, *Films that Work*, pp. 19–34.

21. Vinzenz Hediger and Patrick Vonderau, 'Record, Rhetoric, Rationalization: Industrial Organization and Film', in Hediger and Vonderau, *Films that Work*, pp. 35–50.

22. 'Introduction: Utility and Cinema', in Acland and Wasson, *Useful Cinema*, pp. 1–14.

23. For instance, Hugh E. Agnew, *Outdoor Advertising* (New York and London: McGraw-Hill, 1938); Anon., 'Ad Slides: Good and Bad', *Reel and Slide*, 14 September 1919.

24. Jeffrey Klenotic, 'Advertising', in Richard Abel (ed.), *Encyclopedia of Early Cinema* (London and New York: Routledge, 2005), pp. 7–8.

25. André Gaudreault, *Film and Attraction: From Kinematography to Cinema* (Urbana and Chicago: University of Illinois Press, 2011 [2008]), pp. 64–8. Cf. Yvonne Zimmermann's chapter in this volume.

26. Anon., 'AAAA's Committee Declares Screen Ads Are Yet Experimental', *Motion Picture Herald*, 9 May 1931.

27. Watterson R. Rothacker, 'System in Motion Picture Advertising', *Motography* vol. 5 no. 5 (May 1911), pp. 71–2. See also the advert, 'Declaration of Independence', *Exhibitors Herald*, December 1919.

28. Anon., 'Ad. Film Folks Meet To Discuss Organization', *The Moving Picture World*, 29 August 1914; Anon., 'Alexander and Others Cited for Monopoly', *Motion Picture Herald*, 28 March 1942; Anon., 'US Finds Monopoly in Ad Film Industry', *Motion Picture Herald*, 3 July 1943.

29. Ibid.

30. James R. Beniger, *The Control Revolution: Technological and Economic Origins of the Information Society* (Cambridge, MA: Harvard University Press, 1986), pp. 264–71. Cf. Miriam R. Levin (ed.), *Cultures of Control* (Amsterdam: Harwood, 2000).

31. Steven Tadelis, 'What's in a Name? Reputation as a Tradeable Asset', *American Economic Review* vol. 89 (June 1999), pp. 548–63.

32. Jane M. Gaines, *Contested Culture: The Image, the Voice, and the Law* (Chapel Hill: University of North Carolina Press, 1991); see also Paul H. Rubin and Tilman Klumpp, 'Property Rights and Capitalism', in Dennis C. Mueller (ed.), *The Oxford Handbook of Capitalism* (Oxford and New York: Oxford University Press, 2012), pp. 204–19.

33. The argument here is based on a strand of innovative research on advertising and marketing theory originating in economic sociology. See, for instance, Antoine Hennion and Cecile Méadel, 'Artisans of Desire: The Mediation of Advertising between Product and Consumer', *Sociology Theory* vol. 7 no. 2 (Autumn 1989), pp. 191–209; Hans Kjellberg and C.-F. Helgesson, 'On the Nature of Markets and their Practices', *Marketing Theory* vol. 7 no. 2 (2007), pp. 137–62; Detlev Zwick and Julien Cayla (eds), *Inside Marketing: Practices, Ideologies, Devices* (Oxford and New York: Oxford University Press, 2011).

34. A problem of many advertising histories lies, one might argue, in their attempt to model rationalist assumptions of neoclassical economics into the contingencies or dead-ends of history.

35. *Reel and Slide*, for instance, the official organ of the Screen Advertiser's Assocation of the World, regularly commented on institutional needs and requirements, as would *Business Screen* starting in the late 1930s. See Harry Levey, 'Editorial', *Reel and Slide* vol. 2 no. 1 (January 1919). In his unpublished dissertation, Jeremey Groskopf provides an excellent survey of these debates. Jeremy W. Groskopf, 'Profit Margins: The American Silent Cinema and the Marginalization of Advertising' (dissertation, Georgia State University, 2013).

36. See the remarkable, yet untranslated book by Ralf Forster, *Ufa und Nordmark: Zwei Firmengeschichten und der deutsche Werbefilm 1919–1945* (Trier: Wissenschaftlicher Verlag Trier, 2005).

37. Research by Yvonne Zimmermann, for instance, conducted in the framework of the Swedish research project Advertising and the Transformation of Screen Cultures (2014–16), sheds light on the blurred boundaries between educational, promotional and experimental forms.

38. For instance, *The Film Daily* in 1938 divided the 'commercial field' into four 'types of non-theatrical films': institutional films, sales and dealer-instruction films, sponsored films and short length ad-films. Francis Lawton, 'Motion Pictures for Management and Selling', in Jack Alicoate (ed.), *The Film Daily Year Book of Motion Pictures, 20th Annual Edition* (New York: The Film Daily, 1938), p. 683. See also Lucy Česálková, 'Kinobarons and Noble Minds: Specifics of Film Exhibition in Czechoslovakia Beyond Commercial Entertainment', in Richard Maltby, Philippe Meers and Daniël Biltereyst (eds), *Routledge Companion to New Cinema History* (forthcoming 2016).

39. Publicity was the press agent's work of arranging free exposure, and exploitating the miscelleaneous category of promotions, according to Gaines, *Contested Culture*, p. 40. See also Suzanne Mary Donahue, *American Film Distribution: The Changing Marketplace* (Ann Arbor: UMI Research, 1987), p. 75. Janet Staiger relates this famous distinction back to Robert Cochrane, Vice-President of Universal Studios, in her seminal essay 'Announcing Wares, Winning Patrons, Voicing Ideals: Thinking about the History and Theory of Film Advertising', *Cinema Journal* vol. 29 no. 3 (Spring 1990), pp. 3–31.

40. Groskopf, 'Profit Margins', pp. 7–8.

41. Ibid., pp. 172–218.

42. Forster, *Ufa und Nordmark*, pp. 10–20.

43. Anon., 'Business Looks at Screen Advertising', *Business Screen Magazine* vol. 1 no. 6 (1939), pp. 17–18.

44. *Business Screen Magazine* vol. 2 no. 6 and 7 (1940) includes rivalling ads by Paramount Pictures and J. Walter Thompson, respectively (p. 222 and p. 219).

45. Cf. Pamela Walker Laird, *Advertising Progress: American Business and the Rise of Consumer Marketing* (Baltimore and London: Johns Hopkins University Press, 1998).

46. Elsaesser, 'The Place of Non-Fiction Film', p. 22.

47. Devon Overpeck, 'Subversion, Desperation and Captivity: Pre-film Advertising in American Film Exhibition Since 1977', *Film History* vol. 22 no. 2 (June 2010), pp. 219–34.

48. Marchand, *Advertising the Amercian Dream*, p. 104.

49. Fritz Machlup, *The Production and Distribution of Knowledge in the United States* (Princeton, NJ: Princeton University Press, 1962), pp. 207–94.

50. See, for instance, Arthur Asa Berger, *Television as an Instrument of Terror: Essays on Media, Popular Culture, and Everyday Life* (New Brunswick and London: Transaction, 1980), p. 143; Guy Cook, *The Discourse of Advertising* (London and New York: Routledge, 2001 [1992]), pp. 133–4 (quote taken from this source).

51. Groskopf, 'Profit Margins', p. 54. Trade journals such as *Exhibitors Herald*, *Moving Picture World*, *Sponsor*, *Variety* and others frequently brought up the term in either defensive or accusing ways, at least since the 1920s. More recently, Pinboard-founder and blogger Maciej Cegłowski noted, 'Advertising is like a flu, it always changes in order to avoid resistances' (http://idlewords.com, last accessed 15 January 2016).

52. Hediger and Vonderau, 'Record, Rhetoric, Rationalization', p. 46.

53. Bert Hogenkamp, 'A Strategically Weak and Parasitic Form? Reflections on the History of Corporate and other Useful Media in the Netherlands', talk delivered at the Faculty for the Humanities, Vrije Universitet Amsterdam, 6 November 2015.

54. Rotzoll, 'The Captive Audience', p. 72.

55. Luis Araujo, 'Markets, Market-making and Marketing', *Marketing Theory* vol. 7 no. 3, p. 222.

56. Waller cites Rick Altman, *Film/Genre* (London: BFI, 1999), pp. 62–8. Altman, however, does not consider advertising a genre, arguing that its 'primary discursive role' is in 'pitching products to potential purchasers', rather than constellating communities of viewers – for Altman, the only true indication of genre cinema. Raphaelle Moine has differentiated this position by stressing the notion of 'cinema genre', hence, the broader sphere of generic activity taking place outside Hollywood mainstream entertainment. Raphaelle Moine, *Cinema Genre* (Malden, MA: Blackwell, 2008).

57. The idea that 'trade follows the film' was widespread in the 1920s, and points to how the film industry's ideas about its own function within an emerging consumer society and consumer culture was itself historically variable. Thanks to Joel Frykholm for pointing this out to me.

58. George E. Marcus, 'Ethnography in/of the World System: The Emergence of Multi-Sited Ethnography', *Annual Review of Anthropology* vol. 24 (1995), pp. 95–117; 'Introduction', in Marcus (ed.), *Para-Sites: A Casebook Against Cynical Reason* (Chicago and London: University of Chicago Press, 2000), pp. 1–14.

59. Marcus, *Para-Sites*, p. 8.

60. Martin Quigley, 'Advertising on the Screen', *Motion Picture Herald* vol. 103 no. 1 (4 April 1931).

61. Levey, 'Editorial'.

PART 1
HISTORIES AND
APPROACHES

Advertising and Film: A Topological Approach

Yvonne Zimmermann

This chapter is concerned with outlining a framework for the study of advertising film: a framework that embraces research into the objects, screens and practices of moving-image advertising. I suggest a topological approach and consider what the question 'Where is advertising film?' can contribute to conceptualising the ephemeral practice of advertising with moving images. I focus on the exhibition and consumption of advertising film in different times and *dispositifs* to outline the productivity of a topological approach in more detail. There are other related topics that would be worth considering, such as the place of advertising in production culture, but they are outside the scope of the present chapter.

The chapter ties research on moving-picture advertising into recent debates by addressing the notions of topography and spectatorial experience. These two aspects have become core interests of film studies, not least as a consequence of the fundamental changes in the media sphere. Mobile media, satellite signals, cable, digital channels and global digital networks have increased and altered the spaces, places and trajectories of moving images. With media progressively converging, moving images have transgressed traditional media boundaries and become ubiquitous and ever present. These modified constellations challenge media studies, and film studies in particular, since film studies' classical central object – the cinema – is no longer the primary site of film consumption. A focus on the largely under-researched object of advertising film can further contribute to the field, not only by refining our historical knowledge and current understanding of this ephemeral media practice, but also by eventually speaking to questions raised by digital technology.

DEMARCATING THE OBJECT OF STUDY

Although the focus of this chapter is on the spatial dimensions of moving-picture advertising, responding to the question of 'Where is advertising film?', it still seems useful to begin with the ontological, Bazinian question of 'What is advertising film?', if only to delineate the very object of study considered here. At the same time, this is an admission that it is impossible to separate clearly the 'where' from the 'what' (and the 'when'), as will become evident later in this chapter. The 2009 Amsterdam Workshop on advertising film displayed the vastness and richness of the field: under the umbrella of the term 'advertising film', scholars and archivists presented moving images that varied in format (celluloid, video, digital), in length (from one-minute clips and shorter to feature length), in representation modes (fiction, nonfiction, animation), in style, in rhetoric and in audience address. Defining advertising film is tricky, given the ubiquitous yet ephemeral, multiform, shape-shifting, performative and transgressive character of moving-picture advertising. The elusiveness of this media practice makes it difficult even to determine the very object of study and to demarcate the research field.

In the history of advertising film production, a basic distinction would be made between advertising film in a narrow sense and advertising film in a broad sense.[1] This distinction, as simple as it is, can still help to conceptualise the object of study today. Advertising film in a narrow sense includes short movies, often called 'commercials', 'spots' or simply 'ads' that advertise a product, brand, service, or behaviour. If the predominant purpose of commercials is to raise sales, the aim of advertising in business practice can also be to out-compete other companies, as Michael Schudson argues in his classic 1984 study *Advertising, the Uneasy Persuasion*.[2] Building a brand and ensuring customer loyalty are other objectives of commercials. Even if commercials in the western world pursue different aims in the short run and have symbolic and cultural utility that transcends the mere selling of merchandise, as Schudson claims, in the end and from the advertisers' perspective, they serve the capitalist logic of economic growth. For several decades, the prevalent places of commercials or spots were cinema and television. The last twenty years or so have seen a fundamental diversification of channels for motion-picture advertising: the mobilisation and multiplication of screens, 'the explosion of cinema',[3] 'the dislocation of television screens'[4] and the emergence of social media networks have provided commercials with the potential to inhabit virtually any screen, whether private or public.

To label this probably most blatant category of advertising films *commercials* or *spots* helps to distinguish it from a second body of advertising moving images: that is, advertising films in a broad sense, understood as a rhetorical type of moving image that intends to influence audience opinions, attitudes and behaviour. Such films are 'made to persuade', to quote the theme of the eighth Orphan Film Symposium, held in New York in 2012. Moving-picture advertising in the broad sense has a rhetorical 'brief' and the 'charge' to affect spectatorial thoughts and actions, to borrow two terms art historian Michael Baxandall (1985) uses to reconstruct the historical intentions behind art in order to explain its formal appearances. Historically, the broad category of advertising film overlaps to a large degree with another prominent category in film history, the (sponsored) documentary, and embraces a variety of genres: it includes travelogues and tourist films, industrial and corporate films, many *Kulturfilme* (cultural films) and educational films, social and political campaign films, as well as sanitation and recruitment films. Such moving pictures would normally range from ten or twenty minutes to feature length, be predominantly instructional in tone and often pursue their advertising goals in a discreet and indirect manner (without mentioning either commissioner or product/brand).

Two other types of advertising films that specialise in advertising movies – the trailer and the making-of – can also be added to this category. Finally, more recent audiovisual forms of buzz and viral marketing that work through social media networks can be incorporated into the category of advertising film in a broad sense as well.

To include these highly ephemeral and complex forms of moving-picture advertising into the study of advertising film is to acknowledge not only the impressively wide range of historical and current screen advertising practices that go way beyond the explicit advertising of brands, products and politicians; it is also to acknowledge the pivotal role that these implicit, latent advertising forms played and play in shaping media culture and consumer culture and in building communities and identities. From a historical perspective, these films often interlaced consumer education and civic education. They were the products and promoters of a joint venture of business and state, of corporation and nation, of an alliance of capitalism and democracy that has made advertising pervade our daily life.

IS ADVERTISING FILM A GENRE?

The question whether moving-image advertising can be conceptualised and studied as a genre lends itself to vivid debates. Such debates are often undermined by category misunderstanding and may benefit from a clarification of the term 'genre' and its various semantic implications. It is quite obvious that the question of genre is appropriate only in regard to advertising films in the narrow sense – that is, to commercials or spots – and is not relevant for the discussion of advertising films in a broader sense, given the generic diversity that characterises this latter category. To decide whether commercials or spots constitute a genre depends on how genre is defined. The German language distinguishes between the term '*Genre*' and the term '*Gattung*'. This distinction may be helpful to frame the complex phenomenon of advertising film more precisely. Following Knut Hickethier's comments on genre theory and analysis, the German term '*Genre*', on the one hand, describes a formal or structural category that includes films that share a story formula, narrative convention, a particular milieu, specific character and conflict constellations, or specific emotional and affective constellations.[5] The German term '*Gattung*', on the other hand, refers to particular modes of representation (fiction, nonfiction, animation film) or to specific functions and uses of films. *Gattung* is therefore a predominantly pragmatic category. If we relate this to advertising film, we can state that, essentially, advertising film is defined by the function it performs, namely advertising, and not by intrinsic properties that perform this function. It is, therefore, primarily a *Gattung*, a functional and thus pragmatic category, rather than a *Genre* that builds on intrinsic properties. Yet, this general classification of moving-picture advertising as *Gattung* (or what could translate as 'pragmatic genre') does not preclude the possibility of commercials forming distinct bodies of films that share formal features and thus qualify as *Genre* (or what could be termed 'formal genre'). Indeed, there are commercials that do share story patterns, character constellations and other similarities in form and content and thus do qualify not only as a pragmatic genre, but also as a formal one.

In a larger perspective, moving-picture advertising can be understood as a pragmatic subgenre of the category of *Gebrauchsfilm* (utility film), or what in Anglo-Saxon media studies would be called *useful cinema*. This research field has recently emerged both in Europe and in the USA and has been very productive for the study, preservation and presentation of ephemeral or orphan films – that is, neglected moving images such as science and industrial films, educational films, newsreels and home movies. Among the pioneering studies in the field are *Films that Work* edited by Vinzenz Hediger and Patrick Vonderau (2009) on the use of moving images in industrial contexts, Charles R. Acland and Haidee Wasson's anthology *Useful Cinema* (2011) on functional films in classrooms and civic circuits and the two collections of essays on educational and classroom films *Learning with the Lights Off* (Orgeron *et al.*, 2012) and *Lights! Camera! Action and the Brain* (Bahloul and Graham, 2012). The concept of useful cinema refers to a wide range of films beyond the commercial mainstream and beyond the art film canon; it includes a large body of films that were neither primarily produced as commodities to make money with or as pieces of art, but that were used as instruments to produce knowledge and to influence audiences in the context of an 'ongoing struggle for aesthetic, social, and political capital'.[6]

To approach screen advertising within the theoretical and methodological framework of useful cinema studies[7] means to acknowledge the pragmatic logic of advertising film as being not an end in itself (to make money or art), but a *means* to influence minds, shape tastes and affect behaviour. Inducing cooperation on the part of customers, workers, citizens and authorities with the advertiser is among the predominant missions of motion-picture advertising. In other words, advertising films, like *Gebrauchsfilme* in general, are not commodities, but instruments in the service of the advertiser. The exploitation logic of commercials, therefore, differs from that of mainstream cinema and the entertainment industry: instead of *making* money with the production, distribution and exhibition of moving pictures, advertisers *pay* money for their films to be exhibited and watched. This general rule primarily applies to commercials, whereas in historical practice less explicit forms of advertising films such as instructional documentaries, cultural films and other sponsored movies with educational value could find audiences for free in commercial cinemas, classrooms and other non-theatrical venues. Still, the question of 'Who pays for screen space?' can be helpful when trying to locate advertising film; even more so since the identification of motion-picture advertising has become increasingly challenging in today's media landscape, not least because of buzz or viral marketing strategies that use digital social networks as platforms to spread advertising in disguise.[8]

WHY SPACE MATTERS

Digitisation and cinema's loss of indexicality have not only contested the very concept of cinema and its material condition, film's chemical and photographic base;[9] digital and mobile media are also widely perceived as having plunged cinema as the predominant site of filmic experience into a crisis. As Francesco Casetti has put it, cinema begins to disentangle itself both 'from its exclusive medium (film – projector – screen) and from what has long been its privileged place (film theatre)'.[10]
Cinema screens dislocate, and filmic experience relocates to find new media and new environments. Rather than perceiving cinema in the digital era as being threatened in its very existence, André Gaudreault and Philippe Marion diagnose a 'kinematic turn', a shift from the medium of cinema to a convergence of moving-image media, arguing

that cinema has always been more an 'evolving patchwork of "federated" cultural series' than a static form with a fixed identity.[11] The authors see in today's media landscape an eerie reflection of early cinema with roots in an intermedial mash-up culture in the late nineteenth century. Gaudreault's theory of 'cultural series' draws attention to the variety of cultural practices that moving images were part of in the 1890s and 1900s – such as stage entertainment, photography, magic lantern and lecture, to name but a few – before they were perceived to form their own separate cultural series – cinema – around 1910.[12] If the so-called digital revolution and mobile media have put the place of filmic exhibition and experience into question,[13] the notion of cultural series can serve as a conceptual directory to a topological approach. And advertising film lends itself as a paradigmatic object of research to illuminate and explore the many sites of moving images, with cinema being but one among many others.

Across the humanities and social sciences the spatial turn has fostered an understanding of space as *produced* (and not given), and has called attention to the role of space in the construction and transformation of social life.[14] Also in media and cinema studies, space has been acknowledged as a central methodological and analytical category. Most notably, the spatial turn has fostered a better understanding of the *site-specificity* of moving images. In the introduction to their collection of essays on the spaces of filmic knowledge Vinzenz Hediger, Oliver Fahle and Gudrun Sommer claim that film cannot be understood without an examination of the places of the moving image.[15] The spatial and experiential transformation of the exhibition sites of moving images through digital media have also prompted a re-evaluation of space and exhibition sites in cinema history. In his essay 'The Place of Space in Film Historiography' (2006), Robert C. Allen draws on geographer Doreen Massey's relational notion of space –that is, that space is a product of interrelationships and interactions, constructed through embedded material practices and in itself eventful, to elaborate a theoretical and historiographical model that would take the multiform experience of cinema into account.

To contribute to this scholarship by studying advertising film within a spatial framework is significant for at least three reasons. First, the more ubiquitous and ephemeral an object of study is, the more attention has to be paid to retracing and locating it. Space matters, as Barney Warf and Santa Arias remind us, 'not for the simplistic and overly used reason that everything happens in space, but because *where* things happen is critical to knowing *how* and *why* they happen'.[16] The mapping of the sites and networks of moving-image advertising is thus essential to an understanding of advertising film. Second, I argue that looking at the place of advertising film in cinema and on television sheds new light from a different, so far neglected angle on these traditional sites of moving-image exhibition, and recalls spectatorship and experience into question. Finally, a cartography of moving-image advertising will reach beyond the classic domains of cinema and television and their correspondent studies. It will expand into the vast territory of non-theatrical film and useful cinema, which includes advertising films as 'other' to the predominant cultural series of cinema and television. Such an approach can essentially contribute to a larger film-historical project: to an archaeology of moving images in the many cultural series and institutional practices that shaped and informed private and public life. Given the manifold intersections of moving images with other media in these spaces, such an endeavour is at the same time an archaeology of intermediality.

ADVERTISING'S PLACE IN COMMERCIAL CINEMA

Exhibition and consumption present a vast territory to map the past and present sites of moving-image advertising, from cinema and television to the internet and mobile phones, from town and union halls to libraries and sports stadiums, from city squares to private and public transportation. I suggest that we put the building of a typology of the sites of screen advertising on the agenda of advertising film studies. It is evident that all studies of films, whether advertising or not, can benefit from attention to the context of their exhibition. But there is more at stake in a typology of the sites of moving-image advertising than learning about exhibition context. Arguing in the line of Warf, Arias and others, exhibition sites are not containers for films to be screened; rather, exhibition sites are *produced* by the films on screen just as much as the *films* are produced by the exhibition sites. Exhibition sites co-produce the screened objects. In this sense, exhibition sites are formative in that they format the films to be screened and, as a consequence, they are also normative. A typology of the *sites* of moving-image advertising will therefore produce a typology of the *forms* or *formats* of advertising film.

To illustrate this point, I focus in the following on the exhibition site of cinema and draw on two studies, one published in the USA in 1916, the other in Europe in 1949. The first provides an insight into moving-picture advertising's struggle for a place in commercial cinema, the second a reference for its successful institutionalisation.

Journalist and self-proclaimed expert in motion pictures Ernest A. Dench's 1916 *Advertising by Motion Picture* is a handbook for advertisers published in a transitional period of cinema history, when the era of the nickelodeons was on the verge of declining and movie theatres, specifically built for the purpose of screening moving images, were becoming the predominant site of film exhibition, offering longer and better programmes and more comfortable surroundings. The institutionalisation of cinema was on its way, with the star system being introduced and the feature film slowly becoming the standard format of fictional entertainment. Yet, as Dench perceived it, in 1916 'the motion picture has not reached maturity'[17] and advertising film in particular 'is practically only in its infancy today'[18] and therefore still negotiating for a place in cinema. Slide advertising seems to have been institutionalised as an advertising practice by then, given the regular projection of a series of twelve slides at most in the intermission and standard rentals varying from $5 to $10 per month, according to size and location of the theatre.[19] The exhibition of motion-picture advertising, however, was not standardised. Dench deplores this situation: 'What is sapping the progress of film advertising is that no systematic method of circularizing exists, for, naturally, this end of the process is as important as the picture itself.'[20]

Piecing together Dench's scattered remarks on advertising film exhibition in commercial cinemas in the first half of the 1910s, the following picture emerges: if advertising films were screened, they were part of the regular cinema programme and placed at the end of it as an extra reel. Most programmes changed daily and had an average length of two hours. Advertising films were a supplement to the regular programme for which the advertiser paid a fee to the exhibitor. Rentals varied from $12.50 to $50 per week – a considerable range compared to the average costs of a one-reel industrial film that amounted to $500 for the negative and to $100 for each print. Only one advertising film was screened per programme, and the standard length was one reel – that is, eleven to eighteen minutes, depending on projection speed. One reel was still the standard film length in cinema exhibition at that time (although films with two and more reels were becoming more customary). We also learn from Dench that the most common type of advertising film was the 'industrialog, portraying the process by which certain goods are manufactured',[21] or what cinema studies call fabrication film or process film today to designate a highly standardised genre within the category of the industrial film that typically demonstrates the trajectory from raw material to product and consumption step by step.[22] This instance underlines that advertising films in the broad sense must be included in the study of moving-image advertising in order to capture the full range of advertising forms and practices.

Dench's manual attests to a variety of experimental practices to bring advertising films into cinemas, among them, for example, a weekly newsreel produced by a company that in the first half comprised topical events while the remaining portion was a booster for the firm's goods and was offered to exhibitors for free.[23] In the struggle for an institutionalised place in commercial movie theatres, Dench suggests that advertising motion pictures imitate established film genres and insert advertising points into comedies, dramas, serials and newsreels, thus combining advertising with entertainment and instruction. Dench also advocates that movie stars be coaxed to feature in advertising films. The strategy was to blend advertising films into the regular cinema programme. Hence the films adapted to movie-theatre pictures in length (one reel), in style (documentary, comedy, drama, newsreel) and in marketing (star system). As advertising film had not (yet) carved out its own separate place in cinema, we can conclude it had not (yet) found its own separate formula, the commercial.

INSTITUTIONALISED COMMERCIALS IN 1940S CINEMA IN WESTERN EUROPE

The second example to illustrate the formative and formatting power of space in the cinema exhibition practice of advertising films is situated in Western Europe in the late 1940s and paints a different picture. In a manual for advertisers titled *Die Grundlagen der Filmwerbung* (*Fundamentals of Advertising Film*), published by the Swiss Advertising Association in 1949, there is a table that draws a transnational comparison between the theatrical exhibition of commercials in seven European countries or regions, namely Switzerland, Belgium, England, France, Holland, Italy and Scandinavia.

Country	Length of films (in metres)	Number of advertising films per running week	Placement in the programme	Method of cost calculation
Switzerland	Up to 120m	1	Programme of shorts	Price per film Consistent price for all cinemas in a list
Belgium	10–70m	3–6 in total 150m	Intermission	Price per metre according to cinema category
England	65–70m	1	Programme of shorts	Price per metre according to cinema category
France	10–70m	3–6 in total 150m	Intermission	Price per metre according to cinema category
Holland	50–120m	1	Programme of shorts	Price per metre individual per cinema
Italy	30–100m	1–3 in total 120m	Partly intermission, partly programme of shorts	Average price per film according to selection of cinema
Scandinavia	35–70m	1–4 in total 140m	Intermission	Price per metre individual per cinema

The table considers four features for comparison: the length of the films, the number of commercials screened per week, the place of the commercials in the programme and the method of cost calculation. The comparison in film length shows a range between 10 metres and 120 metres per commercial, equalling a running time between twenty-two seconds and four minutes and twenty-four seconds (at a projection speed of twenty-four frames per second). The average length is 70 metres (two minutes and thirty-five seconds). Commercials are longest in Switzerland and Holland, and shortest in France and Belgium. From this information a contemporary advertiser with transnational marketing ambitions would have taken the advice to commission a commercial of 70 metres in length in order to have the largest possible theatrical distribution options. The number of commercials screened per theatrical week ranges from one in Switzerland, England and Holland to up to six in Belgium and France. We can deduce from the table that the total length of the commercial programmes is between 120 and 150 metres (four minutes and twenty-four seconds to five minutes and thirty seconds). The third column locates commercials in the cinema programme and assigns them two possible slots: either in the programme of shorts that precedes the screening of the feature film or in the intermission. Commenting on this situation the manual notes that 'a completely satisfying placement of the film in the programme' only exists in Switzerland, England, Holland and, to some extent, in Italy:[25] that is, in those countries that grant commercials a place *within* the movie programme. Being part of the cinema programme meant that commercials were screened in the dark and addressed a seated audience that (eventually) was in an attentive and receptive mode. Or, as Dench puts it in his study, 'you obtain a hundred per cent attention, for folks, in the darkened hall, must concentrate upon the screen'.[26] The last column lists cost calculation for cinema exhibition (either per metre or per film and whether depending or not on the movie theatre category), reminding us that, in the case of cinema commercials, advertising space is paid-for space.

The table is instructive in many ways and inspiring for further research. First of all, it tells us that there *was* a place in cinema for commercials in Western Europe; that there *was* a programme section assigned to films that use explicit rhetoric to advertise brands and products. With Dench's study at the back of the mind one can conclude that, at some point in time, both the commercial as a separate type of film and its separate place in cinema had been institutionalised (in Western Europe at least), although the details of this process are largely obscure and await further study. This institutionalisation is no matter of course, not even in the capitalist stronghold of the USA, where, despite the occasional inclusion of advertising films in the early days of cinema programmes, commercials had no lasting place in regular movie theatres. Commercials came and went from American screens from 1894, as Kerry Segrave's study on product placement in Hollywood films illustrates,[27] but did not gain acceptance on American screens until the mid-1970s.[28] After the institutionalisation of cinema, moviegoers in the USA came to expect, as Douglas Gomery writes, one feature, a couple of shorts, a newsreel and possibly a stage show, but no commercials. Commercials continued to be largely absent from movie screens in the USA when, in the early 1930s, the double feature was introduced as a programme formula that would function as the standard in movie exhibition through the 1940s.[29]

Regarding the formative and formatting power of space, the table shows that the granted place in the programme regulates the length of the commercials.[30] This, in turn, affects narrative; it affects what stories commercials tell and how they tell them. To advertise a product in twenty-two seconds or in four and a half minutes makes a difference in scope and pace, in rhetoric and audience address. Swiss commercials from that period, for example, are epic, often veritable mini-features starring vernacular stage and film stars in short comedies, detective stories and melodramas (thus pretty much following the formula that Dench suggests). Whether screened as a stand-alone item in the commercial programme or together with up to five other spots competing for audience attention also affects form and rhetoric. The same applies for a screening slot in the dark with a seated audience compared to during the intermission when the lights are on and audience attention is distracted from the screen.

The space of cinema produces a public arena that attracts, involves and interacts with audiences of particular social formations in terms of gender, age, race, ethnicity and religion. From an advertising perspective, these are target audiences and, as such, they also affect the commercials: they affect both *what* is advertised and *how* it is advertised. From this point of view, the table reflects on how commercials are co-produced by their position in cinema and how commercials, in turn, also co-produce the experiential space of cinema in interaction with audiences, thus pointing to the complex, heterogeneous interrelationships that produce space.

RECONSIDERING PROGRAMME AND SPECTATORSHIP IN CINEMA HISTORY

Furthermore, and probably most importantly, the table calls attention to the question of the programme and to advertising film as a programme category. In explicating this point, I refer to the typical cinema exhibition practice in Switzerland that, from the 1930s to the early 1970s, remained rather constant and was, at least in the German-speaking part of the country, modelled after cinema exhibition in Germany. During this period commercials were but one of three distinct categories of advertising film (both in the narrow and broad sense) in regular cinema programmes. The second category consisted of trailers[31] and the third category comprised so-called *Kulturfilme*, cultural films that explore foreign and local cultures, customs, landscapes, art, science, architecture, industry and manufacturing. One such short, predominantly nonfiction film of an average length between ten and twenty minutes, would be screened before the main feature. The *Kulturfilm* category calls to mind the one-reel process film in early cinema advertising practice that Dench mentions. Cultural films were screened for free, but to qualify for the *Kulturfilm* category they had to comply with certain conditions: the films had to renounce explicit advertising and the disclosure of sponsors (this stipulation has resulted in the sponsorship of cultural films being often overlooked). Instead, they resorted to discreet and indirect ways of promoting modernisation, consumerism, gender roles, bourgeois culture and citizenship. This illustrates the normative and formative power of space. With this third category, cinema offered a place for advertising in disguise of bourgeois civic education, which, in turn, also advertised bourgeois values and culture. The *Kulturfilm* was institution-alised in German cinemas in 1926 (when tax breaks motivated cinema owners to screen cultural films) and adopted in Austria and Switzerland (and other European countries at certain points in time) to domesticate the institution of cinema by counterbalancing entertainment with education in the above-mentioned sense.[32] All three categories of advertising film, together with the newsreels (which, contrary to Dench's hopes, remained free of commercials, but, of course, could also have indirect advertising aspects),[33] were part of the so-called *Beiprogramm* – that is, the programme of shorts that preceded the screening of the main attraction, the feature film – which, for its part, may or may not have included product placement. In interaction and exchange with other advertising media and practices present in the space of cinema, such as cinema billboards, advertising slides and giveaways, advertising film in its multiple shapes co-produced cinema as a hybrid multimedia advertising space.

A topological enquiry of advertising film shifts the focus from the single space in cinema that has been researched in depth so far – that of the feature narrative – to the largely under-researched field of the programme of shorts and, in so doing, calls for a reconsideration of the programme formula of cinema. As I have argued elsewhere,[34] research into historical programming has predominantly been concerned with early cinema,[35] with avant-garde and experimental film[36] and with television.[37] With the industry-wide institutionalisation of the full-length feature film in the mid-1910s, scholarly interest in theatrical programming has largely come to an end. Even though scholarship on exhibition and presentation in commercial cinema has increased and research into cinemagoing and movie memories proliferates,[38] these studies predominantly focus on cinema's main attraction: the movies – that is, mainstream feature films and their importance in daily life as social practice and object of remembrance. Nico de Klerk's essay on nonfiction films in commercial cinema theatres in the Netherlands in the 1930s is a rare exception in that it considers the programme of shorts in more detail.[39] De Klerk mentions musical shorts and singalongs to have been regular components in the programme of shorts in Dutch cinemas (some of them might also have had an advertising aspect), whereas in Switzerland, at least to my knowledge, they did not have a standard place in commercial movie theatres – an example that points to the need for comparative transnational research (see below). Research into advertising film and the programme of shorts highlights that cinemagoing was (and still is) more than watching movies: it included the experience of a variegated programme of shorts, plus a feature or two. Thus, advertising films teach us *not* to reduce cinema to a space for feature-length movies and suggest instead that we reconsider cinema in the light of programme variety.

Concurrently, advertising films call film consumption and spectatorship into question. Studies on film reception and spectatorship in 'classical' cinema centre on the reception of narrative feature film and foreground diegetic absorption, 'attendance'[40] and 'individual spectatorship'[41] in distinction to the early cinema mode of collective audience. Spectatorship of the programme of shorts is neglected, and with it possible alternative forms of attraction, distraction and diversity. Even if such different forms of address and attractions predominantly acted as a foil to the feature to maximise their difference, as de Klerk argues, the following question may still be worth considering: what if early cinema's paradigm of attraction and pre-classical forms of direct audience address and collective spectatorship were *not* expelled from cinema by the introduction of feature narratives (to go underground in non-theatrical venues before resurfacing in the post-cinema area), but continued to exist – in modified forms – in the programme of shorts?[42] The assumption that there were remnants of early cinema in the programme of shorts needs to be validated by further research, but I think it is safe to say that advertising films and commercials, in particular, do attest to the co-existence of different modes of audience address and spectatorship in movie theatres, to a heterogeneity of forms of film consumption and experience and, as a consequence, to a practice of mode switching in institutionalised cinema.

TRANSNATIONAL COMPARATIVE RESEARCH

To conclude this short transnational exploration of the space of advertising film in commercial cinema, let us return to the table and take up what is probably its most compelling feature: its comparative approach. The table illustrates national differences as well as similarities between some European countries and regions and draws attention to the need for comparative transnational studies of the spaces of advertising film in cinema (where the programme of shorts could serve as comparative object of study), but also on television (where the introduction of commercials and their place in the programme flow of state-regulated public broadcasting and commercial television might be a reference for comparison). Here is not the place to further elaborate on such projects which, in terms of methodology, might profit from Andreas Fickers and Catherine Johnson's thoughts on a comparative approach to transnational television history.[43] Suffice it to say that the presentations at the second International Workshop on Advertising Film, held in Stockholm in 2012, revealed compelling national dissimilarities (as well as similarities) regarding the historical place of advertising film in cinema and on television within Europe, between Europe and the USA and between capitalist and non-capitalist countries; these findings call on future studies of advertising film to invest in transnational research.[44]

EXPANDING THE FIELD

A mapping of the sites of advertising film expands beyond cinema and television into fields that for many years were blind spots in film history. Recent studies have started to chart this territory; they have mined the home movie and excavated amateur film practices,[45] they have explored film in the museum and the gallery[46] and they have traced distinct uses of moving images in schools, universities, science, business, surveillance and the military. Or, to formulate it with Gaudreault's notion of cultural series, they have started to retrace the place of moving images in the many cultural series and institutional practices other than cinema that have included moving pictures in their concerted use of various media. Thomas Elsaesser has hinted at a possible relation between new technologies and the increasing academic recognition of this field:

> Even before the advent of digitization, it was obvious that the cinema also existed in what one might call an expanded field. ... What is new – and perhaps a consequence of the new digital media – is that we are now willing to grant these uses the status of parallel or parallax cinema histories.[47]

Since the rise of digital technology and media, it has become customary to break down film history into the three successive periods of early cinema, cinema and post-cinema.[48]This periodisation suggests a linear history of one cinema evolving from the previous. But, as Gaudreault and others have argued, institutional cinema cannot be understood as having grown out of early cinema's diverse practices around the *kinematograph*. Likewise, post-cinema cannot sufficiently be explained by mere transformations of the institution of cinema. Scholars have pointed out the parallels between pre-classical and post-classical forms of spectatorship, between early modern and postmodern forms of distraction and diversity, between new media and old media.[49] Even if it is not their intent, these comparisons demonstrate that cinema cannot provide historical explanations for the post-cinema condition in which – we sometimes have to remind ourselves – cinema still exists.

Instead, we have to look for answers elsewhere. The expanded field of 'useful cinema', 'non-theatrical film', or 'other cinemas' provides alternative grounds for media archaeology to excavate the spaces, networks and flows of moving images within institutional practices at the crossroads of other media and cultures; it presents alternative grounds in which moving images in alternative media constellations provided 'possible futures' for media practices to eventually resurface in the era of post-cinema. This is also to state that, since the early days of the *kinematograph*, moving images have never stopped being also part of other cultural series and media constellations, even after moving images found their 'own' and 'proper' space in the institution of cinema. The institutionalisation of cinema has not rendered these alternative practices extinct, but obscured them until cinema itself has become part of other media constellations as well.

It is within this framework that the topological study of advertising film can essentially contribute to a media archaeology of the digitally expanded places of moving images, to a media archaeology of the post-national 'space of flows'[50] and today's mediascape.[51] It might be particularly interesting to retrace the place of advertising film within the institutional context of the advertiser, of corporations, business organisations, non-profit organisations and other commissioners. To take the example of the business world, one could focus on the place of advertising film within different industrial sectors[52] or within a single corporation and centre on screen advertising as part of the corporate media mix (*Medienverbund* in German) to study moving images in relation to other media, thereby examining both the various levels of inter-, trans- and cross-media relations and exchanges and what Raymond Bellour calls 'the passages of the images':[53] that is, the exchange and collision between different media images (cinema, photography, video and the digital). Individual products or individual advertising campaigns, their spaces and trajectories over time or at a certain moment in time, could be the objects of such institutionally framed studies. Since screen advertising is not an exclusive business practice, but widespread among non-profit organisations ranging from health organisations and educational boards to political and social interest groups, there is a large variety of institutional spaces to put the research focus on.

A second point of departure from a topological perspective could be to undertake explorations into the place of advertising film within the cultural series of exposition. The multimedia spaces of expositions, fairs and trade shows are alternative *dispositifs* that lend themselves to a study of the role of moving-image advertising (in interrelation and exchange with other media) in experimenting with production and exhibition technology and in co-producing alternative experiential spaces and public spheres. Outdoor spaces with their transformation into mediascapes constitute yet another cultural series to explore moving images, intermediality and media convergence. Shibuya Crossing in Tokyo and Times Square in New York City would be emblematic places in the eastern and western world for this endeavour. Among many aspects, such an enquiry could reflect anew, in a different setting and timeline, on the transition of still image to moving image upon considering the transformation of billboard advertising to moving-picture advertising. And it might have us re-examine to what extent the multiplication of screens in urban environments and public spaces is, in fact, a transformation of pre-existing billboards and screens to digital screens.

Moreover, places like Shibuya Crossing and Times Square could also be studied as a mediascape of attraction in which media exposes itself and creates a self-reflective media space, a meta-mediascape, so to speak, in which advertising film itself is on display.

ADVERTISING FILM AS PERFORMANCE

The last section of this chapter responds to the question of 'When is advertising film?' rather than to the question of 'Where is advertising film?', even though the approach is still topological.[54] Issues of time and temporality surface when setting out the pragmatic essence of moving-image advertising: its persuasive rhetoric, or, if you will, the 'advertising' part in moving-image advertising. In the case of commercials, the answer is simple: the 'advertising' is in the film; persuasive rhetoric is part of the cinematic text. However, persuasive rhetoric is not necessarily a textual feature; it can also be a contextual factor. The institutional framing of a film screening, the embedding of moving images in a marketing event and its accompaniment by performative activities such as lectures can provide external advertising rhetoric and turn the screened film into an advertising film. In these moments, the exhibition of an advertising film has the character of a performance. This particular *dispositif* evokes early cinema again, when live music, sound effects and lectures would add meaning to and complete the projected film. The instance calls attention to the highly ephemeral character of advertising-film exhibition as a live event and a performance, and to the particular experiential space that it creates. A map of advertising film will also have to hold on to and register those ephemeral moments when moving-picture advertising is a performance, which is only possible when focusing on the very moment of exhibition.

In lieu of a conclusion, I return to cinema's contested future in the digital era. One of the goals of topological research into advertising film would be to contribute to illuminating a topography that is composed of the various cultural series that moving images were and are part of. In such a landscape, cinema would appear only as one among many other cultural series. To de-centre the place of cinema this way could be a conceptual tool that averts us from looking at moving images beyond cinema merely from the vantage point of cinema and from perceiving it as *other* than cinema. In expanding André Gaudreault's methodological claims for the study of early *kinematography* into later periods,[55] I argue that it would be preferable to look at moving images not only *before* cinema, but also *beyond* cinema (and, if you will, *post*-cinema) from the perspective of the other media and cultural spaces that moving images are part of. However, linking cinema to other cultural series and media constellations and studying it as one node in a ramified network of moving-image practices is to integrate cinema into the larger picture of moving-image culture. Even if such cartography does not challenge cinema's historical status as the primary site of feature-film exhibition and consumption, it still shifts perspectives given the scale and scope of moving images that circulated for other than entertainment purposes. Advertising film is one case in point. This is not to derogate the space of cinema, but to advocate for the place of the moving image in the twentieth and early twenty-first century and for studies that invest in exploring its place.

NOTES

1. See, for example, in the context of Switzerland, the issues on advertising film published for *Schweizer Reklame und Graphische Mitteilungen* (1937) and *Die Grundlagen der Filmwerbung* (1947).

2. Michael Schudson, *Advertising, the Uneasy Persuasion: Its Dubious Impact on American Society* (New York: Basic Books, 1984).

3. Ji-Hoon Kim, 'The Post-Medium Condition and the Explosion of Cinema', *Screen* vol. 50 no. 1 (Spring 2009), pp. 114–23; Francesco Casetti, 'Die Explosion des Kinos: Filmische Erfahrung in der post-kinemaotgraphischen Epoche', *Montage AV* vol. 19 no. 1 (2010), pp. 11–35.

4. William Boddy, '"Is It TV Yet?" The Dislocated Screens of Television in a Mobile Digital Culture', in James Bennett and Niki Strange (eds), *Television as Digital Culture* (Durham, NC: Duke University Press, 2011), pp. 76–101.

5. Knut Hickethier, 'Genretheorie und Genreanalyse', in Jürgen Felix (ed.), *Moderne Film Theorie*, 2nd edition (Mainz: Bender, 2003), pp. 62–96.

6. Charles R. Acland and Haidee Wasson (eds), *Useful Cinema* (Durham, NC, and London: Duke University Press, 2011). The term 'useful cinema' is one of several designations for this emerging research field. 'Non-theatrical' is another term that is widely used. It refers to the production, circulation and exhibition of all sorts of moving images beyond commercial cinema circuits. See also Anthony Slide, *Before Video: A History of the Non-Theatrical Film* (New York: Greenwood Press, 1992) and Dan Streible, 'Introduction: Nontheatrical Film', *Film History* vol. 19 no. 4 (2007), pp. 339–43. Equally inclusive is the term 'other cinemas' in its embracing all films outside the mainstream of commercial cinema such as amateur, educational, industrial and other sponsored films (see 22nd International Screen Studies Conference 2012 dedicated to *other cinemas*). Other terms are more specific: Barbara Klinger's 'extra-theatrical' cinema describes cinematic experience beyond the multiplex (Barbara Klinger, *Beyond the Multiplex: Cinema, New Technology, and the Home* [Berkeley: University of California Press, 2006]). The term 'expanded cinema' emerged in the experimental film movement in the 1960s and refers to moving images within the art scene (see Gene Youngblood, *Expanded Cinema* [New York: E. P. Dutton, 1970]). Similar to that is Raymond Bellour's use of *autre cinéma* to describe media installations in the gallery (Raymond Bellour, 'D'un autre cinéma', *Traffic* no. 34 [2000], pp. 5–21).

7. See Yvonne Zimmermann (ed.), *Schaufenster Schweiz: Dokumentarische Gebrauchsfilme 1896–1964* (Zurich: Limmat, 2011).

8. On virality as a theory of contagious assemblages, sociological events and affects in network cultures see Tony D. Sampson, *Virality: Contagion Theory in the Age of Networks* (Minneapolis: University of Minnesota Press, 2012).

9. See, among others, Philip Rosen, *Change Mummified: Cinema, Historicity, Theory* (Minneapolis: University of Minnesota Press, 2001); Tom Gunning, 'Before Documentary: Early Nonfiction Films and the "View Aesthetic"', in Daan Hertogs and Nico de Klerk (eds), *Uncharted Territory: Essays on Early Nonfiction Film* (Amsterdam: Stichting Netherlands Filmmuseum, 1997), pp. 9–24; Mary Ann Doane, 'The Indexical and the Concept of Medium Specificity', *Differences: A Journal of Feminist Cultural Studies* vol. 18 no. 1 (2007), pp. 128–52; David Norman Rodowick, *The Virtual Life of Film* (Cambridge: Harvard University Press, 2007).

10. Francesco Casetti, 'Filmic Experience', *Screen* vol. 50 no. 1 (2009), p. 62.
11. André Gaudreault and Philippe Marion, *The Kinematic Turn: Film in the Digital Era and its Ten Problems*, trans. Timothy Barnard (Montreal: Caboose, 2012), p. 32.
12. André Gaudreault, *Film and Attraction: From Kinematography to Cinema*, trans. Timothy Barnard (Urbana and Chicago: University of Illinois Press, 2011 [2008]).
13. See the numerous essays that retrace cinema and filmic experience in today's multimedia environment (Casetti, 'Filmic Experience'; Casetti, 'Die Explosion des Kinos'; Casetti, 'Rückkehr in die Heimat: Das Kino in einer post-kinematografischen Epoche', in Irmbert Schenk, Margrit Tröhler and Yvonne Zimmermann [eds], *Film – Kino – Zuschauer: Filmrezeption/Film – Cinema – Spectator: Film Reception* [Marburg: Schüren, 2010], pp. 41–60; Malte Hagener, 'Where Is Cinema [Today]? The Cinema in the Age of Media Immanence', *Cinema & Cie* no. 11 [Autumn 2008], pp. 15–22; Francesco Casetti and Sara Sampiero, 'With Eyes, With Hands: The Relocation of Cinema Into the iPhone', in Pelle Snickars and Patrick Vonderau [eds], *Moving Data: The iPhone and the Future of Media* [New York: Columbia University Press, 2012], pp. 13–32; Alexandra Schneider, 'Kann alles ausser Popcorn, oder Wann und wo ist Kino?', in Philipp Brunner, Jörg Schweinitz and Margrit Tröhler [eds], *Filmische Atmosphären* [Marburg: Schüren, 2012], pp. 91–106).
14. Barney Warf and Santa Arias (eds), *Spatial Turn: Interdisciplinary Perspectives* (Florence: Routledge, 2008).
15. Vinzenz Hediger, Oliver Fahle and Gudrun Sommer, 'Einleitung: Filmisches Wissen, die Frage des Ortes und das Pensum der Bildung', in Gudrun Sommer, Vinzenz Hediger and Oliver Fahle (eds), *Orte filmischen Wissens: Filmkultur und Filmvermittlung im Zeitalter digitaler Netzwerke* (Marburg: Schüren, 2011), p. 9.
16. Warf and Arias, *Spatial Turn*, p. 18 [emphasis in the original].
17. Ernest A. Dench, *Advertising by Motion Pictures* (Cincinnati: The Standard Publishing Company, 1916), p. 203.
18. Ibid., p. 156.
19. Ibid., p. 201.
20. Ibid., p. 162.
21. Ibid., p. 47.
22. See Gunning, 'Before Documentary', pp. 17–18; Zimmermann, *Schaufenster Schweiz*, pp. 266–85.
23. Dench, *Advertising by Motion Pictures*, pp. 62–3.
24. Chart reproduced from Schweizerischer Reklame Verband (ed.), *Die Grundlagen der Filmwerbung: Eine Wegleitung für Auftraggeber* (Zurich [1949]), p. 20 (translated by the author).
25. Ibid., p. 18.
26. Dench, *Advertising by Motion Pictures*, p. 198.
27. Kerry Segrave, *Product Placement in Hollywood Films: A History* (Jefferson, NC, and London: McFarland, 2004).
28. Deron Overpeck, 'Subversion, Desperation and Captivity: Pre-film Advertising in American Film Exhibition Since 1977', *Film History* vol. 22 no. 2 (June 2010), pp. 219–34.
29. Douglas Gomery, *Shared Pleasures: A History of Movie Presentation in the United States* (Madison: University of Wisconsin Press, 1992), pp. 77–8.

30. Cinema space and television space were also formative for the use of colour. Colour film became standard for cinema commercials in the early 1940s, whereas television commercials were black and white until the introduction of colour television broadcasting in the 1970s.

31. On American movie trailers, see Vinzenz Hediger, *Verführung zum Film: Der amerikanische Kinotrailer seit 1912* (Marburg: Schüren, 2001); Lisa Kernan, *Coming Attractions: Reading American Movie Trailers* (Austin: University of Texas Press, 2004); Keith M. Johnston, *Coming Soon: Film Trailers and the Selling of Hollywood Technology* (Jefferson, NC: McFarland, 2009).

32. See Klaus Kreimeier, Antje Ehmann and Jeanpaul Goergen (eds), *Geschichte des dokumentarischen Films in Deutschland*, vol. 2: Weimarer Republik 1918–1933 (Stuttgart: Reclam, 2005); Peter Zimmermann and Kay Hofmann (eds), *Geschichte des dokumentarischen Films in Deutschland*, vol. 3: 'Drittes Reich' 1933–1945 (Stuttgart: Reclam, 2005); Ramón Reichert (ed.), *Kulturfilm im 'Dritten Reich'* (Vienna: Synema, 2006); Zimmermann, *Schaufenster Schweiz*.

33. Unlike advertising films, newsreels were commodities. The production of newsreels was a business whose return on investment came from cinema exhibition. In other words, cinema owners paid for newsreels to be part of the programme.

34. Yvonne Zimmermann, 'Nestlé's Fip-Fop Club: The Making of Child Audiences in Non-Commercial Film Shows (1936–1959) in Switzerland', in Schenk *et al.*, *Film – Kino – Zuschauer*, pp. 281–303.

35. Frank Kessler, Sabine Lenk and Martin Loiperdinger (eds), *KINtop: Jahrbuch zur Erforschung des frühen Films* no. 11: Kinematographen-Programme (Frankfurt am Main, Basel: Stroemfeld/Roter Stern, 2002); Thomas Elsaesser, *Filmgeschichte und frühes Kino: Archäologie eines Medienwandels* (Munich: Edition Text+Kritik, 2002); Ivo Bloom, *Jean Desmet and the Early Dutch Film Trade* (Amsterdam: Amsterdam University Press, 2003); Andrea Haller, 'Das Kinoprogramm: Zur Genese und frühen Praxis einer Aufführungsform', in Heike Klippel (ed.), *'The Art of Programming': Film, Programm und Kontext* (Münster: Lit, 2008), pp. 18–51.

36. Malte Hagener, 'Programming Attractions: Avant-garde Exhibition Practice in the 1920s and 1930s', in Wanda Strauven (ed.), *The Cinema of Attractions Reloaded* (Amsterdam: Amsterdam University Press, 2006), pp. 265–79; Ansje van Beusekom, '"Avant-guerre" and the International Avant-Garde: Circulation and Programming of Early Films in the European Avant-garde Programs in the 1920s and 1930s', in Frank Kessler and Nanna Verhoeff (eds), *Networks of Entertainment: Early Film Distribution 1895–1915* (Eastleigh: John Libbey, 2007), pp. 285–94.

37. Raymond Williams, *Television: Technology and Cultural Form* (Glasgow: Fontana, 1974); Toby Miller (ed.), *Television Studies* (London: BFI, 2002); Robert C. Allen and Annette Hill (eds), *The Television Studies Reader* (New York: Routledge, 2004); Jonathan Bignell, *An Introduction to Television Studies* (New York: Routledge, 2004).

38. Melvyn Stokes and Richard Maltby (eds), *Hollywood Spectatorship: Changing Perception of Cinema Audiences* (London: BFI, 2001); Annette Kuhn, *An Everyday Magic: Cinema and Cultural Memory* (London and New York: I.B.Tauris, 2002); Gregory A. Waller (ed.), *Moviegoing in America: A Sourcebook in the History of Film Exhibition* (Malden, MA: Blackwell, 2002); Jon Lewis and Eric Smoodin (eds), *Looking Past the Screen: Case Studies in American Film History and Method* (Durham, NC: Duke University Press, 2007); Richard Maltby, Melvyn Stokes and Robert C. Allen (eds), *Going to the Movies: Hollywood and the Social*

Experience of the Cinema (Exeter: University of Exeter Press, 2007); Richard Maltby, Daniel Biltereyst and Philippe Meers (eds), *Explorations in New Cinema History: Approaches and Case Studies* (Malden, MA: Wiley-Blackwell, 2011); Daniel Biltereyst, Richard Maltby and Philippe Meers (eds), *Cinema, Audiences and Modernity: New Perspectives on European Cinema History* (London and New York: Routledge, 2012).

39. Nico de Klerk, 'The Moment of Screening: What Nonfiction Films Can Do', in Peter Zimmermann and Kay Hoffmann (eds), *Triumph der Bilder: Kultur- und Dokumentarfilme vor 1945 im internationalen Vergleich* (Konstanz: UVK, 2003), pp. 291–305.

40. Janet Staiger, *Perverse Spectatorship: The Practices of Film Reception* (New York: New York University Press, 2000), pp. 11–27.

41. Thomas Elsaesser, 'Wie der frühe Film zum Erzählkino wurde: Vom kollektiven Publikum zum individuellen Zuschauer', in Irmbert Schenk (ed.), *Erlebnisort Kino* (Marburg: Schüren, 2000), pp. 34–54.

42. Miriam Hansen has called attention to the persistence of early cinema exhibition practices through and even beyond the nickelodeon period, claiming that these practices provided the condition for an alternative public sphere (Miriam Hansen, *Babel and Babylon: Spectatorship in American Silent Film* [Cambridge: Harvard University Press, 1991]). A salient example for such an alternative public sphere building on early cinema modes in the context of advertising and marketing is Nestlé's Fip-Fop Club, a film club for children that was immensely popular in the 1930s through the 1950s (see Zimmermann, 'Nestlé's Fip-Fop Club').

43. Andreas Fickers and Catherine Johnson, 'Transnational Television History: A Comparative Approach', *Media History* vol. 16 no. 1 (2010), pp. 1–11.

44. I do not advocate for an Anglo-Euro-American approach in particular, but summarise the conference outcomes. It is understood that the objective must be a topology of advertising film that spans the globe and allows for worldwide transnational comparison as well as for research into the transnational flows of advertising film in digital media channels and social networks.

45. Patricia R. Zimmermann, *Reel Families: A Social History of Amateur Film* (Bloomington: Indiana University Press, 1995); Alexandra Schneider, *Die Stars sind wir: Heimkino als filmische Praxis* (Marburg: Schüren, 2004); Karen L. Ishizuka and Patricia R. Zimmermann (eds), *Mining the Home Movie: Excavations in Histories and Memories* (Berkeley: University of California Press, 2008).

46. Haidee Wasson, *Museum Movies: The Museum of Modern Art and the Birth of Art Cinema* (Berkeley: University of California Press, 2005).

47. Thomas Elsaesser, 'Early Film History and Multi-Media: An Archaeology of Possible Futures?', in Wendy Hui Kyon Chun and Thomas Keenan (eds), *New Media, Old Media: A History and Theory Reader* (New York: Routledge, 2005), p. 20.

48. On the notion of 'post-cinema', see Casetti, 'Rückkehr in die Heimat'.

49. Miriam Hansen, 'Early Cinema, Late Cinema: Permutations of the Public Sphere', *Screen* vol. 34 no. 3 (1993), pp. 197–210; Elsaesser, 'Early Film History and Multi-Media'; Hui Kyon Chun and Keenan, *New Media, Old Media*; Gaudreault and Marion, *The Kinematic Turn*.

50. Manuel Castells, *The Informational City: Information Technology, Economic Restructuring, and the Urban Regional Process* (Oxford: Blackwell, 1989).

51. Arjun Appadurai, *Modernity at Large: Cultural Dimensions of Globalization* (Minneapolis: University of Minnesota Press, 1996).

52. The objects, screens and practices of advertising film depend heavily on 'what' is to be sold to 'whom' and, as a consequence, differ most notably from sector to sector: the place of advertising film in the consumer goods industry, for example, is different from the one in the chemical industry (Yvonne Zimmermann, 'Target Group Oriented Corporate Communication: Geigy Films', in Museum für Gestaltung Zurich [ed.], *Corporate Diversity: Swiss Graphic Design and Advertising by Geigy 1940–1970* [Baden: Lars Müller, 2009], pp. 48–57).

53. Raymond Bellour, 'The Double Helix', in Timothy Druckrey (ed.), *Electronic Culture: Technology and Visual Representation* (New York: Aperture, 1996), pp. 173–99.

54. Thomas Elsaesser has brought up the question of 'when is' in regard to Dada films (Thomas Elsaesser, 'Dada/Cinema?', in Rudolf E. Kuenzli (ed.), *Dada and Surrealist Film* [New York: Willis Locker & Owens, 1987], pp. 13–27) and renewed it in regard to cinema in the age of post-cinema ('Early Film History and Multi-Media').

55. Gaudreault, *Film and Attraction*, p. 63.

2

International Harvester, *Business Screen* and the History of Advertising Film

Gregory A. Waller

> In adapting motion pictures to the educational work of our advertising, this Company [International Harvester] became a pioneer in the field that has no limits in its advertising possibilities ... Our leadership is a beacon for all who follow; it furnishes encouragement for those who are to come after us. This explanation and this encouragement take the form of educational advertising.[1]
>
> *Harvester World*, May 1912

Trumpeting and seeking to shape what it called 'the power of films to sell', *Business Screen: The Magazine of Commercial and Educational Motion Pictures* began publication in September 1938, marking a significant milestone in the business of film advertising in the USA. This periodical would run as *Business Screen* until 1977 and then for eight more years under different titles. As the first and most successful trade magazine covering the field of commercial film-making, this monthly now stands as an essential primary source for the historical study of film advertising and corporate uses of motion pictures and, indeed, for American cinema history broadly and inclusively understood. The searchable online access through the Media History Digital Library to the full run of *Business Screen* – heretofore a periodical quite difficult to find, even in major research libraries in the USA – should transform the way we think about the history of film advertising, industrial film and, more generally, about the contours of what I have called *multi-sited cinema* – that is, the varied and historically specific ways that motion pictures have been put to a host of different uses across a wide range of locations well beyond the commercial movie theatre.

BUSINESS SCREEN BEGINS

Like the other prominent motion-picture trade magazines active in the 1930s, *Business Screen* offers a mix of information, editorial commentary, film reviews, advertising for products and services and highly topical news coverage. Together, this sometimes quite diverse array of print material constitutes a rich discursive field in which the uses and the usefulness, the production and the circulation and the varieties and values of advertising films were defined, assessed and promoted. Nowhere is this more apparent than in the inaugural issue of *Business Screen*, which serves – sometimes quite explicitly – as an industry insider's articulation of the already bustling and well-established business of using motion pictures as an advertising medium. Issue 1.1 is an effective showcase for the magazine and the field at large, filled with full-page advertisements for portable Bell & Howell, Victor and Ampro projectors and Da-Lite Screens; for top-tier non-theatrical producers like Jam Handy, Burton Holmes Films and Wilding Productions; and for major distributors like Modern Talking Picture Service, as well as for innovative delivery formats like General Screen's *Minute-Movies* and new sales-oriented technologies like Flolite's fully automatic, self-contained projector with built-in screen. Articles cover animation and sound slide-films, tout US Steel's latest productions shot in Technicolor, describe successful distribution and exhibition strategies employed by Standard Oil and provide advice on the deployment of film in department stores (complete with a detailed survey of practices in Chicago's major retail stores). Virtually everything in the first issue of *Business Screen* suggests that this modern medium is alive and doing quite well, burgeoning with opportunities for expanding markets and for new uses that businesses large and small might make of motion pictures. Not surprisingly, nothing in the issue challenges the claim (or mantra) that sound motion pictures are 'easily the most perfect of all modern advertising media'.[2]

So preoccupied are trade magazines like *Business Screen* with speaking to the ever-changing present and speculating about the short-term future that they typically have little space (or inclination) to provide historical perspective.[3] But the first feature article in the first issue of *Business Screen* does precisely that, perhaps as a way of legitimating the advertising film's present by acknowledging its past – specifically, by celebrating the motion-picture productions of the International Harvester Company (IHC), deemed 'a pioneer of 1911 [that] shows the way in 1938'.[4] Created in 1902 by the union of the major competing farm machinery companies, IHC quickly came to dominate the North American market, aggressively branching out internationally (opening a factory in Sweden in 1905 and Germany in 1909), and introducing a wide range of new product lines (including trucks in 1907 and tractors in 1908). Almost from its inception, IHC faced legal challenges to its corporate policies that finally led to one of the era's most high-profile government suits, charging International Harvester in April, 1912 with monopolistic activities in violation of the Sherman anti-trust law.[5]

According to the first issue of *Business Screen*, the history of the advertising film was in fact coterminous with the activities of International Harvester, which had been utilising motion pictures for over twenty-five years. As my epigraph indicates, IHC was claiming as early as 1912 a 'leadership' role in the corporate use of motion pictures and had, by 1938, some forty films (totalling 2,800 prints) in circulation, including titles like *The Building of Boulder Dam* (1935) and *Soybeans for Farm and Industry* (1938). The newest wave of IHC sound films – all designed to offer a measure of 'entertainment' value – aimed at providing 'sales promotional background' and 'institutional publicity' rather than seeking to boost direct sales of equipment. What's more, *Business Screen* asserted, *Back to the Old Farm*, said to have been produced by IHC in 1911, stood as a motion-picture landmark since it 'practically dates the application of this medium to industrial and advertising uses except for some isolated experimental attempts'.[6]

Three issues later in 1938, *Business Screen* expanded on this particular claim, describing *Back to the Old Farm* as the 'first dramatic sales film', which applied 'showmanship to selling' and reached 'millions of farmers' in a remarkably cost-effective manner. A detailed summary of the film and ten frame enlargements supposedly taken from the last surviving print resurrect – and canonise – *Back to the Old Farm* and begin to provide commercial film-making with a history that pre-dates the advent of 16mm film and fully mobile projectors. For *Business Screen* – preoccupied with state-of-the-art sales strategies and thoroughly modern equipment – there is even a lesson to be learned from International Harvester's wise decision to 'not plug the product to the exclusion of dramatic interest' in *Back to the Old Farm*.[7] An IHC representative made a similar point in *Business Screen*'s February 1939 issue: the company's films that had proven to be most successful in selling to farm audiences, he declared, 'have been dramatic. *Back to the Old Farm*, the first dramatic sales film, proved the value of drama for this group.'[8]

Perhaps responding to the heightened visibility of the film in *Business Screen*, IHC repackaged *Back to the Old Farm* as a sound film in 1940. Nothing appears to be cut from the original production, though the re-released version opens with a new title: 'HISTORY! A REview Not a PREview.' It also adds a prologue with a folksy company spokesman announcing: 'We are about to show you the first motion picture made by a business company.' His spoken voiceover commentary during the remainder of the film gently mocks the datedness of performance styles and even the accuracy of the original in depicting farm life. But *Back to the Old Farm* is not treated to the parodic ridicule afforded repurposed silent-era films in, for example, MGM's contemporaneous *Goofy Movies* series. I have found no evidence about the distribution of the sound version, but it is worth noting that claims for *Back to the Old Farm*'s supposed status as 'the first industrial motion picture' surfaced again in *Business Screen* in 1950 and two years later in IHC's magazine, *International Harvester Today*.[9]

It ultimately makes little difference whether *Back to the Old Farm* was actually the first 'dramatic sales film' or whether IHC in 1912 had, indeed, found the key to the successful use of motion pictures for advertising purposes. Verifiable or not, these claims still have historical relevance for what they reveal about *Business Screen* and the field it set out to serve in 1938. And these claims, likewise, point us backward to the 1910s to look not for pioneers but for what a film like *Back to the Old Farm* might help us see about corporate uses of motion pictures, material practices related to production and circulation and the media environment within which IHC and other early adopters of advertising films operated.

ESSANAY'S *BACK TO THE OLD FARM*

Released by the Essanay Film Manufacturing Company on 3 September 1912, *Back to the Old Farm* begins with white-collar, thirty-something George behind a desk in a hot, cramped city office planning a vacation.[10] His friend, Frank, arrives and proposes that they accept an invitation to visit the old farm where George had once worked. That night, an intertitle informs us, George, in his small apartment, 'dreams of the old farm of ten years ago'; what then appears on screen is not some picturesque and cherished rural homestead, but a site of non-stop, demanding, physical labour in the fields, the barn and the kitchen. Fed up, despondent and disconnected from the farm family for whom he works, George decides to leave for the city. 'I can't stand the drudgery of farm life,' he writes in his farewell note and departs, even as Molly, the farmer's daughter, implores him to stay.

Awakening from this dream/memory, George is ready to forgo the trip until Frank shows him a photo of Molly. Desire, it would seem, trumps bad dreams. The friends embark and, even before they arrive at the farm, an intertitle affirms: 'How the old place has changed. Time and money have worked wonders, sure enough.' The rest of this one-reeler pictures these wonders, the markers of a new standard of living, including a spiffy automobile that picks up the visitors at the train station, delivering them to a substantial, landscaped brick house, where they are ushered into a well-decorated guest room, complete with attached bathroom and indoor plumbing. George is reunited with Molly, who takes him on a horseback tour of what an intertitle calls a 'revelation in modern farming', including machines for ploughing, harvesting and cultivating the fields; and electric-powered contraptions for separating cream, shelling corn and grinding feed. After this revelatory glimpse of what was then known as 'power farming' in action, George is suddenly free to act on his desire. At midnight the couple elopes, driving off in the farmer's auto-wagon. The following morning, a letter is delivered, appropriately by truck, announcing the elopement and George's promise to return soon to the old farm with Molly.

Thus, almost magically, the farm family in *Back to the Old Farm* moves securely into the middle or upper middle class, as drudgery becomes a distant memory even for the new coterie of servants and hired help. *Back to the Old Farm* doesn't find it necessary to explain where the money came from to buy the products that wonderfully transformed the inhospitable homestead, replacing workhorses with machines and ending the gruelling, non-stop tasks of the farm owners, who, in fact, no longer are required to do any physical labour whatsoever.

In its unambiguous celebration of change understood as progress driven by an investment in the technology and methods of 'modern farming', *Back to the Old Farm* enthusiastically echoes an oft-repeated refrain in much of the advertising for IHC and other farm machinery companies in the 1910s. The keynote is the efficiency and, in fact, the necessity of machines for powering the farm and thereby modernising farming to meet the demands of the twentieth century and to improve the quality of life and economic well-being of the farmer and his family. But no intertitle in *Back to the Old Farm* announces this message. No scene shows IHC sales agents in action. No characters speak for the company. No shots dwell for very long on a cultivator or a cream separator.[11]

Not that the collaboration between Essanay and International Harvester was a tightly guarded secret. As part of the pre-release promotion of the film, a brief item in *Moving Picture World* noted that the Dunham Oak Lawn Farm in Wayne, Illinois, had served as the location for 'an [unnamed] educational moving picture taken by the Essanay Film Company for the International Harvester Company'.[12] An even more extensive account of the filming, written by an IHC employee, appeared in the agricultural trade magazine, *Farm Implements*, which also offered a plot summary of a film identified as *Back to the Old Farm*, including mention of its 'little love story'.[13]

Yet the opening title credit of *Back to the Old Farm* offers the standard design and company logo common to other Essanay films of this period, with no indication that International Harvester was in any way involved with the production. In fact, the only overt references to IHC in the film are the sometimes barely visible signs affixed to certain of the vehicles and machines. I assume that this lack of explicit product pitching and corporate branding, coupled with the narrative and character-driven logic of *Back to the Old Farm*, led *Business Screen* to identify the film as the originator of the 'dramatic sales film'. This claim speaks also to one of the prime motifs running through at least the initial issues of *Business Screen*, which proclaimed as a central credo that 'a "business film" is, in essence, a sales tool'.[14] This tidy definition did not, however, foreclose an interest in what the magazine called the various 'types' – the genres – of business film, a topic that was intimately connected to *Business Screen*'s efforts to take a leadership role in a burgeoning field by promoting best practices. To this end, for example, *Business Screen* warned against too much of what it called 'direct advertising' and praised 'technical quality' measured against the standard of Hollywood. And its reviews of recent releases made use of a quite variegated taxonomy, depending on the intended use of and audience for the film under consideration. Certain titles were identified as 'dealer education' or 'public relations' films; others were categorised as 'educational consumer', 'consumer selling', 'institutional selling', 'business education', 'promotional travelogue', 'public relations with subtle advertising' and so on.[15] This taxonomy testified at once to the multiple uses of business films and to *Business Screen*'s informed knowledge of the broad field of commercial film-making.

DISTRIBUTION

Given equal weight in *Business Screen*'s reviews of new product was what the magazine called 'distribution', meaning how, to whom and by whom a film was (or was intended to be) circulated and screened. For instance, *To the Ladies* (1938), produced by Burton Holmes Films for the Milwaukee Lace Paper Company, was described as being screened or screenable in 'special showings to company salesmen at meetings, to jobbers and dealers and general non-theatrical distribution to women's organizations nationally'.[16] Distribution understood in this way was directly related not only to how a particular title circulated, but also to its target audiences and, hence, to its potential usefulness for certain business purposes.

Tracking, even in a necessarily limited way, the distribution of *Back to the Old Farm* in 1911–12 complicates any easy identification of this title as a 'dramatic sales film'. What becomes readily apparent is that *Back to the Old Farm* was initially promoted, exhibited and reviewed not as an International Harvester film but rather as another in a steady stream of Essanay releases.[17] The company's regular weekly ad in *Moving Picture World* on 7 September 1912 covered four films being released that week: a 'screaming farce-comedy', a 'stirring drama of the Far West', a serious romantic drama based on a popular song and *Back to the Old Farm*, pitched as:

> a bucolic comedy-drama of a young city chap's visit back on the old farm on which he worked when a boy. He finds the old place a marvel of improvement and equipped with splendid machinery entirely up-to-date. Entertaining and of great educational value.[18]

Promotional notices and advertisements for *Back to the Old Farm* often drew directly on Essanay's publicity material (a common practice in this period). For instance, another American motion-picture trade journal, *Motography*, similarly described the film as 'a bucolic comedy-drama' and a 'pleasing and novel, as well as educational production'.[19] Even though *Motography*, at this date, explicitly identified certain motion pictures as 'industrials' or 'advertisements', the magazine used neither of these terms in reference to the 'educational' *Back to the Old Farm*.[20] And, complicating matters a bit further, while the film was deemed to be 'educational', it was not cited in *Motography*'s monthly listing of 'Current Educational Releases', which typically favoured scenics, nature films, literary adaptations and historical dramas.[21]

In terms of situating *Back to the Old Farm* for exhibitors looking to book and promote the film, the *Moving Picture World*'s review is particularly telling since it finds the quite laudable strength of *Back to the Old Farm* to be its 'truthfulness' in contrasting older with more modern ways of farming rather than its 'story' and romantic denouement:

> The story that the picture tells doesn't seem very fresh or vital, but it serves very effectively indeed to contrast the old break-back and kill-soul methods of farming (they are very truthfully shown), with the modern and far easier way of making machinery do the hard physical work on a farm, and these also are essentially truthful. So interesting indeed are these views that they raise the picture to a high place among releases as an offering to the public. The early scenes (they are dream memories of the old farm), are finely acted and there is much art in them. The picture's only weakness lies in that the parts do not hook together very convincingly, and the elopement end was neither necessary to make the picture popular, nor was it good art.[22]

What might we make of the fact that the motion-picture trade press in 1912 did not acknowledge (and perhaps did not even realise) that *Back to the Old Farm* was produced *for* International Harvester? Was there already in place, by this early date, a resistance to screening corporate-sponsored films as theatrical entertainment? The role of IHC would seem to have been newsworthy, if nothing else, and a relevant bit of information for exhibitors. But would the lack of recognition have mattered to International Harvester? The film itself, as I noted, does not announce or underscore its corporate lineage. Perhaps IHC would have welcomed moviegoers seeing a narrativised, 'essentially truthful' contrast between 'the old break-back and kill-soul methods of farming' and modern mechanised farming without theatrical audiences realising that this ideologically charged vision of American agriculture was sponsored by a massive corporation that continued to be under scrutiny for its monopolistic tactics. It could well have made good business sense for both Essanay and IHC if *Back to the Old Farm* was produced and promoted on its initial release as 'educational' rather than as industrial or as, in any way, a 'sales film'.

EXHIBITION

Scattered evidence concerning how *Back to the Old Farm* was actually exhibited in motion-picture theatres reinforces the point that the film was not initially circulated as a production made for (and thereby sponsored by) International Harvester. To cite only a few representative examples: directly upon its release in early September 1912, *Back to the Old Farm* was screened in Seattle, Washington; Springfield, Massachusetts; and Racine, Wisconsin, on bills that included three or more other films drawn from different production companies. This standard exhibition strategy was employed through the rest of the year and into January 1913, during which time *Back to the Old Farm* was variously identified in local newspaper ads as a 'bucolic comedy drama of great educational value' or a 'summer pastoral story by the Essanay Company', or as a film that 'tells of a city chap who longed for the country air and his sweetheart'.[23] Once again, I have found nothing in these ads that identified the film as being in any way associated with International Harvester.

In October 1913, an article in *Harvester World*, IHC's in-house magazine, declared that *Back to the Old Farm* 'has been shown in more than half the picture theatres of the world'.[24] A wishful overstatement, to be sure, but this hyperbolic claim attests to the company's ambition to have *Back to the Old Farm* broadly seen by moviegoers in commercial theatres. What sets this motion picture apart from probably all of the many one-reel comedies, dramas and scenics with which it was billed in American movie theatres is the fact that, within three months of its release, *Back to the Old Farm* began to be distributed and exhibited *outside* the standard commercial film system with a goal of reaching more narrowly targeted 'farm' audiences. In December 1912, for instance, *Back to the Old Farm* served as the concluding attraction for two free shows that drew more than 1,000 spectators to the Mathewson Opera House, a 780-seat multipurpose venue in the small town of Boonville, Indiana. Sponsored by the local IHC dealer, who distributed the complimentary admission tickets, this self-styled 'entertainment' also featured International Harvester's illustrated lecture, *The Romance of the Reaper*. In this instance, *Back to the Old Farm* was identified in the local newspaper as having been 'written by Edwin L. Barker of the IHC Service Bureau'.[25] In other words, the event was unmistakably marked as being arranged and brought to Boonville under the direct auspices of the International Harvester Company. Over the next month, the same show played a number of other Indiana towns, sometimes in theatres, but always with tickets free, 'courtesy of the International Harvester Co. and their local agents'.[26] By December 1913, as part of the company's new education plan, *Back to the Old Farm* was being made available (presumably nationwide) to 'farmers' organisations', distributed directly by IHC for only the cost of shipping.[27]

Once *Back to the Old Farm* became readily obtainable from IHC, the extent of this film's circulation and even its shelf life becomes harder to trace. There's no telling, for instance, how many prints were in use, how long they remained available, or if the film (before its 1940 re-release) might subsequently have been retitled, re-edited, or repurposed as stock footage. Even with such significant gaps, the history of *Back to the Old Farm*'s movement from commercial to non-commercial (and largely non-theatrical) screenings offers what could well have been a common or perhaps a preferred trajectory for 'business' films in the North American market during the 1910s. Edwin L. Barker (who claimed authorship of *Back to the Old Farm*) in fact declared in the March 1913 issue of *Advertising & Selling* that 'many firms have made a mistake in thinking that moving picture theaters are the beginning and the end of moving picture circulation. They may be the beginning but they are far – very far – from the end.'[28]

THE ROMANCE OF THE REAPER

Tracking International Harvester's promotional efforts in the early 1910s through farm implement magazines, the moving-picture trade press, local newspapers and *Harvester World* reveals that there was at least one other, more prominent use IHC made of moving pictures beyond *Back to the Old Farm*. As I noted, when *Back to the Old Farm* was first circulated directly under the auspices of IHC, it served as an added attraction to the centrepiece of the programme, *The Romance of the Reaper*, which was not some macabre gothic fantasy, but a celebratory nonfictional account of the invention and spread of mechanised harvesting machines, a history lesson delivered in the form of a performance that combined spoken narration, lantern slides and moving pictures.[29] This multiple-media show took its title (and no doubt some of its ethos) from a book published by a major New York firm in 1908 that lauded International Harvester as the very best in the 'American way of manufacturing', a forward-thinking company committed to 'free trade' and to aggressive international expansion, all the while being run by 'plain, hard-working' and 'simple-living American citizens'.[30] *The Romance of the Reaper*, in effect, provided the all-important – and far grander – back-story for *Back to the Old Farm*.

The Romance of the Reaper – like *Back to the Old Farm* after its initial theatrical run – was promoted and circulated by IHC's Service Bureau, which described its public-oriented mission not as increasing sales of combines and trucks but as solving the problems and advancing the prosperity of farmers.[31] Created in September 1910, the Service Bureau remained within IHC's advertising department until March 1914, when it was moved to a newly formed, more explicitly 'educational' corporate unit, the Agricultural Extension Department, which had been initiated in part as a way of countering charges that IHC's 'public service' activities were ultimately a scheme to 'put over some "indirect advertising"'.[32] Thus, informing any particular uses of moving pictures by International Harvester were the goals and policies of the Service Bureau, whose public visibility, mission and what we could call 'corporate location' underscores the complex and potentially contentious relationship in this period between promotional activity, advertising campaigns, educational initiatives and public service outreach.

A 1912 account of the Service Bureau's many activities insisted, largely on the basis of *The Romance of the Reaper*, that 'speaking of moving pictures, there is probably not a commercial or industrial concern in the world that has done so much in this line of education and publicity as the IHC Service Bureau'.[33] Delivered for the first time at the Iowa State Fair in August, 1910, *The Romance of the Reaper* was, according to IHC press releases, an ambitious (and entirely self-promoting) show said to include a hundred coloured views and 5,000 feet of motion pictures, all telling 'an interesting story' of :

> the centuries of struggle to raise enough to eat – from the days of the reaping hook down to the invention of the reaper, and the coming of agricultural greatness through perfection of modern binders, gasoline engines, farm wagons, and other improved machines and implements. Pictures show the manufacture of farm machines, from the time the lumber is cut in the woods and the ore dug in the mines, until the machines are at work in the field. Harvesting in various countries of the world is shown, the twine industry is described, and other items of agricultural interest are related and pictured.[34]

Throughout the American Midwest, at state fairs – the major annual public event for rural communities and the agricultural machinery industry – *The Romance of the Reaper* was presented in a large black tent adjacent to International Harvester's exhibit of its equipment. Free tickets to the performance were handed out at the exhibit.

But, significantly, *The Romance of the Reaper* reached its widest audiences as a travelling show that, for more than two years, toured the USA, usually as a two-person operation, with a projectionist and lecturer. (At times, two such units were simultaneously on the road.) It continued to be a mainstay at state fairs, but it was also extensively booked into public halls, schools, colleges and theatres, typically under the auspices of the local IHC agent. For example, *Harvester World* reported that a one-month tour in Missouri during March 1912 covered twenty-four different towns, with two shows daily (each featuring live music and introductory remarks by a 'prominent [local] citizen'), with the afternoon performance for farmers and their families and the evening 'for the benefit of the schools, town officials, ministers and personal friends of the local [IHC] dealers'.[35] *The Romance of the Reaper* was also scheduled as the featured entertainment at conferences or other formal gatherings, like the annual meeting of the Illinois Corn Growers' Association or the North Dakota Industrial Exposition. By the time it was retired from service, *The Romance of the Reaper* was said to have been delivered 3,000 times in all parts of the USA and, while it was most successful in rural small towns, it was even presented at the Museum of Natural History in New York City.[36]

Perhaps not surprising given its wide circulation and the fact that it was often referred to as a 'motion-picture show', *The Romance of the Reaper* (unlike *Back to the Old Farm*) figured prominently in early discussions of motion-picture advertising, like Henry W. Mitchell's 'The Camera as a Salesman', which appeared in *System: The Magazine of Business* (December 1910). An article written for the trade magazine, *Advertising & Selling*, and then reprinted in *Motography*, singled out *The Romance of the Reaper* as a successful example of the 'peculiar and unique grip of the new art of moving picture advertising' precisely because in this show the 'advertising side' is less prominent than the 'educational purpose'.[37] The head of IHC's advertising department called this approach 'indirect advertising' or 'educational' advertising, claiming in regards to *The Romance of the Reaper* that:

> we have carefully cut all direct advertising and are emphasizing the interesting points of the story. While we still show some of the processes relative to the manufacture of modern machines, yet, you can see, that all this has its place in the story, and helps to give it a more or less universal appeal. 'The Romance of the Reaper,' as it is now presented, is a big illustrated entertainment, with an undercurrent of the best publicity.[38]

There is scant evidence available to test this claim about the relative quotient of entertainment and advertisement. An article on the performance in the small town of Cloverport, Kentucky, however, offers at least a glimpse of how *The Romance of the Reaper* might have been received. While fully aware that the show promoted the interests of International Harvester and might even lead to sales of IHC machines, the local newspaper insisted that *The Romance of the Reaper* had offered a 'thrilling', at times beautiful, and even quite humorous experience for the audience, who along the way learned much about the invention of the reaper and acquired a fuller appreciation of the international and domestic operations of the International Harvester Company, then under attack by the State of Kentucky for allegedly monopolistic activities.[39] Along the same lines, articles in *Harvester World* touted the 'indirect' advertising benefits of *The Romance of the Reaper*, which was said to have created a 'deeper and more wide-spread respect for the International Harvester Company of America'.[40]

The success of *The Romance of the Reaper* presumably led International Harvester to invest in additional illustrated lectures that promised to include even less material identifiable as company advertising. IHC attempted to market in 1914 what it pitched as an innovative hybrid form of educational entertainment and 'indirect' self-promotion, which the Service Department named the 'industrialog'. This experiment was short-lived, and IHC's use of motion pictures became less ambitious and somewhat more utilitarian by the end of the decade when, for example, it was using *Tractor Farming* (1919) and other 'educational' films of 'popular interest' that 'do not advertise directly' to help create a potential market for tractor dealers.[41]

CONCLUSION

Following a prompt in the first issue of *Business Screen* I have, in this chapter, revisited *Back to the Old Farm* as a way to think historically about the advertising film in the USA and about the role played in this history by International Harvester, a major American corporation with a longstanding investment in deploying motion pictures. Going back to *Back to the Old Farm* complicates any simple genealogy of film used for the purposes of selling, promoting and publicising. But I would argue that there is no revisiting *Back to the Old Farm* as a purportedly pioneering 'sales' film without expanding the conversation to include the discursive terrain occupied by *Business Screen* and without taking into account *The Romance of the Reaper*, IHC's widely presented multiple-media travelling show. Greater consideration than I have been able to provide here is due, most notably, to the non-Hollywood film industry that *Business Screen* addressed in 1938 and to the full breadth of International Harvester's extensive promotional and advertising efforts in the 1910s – efforts related, in turn, to this period's lively discourse in a host of trade journals, general-interest magazines and instructional guidebooks about the role and practice of American advertising.

Moving from *Business Screen* to *Back to the Old Farm* runs the risk of suggesting that the history of motion-picture advertising in the USA might be reduced to the efforts of a handful of major corporations. However, this return to a supposedly pioneering instance also has the benefit of bringing distribution strategies and exhibition practices squarely to the fore. And rightly so. Writing the history of multi-sited cinema depends, in part, on investigating – so far as is possible – how useful cinema was actually put to use.

Equally important, a look back to *Back to the Old Farm* and *The Romance of the Reaper* foregrounds another essential historical issue: the generic identity of these corporate-sponsored productions. The distribution of and period discourse concerning *Back to the Old Farm*, as I have shown, reveals not so much what *Business Screen* called the prototypical 'dramatic sales film', but instead a one-reel motion picture that was promoted and exhibited both as a bucolic Essanay comedy with educational aims and as an International Harvester film about old and new methods of farming. In other words, situating *Back to the Old Farm* and *The Romance of the Reaper* in their original historical context brings certain basic questions about genre to the fore. What makes a film identifiable as an advertisement? To what extent does sponsorship itself determine a film's genre? How much does generic identity depend on when and where a film is exhibited? What is at stake in ascribing a film to a particular genre or in denominating – inventing – a genre? Such questions suggest a process much like what Rick Altman calls 'genrification', the pragmatically driven, historically grounded, sometimes quite contentious activity of generically identifying individual films and constituting genres. This process might turn out to be just as central to the history of the advertising film, the business film and the sales film as it is to the history of the classical Hollywood cinema.[42]

NOTES

1. 'Making the Most of the Lecture', *Harvester World* vol. 3 no. 5 (May 1912), p. 21. I would like to thank Laura Farley, Reference Archivist for the McCormick-Harvester Collection, housed at the Wisconsin Historical Society, for her generous assistance. This archive is to be commended for making important parts of the McCormick-Harvester Collection accessible online.
2. 'New Dimensions in Advertising', *Business Screen* vol. 1 no. 1 (1938), pp. 17–18.
3. An obvious exception is 'Motion Pictures: Not for Theatres', the series that Arthur Edwin Krows published in *Educational Screen*, between September 1938 and June 1944. Note that Krows also refers to International Harvester as a non-theatrical pioneer of sorts ('Motion Pictures: Not for Theatres, Part 27', *Educational Screen* 20 [May 1941], pp. 200, 223). An interesting precursor is Terry Ramsaye's serialised history of the movies, which began running in *Photoplay* in April 1922 under the title, 'A Romance History of the Motion Picture'.
4. 'International Harvester: A Pioneer of 1911 Shows the Way in 1938', *Business Screen* vol. 1 no. 1 (1938), pp. 14–16.
5. The grounds for the government's suit against International Harvester are detailed at length in the Department of Commerce and Labor, Bureau of Corporation's 3 March 1913 report, *The International Harvester Co.* (Washington, DC: General Printing Office, 1913). For a sense of 'agricultural industrialism', see Deborah Fitzgerald, *Every Farm a Factory: The Industrial Ideal in American Agriculture* (New Haven, CT: Yale University Press, 2003). For a sample popular history of IHC, see D. H. Wendel, *150 Years of International Harvester* (Osceola, WI: Crestline, 1993).
6. 'International Harvester: A Pioneer of 1911 Shows the Way in 1938', p. 15. Later issues in the first volume would highlight the efforts of other corporate pioneers and thus help to construct a history for commercial film-making: 'General Electric: A Visual Pioneer', *Business Screen* vol. 1 no. 5 (1939), pp. 17, 42; vol. 1 no. 6 (1939), pp. 23–4, 36, 38; and 'The Tractor Dealer Tells 'Em with Motion Pictures: A Brief History of the Caterpillar Tractor Company's Twenty Year Film Program', *Business Screen* vol. 1 no. 7 (1939), pp. 23–4.
7. 'The Birth of the Sales Film', *Business Screen* vol. 1 no. 4 (1938), pp. 16–17.

8. J. W. Gafill, 'Speak Your Audience's Language', *Business Screen* vol. 1 no. 7 (February 1939), p. 18.
9. 'Since 1911, International Harvester Co. Has Pioneered the Use of Farm Films', *Business Screen* vol. 4 no. 11 (1950), p. 29; 'Film Clips: IH's First Film Had the Old Blend of Romance and "Sell"', *International Harvester Today* vol. 4 no. 3 (November–December 1952), pp. 29–30.
10. Based in Chicago when *Back to the Old Farm* was filmed, Essanay had gone into business in 1907. The company opened a second studio facility in Niles, California, in 1912. My discussion of *Back to the Old Farm* is based on a 16mm copy of the film, checked against the 1940 re-release and contemporaneous written descriptions. Thanks to David Drazin for posting his copy to YouTube complete with an excellent original piano score: http://www.youtube.com/watch?v=Bow99bzHfiM
11. An article by James H. Collins from *Printers' Ink* that was reprinted as 'Advertising via Moving Pictures', in *Moving Picture World* vol. 6 no. 11 (March 1910), pp. 422–3, claims that when Essanay shot films for companies like IHC, it offered not 'a glaring advertisement' but rather a 'general impression which is very lasting' since the name of the company appears on the machines filmed and on 'the "title" which precedes each picture'.
12. *Moving Picture World* vol. 13 no. 6 (10 August 1912), p. 460.
13. J. E. Buck, 'Ancient and Modern Methods of Harvesting Photographed in Motion Pictures', *Farm Implements* vol. 26 no. 7 (31 July 1912), p. 42. I have not located any actual contract between IHC and Essanay that might help explain the precise financial arrangement between the two companies and particulars concerning control over the film's production and its short- and longer-term distribution.
14. 'The Birth of the Sales Film', p. 17.
15. See 'Brief Reviews of Current Releases', *Business Screen* vol. 1 no. 1 (1938), pp. 37, 62; and 'Brief Reviews of Recently Released Motion Pictures and Slide Films', *Business Screen* vol. 1 no. 2 (1938), pp. 40–1.
16. 'Brief Reviews of Current Releases', p. 37.
17. *Making Hay with Modern Machinery* (sometimes referred to as *Making Hay with New Machinery*), another Essanay film sometimes identified as an IHC production, was released by Essanay as a split-reel with the comedy *Accidental Bandit* on 20 August 1913 (*Motography* vol. 10 no. 3 [23 August 1913], p. 4).
18. *Moving Picture World* vol. 13 no. 10 (7 September 1912), p. 935. There is also no hint of the IHC connection in the plot summary Essanay circulated promoting the film, where the only bit of modern machinery actually mentioned is a 'new auto-wagon'. See, for example, *Moving Picture World* vol. 13 no. 9 (31 August 1912), p. 906.
19. 'Photoplays from Essanay's [sic]: Some Coming Features', *Motography* vol. 8 no. 5 (31 August 1912), p. 173. See also the promotional notice in *Moving Picture World* vol. 13 no. 10 (7 September 1912), p. 985.
20. For example, *Motography* identified Edison's *The Manufacture of Paper* (released 10 September 1912) as an 'industrial' and noted that a branch of the Southern Pacific railroad in Texas 'is the first system in the United States to start a continuous advertising campaign through the motion picture medium' ('Advertise Roads by Pictures', *Motography* vol. 8 no. 7 [28 September 1912], p. 248). In *Motography*'s 'Complete Record of Current Films', from 14 September 1912, *Back to the Old Farm* is listed as a 'drama' (*Motography* vol. 8 no. 6 [14 September 1912], p. 231).

21. 'Current Educational Releases', *Motography* vol. 8 no. 6 (14 September 1912), p. 201; 'Current Educational Releases', *Motography* vol. 8 no. 8 (14 October 1912), pp. 285–6.

22. *Moving Picture World* vol. 13 no. 12 (21 September 1912), p. 1174.

23. Advertisements for the Bijou, *Springfield [MA] Daily News*, 7 September 1912, p. 5; for the Clemmer Theatre, *Seattle Daily Times*, 8 September 1912, p. 27; and for the Bijou, *Racine [WI] Journal News*, 10 September 1912, p. 9. See also, for example, advertisements for the Princess Theater, *Lexington [KY] Herald*, 13 September 1912, p. 7.

24. E. L. Barker, 'Batting It Up to Our Own Family', *Harvester World* vol. 4 no. 10 (October 1913), p. 12.

25. 'Free Entertainment', *Boonville [IN] Standard*, 6 December 1912, p. 2; 'Interesting Exhibit', *Boonville [IN] Standard*, 20 December 1912, p. 2.

26. 'Romance of the Reaper', *Madison [IN] Herald*, 17 January 1913, p. 2; the same two-hour show combining *The Romance of the Reaper* with *Back to the Old Farm* played in Idaho Falls, Idaho, in January 1913 (*Idaho Register*, 14 January 1913, p. 1). A notice in *The Implement Age* suggests that a similar show concluding with the 'delightful little drama', *Back to the Old Farm*, was presented several times in Wisconsin ('IHC Lecturers Entertain Wisconsin Audiences', *The Implement Age* vol. 42 no. 4 [26 July 1913], p. 11).

27. *Ardmore [OK] Daily Ardmoreite*, 12 December 1913, p. 8.

28. Edwin L. Barker, 'Picture and Lecture Publicity', *Advertising & Selling* vol. 22 no. 10 (March 1913), p. 57.

29. Rick Prelinger identifies *The Romance of the Reaper* as a one-reel film in his *Field Guide to Sponsored Films* (San Francisco: National Film Preservation Foundation, 2006), p. 79, though I have come across only references to this title as an illustrated lecture that included moving pictures.

30. Herbert Newton Casson, *The Romance of the Reaper* (New York: Doubleday, Page & Co., 1908), pp. 101, 121. The first four chapters of this book had appeared as a series of four articles for the popular monthly periodical, *Everybody's Magazine*: 'The Romance of the Reaper', *Everybody's Magazine* vol. 17 no. 6 (December 1907), pp. 755–66; vol. 18 no. 1 (January 1908), pp. 59–70; vol. 18 no. 2 (February 1908), pp. 196–207; vol. 18 no. 3 (March 1908), pp. 400–11.

31. See the information on the Service Bureau included in most IHC publications of the period, like *The Golden Stream* (Chicago: International Harvester Company of America, 1910), pp. 66–7.

32. 'IHC Service Bureau', *Harvester World* vol. 1 no. 12 (September 1910), p. 5; 'A New Department', *Harvester World* vol. 4. no. 3 (January 1913), p. 16.

33. 'The IHC Service Bureau', *Harvester World* vol. 3 no. 7 (July 1912), p. 28.

34. 'The Romance of the Reaper', *Farm Implements* vol. 24 no. 8 (30 August 1910), p. 48. Later descriptions usually put the amount of moving-picture footage as 2,000 feet.

35. 'Making the Most of the Lecture', *Harvester World* vol. 3 no. 5 (March 1912), p. 21.

36. 'Passing of "The Romance of the Reaper"', *Harvester World* vol. 4 no. 11 (November 1913), p. 6; *Daily Paper* [New York City], 29 March 1913, p. 3. In 1930, IHC produced and distributed a twenty-six-minute sound film, entitled *The Romance of the Reaper*, filmed at the 'Old McCormick Homestead' in Virginia by the Fox–Case Corporation. It is not clear whether any of the footage was drawn from the moving pictures used with the illustrated lecture. Scenes from the lecture might well have been reshot for the 1930 film, which included no synchronous dialogue. Viewable at: http://content.wisconsinhistory.org/cdm/ref/collection/p15932coll3/id/0

37. Joseph B. Baker, 'Examples of Motion Picture Advertising', *Motography* vol. 5 no. 6 (June 1911), pp. 133–6.
38. Edwin L. Barker, 'Industrial Moving Pictures', *Motography* vol. 6 no. 3 (September 1911) pp. 139–40. This article is identified as being reprinted from *The Novelty News*.
39. '"The Romance of the Reaper" As Pictured to Cloverport and Breckinridge County Last Week. Beautiful Field Scenes of the World and the Making and Working of Farm Machines Were Given in the International Harvester Company's Show Thursday Night. Brief Sketch of McCormick', *Breckinridge [KY] News*, 29 November 1911, p. 1.
40. E. J. Ortmeyer, 'On Booking The Romance of the Reaper', *Harvester World* vol. 4 no. 3 (March 1913), p. 5.
41. 'Cracking the Hard Shell Tractor Prospects', *Harvester World* vol. 10 no. 9 (September 1919), p. 16.
42. See Rick Altman, *Film/Genre* (London: BFI, 1999).

3

Selling Machines: Film and its Technologies at the New York World's Fair

Haidee Wasson

This chapter examines the use of film and its technologies during a telling and particularly rich event: the World's Fair of 1939 and 1940 held in New York City.[1] Dubbed the 'World of Tomorrow', the fair boasted over thirty-four purpose-built movie theatres, constituting an unusually dense clustering of films and their spaces. These theatres showed hundreds of documentary, industrial, publicity and advertising films, often continuously from morning until night. Yet, what may seem at first glance to be an impressive if conventional iteration of cinema's apparatus – film, projection, dark room, seated audience – the fair provides an opportunity to expand our understanding of film exhibition and display beyond what we tend to think of as discrete theatres and towards a distinctive but enduring development of film performance and projection scenarios. At the fair, many more moving images appeared in venues that could in no way be deemed theatrical but instead made use of walls, floors, ceilings, small booths and boxes as sites for images big and small, continuous and discontinuous, silent and not.[2] Such film display devices played in large halls, small galleries and walkways designed expressly to facilitate steady human traffic.[3] Moving images addressed a range of spectatorial dispositions, as much the fleeting glance as the focused gaze. The varied modes of watching also entailed navigating elaborate multi-medial exhibits wherein a visitor's eye ambled across texts, still images, objects, maps, diagrams, working machines and perhaps eventually a projected piece of film. Even whole theatres can be understood as but one display technique integral to multi-modal exhibition designs, partial elements of much larger and elaborate themed environments. Such spaces embodied corporate image and aspiration, employing a range of expressive tools and espousing the virtues of technological progress: streamlined architecture, elaborate motorways, moving sidewalks, rocket launches, frozen forests, talking cars and wise-cracking robots!

Considering the whole of the fair's expanded scenario for film performance, there existed a dynamic tapestry of celluloid formats, techniques and processes – silent, sound, colour, 3D, black and white, animation, live action, 35mm, 16mm and 8mm. Some film projectors were concealed and some were foregrounded, some worked by front and others by rear projection. Some films showed as automated loops, some ran by the push of a button and still others as parts of unique hybrid–live performances. Some were designed and featured as sizable, spectacular augmentations of a purpose-built environment and still others were more ambient, blending in with other whirling, winding, flashing and buzzing attractions. In what follows I suggest that this richly textured, highly diversified expanded apparatus can be thought of as a form of 'exhibitionary cinema', extending cinema's relevance well beyond the Hollywood-dominant movie theatre or the generalisable 'non-theatrical' realm towards spaces specifically built to promulgate the ideals of industry and the related, ascendant empire of consumption. At the fair, cinema became a relatively elastic apparatus, shaped by the rising tide of corporate communications and transformed into a machine that sold all manner of idea and thing. This selling machine should not be understood merely as a body of films but needs to be conceived as but one element within a particular, sometimes experimental alignment of words, images, sounds, machines and projections situated within a whole display ecology. These spaces invited onlookers to marvel at the wonders of modern industry, to admire the research prowess of American corporations and to ponder a powerful and enduring invitation: consume.

This chapter builds on the important work of film and media scholars expanding the kinds of films we examine, and the methods we use to consider their importance.[4] It also presupposes that we must equally be adept at assessing the complex scenarios in which these films appeared and the devices that made them visible.[5] Doing so can help us to develop a more fulsome and engaged understanding of the particularities of moving-image advertising, its technologies and techniques and – most important – why and in what ways it mattered. In keeping with this, I will frame cinema less as an apparatus for entertaining or narrating or educating and more as a complex, multiply articulated *machine that sells*. By approaching exhibitionary cinema through the lens of industrial and corporate practice, I seek to contribute to recent work on expositions and exhibitions that tends to focus on art, interactivity, immersion, or the progressive humanist ideals of connection.[6] In what follows, I use the fair as a case study for mapping the ways in which cinema was being appropriated by a new generation of advertising and public relations experts, as well as industrial designers, interested in exploring what they deemed a productive interface between moving images, sounds and selling. The chapter will begin by providing an overview of film at the fair, surveying a range of exhibition scenarios and devices, and then focus on but one: small projection machines. I will conclude with a discussion of what this research suggests for future work on moving images, sounds and advertising.

Before discussing the fair, it is helpful to provide a brief context for this approach to writing film history. Film historians of American cinema have shown that the late 1920s and the 1930s played host to considerable technological transformation. Alongside the well-known shift to synchronised sound, industries were also realigning, building links among the telephone, radio, recorded music, publishing and film industries. The electrical utilities served as key players in the corporate realignments underway, expanding necessarily what we think of when we consider the film industry proper.[7] These corporate and technological shifts changed what films looked like as well as the conditions in which they were shown. Indeed, while movie theatres had, for several decades, served as the primary retail interface between the film business and its consumers, these prominent spaces of cinema became more complex, incorporating new technologies that enabled electronically reproduced and amplified sounds to fill cavernous palaces and modest halls alike.[8] Live radio broadcasts from movie theatres during the 1930s promoted made-in-Hollywood wares and further instituted select flagship theatres as epicentres for unique but also dispersed, broadcast events. Yet this period, which can seem at one glance to mark the consolidation of the theatre's place in the powerful and seemingly dominant cinematic apparatus, also facilitated a slow, concurrent and distinct transformation, one that I will argue is crucial for understanding the interface between advertising and cinema.

Determined efforts to make cinema into architectural spectacle during this period by way of the sophisticated picture palace were also accompanied by a vocal if motley crew of engineers, designers, manufacturers and technophiles committed to creating another, radically different kind of cinema. This other kind of cinema was portable, easy-to-use and adaptable. It often relied on substandard film gauges (8mm and 16mm, among others), as well as a family of smaller machines: cameras, but, notably, projectors. Hundreds of screen types filled out this more malleable apparatus; they came in varied sizes and were made of a range of materials. Growing out of previous and cognate screen practices, such screens stood freely or could be mounted on walls, desks, ceilings and even on moving vehicles. This newly expanded apparatus asserted that cinema need not be confined to Hollywood, theatres, feature films, stars, or to big budgets. Cinema could serve a wider range of purposes, affording a shifting assemblage of production, distribution, display and performance techniques that were highly adaptive to an evolving media ecology and the institutions that shaped them.[9] This kind of cinema was poised directly against the institutional and structural monumentality of the Hollywood-sanctioned movie theatre and the regulatory structures that controlled what could appear there. This other apparatus enabled another kind of media infrastructure, one that allowed films to be seen in a vast range of other spaces and contexts. It also enabled a degree of rearrangement, experiment, provisionality, hybridity and a series of additional uses for celluloid and projector. Included among these were the ascendant communications needs of American industry.

Interior of the Communications
Building, Design by Deskey
(*Business Screen*, 1938)

Cinema's expanded apparatus facilitated and accelerated the use of moving images and sounds by American corporations (and foreign industries operating in the USA). By the late 1930s, such companies included Bell Telephone, John Deere, International Harvester, General Mills, Shell Oil, Renault, Ford Motor Company, General Motors, Chrysler Motor Corporation, Consolidated Edison, Westinghouse, Radio Corporation of America, Coty Cosmetics, US Steel and Republic Steel.[10] To be sure, some of the films made by these companies showed in commercial movie theatres, but many more showed in multipurpose spaces and in provisional venues carved out on factory floors, lunchrooms and boardrooms, in retail outlets, social clubs and at industrial fairs and exhibitions. People gathered in temporary and re-purposed spaces to watch public relations, advertising and training films, among others. The World's Fair built on these extant practices but it also amplified them, using an event-based logic that had long permeated large-scale industrial exhibitions and fairs, as well as emergent exhibition techniques that also employed small-scale adaptable displays. The discussion that follows works to mind the difference between the exceptional monumentality of the fair, and the more prosaic modes by which media and messages circulated, but also to note the ways in which film and other media allowed a degree of traffic across these categories.

CINEMA IN THE 'WORLD OF TOMORROW'

Cultural historian Warren Sussman shows that the 1939 World's Fair in New York boldly continued the convention of all modern fairs: to display the triumphs of state, science and industry. Initially conceived as a way to help kick-start the New York City economy, the fair was thus incorporated by individuals constituting an audacious display of wealth and power, including the heads of twenty-three banking and trust companies, fifteen Wall Street firms and eight insurance companies, as well as the presidents of such corporate behemoths as Standard Oil, General Electric, General Motors, CBS and NBC, among others.[11] Fifteen politicians joined the fair's forty-six-member Board of Directors, including New York City mayor, Fiorello LaGuardia. President Roosevelt spoke at the fair's opening-day celebration, the first televised presidential address in American history. Municipal, state and national government entities built modest and elaborate pavilions. During this tumultuous period of American history, the fair corporation, the administrators working on its behalf and the exhibitors all worked to present a reassuring message to visitors: that after almost a decade of economic hardship, government and industry were successfully building a new world based on private enterprise buoyed by goals of abundance, efficiency, self-fulfilment, technological innovation and consumerism.[12] To be sure, the event's vast size entailed that exhibits and concessions pursued this broad imperative in many ways, each differently shaping common cultural refrains. Robert Rydell and others remind us that the fair inflected its utopianism with normative ideals of the body and the family, many of which were undergirded specifically by eugenics and, more generally, by the racism that permeated the culture at large. The future woman was differently modern, at times appearing as a kind of commodified spectacle, enshrouded virtuously in a sanitised world of home appliances, convenience foods and beauty products and at others offered up as a kind of progressive and sexually liberated figure in the numerous nudie and peep shows that populated fair concessions.[13] The 'World of the Future' was predictably complex.

Yet, general trends can be identified, including the prominent strategies of address employed by American corporations. Historian Roland Marchand argues that while fairs had, up until New York, long served as sites for businesses to sell their wares, the 1939 fair marked a clear shift away from an exclusive emphasis on the selling of things and also included forwarding a particular and carefully crafted corporate image.[14] General Motors, Ford Motor Company, Westinghouse, RCA and AT&T each commissioned monumental if temporary signature buildings that embodied their respective corporate visions while employing the latest practices of industrial architecture: they were modern, streamlined and efficient. In addition to architecture, contemporary techniques of exhibition design inside and outside these buildings completed the vision. Whole building interiors and also surrounding grounds became blank canvases upon which to pursue the ideal of persuasive corporate communication. Film was but one part of this whole exhibition environment, one that didn't just feature moving images but all manner of moving things. One study of this fair's exhibition techniques indicates that 77 per cent of exhibits employed some sort of moving parts in their exhibits.[15] Suitably then, motion pictures, ever-changing projection slides and vibrant, imaginative lighting (particularly at night) appeared throughout the grounds. Buildings constructed of glass, exterior and interior moving platforms and ramps, electrical staircases and even curtains of water underscored the perpetual, controlled movement of all things at the fair: progress.

Trained as an architect, Donald Deskey served as a prominent industrial designer, who, among other high-profile commissions, completed the art deco interiors for Radio City Music Hall, which included the largest movie theatre in the world upon its opening, seating over 6,000. Along with a new generation of other notable industrial designers such as Walter Dorwin Teague and Norman Bel Geddes, Deskey worked on the prestige buildings and exhibits that populated the grounds. Film suited what Deskey dubbed 'industrial showmanship'. In 1938 he wrote:

> Every device for the dramatic presentation of products and ideas is being probed. The motion picture is being used in many cases as an important part of the display. However, the use of the sound film alone in a standard theatre setting is nothing new to the visitor from the crossroads. But as an instrument for the visualization of ideas, it is being incorporated into more elaborate mechanical devices; stage presentations for industry with the motion picture as an integral part.[16]

Affirming Deskey's enthusiasm for the wide uses to which film technologies could be put, a range of exhibits integrated projectors, large- and small-scale images and hidden and highly visible screens. As pictured above, select films played continuously, often as one moving element of spectacular wall displays, rather than as stand-alone events or as unique shows. Film was one material among many used for innovating display techniques, servicing a multimediated design ecology predicated on the persistent march of progress, fuelled by advertising logics which presupposed the incessant buying and selling of things.

The 'industrial showmanship' that Deskey called for placed film in service of a rising common sense within American industry. Effective communications plans entailed selling products and also selling the very idea of private enterprise itself. Principles of showmanship were thus enjoined to techniques that promulgated not simply the quality of a particular steel gadget or the benefits of a specific cleaning product; rather, on the pages of popular magazines and across many other outlets one could increasingly find what today we would call 'public relations' campaigns extolling the importance of steel for building safe school buses and resilient bridges or declaring the crucial role of chemistry for bettering everyday life for Americans.[17] In short, businesses began selling the very idea of business. Using film to tell generalisable stories (Why oil is good for everybody!) and also to sell specific products across an expanding display infrastructure appealed to an increasing number of manufacturers and retailers. This was true in part because this infrastructure allowed them access to groups of people willing to gather for a show (audiences), but also because it allowed for new and sometimes automated ways of forwarding sales messages through narrative, movement, sounds, rhythm, visual effects, projected light – in short, through many of the distinct formal qualities of cinema, which were understood by some as particularly effective at securing favourable consumer attention. Like other media forms, this expanded cinema enabled a site-specific targeting of messages, capable of articulating to both attentive and also distracted consumers, wherever a projection device might be set up. Expanded film scenarios in the late 1930s also likely possessed the basic appeal of novelty as modes of modern messaging (movies on a wall, in an office, at the store!).

At the fair, in addition to nineteen governments (e.g. Russia, Britain, France, Brazil, the USA) that showed films in their pavilions, many more private corporations made and showed films, among them Coca-Cola, US Steel, Greyhound, Westinghouse, Coty Cosmetics, various elements of the oil industry and Eastman Kodak. But the American automobile industry provides a particularly interesting and telling cross-section of film use. Orchestrated by Ford, GM and Chrysler, cinema exhibits ran the gamut from small and incidental to big and spectacular, shaping elaborate exhibits which, as Alice Goldfarb Marquis has claimed, 'flamboyantly reflected the car's central role in American life'.[18] Long before the fair, the Ford Motor Company began an in-house film programme in 1914; General Motors began making sales and promotional films in 1924. Ford, Chrysler and GM used film in multifaceted ways during the 1920s and 30s: screen magazines, training films, worker education, publicity and advertising. Some of these titles enjoyed broad release and appeared in commercial theatres. Some showed primarily in factories, car dealerships, or company social clubs; still others travelled to churches, men's or women's clubs, YMCAs and schools. Lee Grieveson's study of Ford's film programme has shown that the company's films were among the most widely seen of the silent era.[19] 'Car movies' were a familiar genre to Americans who, during the 1920s and 30s, saw the national highway programme connect more and more communities, witnessed the first trends towards suburbanisation and drove to the first car cinemas (the first drive-in opened for business in New Jersey in 1933).

Ford, Chrysler and GM each projected films in theatres at the fair. Yet, they also used film technologies to explore acoustic and spatially multidimensional exhibition techniques. Indeed, a family of technologies operated in a kind of partial and para-cinematic way, linking still and moving displays, flashing lights and electrically amplified sound to each other in vast display environments. Collectively, this amounted to a distinct kind of corporate experiment, a new kind of interface between corporate and consumer desire. Cinema was a modern machine, used creatively and imaginatively in service of other machines – in this case, automobiles – to induce both wonder and desire.

Under this rubric, General Motors commissioned Norman Bel Geddes to design what was called 'Futurama', featuring a moving 1,586-foot 'chair train' that mobilised thousands of seated spectators daily, carrying them through the whole of the pavilion's several hundred elaborately designed futurist dioramas. Futurama illustrated the highway-saturated future of 1960. Seated spectators enjoyed aerial views of highways and 50,000 miniscule cars, 10,000 of which zipped around the expansive installation. As the future was air-conditioned, riders enjoyed the fifteen-minute ride in relative comfort. A recorded lecture, secured optically on 150 unique filmstrips, played from a nearby control room in accordance with where each group of four riders was in relation to the unfolding show.[20] The ride combined the latest sound inscription, reproduction and amplification technologies, the very ones being used in film theatres as well as in the new portable sound film projectors that littered the fairgrounds.[21]

Futurama was not the conventional apparatus we have long prized as film historians, yet technologies of cinema undeniably shaped the ride experience at its core. It embraced mechanical movement and reproduced sound; its iconography echoed that of the much older ride films like Hale's tours, and also presaged the roll-out of Cinerama's widescreen, which presented theatrical cinema as a form of panoramic travel. Celluloid strips with recorded sound ran continuously throughout the ride, synching voiceover and sound effects to unfolding scenes. Futurama was also featured in a subsequent General Motors film called *To New Horizons* (Jam Handy, 1940), which fashioned the automobile and its highways-to-come as the peak of an evolutionary model of human transportation. The on-site fair exhibit was integral to the film, which included extended footage of the ride and elaborated on its themes, making the film a kind of extension of the exhibit. *To New Horizons* showed at the fair in its second year and was widely distributed afterward. In this case, a public relations campaign across media worked to normalise a particularly corporate form of urban planning primarily by way of predicting efficient, accessible, elaborate highway systems, intelligible only if automobiles were normalised as affordable, necessary consumer goods.

In addition to Futurama, GM also boasted the largest conventional theatre at the fair with 650 seats, which provided the venue for another previously circulated GM film – an animated short called *A Coach for Cinderella* (Jam Handy, 1936), which generously upgraded the heroine's pumpkin coach to an eight-cylinder sedan, assembled by flying and floating forest creatures. Likewise, Ford featured a 16mm film entitled *Symphony in F* (Audio Productions, 1940), which depicted everyday scenes in a Ford factory and ended with a stop-motion animation segment of its most recent model self-assembling without human or factory assistance. This film also includes a long segment documenting Ford's on-site exhibit, which included a rotating diorama illustrating the multiple phases of car manufacturing. A mountain-shaped evolutionary narrative shows the procurement of raw materials (usually from exoticised foreign locations with indigenous workers) at the bottom, evolving upward towards the highly civilised industrial logics (and white workers) that directly result in the assembly of a finished car. The film here functioned as a stand-alone media text, but as one integrally linked to a site-specific exhibit, extending that exhibit's reach beyond the fair site.

Magical cars were commonplace at the fair. Each auto company showed films in which automobiles miraculously became whole from parts, whether by animation or stop-motion. The theme of the magical automobile with the powers of self-construction resonates with the insight of Marchand who has suggested that such magic was a common element of the messages promulgated at the fair.[22] Perhaps nowhere was this magic more fully manifest than in Chrysler's 3D film, which became known as the most popular and most spectacular film at the fair. *In Tune with Tomorrow* (John Norling, 1939) billed as '10 Minutes of Magic', was one part of a five-part exhibit, or as Chrysler called it a 'Five Star Show'. The exhibit included a 'Rocket Port of the Future', which featured a fifteen-minute sound film entitled 'History and Romance of Transportation'. The film was projected onto a large silhouetted map of the world. A live on-stage rocket launch served as a finale for the film. Richard Griffith notes that as the film was incomplete without the live launch, it was essentially useless for post-fair viewing.[23] It is worth noting that live sound effects were also used. Another section of Chrysler's five-part exhibit featured a 'Miracle Plymouth', billed as a 'talking car' that responded to questions and claimed to perform 'amazing feats of magic'. The 3D film, *In Tune with Tomorrow*, ran for a total of seventeen minutes and began with a 2D, seven-minute didactic introduction by Major Bowes, a popular radio host, who explained how the 3D effect was achieved. The 3D portion of the film begins with a shot of the half-mile-long assembly-line at a Detroit-based Plymouth plant, but then quickly takes viewers to the story's main stage, where each part of the soon-to-be car is animated by stop-motion. For roughly ten minutes, viewers watch as the various parts of the car fly towards the screen and then seemingly beyond it, eventually settling into a completed on-screen car. The bits and pieces zoom through the air to upbeat, peppy music written specifically for the film.[24] Visitors to the exhibit donned bi-coloured glasses, shaped like the front grill of a car, with lenses where the headlights would normally be. The eyewear doubled as a souvenir; viewers were encouraged to take them home. Apparently, the stereoscopic effect succeeded, though the appeal was often described with a familiar, if contradictory, pull between pleasure and pain. One viewer reported: 'You [still] hear the howls of delight when a cam shaft hits you in the eye.'[25]

According to statistics issued by the fair, the Chrysler theatre was the busiest of all exhibits, with a frequently filled auditorium. According to several sources, there was a 'waiting line for every performance'. The theatre was in continuous operation from 10am to 10pm. An estimated 12,000 per day watched the seventeen-foot-wide screen.[26] *In Tune with Tomorrow* clearly furthered the fair-wide appeal to magic and wonder through its use of novel display technologies and techniques; the magic of the car coincided with the magic of the multidimensional film screen. It should also be pointed out that this film, along with the other car films discussed, presented a context of labourless production and fantastical, automatic assembly. Sidestepping a decade of labour strife, these films celebrated various animation techniques and stereoscopic delights, appealing to customers of the growing car industry. Workers did not fare so well.

SMALL SCREENS

Beyond the more spectacular environments seeking to transform fairgoers into consumers (or perhaps affirm them as consumers) resides a somewhat humbler iteration of cinema's selling machine: the small film screen. Despite the thirty-four different medium and large dedicated auditoria that showed films during the fair's typical day, many more small portable projectors operated throughout the fairground, animating small theatres, restaurants, outdoor gardens, open-air theatres and individual projection rooms, as well as 'various other unique locations'.[27] According to *Business Screen*, 130-odd small projectors operated on a near-continuous basis ten to twelve hours per day, seven days a week. Still another source indicates that roughly 75 per cent of these small projectors operated not just continuously but automatically, without the intervention of an ever-present projectionist.[28] Some of these diminutive screens measured no more than twelve inches. Some worked with rear-projection technologies. For instance, twenty such rear-projection units appeared throughout the fairgrounds, promoting current fair events on film, showing fairgoers at one location what was happening at another.[29] Some spectators sat but many stood or simply walked past moving images. A whole range of projection technologies illuminated mannequins, multi-screened installations and large improvisational screens such as ceilings. One exhibit placed a small screen underneath a thin sheet of water in order to create the illusion of viewing magnified cells in water.[30] Portable film projectors showed old American silents in the concession area and also provided a kind of rolling text panel to accompany exhibits and to replace conventional didactic labels.[31] As mentioned earlier, many projectors worked automatically and continuously, while some were user-operated by push-button.

The broader context for the use of these smaller devices is punctuated by the publication of *Business Screen*, starting in 1938. The magazine promulgated and normalised the use of such portable technologies, regularly recommending new uses for film, projectors and screens in the context of day-to-day business and retail operations. In the first issue of the magazine, Gilbert Rohde, a regular contributor, declared: 'I think that the motion picture will be taken as a matter of course in selling in the future. No one will think of planning an office without a projection screen in comfortable view of the executive's desk.' For the business world, film is on the 'threshold of discovery as a new medium'.[32] Film advertising and its virtues appeared frequently throughout issues of *Business Screen*, crafting cinema as a natural salesman, using such phrases as 'salesmanship in a can', 'sells with the pace of today', 'dynamic messaging', each invoked to highlight the ostensibly superior power of expression based in mechanised movement above other more widespread, accessible but formally static media. Portable projectors, marketed directly to salesmen, were also declared a magical modern aid to salesmanship. For instance, the 16mm DeVry 'Challenger' harnessed the might of a 'machine-powered salesforce', using the tagline 'momentum'. The projector was likened to a rushing locomotive, forcing its directed light beam – wherever you willed it to appear – to blast through a potential buyer's inertia, the same way a train bursts through a static landscape.[33] It should be no surprise that the magazine took great interest in the fair and devoted its second full issue to the event.

Business Screen hosted a range of advertisements and articles about machines that sell: some featured motion pictures with and without sound, others featured film slides with sound. Examples include products such as the 'Explainette', the 'Illustravox' and the 'Automotion' machine, sold to retailers and merchandisers as automatic image machines that enhanced selling techniques. Some of these required the constant control of an operator, while others were fully automatic. The Flolite, for instance, was a stand-alone unit that claimed to be a 'miniature theater' allowing 'brilliant pictures even in broad daylight'. It was a rear-projection console system operating with a looping mechanism that allowed the device to repeat a film as many times as desired. The screen was quite small at twelve inches by fifteen inches.[34] The unit weighed eighty-five pounds and was sold as suitable for 'retail, food, drug and cigar stores, department stores, car depots, window and store displays, hotel, theater and club lobbies, conventions, public buildings and numerous other similar places'.[35] The 16mm Victor Animatograph 'All in One', also known as the Victor 33, invited 'industrial and commercial users to more profitably employ the greatest of all modern sales tools'. A sound projector, the 'All in One' announced that it was compact and self-contained during operation. It came with a 'small handy microphone' providing 'loud speaker facilities for sales talks, announcements, comments and demonstration spiels'. The '33' also included a 'phono-record turntable' to provide musical background for silent films or 'for entertainment during reel changes, banquets, etc.'. This same device was later sold not as the 'All in One', emphasising a kind of total business machine, but as the 'Add it On', emphasising more its modularity and adaptability to differing needs. Either way, regardless of what the device was called, here was a projector marketed to salesmen, designed and sold to perform multiple functions, including operating as a stand-alone sound machine. Showing a film was but one element of the machine's utility to the more general task of selling.

One of the more interesting and less understood aspects of what I am crafting as cinema's selling machine is the use of rear-projection units. Such devices rose in use at the fair and elsewhere during this period precisely to overcome the challenges of daylight projection, or, in other words, to overcome the need for spaces that were dark. Because conventional projector and screen relations dictated a projector on one side of the room and a screen on the other, film projection required very particular spaces that were free of visual impediments such as columns or other obstructions, and also relatively dark in order for the image to appear legible. Rear-projection units promised to overcome this problem, offering a theatre-in-a-box, one that could be used anywhere the box could be put.

The application of rear-projection logics to create cinema consoles for daylight viewing was, by 1939, a reasonably common sight in train stations, nightclubs and diners used for advertising, product demonstration and stock quotes throughout the USA.[36] Such devices have deep links to the use of film for advertising, but also early configurations of sound and music in the form of sound shorts (soundies), as Andrea Kelley has shown.[37] Such booths were operating in the USA, as well as in the UK and Germany from the early 1930s.[38] These booths were also amply evident at the fair. In his report cataloguing and commenting on fair films, Richard Griffith regularly mentions 'booth projected' films, offering opinions on this specific mode of display. Griffith's comments indicate his plain sense that daylight booths worked well for a particular kind of film, preferably short, 'sensationalist' and 'lithographic', by which he seems to have meant films that borrowed from the more sparse graphic principles of modern poster design. He deemed more didactic and lengthy films best left to conventional projection scenarios.[39] He cited the poster films of the Empire Marketing Board as positive examples of this daylight cinema, short films that worked with clean simple lines.[40] Most 'booth films' worked on the repetitive principle enabled by looping, running continuously without need of constant operator attention. They also worked on the principles of a peripatetic distracted viewer, or at best, on the temporarily attentive one.[41]

Another such device was the Kodak Business Kodascope, first marketed in 1928, which Kodak claimed could be carried in a 'case as small as the average sample case'.[42] The screen reflected light in the normal way but because it was translucent the projected image could be seen from either side, front or back.[43] The Kodascope further promised quick set-up (less than half a minute), adaptability to all modern offices (including those fully lit and with glass partitions) and a screen five-and-a-half inches by seven inches, which Kodak suggested was large enough considering the 'close range at which it is viewed' and comparable to 'a full page illustration in the average-size book'.[44] Kodak claimed that the projector and bulb were sufficient to illuminate a thirty-inch by forty-inch screen, thus rendering the device adaptable, good for 'a one-man (sic) audience or a group'.[45] The machine was frequently displayed in Kodak's advertising atop a desk. Other rear-projection business machines include the 'Merchandiser', a small, table-top or mounted, rear-projection screen that used 16mm film. The unit itself was designed to resemble a photographic camera: the screen appeared in a cone that resembled a lens jutting out from a plastic box. The portable machine worked automatically on a loop, repeating a short message over and over again. Its small size and self-contained set-up meant that it could be placed anywhere in any kind of retail space: in a window, on a counter, in a showroom, alongside

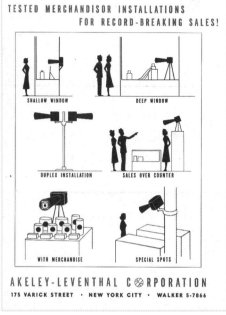

another display, day or night. This flexibility featured in its sales literature. The company, Akeley-Leventhal, also claimed superior reliability, smooth operation and easy film changes.[46] Montgomery-Ward used the device across its national chain of department stores. At the fair, the smallest of these devices were used in exhibits to integrate screens into product displays in some unusual ways. For instance, the makers of Bromo Seltzer placed a small, rear-projection unit inside an over-sized bottle of its antacid.[47]

TOWARDS CINEMA'S FUTURE

Grover Whalen, the fair's president and public figurehead during its first year, extolled publicly that at the fair,

> [a] new high mark in the use of motion pictures for educational purposes, for the betterment of living conditions, for the advancement of science, for the improvement of health, and for the distribution of the products of industry, will be reached.[48]

Film, according to Whalen, worked in perfect harmony with the new frontier that the fair itself sought to realise: modern, moving, efficient, automatic and electric. The uses of cinema Whalen refers to here include the familiar call to education, but more important and less understood is the use of cinema in this rising tide of corporate communication, publicity and the overlapping category of advertising films. By 1939, there was a growing network of production companies emerging to make publicity and advertising films (Jam Handy and Audio Productions being key examples) and so too did advertising agencies begin to open film divisions.[49] Even the advertising industry used film to promote itself. In 1933, the Advertising Federation of America and the American Association of Advertising Agencies made a film called *Golden Years of Progress*, shown at the Chicago World Fair (1933–4). The film extolled the virtues of advertising as an industry, contributing – so it was claimed – to an increased standard of living for all.[50]

The use of cinema at the New York World's Fair marks an exceptional event that incorporated extant activity and also signalled the way towards future trends. In the post-war period, the use of film at exhibitions and expositions continued to grow and diversify. Indeed, the use of small machines and big ones in 1939 indexes a crucial way in which moving images and the many technologies that facilitated their performance were being harnessed to the imperatives to sell, both through techniques specific to what I am calling 'exhibitionary' impulses in film's unique expressive capacities (spectacle, narrative, visual effects) and through articulating cinema's specificities to hybrid media spaces and experiments in industrial design. In some instances, this plainly entailed dis-articulating what we commonly think of as the cinematic apparatus, and re-articulating it to pursue many other display and performance scenarios which thrived far beyond the movie theatre.

The corporate use of projectors at this fair shows us that film and its family of technologies were being eagerly appropriated by a range of business interests seeking to master a changing audiovisual landscape, harnessing the powers of light and dark, sound and silence to their respective agendas. It also shows us the powerful adaptability of celluloid, projector and screen as a kind of exhibitionary triumvirate, used creatively to envision a particular kind of automated, efficient future in which screens purveyed not just the impulse to sell, but also a sense of connectivity and technological savvy and a persistent link to a panoply of other technologies – automobiles, refrigerators, electricity, radios, televisions, cameras.

To be sure, the 'World of Tomorrow' was a particularly corporate, governmental and technological utopia wherein alliances across machines came to aid and abet a distinct form of advertising. This iteration of advertising was multidimensional, highly adaptable to a range of spaces and purposes, and announced a common sense for a new kind of cinema in sometimes fantastical but also banal terms. This other kind of cinema provided a new set of materials not just for artists or the entertainment industry, but for all industries. Advertising films were part of this broader family of films, visual forms and viewing technologies that should not be readily reduced or understood by resorting to the received methods used to understand films as discrete texts shown to audiences gathered to see a show.

Michael Cowan has written recently about the clear overlap between canonical experimental film-makers like Walter Ruttmann and the emergent field of motion-picture advertising, showing the ways in which strands of contemporary psychology and ideas about attention shaped film experiments in the field of advertising in Germany during the 1920s and 30s. In the American context, the experimental impulse to merge the worlds of moving pictures and advertising is also deeply revealing of the ways in which films and film technologies were being integrated by artists, including within disciplines distinct from those we easily and readily associate with cinema: architecture, commercial exhibition practices, industrial design, corporate speech and publicity. This brief glimpse of the World's Fair demonstrates that thinking about moving-picture advertising requires us to include among our key questions: how was the film shown? With what other media? On what kind of viewing device? As a part of what media ecology, design concept and corporate campaign? What distinct epistemologies were invoked or asserted? To be sure, some advertising films were rather conventionally shown, if not in movie theatres then in theatre-like scenarios, with seated audiences facing a screen where discrete texts called films appeared from beginning to end. Nevertheless, we must also presume that a range of films appeared in widely varied settings, augmented by other technologies of showmanship and display, articulated to spatial, ecological and spectatorial conditions hitherto underexplored. This includes but is not limited to salesrooms, shop windows, boardrooms, department stores, factory floors and industrial expositions. Thinking about the specificities of advertising film requires that we consider an expanded technological apparatus, diversified viewing scenarios and the distinct institutional imperatives undergirding them. These other contexts, and their technological and performative articulations, will help us to identify more fully the specificities of the stylistic and formal properties of these films, which will include, most certainly, the short but also the small and the looped, the spectacular and the banal, the complete but also the partial and the complementary. It will also require us to learn more about the fields of industrial and graphic design, and the long history of exhibition techniques broadly defined. Lastly, expanding the methods we use to investigate this rich area will help to insert cinema into other visual and audile strategies, cross-media modes of advertising and techniques of selling, where it has clearly had a long life and a lasting impact.

NOTES

1. The New York World's Fair actually ran for six months (from May to October) in 1939 and again in 1940.
2. Reports vary on how many projectors of which type were in operation at the fair. The magazine *Business Screen* estimated that 130 portable projectors operated throughout the fairgrounds. 'The World's Fair Survey of Motion Pictures and Slidefilms at the Fairs', *Business Screen* vol. 2 no. 1 (1939), pp. 21–5, quoted in Claude Collins. 'Introduction', *Films Exhibited at the World's Fair 1939: A Survey* (1940) [Box 398, File 10: New York World's Fair 1939–1940 Collection] Manuscripts and Archives Division, New York Public Library (NYPL), II. Other sources suggest a far more striking figure of 10:1, indicating that portable machines were by far the dominant type of projector; this estimate can be found in 'Exhibitors Projection Committee, New York World's Fair 1939' (17 March 1939) [Box 309, File 11; New York World's Fair 1939–1940 Collection] Manuscripts and Archives Division, NYPL.
3. For an excellent discussion about movement, films and film-display machines in earlier German industrial fairs, see Michael Cowan 'From the Astonished Spectator to the Spectator in Movement: Exhibition Advertisements in 1920s Germany and Austria', *Canadian Journal of Film Studies* vol. 23 no. 1 (Spring 2014), pp. 2–29.
4. This is an ever-expanding area. Particularly important publications include Vinzenz Hediger and Patrick Vonderau (eds), *Films that Work: Industrial Film and the Productivity of Media* (Amsterdam: Amsterdam University Press, 2009); Charles R. Acland and Haidee Wasson (eds), *Useful Cinema* (Durham, NC: Duke University Press, 2011); and Devin Orgeron, Marsha Orgeron and Dan Streible (eds), *Learning with the Lights Off: Educational Film in the United States* (London: Oxford University Press, 2012).
5. This argument has been more fully elaborated in my previous essays. Please see 'The Protocols of Portability, *Film History* vol. 25 no. 1–2 (2013), pp. 236–47; 'The Other Small Screen: Moving Images at New York's World Fair, 1939', *Canadian Journal of Film Studies* vol. 21 no. 1 (Spring 2012), pp. 81–103.
6. See, for instance, Beatriz Colomina, 'Enclosed by Images: The Eameses' Multimedia Architecture', *Grey Room* no. 2 (Winter 2001), pp. 5–29; Fred Turner, *The Democratic Surround: Multimedia and American Liberalism from World War II to the Psychedelic Sixties* (Chicago: University of Chicago Press, 2014); Janine Marchessault, 'Multi-Screens and Future Cinema: The Labyrinth Project at Expo '67', in Janine Marchessault and Susan Lord (eds), *Fluid Screens, Expanded Cinema* (Toronto: University of Toronto Press, 2007), pp. 29–51; Alison Griffiths, *Shivers Down Your Spine: Cinema, Museums, and the Immersive View* (New York: Columbia University Press, 2013).
7. Donald Crafton, *The Talkies: American Cinema's Transition to Sound, 1926–1931* (Berkeley: University of California Press, 1999); Steven Wurtzler, *Electric Sounds: Technological Change and the Rise of Corporate Mass Media* (New York: Columbia University Press, 2008).
8. Emily Thompson, *The Soundscape of Modernity: Architectural Acoustics and the Culture of Listening in America, 1900–1933* (Cambridge: MIT Press, 2002); Ross Melnick, *American*

Showman: Samuel 'Roxy' Rothafel and the Birth of the Entertainment Industry, 1908–1935 (New York: Columbia, 2012).

9. For more on this see my 'Suitcase Cinema', *Cinema Journal* vol. 51 no. 2 (Winter 2012), pp. 150–4; and 'Moving Images: Portable Histories of Film Exhibition', in John Nerone (ed.), *The International Encyclopedia of Media Studies: Media History and the Foundations of Media Studies* (London: Wiley-Blackwell, 2013), pp. 367–84.

10. See, for instance, Lee Grieveson, 'The Work of Film in the Age of Fordist Mechanization', *Cinema Journal* vol. 51 no. 3 (Spring 2012), pp. 25–51; Sara Sullivan, 'Corporate Discourses of Sponsored Films of Steel Production in the United States, 1936–1956', *Velvet Light Trap* no. 72 (Autumn 2013), pp. 33–43; Greg Waller, 'Free Walking Picture – Every Farmer is Welcome: Non-theatrical Film and Everyday Life in Rural America during the 1930s', in Richard Maltby, Melvyn Stokes and Robert C. Allen (eds), *Going to the Movies: Hollywood and the Social Experience of Cinema* (Exeter: Exeter University Press, 2007), pp. 248–72.

11. Alice Goldfarb Marquis, *Hope and Ashes: The Birth of Modern Times 1929–1939* (New York: Free Press, 1986), p. 190.

12. See Warren Susman, *Culture as History: The Transformation of American Society in the Twentieth Century* (Washington, DC: Smithsonian Institution Press, 2003), particularly chapters 9, 10 and 11.

13. For more on this, see Robert Rydell, *World of Fairs: The Century-of-Progress Expositions* (Chicago: University of Chicago Press, 1993); and also Christina Cogdell 'The Futurama Recontextualized: Norman Bel Geddes's Eugenic "World of Tomorrow"', *American Quarterly* vol. 52 no. 2 (June 2000), pp. 193–245.

14. Roland Marchand, 'Corporate Imagery and Popular Education: World's Fairs and Expositions in the United States, 1893–1940', in David Nye and Carl Pederson (eds), *Consumption and American Culture* (Amsterdam: VU University Press, 1991), pp. 18–33.

15. The trend towards active demonstration and dynamic illustration of products and principles, as opposed to static display, is well-documented in New York Museum of Science and Industry, *Exhibition Techniques: A Summary of Exhibition Practice, Based on Surveys Conducted at the New York and San Francisco World's Fairs of 1939* (New York: New York Museum of Science and Industry, 1940), p. 21.

16. Donald Deskey, 'Industrial Showmanship', *Business Screen* no. 2 (1938), p. 17.

17. For more on this, see Roland Marchand, *Creating the Corporate Soul: The Rise of Public Relations and Corporate Imagery in American Big Business* (Berkeley: University of California Press, 1998) and William Bird *'Better Living': Advertising, Media, and the New Vocabulary of Business Leadership, 1935–1955* (Evanston, IL: Northwestern University Press, 1999).

18. Marquis, *Hope and Ashes*, p. 197.

19. Grieveson, 'The Work of Film in the Age of Fordist Mechanization'.

20. For a technical description of Futurama see Schuyler Van Duyne, 'Talking Train Tour, World's Fair Exhibit', *Popular Science* (July 1939), pp. 102–5.

21. For more on the relationship of Bel Geddes, Futurama and the immanent building of the interstate highway system, see Paul Mason Fotsch, 'The Building of a Superhighway Future at the New York World's Fair', *Cultural Critique* no. 48 (Spring 2001), pp. 64–97.

22. Marchand, *Creating the Corporate Soul*. Cf. Michael Cowan's chapter in this book.

23. For more on this see Richard Griffith, *Films of the World's Fair, 1939* (New York: American Film Center, 1940), pp. 61–3.

24. The score was written for the film by George Steiner and Phillip Sheib.

25. 'The World's Fair Survey of Motion Pictures and Slidefilms at the Fairs', *Business Screen* vol. 2 no. 1 (1939), pp. 21–5.

26. In its first year the film was in black and white. And, in 1940, a Technicolor version of the film was produced and the title changed to *New Dimensions*. In 1953, RKO bought the rights to the film and re-released it as part of the well-known 3D cycle of that decade. Now you can find it in bits and pieces on YouTube.

27. Collins, 'Introduction', *Films Exhibited at the World's Fair 1939*.

28. 'The World's Fair Survey of Motion Pictures and Slidefilms at the Fairs', *Business Screen* vol. 2 no. 1 (1939), pp. 21–5. Bell & Howell conducted this survey sharing its information with *Business Screen*. At the Chicago fair of 1934, it was estimated that of the hundred 16mm projectors in use on the grounds, sixty-one of them were silent, nineteen used the recent sound-on-film technology and eleven used the soon to be obsolete sound-on-disk models. Seventeen were manually operated and seventy-four were in automatic and continuous use. 'Report of the Committee on Non-Theatrical Equipment', *Journal of the Society of Motion Picture Engineers* vol. 24 no. 1 (January 1935), pp. 23–6.

29. Press release 'Movies-1' (13 March 1939) [Box 398; File 7: New York World's Fair 1939–40 Collection], Manuscripts and Archives Division, NYPL, 7pp.

30. Projection on ceilings and under water at the fair is discussed in Carlos E. Cummings, *East is East, West is West* (Buffalo, NY: Buffalo Museum of Science, 1940), pp. 255–8. For examples of unrealised proposals for screen experimentation consult the New York World's Fair 1939–40 Collection, Manuscripts and Archives Division, NYPL.

31. Cummings, *East is East*, p. 258. Old American films starring Charles Chaplin, Mary Pickford, Fatty Arbuckle and Lon Chaney played daily in the Amusement Area of the fair in a one-hour show, in a small theatre seating forty-eight. Admission was charged (Collins, 'Introduction', *Films Exhibited at the World's Fair 1939*, p. 12).

32. Gilbert Rohde 'Films Rediscovered', *Business Screen* no. 1 (1938), p. 1.

33. See, for instance, 'Momentum' [DeVry Corporation Advertisement] *Business Screen* no. 5 (1939), p. 29.

34. 'Flolite' [advertisment], *Business Screen* no. 1 (1938), p. 8.

35. Ibid.

36. Ian Aitken, *Film and Reform: John Grierson and the Documentary Film Movement* (London: Routledge, 1990); Michael Cowan, *Walter Ruttman and the Cinema of Multiplicity: Avant-garde, Advertising, Modernity* (Amsterdam: Amsterdam University Press, 2014).

37. Andrea Kelley, '"A Revolution in the Atmosphere": The Dynamics of Site and Screen in 1940s Soundies', *Cinema Journal* vol. 54 no. 2 (Winter 2015), pp. 72–93.

38. During the 1930s, the Society of Motion Picture Engineers established a Projection Screens Committee and began publishing its report regularly in the association's journal in September 1931. For information about such screens, see, for instance, 'Report of the Projection Screens Committee', *Journal of the Society of Motion Picture Engineers* vol. 18 no. 2 (February 1932), pp. 248–9.

39. For more on this, see Griffith, *Films of the World's Fair, 1939*.

40. See also Aitken, *Film and Reform*.

41. For more on the development of rear-projection systems, see my 'The Other Small Screen'.

42. 'The Eastman Business Kodascope', *Journal of the Society of Motion Picture Engineers* vol. 12 no. 36 (September 1928), p. 1175.

43. Such translucent screens were widely used by the Navy on ships which needed to maximise viewing space deckside and so arranged sailors on both sides of the screen.
44. 'The Eastman Business Kodascope', pp. 1176–7.
45. Ibid., p. 1177.
46. Developed by Akeley-Leventhal, a company founded by Carl Akeley, the well-known explorer and developer of cameras suitable for capturing images of nature. [Advertising Pamphlet] Akeley-Leventhal Corporation (1939), New York World's Fair 1939–40 Collection, Manuscript and Archives Division, NYPL.
47. This display featured an animated short with a six-foot-by-eight-foot screen made to appear as the label of an over-sized bottle of the antacid medication ('The World Fairs' Best Salesman!', *Business Screen* vol. 1 no. 8 [1939], pp. 17–19).
48. Grover Whalen, 'New Fields For Films at New York's Fair', *Business Screen* vol. 1 no. 2 (1938), p. 15.
49. See, for instance, S. H. Walker and Paul Sklar, *Business Finds its Voice* (New York: Harper and Brothers, 1938), a short book which grew out of a series of well-received articles initially published in the widely read *Fortune* magazine, which claims that five American advertising agencies opened up film arms by 1938. See also 'The ABC's of Agency Film Activities', *Business Screen* vol. 1 no. 6 (1939), p. 18. For information about Jam Handy, see Rick Prelinger, 'Eccentricity, Education and the Evolution of Corporate Speech: Jam Handy and his Organization', in Hediger and Vonderau, *Films that Work*, pp. 211–20.
50. Walker and Sklar, *Business Finds its Voice*, p. 42.
51. Ibid.

4
Selling the Motion Picture to the *fin de siècle* American Public

William Uricchio

By 1902, Sears, Roebuck & Company's *Consumer's Guide* could boast of the motion picture: 'Of all forms of public entertainment, there is one that leads. All others follow.' One of America's two largest mail-order retailers, Chicago-based Sears distributed millions of catalogues per year in this period, whetting appetites for every imaginable consumer good in cities and on farms across the USA and Canada. The Spring 1898 *Guide* (No. 107) included in its Department of Special Public Entertainment Outfits and Supplies the Optigraph, a motion-picture projector produced by Chicago's Enterprise Optical Company, as well as dozens of films.[1] More to the point, it wrapped these artefacts in a surround of descriptions, illustrations and testimonials, carefully portraying the new medium in terms of its economic and technological operations and even – for those many readers who had yet to see a projected film – a description of the motion-picture experience. Sears, Roebuck & Co.'s main mail-order competitor, Montgomery Ward & Co., issued a special forty-page pamphlet in 1898 entitled *Catalogue of Magic Lanterns, Stereopticons and Moving Picture Machines* (and, by 1900, Sears would issue its own fifty-page moving-picture catalogue).[2] Together, these publications offered the American and Canadian public a portrayal of the moving-picture medium and programme with a level of detail unmatched by anything outside the trade press. They brought this portrayal to many millions more readers than the best-selling newspapers of the day, whose circulations peaked at 200,000 or 300,000.[3] And they brought it to a public that lived in the small towns, farms and hinterlands far outside the zones of what we take to be the period's burgeoning film culture.

This chapter explores how the motion picture was sold to the public in the pages of the Sears, Roebuck & Co.'s *Consumer's Guide*, arguing that, more than any other depiction in the period, this one defined the horizon of expectations that greeted the new medium. While the theme of the collection within which this chapter appears is *films that sell* – that is, *the advertising film* – understanding how film itself was sold goes a long way towards helping us understand the medium's reach and status, particularly during its earliest years. True, 'the seller' in this particular chapter is a paper-bound mail-order catalogue and not the motion picture, but, as we will see, its penetration of the American and Canadian consumer market and its detailed portrayal of the motion-picture medium help to situate film within the technological and economic frames that informed the viewing practices of its public. Understanding these frames can help to qualify our understanding of the period's conditions of popular reception and offer insight into the associations underlying film-based advertisements in the early cinema period. This chapter, then, re-purposes the meaning of the phrase 'advertising film' by shifting 'advertising' from adjective to verb. But it does so in order to cast new light on film's work as medium, including its promotional endeavours.

What, then, did the general North American public know about the motion picture in the medium's earliest years? The motion picture as technology and experience was, of course, occasionally described in venues outside the trade press, ranging from stories in the newspaper (generally well documented by early cinema historians) to coverage in specialised journals. Regarding the latter, for example, an 1897 edition of *Scientific American* contained a cover story on the production, exhibition and the inner mechanics of 'photography as an adjunct to theatrical representation', intermingling images of the projected moving picture (a Biograph exhibition[4]) and coin-in-the-slot peep show (Casier's Mutoscope for production process and mechanics[5]). But the Sears & Roebuck *Consumer's Guide*, despite a few passing mentions, has remained largely on the margins of scholarly attention.[6] I have argued elsewhere (and will recall some of those arguments here) that not only did the *Guide* offer a robust depiction of film as an experience, an economic opportunity and technology; it also located it within a larger constellation of media practices.[7] Thus, the positioning of the moving-picture apparatus in a contiguous section that included not only magic lanterns and stereoscopes, but also graphophones, photographic cameras, books and printing technologies, (digital) musical instruments, telegraphs and telephones, and games offers an insight into the period's conceptual categorisation of the new medium.

EXPERIENCE

> Moving-picture exhibitions have been during the past year one of the most popular attractions in the large cities, but the cost of outfits has been so great that as yet few people outside of the larger cities have seen them.[8]

One popular-culture expression of this experiential disparity between city and country dwellers took the form of Uncle Josh, who famously misunderstood the film experience in *Uncle Josh at the Moving Picture Show* (Edison, 1902). America's caricature-of-a-rube serves as a reminder of the complexity of characterising audience composition. The chance of coming across travelling exhibitors certainly enabled the occasional encounter with moving pictures outside cities, but, generally speaking, period discourse suggests that exposure to the new medium was primarily in urban settings. Might this, then, give credence to the period's many depictions of 'yokels' and 'country bumpkins' reacting in panic to the moving-picture image? Stephen Bottomore has discussed the 'train effect' with characteristic rigour, taking on the various insights of Tom Gunning, Yuri Tsvian, etc. regarding the period's reception.[9] The Sears, Roebuck & Co.'s *Consumer's Guides* offer yet another piece of evidence that helps to complicate our understanding of the horizon of expectations that met the new medium.

By 1907, some 6 million 1,200-page-plus Sears catalogues[10] (and millions more Montgomery Ward catalogues) per year cycled their way through a population that was still predominantly rural.[11] One business historian went so far as to claim that for much of rural America, 'the Sears catalogue and the bible were the only two pieces of literature in the home'.[12] It is fair to assert that no other representation of the nascent film medium reached as large or as diverse a public. And certainly, outside the trade press, no descriptions of the medium, its physical components and economic models, were more fulsome. Although we, as a field, have attended carefully to urban experiences of film, these catalogues established a horizon of highly detailed expectations that penetrated every nook and cranny of the land. And, as Calvin Pryluck suggests, representation often led to reality. In their address of show business novices, the Sears *Guides* resulted in the opening of motion-picture entertainment venues where none had previously existed.[13]

What, then, did a reader of the 1898 *Guide* in St Armand, Quebec or Oakley, Mississippi, learn about the moving picture? First and foremost, an affective stance: incredulity ... 'So life-like, so true to nature and so perfect in every detail, with such life-like motions are the pictures as projected by these machines, that the audience can scarcely realize that what is before them is but a picture.'[14] But the text goes on to invoke cinema's primal scene, describing the exhibition of a film to those who have never seen one before:

> To illustrate more fully we will describe a scene as it is now exhibited in the theatre or opera house. The drop curtain has fallen for the intermission, when suddenly the house is darkened and before the eyes of the audience a huge window appears to open. Through it they see a bit of a meadow landscape with a forest in the background from which to a point close by the window stretches a section of railway line on an embankment. A number of men are engaged in repairing the roadbed. There appears in the distance, just emerging from the woods, a cloud of white smoke, which within a few seconds shapes itself into the outline of an approaching train, and in another moment what appears to be a real passenger train is rushing by at a tremendous rate. Every detail of motion is clearly defined, and even the rapid rise and fall of the piston rods can be plainly seen. In a twinkling the whole scene disappears, the theatre is again lighted up and before the audience hangs only the drop curtain.

And there it is ... the window on the world, the train and the stuff of lore. Perhaps the train scene was simply an arbitrary choice on the part of the *Guide*'s writers, or perhaps it was selected because of its dramatic efficiency, or perhaps it was deployed because of its resonance with the 'train effect'. While we will never know, this particular exemplification suggests that many millions of readers were well prepared for what was to come. One of the film subjects that buyers could choose from, #21256 – *Passenger Train*, is illustrated, showing a locomotive approaching the screen and, according to the accompanying caption, 'going at a high rate of speed, taking up and throwing off mail bags, and showing good smoke effect'. Of course, the drawn image, consistent with the other drawn illustrations of photographic slides and films, suggests nothing particularly alarming; but as promised, it is legible in every detail.

In the context of the many accompanying testimonials from satisfied customers, details of how the moving picture worked, both technically and economically, and the larger context of the *Guide*'s Department of Special Public Entertainment Outfits and Supplies (all of which we will consider), these descriptions of the new medium simply added an affective dimension to a remarkably robust portrait of the new medium.

TECHNOLOGY

Sears, Roebuck & Co.'s motion-picture projector was the Optigraph, manufactured by the Chicago-based Enterprise Optical Company (patent still pending in 1898).[15] Curiously, Alvah Roebuck was the principal owner of the Enterprise Optical Company, having sold his interest in Sears, Roebuck & Co. to Richard Warren Sears in 1895 for roughly $20,000.[16] Consistent with its policy of explaining its products (and extolling their qualities), the *Guide* offered an elegant summary of the projector's operation:

> The principle of the OPTIGRAPH MOVING-PICTURE MACHINE is the Magic Lantern, only the pictures appear on a transparent film and pass before the lens in rapid succession. The film is a long, transparent celluloid tape, the standard length of which is 50 feet, with a series of photographs taken at the rate of 20 a second; and to produce animated movements, the films must be moved past the projecting lens at the same rate of speed with a fractional stop and division made between each picture. On each 50-foot film there is a series of about 750 photographs, each one slightly different from the other…. For simplicity, easy action, noiselessness, quality of material and workmanship, the OPTIGRAPH MOVING-PICTURE MACHINE has no equal.[17]

This explanation by way of the magic lantern can be accounted for in several ways. Its technology was widely understood (Sears also sold toy magic lanterns); the presumed buyers for the Optigraph were showmen already equipped with lanterns; and, perhaps most importantly, the Optigraph required a lantern for its operation. The machine was, in fact, an attachment. Said the *Guide*,

> The Optigraph can be attached to any lantern, sciopticon or stereopticon, and when once set in place either the lantern of the Optigraph Moving-Picture Machine can be used at will, the change from one to the other requiring but a moment's time.

And yet, the moving-picture machine was also a world away from the 'ordinary' magic lantern, as the *Guide* asserted in a harsh but revealing analogy. 'In comparison, the Optigraph Moving-Picture Machine is as far superior to the ordinary magic lantern or stereopticon as the graphophone is to the crude toy doll which but imperfectly utters the one word "Mamma".'

The *Guide* missed no opportunity to remind its readers of several key features of the Optigraph (in contrast to other machines), namely, that the apparatus was noiseless, flicker-free and well built. Offering the 'Opinion of an Expert Mechanic', the *Guide* printed a testimonial from Albert Tuerk, maker of clock movements, inventor of culinary timing devices and, by 1902, manufacturer of a peanut vending machine that Sears would promote on the same pages as its Optigraph machines. Mr Tuerk confirmed Sears' claims, saying,

> Your machine throws a very steady picture, is free from the unpleasant flickering as well as being almost noiseless, all of which are very unpleasant features with other machines which cost three or four times as much money. Take it all in all it is a 'Little Gem'.

In 'An Opinion From One Who Has Had a Wide Experience in This Class of Goods', Chicago's George Kleine further testified to the smoothness of its operation, the novelty of its shutter and the ingeniousness of its rewind system.[18]

A little gem of an attachment for the lantern; a qualitative improvement over previous projected entertainment technologies; an apparatus so simple that a child could operate it ... the Optigraph could be had for somewhere between $25 for the base model and $154 for 'the works' – including a portable gas-making and calcium light outfit, ten twenty-five-foot films, a lamp house, lens and 1,000 'mammoth' (18 x 24 inch) posters and an equal number of tickets. Little wonder that numerous customer testimonials found it, like Mr J. E. Whitshaw of Wiley, Alaska, 'to be satisfactory in every particular'. Writing in the October 1957 volume of the *Journal of the Society of Motion Picture and Television Engineers*, Don Malkames noted that this 'ingenious little mechanism, not much larger than your fist, gave very acceptable projection and probably more of them were sold than all other makers combined'.[19] He added that the Optigraph was actually the first model of the Motiograph, which superseded it in 1908 and 'is still considered one of the finest projectors manufactured today'.[20]

ECONOMICS

Sears, Roebuck & Co.'s Department of Special Public Entertainment Outfits and Supplies filled twenty-one pages of the Spring 1898 *Consumer's Guide* with descriptions, illustrations and testimonials regarding its Graphophone Talking Machine (with concert horns, tubes, coin-in-the slot and stenographic configurations), its Special Lecture Outfits (high-powered magic lanterns), its Optigraph Moving-Picture Machines and, of course, gas-making equipment, recordings, films and featured slide shows (the Klondike gold fields and the Cuban War). Just as interesting is the larger cluster of media forms within which the Department of Special Public Entertainment Outfits and Supplies was situated, including clocks, optical goods such as eye-glasses, microscopes, binoculars and telescopes, drawing equipment, cameras and photographic supplies, telegraphs and telephones, musical instruments, music boxes and perforated disks, organ rolls, sheet music, books (over fifty-seven pages of titles!), stationary and writing materials, albums, games, artist materials and typewriters.

In all, nearly one hundred consecutive pages chart the contours of what might broadly be considered the period's media constellation.[21] From a contemporary perspective, this cluster is striking in several regards (besides the prescient inclusion of games). First, the items for sale enable both the 'reading' and 'writing', the production and consumption, of word, sound and image. Second, they demonstrate conceptual contiguity between analogue production and playback systems and binary or digital systems such as the telegraph, organ rolls and perforated music disks. All are simply ways of storing and playing back information. Third, given the tropes of the day, even clocks, telephones and telescopes figured prominently in proto-science fiction notions of the televisual evident in such terms as the *telectroscope* and *telephonoscope*, thus making sense in this configuration.[22] Finally, a point to which we shall return, they demonstrate that multimedia experiences involving recorded sound, still and moving images and performance enjoyed a taken-for-grantedness in the period.

Who then, was the intended customer for the Optigraph? The appearance of home entertainment magic lanterns in the section just *outside* the Department of Special Public Entertainment Outfits and Supplies' pages – where 'Juvenile Magic Lantern Outfits' could be had for as little as $0.75 and more advanced machines cost between $43.65 for their highest grade magic lantern or $98 for a stereopticon – suggests a distinction between amateur and professional. These latter machines and accompanying slide sets were targeted for home use and fundraising purposes, although Sears noted that they could also be used by professionals. The Department of Special Public Entertainment Outfits and Supplies' pages that follow, however, make clear their address of professionals-in-the-making.

> It has been demonstrated to us that the public entertainment business is a very profitable field and an opportunity for making big money with a very small amount invested, but it seems that there has been but a very limited amount of energy expended in this direction owing to the lack of knowledge as to what is required to complete a suitable outfit for public entertainment, and more important still, how to start the work successfully.... We have made a special effort and are glad to be able to inform our patrons that we have made everything connected with the work so simple that anyone can understand it.

Each outfit came with a book of instructions offering not only technical information, but also advice on how to advertise and secure the use of halls, churches and opera houses. As the *Guide* put it,

> we furnish the business proposition, we furnish all material, we furnish all the knowledge of the subject in hand, we furnish the methods for conducting the business, we furnish all the business experience: in fact, we furnish all that is necessary and all the exhibitor has to do is to follow our instructions.

Again and again, the *Guide* reminds its readers to ask if they have any questions whatsoever: 'We are in business to keep you well informed and supplied with the best goods.'

Although the main target of its address seems to have been newcomers eager to enter the entertainment business, Sears cast a wide net, noting that its pricing of the Optigraph brought it 'within the reach of even private individuals for home entertainment'. And it also appealed to those already in business, describing the moving-picture machine as:

> a boon to the manager of a theatre, a powerful auxiliary to his stage effects, a most entrancing divertissement from the usually tedious intermission, and a most excellent means of giving entertainment for profit without any other assistance. To magic lantern exhibitors and lecturers, it affords a means of renewing interest in their work, drawing crowded houses: in fact increasing several times the usual receipts.

The bottom line was clear and oft repeated: 'As an opportunity to make big money on small capital, we know of nothing so promising at the present time.' Indeed, for those who did the maths, the many testimonials for the Optigraph, Graphophone and magic lantern suggested that one could recover the device's purchase price with one evening's paid admissions! The headline to the Optigraph section boldly asserted: '$20.00 to $25.00 Can Be Made Every Evening With the Optigraph Moving-Picture Machine, Only $25.00 ... A BOON to LECTURERS and the GREATEST MONEY-MAKING ATTRACTION ever exhibited.' And as if to confirm these claims, testimonials from places like Frazier, Wisconsin, and North Craftsbury, Vermont, exclaimed: 'Highly Pleased With the Outfit' ... 'Has Crowded Houses at Every Entertainment' ... 'Crowds Every Night'. The economic lure of the moving-picture business rippled through the land, with readers by the million doubtless wondering if it was too good to be true ... or exactly the opportunity that they had been waiting for.[23]

EXHIBITION

Along with the Optigraph Moving-Picture Machine, Sears included an inventory of films available in twenty-five-, fifty- and 150-foot lengths. Although the *Guide* said, 'we can furnish almost any film made by any manufacturer', it also offered specific subjects for sale and suggestions regarding their use. Of its special films at the 'heretofore unheard of low price of $5.00 each' it said,

> These films are of first quality in every respect, and are made in lengths of about 25 feet each, the subject being so arranged that the ends may be joined together, which enables the operator to repeat the films, and the audience will not know that a similar act has been repeated by the same film.

Charles Musser, in his discussion of the Chicago film scene, tells us that Sears had close ties with William Selig, presumably the source for some of these films.[24] The film stock is specified as being made by Eastman, and 'a full description of the views will accompany each film, and as these descriptions are interspersed with witty jokes and funny sayings, it will prove of great assistance to the exhibitor in entertaining his audience'.

And the $5.00 films? They included the previously mentioned *Passenger Train*, *Serpentine Dance*, *Shooting the Cog Railway*, *State and Madison Streets*, *Chicago* and *Kissing Scene* – a 'side-splitting burlesque' on John Rice and May Irwin's famous scene with 'two corpulent ... people'. Some fifty-foot films were priced at $8.00, while 'other concerns charge $10.00 to $15.00 for films of this grade. These films must not be compared with the copied films that are made on inferior stock and sold by some concerns.' However, *copyrighted* fifty-foot films such as *Annabelle Serpentine Dance*, *Black Diamond Express* and the Rice and Irwin *Kiss Scene* sold for $10.00; and 150-foot films such as the *Corbet [sic] and Courtney fight* and *McKinley and Cleveland Going to the Capitol* could be had for $30.00. Sears also had a few subjects 'taken for advertising purposes', such as its 800 employees leaving the store for lunch, for which it charged $3.00 – the advertisers (Sears!) 'paying for the balance of the cost'!

What constituted an exhibition? As we've seen, it could be as simple as showing a film on the drop curtain during a theatrical intermission; or it could involve moving between a lantern or stereopticon exhibition and moving-picture exhibition, with accompanying 'witty jokes and funny sayings'. But the advertising posters, particularly those built around particular subjects such as the sinking of the *Maine*, the war in Cuba and the search for gold in Alaska, suggested a more programmatic approach. Drawing on the three main endeavours of the Department of Special Public Entertainment Outfits and Supplies – the Graphophone Talking Machine, the photographic slide illustrated lectures and the Optigraph Moving-Picture Machine – the *Guide* emphasised recombinatory permutations:

> We have arranged for Klondike (Lecture) and Moving Pictures. Graphophone and Moving Pictures. Graphophone and Klondike Lecture or Graphophone, Klondike and Moving Pictures, Cuban and Graphophone, Klondike and Graphophone. We had so many calls for such combinations that we were compelled, at considerable expense, to have these different combinations made. They are beautifully illustrated with appropriate engravings and have proven a great drawing card.

As noted earlier, the Optigraph was presented in part as a way to bolster flagging interest in illustrated lectures, echoing suggestions also offered for the Graphophone's use. In this sense, Sears saw the combined use of all three technologies, plus the performative powers of the lecturer, as working ideally in tandem, each complementing the other in the creation of a multimedia spectacle. But it is also clear that Sears saw value in promoting a topical subject – in this case, the Klondike and Cuba – by offering a wrap of photographic slides and lecture notes, patriotic music, films and even books. Perhaps Sears saw a growing market in texts. Certainly, the many pages devoted to books, sheet music, recorded music and slide sets (nearly two-thirds of the roughly one hundred pages in the extended media section) suggest that Sears saw a profit in this sector. However, if the company had ambitions to grow its film sales to anything approximating these other media, fear of Edison apparently quashed them. Charles Musser reports that Edison sued Sears for its film sales in April of 1900 and, indeed, with lasting impact: *Guide* No. 112 (early 1902) featured no films for sale, stating instead 'film titles upon request'.[25]

CONCLUSION

Although I have focused this chapter primarily on the Spring 1898 issue of the Sears, Roebuck & Co.'s *Consumer's Guide* (No. 107), much of its copy was recycled in No. 108 the next autumn and, indeed, the recycling of text and images continued for several years. This is to say that tens of millions of copies of the *Guide* circulated throughout the USA and Canada during the formative years of the film medium, targeting rural and urban populations and reaching any community with a postal service. Montgomery Ward, Sears' older sibling in the mail-order trade, also distributed some 3 million catalogues per annum as of 1904 and, as noted, also had a media section including the remarkably similar Optiscope animated-picture machine and virtually the same descriptive prose. Each company also produced specialised catalogues on their media holdings as well as instructional guides for those interested in entering the business. These documents, plus any surviving records regarding sales, merit much closer attention if we wish to understand how the new medium of the motion picture appeared to the North American public.

I have suggested that Sears (like the catalogues I've seen from Montgomery Ward) took an inclusive approach to its readership, encouraging them to enter the exhibition field – and in the process 'make big money'.[26] Read against today's internet-based retail endeavours, one is struck by Sears' address of its readers in first person plural, by its constant offers of help and additional information and by its heavy reliance on testimonials of other (satisfied) customers. Descriptions, illustrations, exemplifications and reassurances combine to create a feeling of a supportive community, always within easy reach. And, as we have seen, they provide a nuanced understanding of the moving picture as an experience, an economic activity, a technology and a textual system. The new medium's interdependencies with existing media – whether conceptual, technological, or operational – are pronounced, as are the *Guide*'s simultaneous attempts to create a delicate balance, distinguishing film from its siblings and generating an aura of the new.

The moving picture was sold to the broad public above all as a business proposition, a way to get rich quick, to make big money. But it offered more. The self-evident qualities of the proposition are endlessly repeated: recoup the investment in a few nights; create an honourable occupation as a self-employed businessman; entertain and inform those many who seek contact with the world around them. The activities of Sears' Department of Special Public Entertainment Outfits and Supplies serve to remind us of the expansive semantic valence enjoyed in the period by terms like 'entertainment'. The film subjects selected for profiling include a fair measure of 'side-splitting' comic encounters, boxing matches and the like, but the unfolding dramas of the day, such as the war in Cuba and gold mania in Alaska, attracted the *Guide*'s main attention. For much of the USA and Canada, beyond the reach of big-city papers and hearing only belatedly and third hand the dramas of the fast-unfolding century, the motion picture, together with the latest photographic slide set, lecture and even sound recordings, provided ways to connect with the world, to be part of it. And the invariably impeccably attired showman depicted in the *Guide*'s illustrations drew back the curtain and illuminated the world for the multitude sitting in the shadows. The promise of respectability, money and the keys to the portal of the bigger world all beckoned in the form of the moving picture. And, best of all, promised the Sears *Guide*, it required no previous experience, no public-speaking ability, nothing but vision and a modest amount of money.

If the terms of engagement for potential buyers of the Optigraph were clear, so too were the operations of the new medium to those many more who only dreamed of it. What it looked like, how its mechanics related to the well-known magic lantern, the details of what each bit of gear and each film cost … and what each was likely to produce – all of the specifics were available. Vivid descriptions and illustrations, the compelling testimony of others and the knowledgeable authority of the *Guide*'s anonymous authors – all combined into a vivid portrait of the medium that went far beyond what would appear on the screen. The selling of cinema? At this defining moment for the medium's cultural position, it behoves us to look more closely at this set of representations.

NOTES

1. Sears, Roebuck & Co., *Consumer's Guide No. 107* (Spring 1898): https://archive.org/details/consumersguideno00sear

2. Montgomery Ward & Co., Department of Magic Lanterns, Stereopticons, Moving Picture Machines, *Catalogue of Magic Lanterns, Stereopticons and Moving Picture Machines* (1898): https://archive.org/stream/catalogueofmagic00mont#page/n1/mode/2up; Sears, Roebuck & Co., *Special Catalogue of the Optigraph Motion Picture Machines, Calcium Light Outfits, Films for Moving Pictures* (Chicago, 1900): https://www.flickr.com/photos/10216389@N08/sets/72157632317572986/

3. By 1900, the American average for newspaper circulations was 15,000 copies, with the nation's largest papers enjoying circulations in the low hundreds of thousands. See Paul Starr, *The Creation of the Media: Political Origins of Modern Communications* (New York: Basic Books, 2004), p. 252.

4. The caption specifies 'Biograph' and presumably refers to American Mutoscope and Biograph, whose facilities the article's author visited in New York.

5. 'The New Art of Moving Photography', in *Scientific American* vol .76 no. 16 (April 1897), pp. 248–50, as well as the issue's cover. The article acknowledges the assistance of W. K. L. Dickson and Herman Casier. The unknown author seems to have been more impressed by the Mutoscope's elegant mechanics than the Bioscope's.

6. Significant mentions of Sears' system include Soterios Gardiakos' collection of Optigraph photographs and advertisements in his *The Optigraph 35mm Movie Projector, 1898–1907* (Aurora, IL: Unigraphics, 2006); Calvin Pryluck, 'The Itinerant Movie Show and the Development of the Film Industry', in Kathryn Fuller-Seeley (ed.), *Hollywood in the Neighborhood: Historical Case Studies of Local Moviegoing* (Berkeley: University of California Press, 2008), pp. 41–2; André Gaudreault (ed.), *American Cinema, 1890–1909: Themes and Variations* (New Brunswick, NJ: Rutgers University Press, 2009), p. 70; Rick Altman, *Silent Film Sound* (New York: Columbia University Press, 2004); Stephen Bottomore, 'The Panicking Audience?: Early Cinema and the "Train Effect"', *Historical Journal of Film, Radio and Television* vol. 19 no. 2 (1999), p. 180; Charles Musser, *The Emergence of Cinema: The American Screen to 1907* (Berkeley: University of California Press, 1990), pp. 292–3; some Sears catalogue materials relevant to Edison's copyright claims are included in the *Edison Papers* edited by Musser; and Raymond Fielding includes two relevant *Journal of the Society of Motion Picture and Television Engineers* reprints in his *A Technological History of Motion Pictures and Television: An Anthology from the Pages of the Journal of the Society of Motion Picture and Television Engineers* (Berkeley: University of California Press, 1967). For an excellent discussion of the cultural import of the Sears *Guide*, including its entertainment section, see Alexandra Keller, 'Disseminations of Modernity: Representation and Consumer Desire in Early Mail-Order Catalogues', in Leo Charney and Vanessa Schwartz (eds), *Cinema and the Invention of Modern Life* (Berkeley, Los Angeles and London: University of California Press, 1996), pp. 156–82.

7. William Uricchio, 'Contextualizing the Apparatus: Film in the Turn-of-the-Century *Sears, Roebuck & Co. Consumer's Guide*'s Department of Special Public Entertainment Outfits and Supplies', in Giovanna Fossati and Annie van den Oever (eds), *Exposing the Film Apparatus: The Film Archive as a Research Laboratory* (Amsterdam: University of Amsterdam Press, forthcoming).

8. *Guide* No. 107 (Spring 1898). Unless otherwise noted, all quotations are from this edition, pp. 193–216.

9. Bottomore, 'The Panicking Audience?'.

10. Catalogue costs varied between 1897 and 1902, depending on the year and catalogue type (general or specialised), from free (although customers were asked to pay $0.15 to help cover postage) to $0.50.

11. In 1900, only nineteen US cities had 200,000 or more inhabitants, and about 15.5 per cent of the population lived in large urban settings. Boris Emmet and John E. Jeuck, *Catalogues and Counters: A History of Sears, Roebuck and Company* (Chicago: University of Chicago Press, 1950), p. 10. By the end of the nineteenth century, approximately 90 per cent of the US population was literate and school attendance was mandatory. Each of the *Guide*'s two annual seasons resulted in some 3 million general catalogues, in addition to smaller circulation runs of specialised catalogues for farming implements, construction and, as noted above, media devices.

12. Sandra Racine, 'Changing (Inter) Faces: A Genre Analysis of Catalogues From Sears, Roebuck to Amazon.com' (PhD dissertation, University of Minnesota, 2002), p. 68. Racine cites *Mr Sears Catalogue* (a 1989 episode of the *American Experience*, WGBH, directed by Edward Gray). Old Sears and Montgomery Ward catalogues (popularly known as 'wish lists') apparently found a second use as toilet paper in outhouses across America.

13. Pryluck, 'The Itinerant Movie Show', p. 41.

14. Compare this assessment with that of the 1898 Montgomery Ward catalogue: 'So life-like, so true to nature, so perfect in detail, such life-like actions are the pictures projected from these machines that the audience can scarcely believe that what they see before them is only a picture.' Given the apparent similarities between Montgomery Ward's Thornward Optiscope and Sear's Optigraph, the similarities in prose between the two competing firms' catalogues here and in note 15 suggest a common source – presumably the Chicago-based Enterprise Optical Company, which I suspect provided both companies with their machines and descriptions.

15. Montgomery Ward & Co. sold the Thornward Optiscope Animated Picture Machine, a device that, at least as visually depicted in their 1898 catalogue, looks remarkably similar to the Optigraph.

16. Musser, *The Emergence of Cinema*, p. 293.

17. The explanation provided on page 10 of the 1898 Montgomery Ward catalogue for its Thornward Optiscope, while remarkably similar, differs in interesting ways: 'A combined Magic Lantern and Animated Picture Machine with which can be used both the regular glass lantern views and the Film Ribbons for producing the animated (or moving) pictures. The principle of the animated Picture Machine is the same as that of the Magic Lantern except that instead of the regular glass lantern slide, there is used a long, transparent celluloid ribbon, the standard length of which is fifty feet, containing a series of photographs taken at the rate of about forty per second. On each fifty feet of ribbon there is a series of about 800 pictures, each slightly different from the other. By means of an ingenious mechanism of the mechanical head of the machine, these pictures are made to pass before the projection lens at about the same speed at which they were taken, with a fractional stop and division between each.'

18. George Kleine also contributed to the 1898 Montgomery Ward *Catalogue of Magic Lanterns, Stereopticons and Moving Picture Machines*, offering a lecture to accompany the fifty-slide set *Land and Naval Battles at Santiago*.

19. Don G. Malkames, 'Early Projector Mechanisms', in Fielding, *A Technological History of Motion Pictures and Television*, p. 101 (originally published in *Journal of the Society of Motion Picture and Television Engineers* vol. 66 [October 1957]).

20. As late as 1915, the Optigraph was still thriving and won a gold medal at the Panama–Pacific Exposition: 'On Thursday, August 12, the Optigraph portable motion picture projector carried off the honors at the Panama–Pacific Exposition by being awarded the gold medal. This remarkable little machine is without a doubt one of the most practical portable motion picture projectors ever displayed. In this machine the trade recognises a long-looked-for medium through which the educational and commercial fields will reap immeasurable gains. The Optigraph has been on the market for the past eleven years and there are literally thousands of these machines in use today; but the 1916 model Optigraph is so far in advance of any of the other models that there is practically no comparison. It has also been approved by the National Board of Fire Underwriters for use in the home, church, school, hall and office. The Optigraph Company, Chicago, 111, is the sole manufacturer of these machines' ('"Optigraph" Wins Gold Medal at San Francisco Exposition', *Motography* [1915], p. 406).

21. For more on this, see Uricchio, 'Contextualizing the Apparatus' (forthcoming).

22. William Uricchio, 'There's More to the Camera's Obscura Than Meets the Eye', in Francois Albera, Marta Braun and André Gaudreault (eds), *Arrêt sur image et fragmentation du temps/Stop Motion, Fragmentation of Time* (Lausanne: Cinema Editions Payot, 2002), pp. 103–20.

23. Alas, we know next to nothing about Optigraph sales figures for this period.

24. Musser, *The Emergence of Cinema*, pp. 292–3.

25. Ibid. Readers were, however, greeted with the news in Sears *Guide* No. 112 that they need have 'no fear of harassing litigation – the courts have ruled the [newly improved 1902] Optigraph is legal!'

26. Montgomery Ward's special 1898 media catalogue offered a slightly more elevated and gender-balanced argument than the general Sears *Guide* of the same year, declaring 'Every man or woman can make a Magic lantern, a Stereopticon or a moving Picture Machine the source of instruction, pleasure and profit.'

5

Early Advertising and Promotional Films, 1893–1900: Edison Motion Pictures as a Case Study

Charles Musser

The extent to which the early motion-picture industry self-consciously used films for advertising and promotional purposes has never been properly recognised. The movies were never 'innocent'. From the very outset, companies did more than make films for sale and profit: the films served other purposes as well and functioned frequently in a duplicitous manner. Audiences may have routinely paid good money to be entertained, informed or even instructed; but many of these films were implicitly – and sometimes explicitly – serving an advertising or promotional agenda. Their underlying purpose was to sell goods and services, and this is nowhere more evident than with the subjects produced at Edison's Black Maria film studio and/or distributed by the Edison Manufacturing Company in the late nineteenth century. The assertion that the predominant function of motion pictures in the kinetoscope era and beyond was to advertise and promote might be debated, but it is not obviously wrong. As early as 1894–5, a film's amusement value, its ability to induce potential patrons to spend 5 cents for a quick look, might be seen as only the necessary precondition for the achievement of this unacknowledged goal.

Although the Edison company exemplified an industry-wide trend, at least in the USA, it may have been more aggressive in these pursuits than many of its rivals. Its pre-eminence in this respect may be explained by a variety of factors. For example, businesses of all kinds may have been eager to trade on an association with the Edison name. Edison and his companies also had unique experience in marketing their own goods and services. And, being first in this field, Edison's film company may have simply occupied it first, assuring its pre-eminence. Moreover, in the wake of the Panic of 1893 and the economic depression that followed, Thomas Edison was determined to off-load his production costs onto other parties – or otherwise minimise film-making-related expenses, often by partnering with celebrities and transportation companies. In this respect, promotional or advertising benefits were emphasised as an important payoff. This might involve, for example, an early use of what we now call 'product placement'. Certainly, other important American film companies pursued similar commercial strategies. The American Mutoscope and Biograph Company rivalled Edison in this regard: it collaborated with the New York Central Railroad in the autumn of 1896, producing *Empire State Express*, which both preceded and sparked the Edison company's ongoing commercial relations with other railroad companies.[1] This is not entirely surprising in that Biograph's first production head, W. K. L. Dickson, had previously been Edison's head of production (as well as co-inventor of Edison's motion-picture system). At least some of the films discussed here can be presently seen on YouTube; they will be indicated with an asterisk (*) after the title of the film. I also provide a number for each Edison film, which is based on a filmography that I published as *Edison Motion Pictures, 1890–1900: An Annotated Filmography*. While this may encourage the dedicated reader to pursue further investigations, the numbers also suggest the relative chronological position of each film. I have identified roughly 1,000 Edison films made in the decade between 1891 and 1900.

PIMPING THE LOVE CHILD FROM THE VERY MOMENT OF ITS BIRTH[2]

Edison's first films from 1893 were designed to draw attention to Edison's newest technology and thus promote it. I have described these films as 'demonstration films'(specifically *Blacksmithing Scene* [no. 16, also known as *Blacksmith Scene**], *Horse Shoeing* [no. 17] and *The Barbershop Scene* [no. 18, aka *The Barbershop**]). The first film made explicitly for commercial exhibition – *Sandow** (no. 26, March 1894) – went further. For this twenty-second motion picture, vaudeville star and famed strongman Sandow was dressed in the bare minimum as he displayed his muscular body before Edison's camera and went through a series of poses. The filming itself was nothing more than a carefully orchestrated media event. All the major New York newspapers covered the story, either sending reporters to Edison Laboratory in Orange, New Jersey, where the filming took place – or making up what transpired for their columns. The story had several possible angles. According to the *New York Herald*:

> The strongest man on earth, to quote the play bills, and the greatest inventor of the age met yesterday at Menlo Park [sic], New Jersey. The meeting was an interesting one, and the giant of brain and the giant of muscle found much to admire in each other. Sandow marveled at Edison's inventions, and the Wizard gazed longingly and enviously at the prodigious muscles of the strong man.[3]

The *Herald* had Edison greeting Sandow at the train station. Although this was a complete fabrication that provided its account with some extra punch, Edison did, in fact, shake hands with Sandow at his laboratory since the strongman had promised to waive his fee if he actually met the inventor.

As the symmetry of the above quote suggests, the event was staged for the benefit of both parties as a criss-cross of mutual endorsements. Certainly it brought attention to Edison's new commercial venture: the kinetoscope, which would debut in little more than a month. This encouraged orders for machines and whetted the interest of potential spectators. At the same time, it was part of Sandow's efforts to promote both his stage career and, more specifically, his book on physical fitness that would appear just one or two weeks later, entitled *Sandow on Physical Training*.[4] Eleven days after its article on Sandow's visit to the Black Maria, the *New York Herald* published a lengthy and glowing review of the strongman's book. Edison's endorsement was thus followed by another. 'A great many books have treated the same topic, but they have not equaled this in perspicuity,' the reviewer remarked.[5] As an extra boost, on the very day of this *Herald* review, the *New York World* published an article on Edison's new kinetograph motion-picture system, featuring frames of Sandow.[6] This attention sold books, and it sold peep-hole kinetoscopes that were the only mechanism to view these films. It also sold the myth of Edison at a time when he faced financial and legal difficulties. Whatever anxieties the inventor must have felt privately, publicly he seemed self-confident, relaxed and carefree.[7]

If Edison faced challenges to his patents, Sandow was being kept in the limelight by challenges to his claim as 'the strongest man in the world' from Louis Cyr and other strongmen.[8] The Edison association, instantiated in the Sandow films themselves, certainly gave the aura of authenticity to the vaudevillian's titles, which were fundamentally promotional and commercial in nature. This motion picture also inaugurated a relationship between newspapers and film-making that was used many times in that first year of commercial production.[9] The visit of heavy-weight champion James J. Corbett to the Black Maria on 7 September, resulting in *The Corbett–Courtney Fight** (no. 54), produced even more copy. Though Edison may have been present, he had to play a more discreet role, given the illegality of prize fighting in New Jersey and other parts of the USA at this time.[10] Nonetheless, the affinities between the world champion of the ring and the world champion of invention were potential subtexts of this event as well.[11] Anticipating a relationship that would become much more common in the twentieth century, reports of filming became a periodic source of news (which sold newspapers) and publicity for stars and producers (which sold films and built careers).

PROMOTING PERFORMERS

One reason so many vaudevillians were eager to appear before Edison's kinetograph camera, initially without compensation, had to do with the promotional nature of such exhibitions. The location of the first kinetoscope parlour was not coincidental. By peering into the kinetoscopes at 1155 Broadway, spectators could see the small moving images of theatrical stars performing just a few blocks away. If, after such a glimpse, they were not inspired to go to the theatre immediately, then perhaps they would go to see 'the real thing' later in the week. Or, correspondingly, patrons who had gone to Koster & Bial's might have their memory of that night stimulated by these life-like, if tiny images. Moreover, as these kinetoscope films were dispersed throughout the country, their exhibition encouraged potential visitors to go to New York in order to see the performers in the flesh. Or else they might wait for the arrival of the touring vaudevillians, musicals and plays to their local venue with heightened expectation. A careful perusing of news items in theatrical journals and elsewhere indicates that business managers in the amusement field took this promotional value very seriously. Theatrical columns reported:

> W. D. Mann, manager of Hoey's new farce, 'The Flams,' has conceived an advertising device for next season. Edison's kinetoscope and phonograph are to be combined in a reproduction of the principal spectacular and vocal features of the new performance, the instrument to be publicly exhibited in the principal cities weeks prior to the play's appearance.[12]

Mann's advertising scheme was hardly original; it merely articulated the kinetoscope's imagined impact on the careers of performers.

Kinetoscope films were excellent advertising for individual performers. If Edison's motion-picture venture had not been so obviously profitable, it may not have been necessary for Edison's kinetoscope agents Raff & Gammon and Maguire & Baucus to pay performers the respectable sums of money they often received for appearing before Edison's camera. Those fortunate headline performers frequently went on to enjoy long and prosperous careers, while many lesser-known figures became more prominent. The extent to which these films contributed to their success in the short term and in subsequent years is, of course, speculative. Robetta and Doreto could only claim to offer one of several 'Fun in a Chinese Laundry' routines on the vaudeville stage during the 1894–5 theatrical season. Two years after they appeared in several Edison films including *Chinese Laundry Scene** (no. 96, November 1894), they were still going strong and called 'old favorites' and 'the two cleverest Chinese impersonators on the stage'.[13] Professor Harry Welton's Cat Circus seemed to enjoy better billing after it appeared before Edison's camera (*The Boxing Cats [Prof. Welton's]** [no. 41]). But when Welton's act faltered, at least one exhibitor attributed the film to being a view of Professor Trewey, the variety performer and concessionaire for the Lumière cinématographe in England.[14] Frank Lawton (*Trio Dance* [no. 103] and Wilson & Waring of *John W. Wilson and Bertha Waring* [no. 107]) went on to be successes in England, where they may have been first seen in Edison's peep-hole machine. Annabelle Whitford, who performed numerous serpentine and butterfly dances before Edison's camera, eventually became the Gibson girl and a star in Ziegfeld's Follies. Hadj Tahar (*Sheik Hadji Tahar*, no. 74) remained an active performer until July 1926, when he died soon after completing his act at the Palace Theater, New York's premiere vaudeville house.[15] This pattern continued in the era of projected motion pictures. J. Stuart Blackton moved up to top-of-the-line vaudeville after the success of *Blackton Sketches, No. 1* (no. 199, August 1896), more popularly known as *Inventor Edison Sketched by World Artist**. He performed for nothing, or rather for charity: his sole personal compensation was the invaluable publicity it gave him.

The earliest kinetoscope films did not promote Edison directly but rather served either as evidence of the inventor's technological wizardry or as the basis for glowing news items about their production.[16] Somewhat later, but even then only very occasionally, did Edison motion pictures become overtly self-promotional in nature. These include *Edison Laboratory* (no. 188, August–September 1896), *Inventor Edison Sketched by World Artist*; and *Mr Edison at Work in His Chemical Laboratory** (no. 334, May 1897). Such direct forms of self-promotion were indebted to the more numerous Lumière films that featured the brothers Louis and Auguste, their family, their customers and their factory. *La Sortie de l'usine Lumière à Lyon* (1895) and its two remakes filled this role most explicitly. But virtually every *cinématographe* programme had at least one picture that featured members of the Lumière family and they were often identified in ads and newspaper copy about the programmes. And since Louis was behind the camera for most of these, Auguste generally became the media star. Edison tried to appear more reticent, less obvious in the way he presented his own mythic figure to the world. It is noteworthy that the only motion picture featuring the inventor from this period was taken at his laboratory (significantly a mock laboratory constructed inside the Black Maria), in which Edison either showed himself to be an awkward actor or chose to burlesque a popular photograph showing him carefully mixing chemicals (in the tradition of *Blacksmithing Scene* or *The Barber Shop*). The Lumière mixture of family films with advertising was potent but avoided by Edison for reasons that seem consistent with the kinds of subject matter fostered by each organisation.

ADVERTISING FILMS PRESENTED ON CITY STREETS

Given these early experiences, it is not surprising that advertising films quickly became one of the more popular genres of early cinema. In large cities exhibitions were given for advertising purposes with films and lantern slides projected from rooftops onto canvases at busy intersections. The stereopticon had been used for advertising purposes since the early 1870s. In Chicago, it was reported that a Mr Van Dusen,

> exhibits in the open air, by means of mammoth views, interspersed with business cards. The views are so pretty that the public is willing to stand the advertisement in order to see the whole of the views. The idea is novel.[17]

By mid-1872, night-time advertising with the stereopticon had become popular in New York City as 'pictures and business cards are alternately thrown on a large screen'.[18] The Stereopticon Advertising Company was soon projecting advertising images in Herald Square.[19] By the summer of 1897 motion pictures had been readily added to the mix of projected images. According to *The Phonoscope*, a trade journal for the motion-picture and phonograph industries:

> A very interesting and novel advertising exhibition is now being given on the roof of the building at 1321 Broadway, facing Herald Square.
>
> Animated films are shown illustrating advertisements. The pictures were all by the International Film Co., 44 Broad Street, and are attracting the attention nightly of thousands of people. As an instance of the enterprise and hustle of the International Film Co., the Democratic Mayor was nominated on Thursday night and on Friday his picture was on the screen at 34th Street.[20]

It was probably not coincidence that the International Film Company was started by two former Edison employees, Charles Webster and Edmund Kuhn. One of their advertising films was *Dewar's Scotch Whisky** (1897). Perhaps the most obvious examples of advertising films among the Edison offerings are *Admiral Cigarette** (no. 362, July 1897) and *Crawford Shoe Store* (no. 362.1). These films and others like them were explicitly made for open-air advertising, but it seems likely that they were also occasionally shown in theatrical and other settings – for example, as burlesque comedies (*Admiral Cigarette* or *Dewar's Scotch Whisky)* or casual street scenes (e.g. *Crawford Shoe Store*).

To exhibit advertising slides and films, J. Stuart Blackton and Albert E. Smith started the Commercial Advertising Bureau in late 1897. *Lickmann's Cigar and Photo*

Store (no. 549) and *North Side Dental Rooms* (no. 550) were two Edison films that were made for this new enterprise in April 1898, shortly before the partners sold the business and began to move into vaudeville exhibition. These two founders of the Vitagraph Company of America – the largest motion-picture producer in the USA between 1906 and 1914 – all but began their motion-picture careers by showing advertising films.[21]

SOME NEWLY PERTINENT FILMS IN THE PAPER PRINT COLLECTION

As Edison paper prints, submitted to the Library of Congress for copyright purposes, have been put back onto 35mm film, the resulting upgrade in quality has revealed an advertising component to many of these titles. For *Corner Madison and State Streets, Chicago** (no. 354), signs for various attractions at Electric Park were paraded in front of the camera. *Sutro Baths, no. 1** (no. 392) displays a large banner proclaiming its hours of operations that would seem an unlikely part of the regular decor. *South Spring Street, Los Angeles** (no. 470) discretely includes a sign for Tally's Kinetoscope Parlor on the left side of the screen. For *Freight Train** (no. 479, January 1898), Horst Brothers went to considerable trouble to put large signs on a series of freight cars, which advertised their special hops. What is striking is the way in which such signage went unacknowledged in catalogue descriptions. The placards for Electric Park would appear to be a random occurrence; the well-framed banner at Sutro Baths appears to be displayed by chance. Or so the unsuspecting viewer (or exhibitor) was led to believe. While not always explicitly advertising films, they were clear examples of product placement.

Just as noteworthy, something approaching half of the Edison films made between the autumn of 1896 and the end of 1900 were subsidised by transportation companies or other organisations seeking publicity. James White and William Heise made films of the onrushing Black Diamond Express with the active participation of the Lehigh Valley Railroad, whose executives were eager to present such images of power and speed as an alternative to those of the Empire State Express, then being shown on the biograph to the benefit of the New York Central Railroad. *Black Diamond Express** (no. 262), which was taken in December 1896, featured a large makeshift sign with the words 'Lehigh Valley Rail Road'. It was so popular that the negative was quickly worn out and the film had to be remade several times over the next few years. *New Black Diamond Express* (no. 817, May 1900) was at least the fourth such negative to be made in as many years. Scenes of Niagara Falls were likewise taken with the assistance of railroad corporations because the site was a favoured tourist destination.

The films made on James White and Frederick Blechynden's tour of the Far West, Mexico and Asia were all made with the cooperation of railroad and steamship companies, which included free transportation and possibly some financial subsidies. They fully recognised that such films promoted tourism. These promotional schemes were, however, more or less covert: the oft-stated claim that such films were a cheap *alternative* to travel deflected attention away from the fact that the films were to a considerable extent made and shown precisely to encourage tourism. Although many actualities such as *Wash Day in Mexico** (no. 450, November–December 1897) were touristic scenes, a substantial number were of company trains and ships: *Sunset Limited, Southern Pacific Railway** (no. 478, January 1898) and *Afternoon Tea on Board S.S. 'Doric'* (no. 567, June 1898), taken for the Occidental and Oriental Steamship Company, are but two such examples. These short, one-shot films served as building blocks for larger programmes, whether as isolated scenes in a variety programme or for incorporation into evening-length travel lectures. It is quite possible that the primary users of these films were the transportation companies themselves, which used them to promote their services. If this was the case, additional sales of prints were seen as a bonus.

Once we look at these early films as advertising and promotional films, there are major implications that become clear. Most films, as images of someone, something, or somewhere, become a form of advertising or publicity. *Roosevelt's Rough Riders Embarking for Santiago** (no. 590, June 1898) helps to promote future New York State Governor and US President Teddy Roosevelt as well as the USA's war with Spain. *Scene on Surf Avenue, Coney Island* (no. 171, June 1896) and *Shooting the Chutes** (no. 173, June 1896) promote and implicitly advertise Coney Island. These early motion pictures embodied a dialectical tension, both acting as a new commodity form and promoting other kinds of services and commodities in the era of an emergent consumer society. In a multiplicity of ways, the motion-picture industry was intensively engaged in the commodification of culture from its earliest years.

NOTES

This chapter is excerpted and adapted from 'Before the Rapid Firing Kinetograph: Edison Film Production, Representation and Exploitation', the introductory essay for *Edison Motion Pictures, 1890–1900: An Annotated Filmography* (Washington, DC, and Friuli, Italy: Smithsonian Institution Press and Le Giornate del Cinema Muto, 1997).

1. Biograph also made groups of films for the US Post Office in 1903 and Westinghouse in 1904, as well as short advertising films of the Gold Dust Twins, mascots for Gold Dust Laundry Powder.
2. This subheading is a friendly nod to those scholars who dabble in biological metaphors when analysing the early years of cinema.
3. 'Edison Perfects His Kinetoscope', *New York Herald*, 7 March 1894, p. 9.
4. Eugen Sandow, *Sandow on Physical Training* (New York: J. Selwin Tait & Sons, 1894).
5. 'Development of a Strong Man', *New York Herald*, 18 March 1894, p. 8E.
6. 'Wizard Edison's Kinetograph', *New York World*, 18 March 1894, p. 21.
7. Gordon Hendricks was, of course, right in claiming that Edison effectively managed an adoring press to build an image that did not neatly correspond to reality.
8. 'The Chance of Sandow's Life', *New York Herald*, 9 April 1894, p. 8; 'Sandow Would Rather Pose' and 'Cyr is the Champion', *New York Herald*, 11 April 1894, p. 12.
9. This relationship of promoting motion pictures while selling newspapers was similar to that relationship between the press and the sporting world. It was quite different from the ways in which cinema was said to function as a visual newspaper.
10. Edison's presence at the filming of the Corbett–Courtney fight went unreported in the press, but Gordon Hendricks located a reminiscence of James Corbett, which suggests the boxer

did meet the inventor on this occasion (*The Kinetoscope: America's First Commercially Successful Motion Picture Exhibitor* [New York: The Beginnings of the American Film, 1966], p. 109).

11. The affinity between the world champion of boxing and the world champion of invention would become explicit in James Corbett's next play, *The Naval Cadet*, in which he played a young inventor, not unlike Edison.
12. 'In the Breezy Roof Gardens', *New York Tribune,* 24 June 1894, p. 11.
13. *Providence Journal*, 16 February 1897, p. 8; *Cincinnati Commercial Tribune*, 20 December 1896, p. 11.
14. The exhibitor who later attributed Welton's act to Trewey was Englishman William Rock. *New Orleans Picayune*, 25 May 1897, p. 14, cited in Sylvester Quinn Breard, 'A History of Motion Pictures in New Orleans, 1896–1908' (MA thesis: Louisiana State University, 1951), p. 31, published in microfiche in *Historical Journal of Film, Radio and Television* vol. 15 no. 4 (Autumn 1995).
15. 'Acrobat Dies After Act', *The New York Times*, 13 July 1926, p. 19.
16. It was, in some sense, unnecessary for Edison to be the frequent or overt subject of his films given that the technology was tied to his name so explicitly: 'Edison's latest wonder, the Kinetoscope', 'Edison's Vitascope' and so forth.
17. 'The Free Stereopticon', *Chicago Tribune,* 1 October 1871, p. 2.
18. 'The Sign Boards of New York', *Scientific American*, 15 June 1872, p. 400.
19. 'Our Bulletin', *The New York Times*, 10 October 1872, p. 1.
20. *The Phonoscope*, August–September 1897, p. 9.
21. Charles Musser, 'American Vitagraph: 1897–1901', *Cinema Journal* vol. 22 no. 3 (Spring 1983), pp. 4–46.

PART II
FORMS AND
PRACTICES

●

6

Advertising and Animation: From the Invisible Hand to Attention Management

Michael Cowan

Although early product-advertising film came in many forms, it is hard to overlook the extensive use of animation. While the earliest film advertisements tended to use live action, the institutionalisation of advertising film in Europe during the 1910s coincided with the adoption of conventions from trick film, and advertising went on to employ nearly every type of animation, from stop-trick and sand animation to silhouettes, experimental abstraction and – the most widespread form of advertising in the 1920s – drawn-character animation. This work includes many films by well-known experimental directors such as Lotte Reiniger, Walter Ruttmann and Dziga Vertov, but it also encompasses an entire army of professional illustrators and animators such as Robert Lortac (France), Peter Eng (Austria), Harry Jäger (Germany) and Victor Bergdahl (Sweden).[1]

If such work is garnering renewed interest today, that interest is certainly due, in part, to the influence of digital technologies, which – following Lev Manovich's call to rethink cinema as a subset of animation – have helped to rekindle interest in the widespread 'graphic' traditions that have always existed within and alongside photographic cinema.[2] The animated advertising film – or what its chief practitioner in Germany, Julius Pinschewer, described as the 'advertising film on graphic basis' (*Werbefilm auf graphischer Grundlage*) – represents an important domain of early animation, but one that has received little attention in animation studies.[3] In what follows, I consider some of the reasons for animation's prevalent role in product advertisements, as well as some of the specific functions that animation assumed

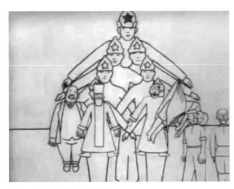

Vertov's *Soviet Toys* (1924)

Bergdahl Stomatol

when used in advertising. Tracing the trajectory of advertising film in Germany from the 1910s to its transformation into a full-fledged industry in the 1920s, I argue that animation served both to thematise issues of consumerist modernity and to forge instrumental images analogous to contemporary developments in graphic design, which were themselves spurred on by the new field of advertising psychology.

TRICKS, CONTROL AND THE 'INVISIBLE HAND'

Writing in 1920, a reporter for the trade journal *Seidels Reklame* argued that a new form of 'film caricature' offered an ideal opportunity for advertisers in their effort to arouse audience interest:

> The very process by which the image emerges over the white screen is extremely interesting and spurs viewers to reflection. It looks as if one of those lightning-sketch painters from the variety stage were drawing the image line by line before the audience's eyes. But the difference is that we do not see the draftsman. The pencil appears to be moved by the invisible hand of a ghost. ... The audience is astonished, for it cannot help but ask itself how this image was recorded.[4]

The writer was most likely describing the work of pioneering animator Emil Cohl. Although Cohl's famous *fantasmagorie* films did often show the artist's hand setting up the image or intervening, their main attraction came precisely when the hand left the frame and characters and objects seemed to move and transform on their own as if propelled by a hidden agency.[5] But the reference to the variety stage situates early advertising more widely within a tradition of attractions and magic tricks that also lay behind the trick films of magician-artists such as Georges Méliès, Segundo de Chomón, Walter Booth and James Stuart Blackton, all of whom had adapted the famous 'lightning sketch' genre to trick film.[6] The work of German pioneer Julius Pinschewer is characteristic here.

After beginning with a few live-action films such as *Die Korsett-Anprobe* (1910), Pinschewer quickly adopted stop-motion and other tricks to create a world of magical

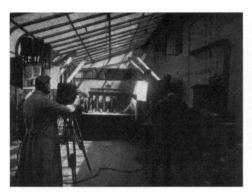

Pinschewer in the studio

Pinschewer's *Tanz der Flaschen* (1912)

Films That Sell

Kupferberg Light advertisement,
Berlin 1926

commodity display, in which products perform dances (e.g. *Tanz der Flaschen* [1912]), sewing kits mend buttons on their own (*Der Nähkasten* [1912]), fairies appear – via superimposition – as tiny figures atop giant champagne glasses (*Sektzauber* [1912]) and paintings come alive by magic (*Das Ahnenbild* [1912]). In such films, Pinschewer sought to visualise commodities that appear – as he put it in an article from 1914 – to be 'guided by invisible hands' as they move about, transform and interact with one another on the screen.[7]

In keeping with the trick film tradition, such films aimed to astonish audiences unfamiliar with the technology behind the display: 'The audience wonders how it is technologically possible, for example, that a coffee pot moves on its own and buttons produced by a certain company line up to spell the company name.'[8]

The use of the 'invisible hand' to describe trick technology also linked animated film advertisements to numerous other forms of animated advertising beyond the cinema, such as the moving automata that were adapted to advertising in shop windows and the animated electric light advertisements. The latter, in particular, were often described as mysterious spectacles, in which words and images unfurl themselves over the night-time skyline as if drawn by an unseen hand. Thus, another writer for *Seidels Reklame*, commenting on the post-war ban on electric advertisements in Berlin, remembered the pre-war animated light spectacles as follows:

> An invisible hand would draw spectacular characters over the building façades: long lines of striking text flared up suddenly, only to disappear after a few seconds as other texts took their place. Colourful animated images appeared on the roof to direct the attention of willing and even unwilling spectators.[9]

Similarly, the author Erich Kästner, after visiting the Leipzig Trade Fair in 1925, described an entire array of animated street advertisements in magical terms, including electric light advertisements written by 'invisible hands' and 'disguised automobiles driven by ghostly hands'.[10]

But if such 'ghostly' hands underscore the link between animation and the conventions of stage magic, they also point towards another issue at stake in filmic animation: namely *control* over the image. In an oft-cited essay, William Schaffer has argued that in animated film every visible frame is 'accompanied by the performance of an *invisible hand*', since the animator intervenes in each individual frame at a level absent in live-action cinematography.[11] The result, Schaffer argues, is a 'paradox of control' in which animators control the image to an unprecedented extent, while also seeing themselves exposed to a division of industrial labour beyond their control (increasingly so as industrial methods are adopted into animation).[12] Schaffer's emphasis on the hand as the ontological ground of animation has not been without its critics.[13] But his identification of control as the key issue in 'graphic' film-making provides a useful entryway for a historical investigation of the use of animation in early advertising. For if contemporary observers invoked the notion of the invisible hand so often to describe advertising spectacles, it is not only on account of its link to trick film, but also on account of the resonances it held with market language and corresponding questions of control within the new capitalist marketplace. Adam Smith's use of the metaphor of the invisible hand to describe a benevolent agency that regulates market forces unbeknownst to its actors is well known.[14] But, as Stefan Andriopoulos has shown, Smith's model of the invisible hand – itself one of many versions of benevolent agencies thought to order the contingencies of human action and history in eighteenth- and nineteenth-century social thought – already had a more sinister counterpart in the gothic literature that emerged during the same period, where the motif of ghostly hands returns obsessively to designate supernatural agencies that thwart individual intentions.[15]

One can find an analogous mixture of phantasmagoric motifs and economic thinking at work in early advertising. Like the work of Méliès, Pinschewer's early films often feature demons, imps and conjurers. The 1912 film *Sektzauber* for Kupferberg champagne, for example, shows a demon figure conjuring up a Kupferberg champagne bottle from an exploding volcano. Like Méliès's *'diable noir'*, who (in the 1905 film of the same title) moves furniture around a hotel room while remaining invisible to the hapless patron, such figures served both as a narrative justification for the filmic tricks and as a means of situating those tricks within a much longer tradition of fantasmagoria and magic display – a tradition they took up, as Pinschewer stated again and again, in order to capture the attention of audiences enchanted by film's special effects. But the trick film also offered a particular level of control over the image and thus, it was hoped, over audience response. Pinschewer described this double valence of the animated image in an article from 1916, when he praised 'the cinematographic trick film, which is particularly interesting for audiences on account of its technique, but which also allows one to place the brand being advertised directly in the centre of the short action being projected'.[16] This centring of attention on the *brand* is a staple feature of advertising film aesthetics from Pinschewer's early stop-trick advertisements to 1920s silhouette advertisements and beyond. And it suggests a broader motivation for the appeal of animation in advertising films; through the presence of the animator's invisible hand, controlling the image at the level of the individual frame and reducing the contingencies

Sektzauber (1912)

Reiniger still from *Das Geheimnis der Marquise* (1922)

of photographic representation, animation seemed to promise a control over spectatorial responses and a focusing of spectatorial attention on the brand.

This control of attention forms part of a broader technology of economic control in the early twentieth century, in which branding and trademarks played a central role. Although trademarks might seem self-evident today, their very presence in advertising was still relatively new in the early twentieth century, having emerged around 1900 when powerful new corporations, such as the National Biscuit Company in the USA and Kupferberg Champagne in Germany, sought to gain control of widening markets by creating a loyal consumer base. In this sense, mass trademark advertising forms a key example of what James Beniger famously dubbed the 'Control Revolution' around 1900, where bureaucratic systems, telecommunications and emerging mass media were enlisted to manage the centrifugal forces unleashed by industrial production methods.[17] Branding helped to manage increased production by stimulating consumption; but it also helped to forge a new *habitus* of consumption marked by affective investments in specific brands. For the companies involved, the mass distribution of identical trademarks promised to wrest market control from middlemen – retailers, wholesalers and department stores – by appealing directly to consumers. And it was precisely this development that led to the emergence of what the economist Viktor Mataja described in 1910 a new 'professional group of advertising experts [*Reklamefachleute*]' (i.e. advertising agencies), who promised to help companies forge effective brands and distribution strategies.[18]

This desire for control over a broad consumer base also forms a key part of the background to the development of film advertising and its expert practitioners such as Pinschewer. The expense of film alone – the production cost of labour-intensive 'trick films', but also and above all the distribution costs – favoured large enterprises such as Kupferberg (champagne) and Excelsior (tyres).[19] But for those who could afford it, film advertising promised to reach broad swathes of the population and expose them – through tricks and animation – to a particular brand in an entertaining way. Thus Pinschewer, in his first published article on advertising film, could cite a 'statistical study', based on the observation of 1,000 screenings in 600 theatres, which showed that 90 per cent of advertising films had elicited positive responses on the part of audiences to the brands shown.[20] The number of visitors in these 600 theatres alone, he continued, amounted to some 58 million people per year stemming from all classes and professions. (By 1926, Pinschewer would boast of his monopolies with theatres totalling 300,000 seats or 3 million viewers per week.)[21] Little wonder, then, that Pinschewer argued in the same article that advertising film was particularly well suited for 'those products that enter into circulation under a specific trademark'.[22] The cinema circuit offered a seemingly ideal distribution platform for advertisements designed to bind a broad public to a particular brand.

But if movie theatres offered an advantageous form of distribution, the cinema also appeared, in the eyes of advertising theorists, as a powerful *dispositif* for controlling spectatorial attention. Whereas newspaper inserts and street advertisements had to compete with dozens of neighbouring advertisements for the attention of distracted readers and passers-by, the darkened space of the theatre promised to focus attention on the product and its trademark: 'Every patron in the movie theatre', Pinschewer claimed in the 1913 article, 'perceives the advertising film shown during the programme and follows its content with excitement and interest.'[23] In this sentiment, Pinschewer was hardly alone; numerous advertising psychologists emphasised the importance of the darkened space of the theatre for focusing spectators' attention. As another industry specialist would put it in 1926:

> One can deliberately oversee the advertisements section of a newspaper; one can more or less avoid the sight of traffic and electric advertisements; one can take off one's headphones during radio advertisements or simply turn off the receiver; but it is not easy to close one's eyes in the movie theatre.[24]

Advertisement for Pinschewer-Film

This is not to argue that we should take the claims of advertisers at face value, and the frequent discussions of dissatisfied or angry audiences in the trade literature of the time offers one indication of just how tenuous advertising's control strategies might have been in reality.[25] But it does suggest that the logic of control was a central motivation for the enlistment film as an advertising medium in the years around World War I and would continue to shape the way in which advertising theorists approached the medium throughout the 1920s. If the invisible hands of the animator promised control over the image, those of distribution specialists promised control over a new marketplace of late capitalism and its flows of consumer attention. It was precisely this double role that characterised the new class of advertising film entrepreneurs such as Pinschewer.

ANIMATED THINGS

This nexus of control helps to account for the predilection for graphic forms in advertising film. But it does not necessarily explain in particular the fixation these films evince with showing products *in movement*. Again and again, Pinschewer's early films display anthropomorphised commodities dancing, marching, mending shirts, pouring champagne, etc. Indeed, it was precisely such films that the reporter for *Seidels Reklame* cited at the beginning of this article had in mind when he wrote that animation served as a perfect form for advertising the new world of consumer things: 'Thousands of objects lend themselves to this kind of advertising, and this kind of advertising lends itself to thousands of objects.'[26] This is a pattern that would last well into the 1920s and 30s – one still visible, for example, in Oskar Fischinger's famous Muratti cigarette advertisements *Muratti Greift Ein* (1934) and *Muratti Privat* (1935), where animated cigarettes perform various group dances to the music. Here, too, filmic advertisements found a counterpart in other forms of 'living advertisements' such as the parades of human cigarettes and other products that could be seen marching in trade fairs or in the city streets of Berlin.

It would be hard to overlook the link between such spectacles of animated commodities and that other form of market magic so critical to modern life: commodity fetishism. Marx's model – in which the labour of production and social relations assume 'the phantasmagorical form of a relation between things'[27] – informed numerous more expansive diagnoses of modernity that sought to explain how the products of human culture seemed to emancipate themselves from human control. From Georg Simmel's model of the 'tragedy of culture' to Georg Lukács's theory of 'reification', modernist thought continually drew upon the Marxian concept of fetishism to explain the process by which the forms of modern culture – technology, bureaucracy, law, etc. – assume an autonomous status while human beings are reduced to 'passive observers'.[28] Even the early Jean Baudrillard could draw on this paradigm when he described consumer culture and its products as a kind of coercive (structural) social system – 'the code by which the entire society communicates and converses' –

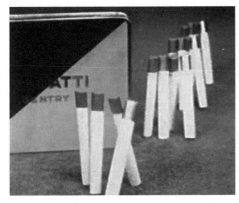

Fischinger Muratti

Ambulatory cigarette advertisement

to which twentieth-century individuals are trained to conform no less than nineteenth-century rural populations were trained for industrial and bureaucratic work.[29]

As powerful as such theoretical paradigms are, however, they cannot account for the particular affective mode in which commodities come to life to address spectators in early animated advertisements: namely their humour. For this, we do better to take a cue from Arjun Appadurai, who famously called for 'methodological fetishism' in the study of things, one that follows the things themselves – their forms, their circulation and, above all, the work they do – rather than reflexively seeking to dissipate fetishistic illusions and reveal the human actors or social networks underneath. The particular humour of early product advertising was part and parcel of a broader culture of humour in early consumer society, which sought precisely to come to terms with the increased agency of material things. Perhaps the best-known articulation of the topos came from the aesthetic theorist and novelist Friedrich Theodor Vischer, who coined the term 'Tücke des Objekts' ('cunning of objects') in his 1879 novel Auch Einer: eine Reisebekannschaft (Another One: A Travelling Acquaintance), in which the protagonist rails against the capacity of everyday objects to thwart the idealistic strivings of thought with their stubborn contingency.[30] Vischer's comedy of 'cunning' objects looked back to his own romantic theories of comedy, where (building on Jean Paul's model of comedy as an 'inverted sublime') he identified the comic with moments in which human thought is forced to come back down, as it were, and attend to the realm of the body and material reality.[31] But by attaching such moments to everyday objects, Vischer also looked forward to an emerging discourse of consumer objects. Product advertising itself was often conceptualised in terms of romantic humour on account of its ability – as one writer for Seidels Reklame described it in 1922 – to 'dissolve seemingly serious values into naught'.[32] But Vischer's humour of cunning objects also provided a template for a broader experience of everyday things in the era of consumerism. Thus, the writer Arnold Zweig, in a humorous feuilleton article from 1923 still resonant with Vischer's view of the cunning object, lamented that consumer objects had 'gone on the attack':

> Threateningly and violently they besiege us, always there, constantly announcing themselves anew – be it because they have run out, because they require restoration, because they need mending, or simply because they are lost. Shifted into the centre of attention, feeding on everyone's energies, they tear open the calm in which innovation takes place. They have banded together and surrounded us; when they shift into attack mode they make us old and tired. We must constantly renew the battle to regain that concentration that used to last through weeks of undisturbed work.[33]

For intellectuals such as Zweig, the experience of everyday objects in consumer society was precisely one of being pulled back down, cast into a stubborn material realm where autonomous theoretical pursuits become impossible.

Early cinema is, of course, full of representations of things assuming their own agency. For theorists such as Béla Balázs and Jean Epstein, this capacity of objects to assume a living physiognomy on screen is precisely what made film an art form, whose defamiliarising close-ups could restore a mode of vision characteristic of children who 'do not yet judge things as tools', but 'regard each thing as an autonomous living being with a soul and face of its own'.[34] Such readings of film's resistance to instrumental vision resonate with an entire strain of modern aesthetics, from Surrealism to Heidegger to contemporary 'thing' theory, dedicated to rediscovering what Bill Brown has called 'the thingness of objects' whose 'flow within the circuits of production and distribution, consumption and exhibition, has been arrested, however momentarily'.[35]

But if the humour of the cunning object resonates with cinema's defamiliarising powers generally, it finds a more specific on-screen representation in slapstick. Méliès's *Diable noir*, itself a proto-slapstick comedy, derived its humour precisely from a spectacle of malevolent objects – chairs, tables and beds – that thwart even the simplest intentions of the unsuspecting hotel guest. And this humour would come to a head in the films of Chaplin and Keaton, which offered, in André Bazin's formulation, 'the dramatic expression of the tyranny of things'.[36] Whereas Chaplin's optimistic comedy consisted in making such tyrannical objects assume new – artistic – functions, it was Keaton, Bazin argues, who 'knew how to create a tragedy of the Object'.[37] Writing some thirty years later, Stanley Cavell could argue that Keaton's comedies offered filmic equivalents of the Heideggerian experience of worldliness, in which the objects of the world, ceasing to function as transparent tools, step forth 'in their conspicuousness, their obtrusiveness, their obstinacy'.[38] One can only imagine what Keaton might have done with some of the uncanny 'things' that inhabited the landscape of early advertising – for example, the 'giant models of packages of Reemstma cigarettes' on display at the 1921 Frankfurt International Trade Fair,[39] or the motorised Walfisch shampoo vehicles riding through the Leipzig Trade Fair the same year. Considering such larger-than-life commodities, it is little wonder that Kästner could describe such trade fairs as the '*Karneval des Kaufmanns*' ('salesman's carnival'); the product trade fair not only had its roots in carnival, but also retained a carnivalesque quality in Bakhtin's sense, where autonomous products and trademarks towered over their human visitors.[40]

It might be tempting to approach such advertising representations as part of the nexus of popular culture by which capitalism creates its own immanent critiques. Many recent histories of animation have highlighted the utopian potential that thinkers such as Walter Benjamin and Sergei Eisenstein saw in cartoons such as *Mickey*

Sherlock Jr (1924)

Walfisch shampoo advertisement – Leipzig Trade Fair, 1922

Advertising and Animation

Mouse with their ability to 'unhinge experience and agency from anthropomorphic identity' through morphing and other tricks.[41] Here, too, however, there is a crucial distinction to be made. For if advertising *evoked* the rebellious objects of slapstick and cartoons, it always did so with a view towards *taming* those objects and reassuring spectators precisely of their instrumental status. This is, no doubt, a central motivation behind the predilection for orderly ornamental dances in advertising films, where the objects such as Pinschewer's champagne bottles or Fischinger's cigarettes arrange themselves in geometrical mass ornaments. Where Siegfried Kracauer saw ornamental 'girl troops' as the expression of an abstract rationality that had transformed man into its raw material, advertising films promised an orderly rationality in the service of the consumer. This topos of the obedient object also informed the rudimentary narratives of many animated advertising films. For example, in a 1927 advertisement by Epoche for the Hamburg gas works, *Umsturz am Nordpol* (*Overthrow at the North Pole*, 1927), an Eskimo family flees in terror before an 'invading army' of animated gas ovens, only to erupt with joy when the ovens end up bringing warmth and modern comfort ('progress') to their cold igloo.[42] Similarly, in a Pinschewer advertisement for Vim cleaning products entitled *Küchen-Rebellen* (*Kitchen Rebels*, 1928), a frustrated housewife struggles to clean her stubborn pots, which then come to life via stop-trick animation. However, the pots' 'rebellion' consists not in a scenario of cunningness, but rather in an orderly procession to the local grocery store to purchase a box of Vim scrubbing powder and dutifully carry it back to the elated housewife. Aimed at middle-class spectators, such advertisements constantly invoked the spectre of the rebellious only to perform its taming on the screen.

This taming of the object was part and parcel of the codes of advertising film and corresponded to the particular brand of reassuring humour such films sought to cultivate. The advertising theorist Fritz Pauli, for example, argued in an article from 1926 that German advertisements displayed a more 'refined' humour than the vulgar slapstick of Felix the Cat: 'Unlike the bawdy humor of American films, these films feature a dignified and unobtrusive humor.'[43] Similarly, the artist Lutz Michaelis could write the following year that animators working in advertising,

Küchen-Rebellen (1928)

should ensure that they do not develop aggressive humour (satire); rather, their figures should be based in a jovial humorous characterisation. (To offer a crass comparison, Wilhelm Busch's caricatures are funny and jovial, while George Grosz's every pen-stroke is caustic and aggressive.)[44]

Such 'jovial' (*bequem*) humour was omnipresent in the animated advertisements of the 1910s and 20s, and this is precisely what separated advertising animation from the provocations of Keatonesque slapstick. Even as these films evoked modernity's 'cunning' objects, they visualised, in scenario after scenario, the transformation of the rebellious object into an obedient commodity.

EXPERTISE

The laments of Vischer and Zweig – that the overwhelming presence of material objects had destroyed 'that concentration that used to last through weeks of undisturbed work' – could also be understood in terms of advertising itself. The period after World War I, in particular, saw an exponential increase in the presence of advertising in Germany as public institutions such as the rail system, streetcars, the post office, subway stations, streets, highways, construction sites and pavements were opened up to advertising for the first time, resulting in a widely observed 'flood of advertising' in the public spaces of the new republic.[45] This went hand in hand with a massive expansion of professional film advertising as new companies such as Deulig, Döring, Epoche, Nordmark, Ufa, Werbedienst, Werbelicht and dozens more got into the business. At the same time, the emergence of portable projectors and daylight screens meant that advertising film was no longer confined to cinemas, but also shown in display windows, trade fairs, on shop floors and advertising vehicles that made the rounds in urban streets. With the return of animated light advertisements after the post-war blackout in the early 1920s, the sight of animated advertising displays became a ubiquitous feature of public space – so much so that a utopian image of

Advertisement for the reklamemobile, 1921

Utopian representation of Berlin 2000
(*Die Reklame*, 1926)

'Berlin in 2000', printed in 1926 in *Die Reklame*, could imagine the city as a giant collection of animated advertising surfaces.

One writer who sought to come to terms with the implications of this new mode of visual culture was Walter Benjamin. Eschewing Zweig's nostalgia, Benjamin argued in his *Einbahnstrasse* (1928) that advertising posed both a new challenge and new possibilities for vision:

> Fools lament the decay of criticism. For its day is long past. Criticism is a matter of correct distancing. ... Now things press too urgently on human society. ... Today, the most real, mercantile gaze into the heart of things is the advertisement. It abolishes the space where contemplation moved and all but hits us between the eyes with things as a car, growing to gigantic proportions, careens at us out of a film screen. And just as the film does not present furniture and facades in completed forms for critical inspection, their insistent, jerky nearness alone being sensational, the genuine advertisement hurtles things at us with the tempo of a good film.[46]

Benjamin's description of advertising 'hitting us between the eyes' prefigures his better-known characterisation of Dada collage and film montage as phenomena that 'hit the spectator like a bullet'. The passage also underscores the relation between the aggressive objects of advertising and the cinema of attractions – the image of the car careening towards the spectator recalling nothing so much as early automobile films such as Cecil Hepworth's *How It Feels To Be Run Over* (1900) – and suggests that Benjamin attached the same utopian hopes to advertising that he did to film as a means of training vision.

Following Benjamin, Janet Ward has rightly emphasised the contribution of advertising to the elaboration of a visual culture of 'shocks' during the Weimar years.[47] At the same time, the very insistence of advertising theorists themselves on distinguishing between advertising and Dada suggest that they understood the visual power of advertising images in ways that went beyond the mere shock of novel impressions. Parallel to the increase in advertising practice in the 1920s, there also emerged a new professional sphere of advertising psychology – one undergirded by new trade publications, university curricula and experimental institutes such as the *Institut für Wirtschaftspsychologie* in Berlin – which saw as one of its central tasks the overhauling of advertising design to achieve a maximum level of control over spectatorial attention. Blending doctrines of suggestion with experimental psychology, theorists such as Walther Moede – head of the *Institut für Wirtschaftspsychologie* and editor of the new journal *Industrielle Psychotechnik* – devised models of advertising images designed to capture the attention, guide the spectator's gaze, stimulate associations and motivate consumer habits.[48] In their writings these theorists conceived of advertising spectatorship as a terrain of 'fleeting glances', which images sought to attract by means of striking visual elements (the so-called '*Blickfang*' or 'eye-catcher') and steer through carefully controlled layouts (so-called '*Blickbewegungslinien*' or 'lines of eye movement') in order to forge lasting associations between needs, pleasures and particular brands.[49] (Indeed, it is no exaggeration to say that the field of advertising psychology, while drawing on many longstanding tenants of experimental psychology and mass psychology, became intelligible as a doctrine of *brand* advertising.)

The result was a new conception of visual culture, in which images struggle for control over attention and the wandering gaze is exposed to constant solicitations by instrumental representations. Here, the invisible hand was no longer that of a magician, but rather the hand of the advertising expert, aspiring to guide the spectator's gaze – as Moede put it – 'in the desired direction'.[50]

Significantly, this new caste of advertising experts sought to define themselves against the world of magic and 'tricks' that had characterised much earlier advertising. 'Tricks', wrote the editor of *Seidels Reklame*, Robert Hösel, in 1926, '... can no longer help us. Today's audiences demand that the advertisement provide them with essential information, that it come to the point.'[51] Hösel's call forms part of a trend towards *Sachlichkeit* (objectivity) – consistently championed by the contributors to *Seidels Reklame* such as Adolf Behne – that found its most famous embodiment in the reductive 'object posters' (*Sachplakate*) of Lucien Bernhard.[52] But the passage is also indicative of a new era of expertise, in which advertising sought no longer to astonish, but rather – according to the dictates of the new advertising psychology – to control and direct visual attention.

Developments in film animation after World War I should clearly be seen in parallel with this professionalisation of print advertising. It was precisely during and after the war that industrialised modes of animation production – where studios were organised along Taylorist principles of industrial efficiency and animators employed labour-saving cel techniques – became the norm in the USA.[53] It was also during this period that drawn animation separated from the tradition of the 'trick film' and the aesthetics of attractions to become an autonomous film genre focused above all on character drawing.[54] This professionalisation of animation forms the context in which the new advertising film companies began to take up animation *en masse*,[55] including the new cel techniques developed in the USA.[56] Like other cultural phenomena coded as 'Americanist', this new culture of professionalised animation provoked an ambivalent reaction. The advertising theorist Hermann Behrmann, for instance, complained that the outsourcing of animation to 'individuals wanting in artistic talent' and working for 'insufficient pay' was creating a market of bad advertising films.[57] Behrmann saw the new vogue for 'artistic' advertising films – he specifically cited

Lutz Michaelis illustration from *Wenn zwei Hochzeit machen* (1927)

Advertisement for Julius Pinschewer's Capitol projector for shopwindows

silhouette film and puppet animation – as a German answer to such 'American' models, which he hoped might replace Taylorised animation studios with the quality work of the 'artist's hand'.[58] Such artistic endeavours by Reiniger, Ruttmann and others remain the most celebrated examples of interwar animated advertisements today. But the vast majority of animators from this period came from the professional world of print illustration and drawn caricature.[59] Artists and illustrators such as Paul Simmel, Wolfgang Kaskeline, Arthur Kraska, Curt Schumann, Lutz Michaelis and numerous others now found work as animators for the many new advertising film companies that emerged after World War I.[60] These companies competed fiercely to have their expertise recognised, and they touted – alongside their monopolies with various theatres – their mastery of the latest animation techniques, such as the so-called combination process (*Kombinationsverfahren*) in which animated figures and live actors were composited on the screen.[61]

At the same time, advertising film itself was increasingly conceptualised within the parameters of the new advertising psychology. On the one hand, the animated images of advertising film appeared to offer an efficacious type of *Blickfang* (eye-catcher). Thus the industrial film-maker Arthur Lassally argued that, with the emergence of the new portable daylight projectors, filmic images would replace posters and cruder forms of animation 'as an eye-catcher [*Blickfang*] in shop windows' and other public spaces.[62] This was, indeed, one of the main arenas for the projection of animated advertising films via portable projectors such as Pinschewer's 'Capitol' projector. On the other hand, theorists argued that film's status as a time-based medium, capable of narrative development, offered ideal conditions for putting the new advertising psychology into practice. Thus, in another article from 1921, C. F. Müller applied the new doctrines of advertising psychology directly onto film when he argued that a good advertising film should 1) include an 'eye-catcher' (*Blickfang*) early on to attract spectators' attention,

Films That Sell

2) communicate a 'need' (*Bedürfnis*) through the scenario to retain attention and arouse interest and 3) introduce the trademark at the end in such a way as to forge a lasting association with a specific brand. This last point, Müller argued, was the key to controlling the actions of spectators after they leave the cinema:

> The cigarette brand ... must be introduced in such a way that it is impressed inextinguishably upon the spectator's attention, which has been carefully prepared by the preceding action in the film. ... In this way, according to the laws of mental association, whenever the spectator of this advertising film subsequently sees an elegant wine bar or hears a dance melody, the brand of cigarettes associated with them through the film will light up in his mind's eye. At the same time, if the need to smoke becomes active in the consumer's mind, this should also call forth memories of the film he saw and with it the relevant brand of cigarettes.[63]

Müller's model – in which the trademark is introduced at the end to be associated with certain needs and their pleasurable fulfilment – offers something of a standard template for advertising films using narrative vignettes such as *Umsturz am Nordpol* and *Küchen-Rebellen*.

To be sure, this was not the only model around. A competing model, emerging in the wake of avant-garde advertising films by Walter Ruttmann, Guido Seeber and Oskar Fischinger, drew on recent psychological research to argue for the use of abstract rhythms in advertising. Elaborated most fully by the advertising theorist Fritz Pauli (who, once again, linked animated film to other forms of animated advertisements such as electric signage), the abstract model relied less on a singular *Blickfang* than on hypnotic repetition, by which – Pauli hoped – consumers could be brought into 'resonance' with the rhythms unfolding on the screen.[64] In the trade literature of the 1920s one can find various 'taxonomies' of the advertising film that include both of these types and others. For example, a 1926 article by the advertising theorist Käthe Kurtzig, published in Walther Moede's journal *Industrielle Psychotechnik*, distinguished three prevalent types of animated advertising: the humorous caricature, the ornamental silhouette (which she saw as the best form for advertising women's products) and the rhythmical 'absolute' film.[65] In every case, however, the animated filmstrip functions as an 'expert' tool for controlling spectatorship: captivating the attention and forging associations with particular brands.

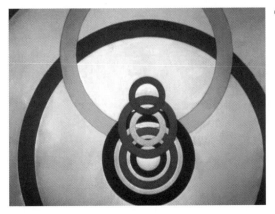

Oskar Fischinger's *Kreise* (1933)

None of this is to argue that the conventions of the 'trick film' completely disappeared in the 1920s. But those conventions are now combined with new forms of expertise and psychological management introduced by applied experimental psychology. Within this context, the invisible hand of the magician is once again subordinated to another invisible hand: that of the advertising expert, whose 'applied animation' would serve to control spectatorship at every level by capturing and directing attention, provoking psychological reactions and stimulating acts of consumption through film. In conclusion, I offer a brief reading of one film, among many, that combines these various moments. Made by Curt Schumann, a prominent member of the new cohort of professional animators in the 1920s, for Kaisers coffee products in 1927, *Gespensterstunde* (*The Ghostly Hour*) uses cel animation to create a phantasmatic world in which the phantom-like products of a Kaiser's grocery store come to life during the wee hours of the night.[66] In its use of the night-time setting and in its specific dramaturgy (such as the tracking over the city's buildings in the opening shot), the film recalls such works of early cinema as *Dream of a Rarebit Fiend* (1906), an Edison trick film based on a comic strip of Windsor McKay, in which the drunken protagonist is plagued in his sleep by a series of 'cunning' objects (culminating in an animated bed that takes him on a harrowing flight over the city). But while *Gespensterstunde* evokes a similar carnivalesque scenario, the film's development works towards transforming such animated objects into obedient commodities. Awoken by their 'leader', a group of Kaiser coffee pots marches down

Gespensterstunde: opening; dance; *Blickbewegungslinie*; trademark

the counter and watches as the various products perform ethnographically marked dances one by one in orderly mass ornaments: a dance of Swiss maidens for 'Kakao', a Chinese dance for 'Tee', etc. With these typological ethnographic dances, the film clearly follows a well-known pattern from ethnographic exhibitions and educational films. But it also inscribes them with a distinctly consumerist gaze: the same imperialist gaze inscribed into the confection shop itself, where the world's products appear lined up in orderly rows at the disposition of the consumer.

But this 'taming' of the object at the level of spectacle is also echoed in the film's narrative. At the end of *Gespensterstunde,* after the dances have been completed, a female 'shopper' emerges from a poster in the store to order products from the animated coffee pot, who tells her (and the film's audience) that only the Kaiser's trademark can guarantee the product's quality. As this exchange plays out, an animated line – quite literally a filmic *'Blickbewegungslinie'* – draws itself across the screen from the woman's eyes to the coffee package, leading our gaze to the space where the trademark should be. In the next shot, the animated pot then jumps onto the package and becomes the Kaiser trademark, telling viewers: 'I must always be present. For only the Kaiser's trademark guarantees quality.' At this point, the trademark is frozen into place, and the other figures also run back to their places as still objects and images. What began with the evocation of the uncanny powers of animation thus ends with the figurative and literal stilling of the rebellious object.

As the focal point for visual attention, the all-important trademark thus not only promises 'quality', but also the pleasures of taming the cunning objects of modern consumer society. At the same time, *Gespensterstunde* transforms the anarchical trick film into a forum for visual pedagogy for the consumer's gaze. Not only does the film culminate with the trademark, thus forging associations between grocery shopping and Kaiser's brand, it also trains the spectator, as it were, *to look for trademarks,* to identify with a brand in the interest of 'quality' consumption. Within this pedagogical scenario, the invisible hand has passed from the magician to the expert: from the phantasmagoria to the laboratories and studios of psychologists and professional animators.

NOTES

1. For a discussion of some of this work, see Donald Crafton, *Before Mickey: The Animated Film 1898–1928* (Chicago: University of Chicago Press, 1982), pp. 217–58.
2. See Lev Manovich, *The Language of New Media* (Cambridge: MIT Press, 2002), p. 252. For the new interest in animation, see Suzanne Buchan (ed.), *Pervasive Animation* (London: Routledge, 2013); Karen Beckman (ed.), *Animating Film Theory* (Durham, NC: Duke University Press, 2014).
3. Julius Pinschewer, 'Von den Anfängen des Werbefilms', *Die Reklame* no. 20 (1927), p. 410.
4. Karl Mischke, 'Die Reklame der Film-Karikatur', in *Seidels Reklame* no. 5 (1920), p. 309.
5. See Crafton, *Before Mickey*, pp. 87–8.
6. Ibid., pp. 49–58. Cf. Haidee Wasson's chapter in this volume.
7. Julius Pinschewer, 'Vom Reklamefilm', *Seidels Reklame* no. 2 (1914), p. 274.
8. Ibid., p. 276.

9. Heinrich Lux, 'Lichtreklame mit Glimmlampen', *Seidels Reklame* no. 7 (1922), p. 109.

10. Erich Kästner, 'Der Karneval des Kaufmanns' (1925), in Klaus Schuhmann (ed.), *Der Karneval des Kaufmanns: Gesammelte Texte aus der Leipziger Zeit 1923–1927* (Leipzig: Lehmstedt, 2004), pp. 172–3. Kästner's contemporaries had no trouble making links between such forms of 'animated' advertisements and filmic animation, as when another writer for *Seidels Reklame* describes his vision of animated light advertisements in London as follows: 'Animals and Machines appear in ten to twenty variations of movement in the manner of trick films' ['Tiere und Maschinen erscheinen zehn bis zwanzigmal variiert in Bewegung nach Art der Trickfilmaufnahmen'] (p. 13). In 1926, yet another writer described animated electric signs 'as if drawn by a mysterious hand' and argued that such spectacles could take a cue from trick film: 'Were the sparkling wine of the Kupferberg light advertisement to flow from the glass back up into the bottle, this would be false in principle, but it would be very amusing and original for the observer of the advertisement. Projecting film in reverse is a rare phenomenon, but it is always met with great applause' ['Wenn bei der Kupferberg-Lichtplakat der Sekt aus der Glase wieder zurück in die Flasche fließen würde, so wäre das ja an sich ganz falsch, für die Beschauer des Lichtplakates aber sehr belustigend und originell. Der rückwärts gekurbelte Film ist zwar selten zu sehen, findet aber immer großen Beifall']. L. von Bialy, 'Das Lichtplakat', *Seidels Reklame* no. 11 (1926), pp. 353–4.

11. William Schaffer, 'Animation 1: The Control Image', in Alan Cholodenko (ed.), *The Illusion of Life II. More Essays on Animation* (Sydney: Power, 2007), p. 466.

12. Schaffer sees this paradox acted out in popular cartoons through what he calls 'allegories of control', where figures of 'controllers' in the cartoon point to the invisible instances of control affecting the image from without (ibid., pp. 471–4).

13. Thomas Lamarre has questioned Schaffer's emphasis on human hands above machines and cel layering (precisely the technology implicated in the industrialisation of animation). See Thomas Lamarre, *The Anime Machine: A Media Theory of Animation* (Minneapolis: University of Minnesota Press, 2009), p. xxix.

14. The metaphor of the invisible hand would be invoked again, periodically, to describe various invisible forces at work in the marketplace. C. Wright Mills would use the metaphor of the 'unseen hand' to describe the massive regulatory apparatus of enterprise capitalism after World War II. See, for example, C. Wright Mills, *White Collar: The American Middle Classes* (New York: Oxford University Press, 1951), p. 189. Alice Gambrell has examined how such economic theories underlie a group of contemporary stop-motion films that reflect on the work of animation. See Alice Gambrell, 'In Visible Hands: The Work of Stop Motion', *Animation Practice, Process and Production* no. 1 (2011), pp. 107–29.

15. See Stefan Andriopoulos, 'The Invisible Hand: Supernatural Agency in Political Economy and the Gothic Novel', *English Literary History* no. 66 (1999), pp. 739–58.

16. Julius Pinschewer, 'Der Film als Werbemittel', *Mitteilungen des Vereins deutscher Reklamefachleute* (1916), p. 117.

17. See James Beniger, *The Control Revolution* (Cambridge, MA: Harvard University Press, 1986), pp. 264–78, 344–56. For an analysis of the rise of trademark advertising in the German context, see Frederic Schwartz, 'Commodity Signs: Peter Behrens, AEG and the Trademark', *Journal of Design History* vol. 9 no. 3 (1996), p. 157.

18. Viktor Mataja, *Die Reklame im Geschäftsleben* (Vienna: Verlag des Niederösterreichischen Gewerbevereins, 1910), pp. 11, 15–17. On this point, see also Beniger, *Control Revolution*, pp. 349–52.

19. On the expense of advertising film, see, for example, Hermann Behrmann, *Reklame* (Berlin: Industrieverlag Spaeth und Linde, 1923), pp. 223–4.

20. Julius Pinschewer, 'Filmreklame', *Seidels Reklame* no. 1 (1913), p. 245.

21. Advertisement for Pinschewer-Film, *Die Reklame* no. 19 (June 1926).

22. Pinschewer, 'Filmreklame', p. 244.

23. Ibid., p. 245.

24. Fritz Pauli, 'Das Problem des Werbefilms', *Die Reklame* no. 19 (1926), p. 616.

25. Thus, the passage by Pauli continues: 'Audiences do not wish to feel cheated, as it were, out of their time or their ticket price. … They wish to be amused, thrilled or educated in an interesting way. When this is the case, they feel entertained and regard the product being advertised with favor' (ibid.). On this point, see also my article 'Absolute Advertising: Walter Ruttmann and the Weimar Advertising Film', *Cinema Journal* vol. 52 no. 4 (2013), p. 68.

26. Mischke, 'Die Reklame der Film-Karikatur', p. 304.

27. Karl Marx, *Das Kapital I*, in Karl Marx and Friedrich Engels, *Werke*, vol. 23, 3rd edition (Berlin: Dietz, 1969), p. 86.

28. Georg Lukács, *History and Class Consciousness,* trans. Rodney Livingstone (Cambridge: MIT Press, 1968), p. 100. For Simmel's link to Marx, see Georg Simmel, 'The Concept and Tragedy of Culture', in David Frisby and Mike Featherstone (eds), *Simmel on Culture* (London: Sage, 1997), pp. 55–75: 'The "fetishistic character" which Marx attributed to economic objects in the epoch of commodity production is only a particularly modified instance of the general fate of the contents of our culture. These contents are subject to a paradox – and increasingly so as "culture" develops – that they are indeed created by human subjects and meant for human subjects, but follow an immanent developmental logic in the intermediate form of objectivity which they take on at either side of these instances and thereby become alienated from both their origin and their purpose' (p. 70).

29. Jean Baudrillard, *The Consumer Society: Myths and Structures*, trans. Chris Turner (London: Sage, 1998), pp. 79–81. 'This fetishistic logic', Baudrillard wrote elsewhere, 'is, strictly, the ideology of consumption' (p. 59).

30. For a reading of Vischer's novel, see Jorg Kreienbrock, *Malicious Objects. Anger Management and the Question of Modern Literature* (New York: Fordham University Press, 2012), pp. 122–72.

31. See Friedrich Theodor Vischer, 'Über das Erhabene und das Komische' (1837), in *Über das Erhabene und das Komische und andere Texte zur Ästhetik* (Frankfurt am Main: Suhrkamp, 1967).

32. G. Schultze-Pfaelzer, 'Die Hauptforman öffentlicher Werbung', *Seidels Reklame* no. 7 (1922), p. 256. According to the writer, this is precisely what separated humorous product advertisements from the more 'serious' forms of publicity such as public service and propaganda films.

33. Arnold Zweig, 'Angriff der Gegenstände' (1923), in *Essays. Zweiter Band. Aufsätze zu Krieg und Frieden* (Berlin: Aufbau-Verlag, 1967), p. 48.

34. Béla Balázs, 'Visible Man', in Erica Carter and Rodney Livingstone (eds), *Early Film Theory: Visible Man and the Spirit of Film* (London: Berghan, 2010), p. 46. Epstein famously argued that film revived a sense of 'animism' familiar from 'certain primitive religions', which 'attributes a semblance of life to the objects it defines'. Jean Epstein, 'Le Cinémaographe vu de l'Etna', trans. Stuart Liebman, in Sarah Keller and Jason N. Paul (eds), *Jean Epstein: Critical Essays and New Translations* (Amsterdam: Amsterdam University Press, 2012), p. 295.

35. Bill Brown, 'Thing Theory', *Critical Inquiry* no. 23 (2001), p. 4. For Brown, such moments form the model for a kind of theory that attempts to resist the sublations of hermeneutic reading.

36. André Bazin, 'Theater and Cinema', in Hugh Gray (ed. and trans.) *What is Cinema?* vol. 1 (Berkeley: University of California Press, 1965, 2005), p. 121.

37. Ibid. For Bazin's reading of Chaplin and objects, see 'Charlie Chaplin', in *What is Cinema?* vol. 1, pp. 145–7.

38. Stanley Cavell, 'What Becomes of Things on Film?', *Philosophy and Literature* vol. 2 no. 2 (1978), p. 250. See also Cavell, 'Leopards in Connecticut', *The Georgia Review* no. 30 (1976), p. 241.

39. J. M. Merich, 'Die III. Frankfurter Internationale Messe', *Seidels Reklame* no. 5 (1920), p. 285.

40. See Kästner, 'Der Karneval des Kaufmanns'. Kästner was hardly alone in describing the trade fair as a carnivalesque event. Numerous were the complaints that these events, with their parades of animated objects, had retained an 'obnoxious carnival character' (*aufdringliche Karnevalscharakter*). Robert Hösel, 'Die Messe und die neue Zeit', *Seidels Reklame* no. 5 (1920), p. 210.

41. Miriam Bratu Hansen, 'Benjamin and Cinema: Not a One-Way Street', *Critical Inquiry* no. 25 (1990), p. 323. See also Esther Leslie, *Hollywood Flatlands: Animation, Critical Theory and the Avant-Garde* (London: Verso, 2002), pp. 80–123.

42. Like the majority of advertising films from the period, this one is now lost. However, a synopsis and illustrations survive in a print advertisement for Epoche. See 'Aus Film-Manuskripten' advertisement, *Die Reklame* no. 20 (1927), p. 421.

43. Pauli, 'Das Problem des Werbefilms', p. 617.

44. Lutz Michaelis, 'Wie entsteht ein Werbetrickfilm?', *Die Reklame* no. 20 (1927), p. 434.

45. On this context, see my article 'Taking it to the Street: Screening the Advertising Film in the Weimar Republic', *Screen* vol. 54 no. 4 (forthcoming).

46. Walter Benjamin, *One Way Street and Other Writings*, trans. Edmund Jephcott and Kingsley Shorter (London: Verso, 1985), p. 89.

47. Janet Ward, *Weimar Surfaces* (Berkeley: University of California Press, 2001), pp. 92–142.

48. Walther Moede, 'Psychologie der Reklame', *Die Reklame* no. 13 (1920), pp. 244–6.

49. Ibid., pp. 244–5.

50. Ibid., p. 245.

51. Robert Hösel, 'Kopf hoch, Charly', *Seidels Reklame* no. 11 (1926), p. 58.

52. Pinschewer himself would later recast his trick films in this light when he described them, in an article from 1927, as 'Advertising films ... which, like "living object poster", brought the brand being advertised closer to observers' ['Werbefilme ... in denen das propagierte Fabrikat, wie in einem "lebenden Sachplakat", dem Beschauer näher gebracht wurde']. Pinschewer, 'Von den Anfängen des Werbefilms', p. 409.

53. See Crafton, *Before Mickey*, pp. 162–8.

54. See Philippe Gauthier, 'A "Trick" Question: Are Early Animated Drawings a Film Genre or a Special Effect?', *Animation* no. 6 (2011), pp. 163–75.

55. Not surprisingly, advertising theorists also began to distinguish between 'trick film' and 'animation' in the early 1920s. Thus, one book from 1923 described a new class of film as 'die gezeichneten Filme, die eigentlich nicht ganz mit Recht Trickfilme genannt werden' ('drawn films that cannot really be called trick films') (Behrmann, *Reklame*, p. 228).

Behrmann identifies the trick film with photographed objects and sees its attraction in the 'Widerspruch zwischen der Photographie als urkundlicher Wiedergabe des Wirklichen und der Unwahrscheinlichkeit der sich abspielenden Vorgänge' ('contradiction between photography as documentary record of the real and the implausibility of the action') (ibid.). Pinschewer too, in the above-cited article from 1927, distinguishes between his early 'Trickfilm' and the 'Trickzeichnungsfilm' of the 1920s. See Pinschewer, 'Von den Anfängen des Werbefilms', p. 409.

56. Lutz Michaelis, for example, described the use of cel animation as the standard process for advertising film in 1927: 'Die Dekoration (Hintergrund) der jeweiligen Szene ist ... eine nur einmalig angefertigte Zeichnung, auf der sich die Karikaturen bewegen' ('The decoration [background] of a given scene is ... a drawing on which moving caricatures are placed') (Michaelis, 'Wie ensteht ein Werbetrickfilm', p. 435).

57. Behrmann, *Reklame*, p. 229.

58. Ibid.

59. Pinschewer, who praised Ruttmann and Reiniger's artistic talents, nonetheless argued that caricature 'is pleasing and comprehensible everywhere in the world and to all classes of the population'. Pinschewer, 'Von den Anfängen des Werbefilms', p. 410.

60. For an overview, see Günter Agde, *Flimmernde Versprechen: Geschichte des deutschen Werbefilms im Kino seit 1897* (Berlin: Das Neue Berlin, 1998), pp. 28–72, especially 59–65.

61. For example, an announcement for the company Epoche read: 'Je verblüffender der Trick in dem zur Werbung verwandten Reklamefilm, desto größer sind die Aussichten seines Erfolges. Ganz neuartig ist das Zusammenspiel einer gezeichneten Figur mit lebenden Menschen und innerhalb einer realistischen Umgebung. ... Wir sind in der Lage, die schwierigsten Aufgaben, die an eine Werbefilm-Produktion gestellt werden können, aufs beste zu erfüllen' ('The more perplexing a trick in a filmed advertising appears, the bigger its chances of success. Entirely new in this respect is the interaction of an animated character with a living human being in a realist setting. ... We have reached a point where we are able to master even the most challenging tasks related to the production of a filmed advertising') ('Eine Reklame durch die "Epoche" – eine Epoche in der Reklame!', advertisement, *Die Reklame* no. 20 [1927], p. 528).

62. Arthur Lassally, 'Filmreklame und Reklamefilm', *Die Reklame* no. 14 (1921), p. 425.

63. C. F. Müller, 'Gedanken über die Reklame durch den Film', *Die Reklame* no. 14 (1921), p. 469.

64. See Pauli, *Rhythmus und Resonanz als ökonomisches Prinzip in der Reklame* (Berlin: Verlag des Verbandes deutscher Reklamefachleute, 1926), p. 38. As another writer put it in 1927, this work sought to 'capture our gaze with suggestive force through the strange rhythms of animated lines' (Max Friedländer, '1000 Worte Werbefilm', *Die Reklame* no. 20 [1927], p. 411.) Pinschewer himself, who produced the films of Ruttmann and Reiniger, also saw such experimental films as a separate category of advertising, 'which limits itself to rhythmical-dynamic design alone' (Pinschewer, 'Von den Anfängen des Werbefilms', p. 410).

65. Käthe Kurtzig, 'Die Arten des Werbefilms', *Industrielle Psychotechnik* no. 3 (1926), pp. 311–14.

66. For a biography of Schumann, see Agde, *Flimmernde Versprechen*, pp. 61–2.

7

More Than Product Advertising: Animation, Gasparcolor and Sorela's Corporate Design

Sema Colpan and Lydia Nsiah

Whenever they screen one of these delightful little colour films in the opening programme of the movies, it attracts the audience's attention, is met with applause and doesn't miss its goal of lasting advertising effectiveness.[1]

Hans Ludwig Böhm

With this plea for coloured, animated, advertising film, Viennese film producer Hans Ludwig Böhm underlines his motivation for making one of the first Austrian advertising films using the three-colour system Gasparcolor. His ad *Morgenstunde* (1935) is about one minute long and combines cartoon animation with cheerful music and a male voiceover.[2] The film plot starts with the close-up of a snoring family (husband and wife with their child) being awakened by a ringing alarm clock. They get out of bed, realise how tousled their hair is and desperately try to fix it. The voiceover comments on the scene: 'hair loss, dirtiness, dandruff …'.[3] There is a knock on the door and a happily smiling shampoo tube appears. It points at its belly, which displays the brand name while the voiceover promises that 'Sorela helps!'. The family bends their heads willingly while the pale pink Sorela tube squeezes its belly and shampoo comes out of its 'head'. The family rubs the shampoo in, and a sliding transition later all three appear with neat hair. The closing sequence is a product shot, focusing on the Sorela tube and its qualities: alkali-free and soapless. Finally, the voiceover repeats the visual message. As the film draws to a close, the brand name is enlarged to take up the screen and is accompanied by the chorus of 'Sorela, Sorela, …'.

Morgenstunde (1935), Collection Austrian Film Museum/Georg Wasner

Morgenstunde (1935), Collection Austrian Film Museum/Georg Wasner

Morgenstunde follows a catchy narrative applied to the sale of consumer goods. It demonstrates an everyday life situation (morning routine at home), detects a morning problem (scruffy hair) and offers a suitable solution (Sorela). The short and entertaining storyline corresponds to the basic narration of contemporary animated advertising films in general. Given its popular advertising argument and the figurative cartoon style, the importance of its role within Austrian advertising film production could easily be overlooked. However, in contrast to the majority of filmic advertisements of the time, *Morgenstunde* is set apart from its contemporaries especially by its remarkable opening titles. Before the plot sets in, the opening title announces 'a new Austrian branch of production: the coloured advertising sound film', followed by the film's credits: its production company Werbe- und Filmdienst Dr H. L. Böhm, the colour system Gasparcolor and the sound system Selenophon are listed along with Gasparcolor's corporate logo – thereby prominently featuring the film's technical qualities. It serves as an advertisement separate from the Sorela narrative and seems to be more of a call to embrace new technologies in advertising. Clearly, this goes beyond advertising in the sense that it is not directed at potential consumers of the shampoo, but it addresses colleagues in the industry instead.

In this case study, we analyse *Morgenstunde* by focusing on this claim of coloured advertising sound film as a new branch of production and highlight its use of filmic technologies such as cartoon and colour.[4] For this we follow contemporary debates, important figures and influencing factors in advertising research, psychology and state-of-the-art film-making. *Morgenstunde* serves as a textbook example for assessing the status of film as advertising medium, while the analysis of the corresponding overall Sorela campaign mirrors emerging discourses on the efficacy of corporate communication in interwar Central Europe.

'THE RISE OF ADVERTISING FROM BOTCH TO SCIENCE'

In the first issue of the journal *Österreichische Reklame*, published in November 1926, the editors called for the increased acceptance and appreciation of advertising. Their intention was to instil a greater awareness among the public by showing how advertising served as an important vehicle for industrial and commercial activities. As such, the hope was for a greater general appreciation of advertising that would eventually allow it to gain a similar level of approval that it enjoyed in 'more advanced' countries. The fact that Austrian advertising had not gained the deserved respect was traced back to a range of factors. Self-criticism referred to crude methods of practitioners that belonged to an earlier or less professionalised period of advertising, general criticism referred to regulatory barriers by the former guild system or to the deficit in freedom of trade in general. Forming an association and launching a trade journal were the initial steps towards the goal of establishing advertising as a practice based on an empirically accepted science.[5] In his article 'The Rise of Advertising from Botch to Science' advertising expert Erwin Paneth compared the slowly evolving 'scientification' in advertising to the early history of natural sciences. Similar to the process that had divided miracle healers and evidence-based medicine many years prior, Paneth claimed research was continuously providing evidence of advertising payoff that was based on the actual implementation of 'natural laws' and not some sleight of hand. Without going into any further detail on these, Paneth optimistically stated that existing prejudices accusing advertising of being of doubtful value could be overturned, if the credo 'truth in advertising' was taken seriously.[6] Hanns Kropff, head of the Zentral-Reklame-Abteilung at the time and chair of the scientific post of the Deutscher Reklameverband, also emphasised the shift towards rationalised consumption and the growing importance of markets.[7] In effect, all of the producer's efforts had to be focused on learning about what the market and the consumer can absorb and what is offered by the competitor to evaluate the market accordingly. In reference to developments in the USA, Kropff stressed that, while focusing on production, companies in Germany and Austria were lacking insight on scientifically collected data on consumer behaviour. Recently developed research methods in applied psychology appeared promising to advertising theorists.[8]

In Austria, one of the earliest institutions investigating anonymous consumer markets was the Österreichische Wirtschaftspsychologische Forschungsstelle (Austrian Research Unit for Economic Psychology). Founded in the early 1930s by Paul Lazarsfeld and Maria Jahoda, it engaged in sales research, carrying out quantitative market surveys for different companies. Apart from its prominent scientists – alongside Lazarsfeld and Jahoda, motivational theorist Ernest Dichter, who worked as a researcher at the unit before moving to the USA – the research unit's list of board members demonstrates the spectrum of interest groups with a stake in the consumer market. It includes big manufacturers and insurance companies, high representatives of political parties and chambers, scientific institutions and spokespersons from the advertising branch.[9]

FILM AS ADVERTISING MEDIUM

In their study on market analysis Kropff and his American co-writer Bruno W. Randolph sketch the necessary preparatory work when planning an advertising campaign and give their view on the advantages and disadvantages of the different means of advertising. According to them, the main challenge advertisers faced when taking film into account for advertising purposes was the assessment of its effectiveness. The approval rates among consumers as well as advertisers fluctuated greatly, which, as they state, might be due to the fact that film was still exploring its forms of expression. While acknowledging the overall efficacy of the film medium, they urge advertisers to consider carefully whether the product suits the potential group of buyers that attend these films in the first place. They also point out that the placing and screening of advertising films can be difficult. Advertisers were at the mercy of the cinema owners as well as at the mercy of the audience, who may, wittingly or unwittingly, reject the advertisement altogether, considering that moviegoers primarily want to view the film programme and not the advertisement. Lastly, Kropff and Randolph advise bearing in mind that the impact of any advertising film is impossible to control.[10]

Advertising psychologist Käthe Kurtzig also points to the fact that working out an impact study on filmic advertisement's effectiveness is rather difficult. On the one hand, statistical data on the filmgoing public was not sufficiently available to adequately reach the target audience. On the other hand, figures revealing the success of filmic advertising were not accessible due to company secrecy. However, as film continued to be part of the advertising media selection of these companies, Kurtzig assumes that the outcome must have been satisfactory. She also reports on two studies. One had tested the effectiveness of film by looking at revenue after using film as the only means of advertising over a specific period of time; the other measured the increase in revenue after adding advertising films to the existing media mix.[11] Moreover, Kurtzig states, the parameters with which one could assess the profitability of film advertising differed from the criteria used for other media.[12] In a special issue of the advertising magazine *Die Reklame*, dedicated to film advertisements, Kurtzig underlines that film as an advertising medium, 'by its nature is more suitable to be put into the service of industrial progress and its practical implementation than other media'. She is convinced that the intensity of its impact, in connection with its versatility, as well as its liveliness, make film into one of the most interesting advertising media:

> For advertising film it's significant ... to not freeze in one form. To a great extent it [advertising film] has an effect, and did have already, by seizing new [film-]artistic movements and bringing them to light. Thus, it gains the versatility enabling it to reach agreement between content and form for ensuring the highest level of efficacy.[13]

According to Kurtzig, film creates awareness and familiarises the audience with the product or brand, as long as it fits into the general advertising campaign and shares the spirit of the brand. This idea of corporate design was partly deduced from psychological considerations. Discussing the advertising campaign for Osram light bulbs, a contributor to *Industrielle Psychotechnik* emphasised the necessity of unity when using different media. The coherence in form translated into distinct means helps to secure attention and arouse interest. It thus serves as a subconscious reminder in the path leading up to the purchase decision.[14]

In his assessment of advertising media, ad expert Niels Cederborg states that the impact of film is much higher than the usually preferred media of press advertising and posters.[15] He advises advertisers to consider film as a more economical advertising medium when planning their budget. Businessman and advertising pioneer Christian Kupferberg also attributes to the moving image a highly promotional effect. He stresses the extraordinarily strong level of persuasiveness that is inherent to the moving image.[16] For *Morgenstunde* producer Hans Böhm, the best setting to create this atmosphere of attention was the movie theatre.

> Nowadays at every turn we encounter advertisement in any form, at home receiving mail or reading the paper, on urban or rural streets, in tram or train, why then not also in theatre and in cinema? It is here where the possibility is given to enthral the prospect in a moment, where he is not distracted by other impressions and has to notice the presented advertisement, if he wants to or not.[17]

As one of the most persistent proponents of advertising film in 1930s Austria, Böhm tirelessly stood up for cinema as an ideal exhibition venue. He stressed the singularity and innovative potential of film for advertising purposes in various articles. As a practitioner, he gained professional experience in photography, focusing on theatre photography and, later, on film, working for film associations in Berlin and London.[18] Born on 14 February 1890 in Vienna, Böhm was fascinated by new technologies at an early age. In 1927 he wrote two articles on emerging sound technologies such as Tri-Ergon, describing their technical particularities and benefits for film.[19] At the same time as avant-garde artists like Hans Richter petitioned for the use of sound and its potential for creating new film forms and narratives,[20] Böhm insisted that 'still we have to find out, which form of expression suits this highly new art genre [sound film], since, as the inventors and patent holders also know, the typical feature film cannot simply become sounding'.[21] In the same magazine, László Moholy-Nagy accentuated the importance of 'the new' for advertisements: 'The attraction of the new, of the not yet used, is one of the most effective factors in advertising design.'[22] He further writes, 'The future optical designer will then no longer be reluctant to tap into scientific findings, which have been already utilised in technical and industrial factories: polarisation of light, interference appearances, subtractive and additive colour mixing etc.'[23] In pointing to the benefits of new technologies, and especially the use of colour for advertisement, Moholy-Nagy in 1927 anticipates what Böhm will realise in the mid-1930s, namely to create effective advertising with the help of 'the new'.

In 1933 Böhm launched his film company Werbe- und Filmdienst Dr H. L. Böhm, curated advertising film screenings, became member of the Verband der Kurzfilmhersteller (Association of Producers of Short Films) and frequently gave lectures on advertising film.[24] Between 1933 and 1936 Böhm produced and submitted about thirty filmic advertisements (and several *Kulturfilme*) to the Viennese Censor's Office.[25] In one of his first articles on film as advertising medium Böhm outlines the importance of filmic advertising in Austria by referring to productions by companies such as the Wiener Persilgesellschaft or sound film commercials by advertising agencies such as Lintas.[26] Stating that Austria follows the German example, Böhm refers to the Ufa and its prominent role in Germany's advertising film production.[27] While he informs the reader about different genres (industrial film, *Kulturfilm*) and techniques (animation, photo-montage), he especially emphasises sound and colour as new and efficient film technologies to attract the consumers' attention. He gives the example of *Ewig Treu* (1933), a German advertising colour film, which had gained quite some popularity in Austria and likely may have been one of the most inspiring examples for local colour film production.[28]

In his screenings, Böhm showed an international selection of advertising films, including a few unnamed British film examples.[29] In these programmes, Böhm gave an overview of contemporary film techniques, paying special attention to animation, photo-montage and Gasparcolor. His aim was not only to showcase international trends in advertising film, but also to promote film as an advertising medium in general and highlight its benefits and challenges for the Austrian branch of film production. In his writings he emphasises short, catchy, humorous and colourful animated films that, in his view, represented the most promising film form for advertising. He mentions Walt Disney's *Silly Symphonies* cartoon series (1929–39) as a leading example, stating that 'the humorous cartoon form ... which has become so enormously popular due to the well-known *Silly Symphonies*, can be utilised for advertising purposes along with puppet animation and stop-motion'.[30]

PROMOTING CARTOONS

Even a mediocre cartoon film offers more film truth [than fiction film]; – and what is most delightful about the masterpieces of Disney is the rhythmically exact, composed, and controlled movement, both in image and in sound.[31]

Hans Richter

In *Hollywood Flatlands* cultural theorist Esther Leslie focuses on the relations between – as its subtitle indicates – *Animation, Critical Theory and the Avant-Garde* and presents an intriguing portrait of the fascination with cartoon film – especially Disney's productions – by artists (e.g. Sergei Eisenstein, Oskar Fischinger, Hans Richter), critical theorists (e.g. Walter Benjamin, Siegfried Kracauer, Theodor W. Adorno) and advertising agents alike.[32] For example, in a special film programme screened in 1929 at the Film Society in London, Jean Epstein's *The Fall of the House of Usher* (1928), John Grierson's *Drifters* (1929) and Sergei Eisenstein's *Battleship Potemkin* (1925) were screened alongside Walt Disney's *The Barn Dance* (1928).[33] Leslie argues that cartoon animation was not only highly appreciated as film entertainment, but also as an art form. Based on lines, cartoons combined the arts of drawing and caricature for constructing rather than reproducing reality. In reference to Alexander Rodchenko and his affinity for the line in 1919, she states, that 'the line ... has revealed a new conception of the world – truly to construct and not to represent' and further points to the use of animation for advertising purposes shortly after the first public presentations of film in 1895.[34] Film pioneer Georges Méliès, for instance, animated letters for adverts as early as 1898.[35]

Within the Austrian context, the oldest preserved animation film, titled *Ideale Filmerzeugung*, was produced in 1914. The seven minute-long film promotes the achievements in film production by the Sascha-Filmfabrik.[36] Stop-motion technique is used to depict the production processes of film in great detail, creating the impression that film was made by machines, without any human intervention. After World War I, Austrian animated film production was revived in 1918, when the Astoria Filmfabrik launched its own animation department. Alongside animator Ladislaus Tuszynski, caricaturist Peter Eng was responsible for producing and promoting animated films.[37] At the Wiener Kinomesse (Viennese Cinema Fair) in 1921, Eng was on site with his Trickfilm-Pavillon, in which he caricatured visitors to show them a short animation of the drawn images the next day.[38] Best known for his *Lausi-und-Mausi* series, Eng made animated advertising films such as *Der Geistige Arbeiter* (1922), *Die Entdeckung Wiens am Nordpol* (1923) and *Ja, warum fahrns denn net?* (1925). The latter, an advertisement for the new city buses in Vienna, was accompanied by a poster series, which was also drawn by Eng and served as a strong mnemonic aid. As noted above, using film as part of a bigger, multimedia advertising campaign was discussed as a promising strategy for successful advertising, as long as the imagery was consistent. Using cut-out animation based on two-dimensional line drawing, Eng's recognisable style is closely interwoven with his practice as a caricaturist. In his film *Lerne Schwimmen!* (1927) he even combines his figurative animation style with a realistic one, juxtaposing live-action recordings of water with drawn animation. The end of the film contains documentary images of the promoted Amalienbad, showing visitors in the well-frequented newly built swimming pool.[39]

In 1920s Austria, such 'moving caricatures' were commonly used in animated advertising films. Accompanied by humorous and absurd moments, which were often marked by unforeseen, witty actions of the animated characters, they contributed to product advertising and the promotion of *Trickfilm* as film form.[40] For ad-industry agents such animated protagonists also had an iconic value. According to advertising expert Fritz Pauli, the highly popular *Felix the Cat* exemplifies an animated character with distinctive design and a potential idol for future animated film advertisements. He recognises a lack of characteristic figures in German-speaking advertising and

Lerne Schwimmen! (1927), WSTLA, Filmarchiv media wien

appeals to practitioners to create such 'heroes' since they attract movie audiences in a systematic and consistent way: the advertising message is incorporated by the animated character itself. If the advertising purpose is masked by such a uniform character, then the product is promoted in the most efficient way. In his rationalistic approach, Fritz Pauli further calls out for tie-in advertising films, which would decrease the advertising budget and simplify the formation of the films. Tyres could then be advertised alongside cars and perfumes alongside toilet articles.

ABSOLUTE ADVERTISING

Alongside the artists Hans Richter and Viking Eggeling, painter and film-maker Walter Ruttmann made so-called absolute films. These films concentrated on the rhythmic orchestration of abstract forms based on scrolls.[41] Ruttmann's animated films were well known and well received by advertising psychologists and film practitioners alike. From an advertising psychologist perspective, Käthe Kurtzig regarded absolute films above all as 'effective due to the rhythmic force of movement, causing the viewer to resonate and not only see and understand the processes on the canvas, but also to experience them'.[42] Cinematographer Guido Seeber even considered absolute films to be the future of animation and the best means for the expression of rhythm.[43] Ruttmann modified his abstract animations for advertising purposes by translating their rhythmic expression into figural forms and, later, even into a realistic and documentary imagery – comparable to Hans Richter's film advertisement for a Cologne newspaper *Der Zweigroschenzauber* (1929).[44] As one of the first artists working in advertising film production, Ruttmann animated products by combining figurative and abstract animation styles. For example, in his ad for Excelsior tyres, *Der Sieger: Ein Film in Farben* (1922), the abstract shapes of his *Opus* series are transformed into more figurative and recognisable forms. Along the lines of caricaturist Harry Jäger's ad for Excelsior (an animated film called *Im Lande der Apachen*, 1920), Ruttmann modified the already familiar 'exotic' scenario.[45]

Ruttmann's hand-coloured animations were widespread and screened in Vienna. On 15 December 1924, as part of a lecture on *Filmkunst* at the Volksbildungshaus Urania (Community College Urania), different animated films were shown, such as slow-motion and time-lapse films, silhouette films and Ruttmann's already-mentioned opus *Lichtspiele*. It was also here that his first sound advertising film for the Deutsche Rundfunk *Tönende Welle* (1928), as well as *Melodie der Welt* (1929), were screened.[46] Most remarkable about Ruttmann's films was his early use of colour. His ad *Der Sieger*, for instance, assembles a wide range and combination of colours, including blue, yellow, orange, red, green, grey and violet.

At the same time the importance of colour was discussed in the field of psychotechnics. Psychologist Hans Hahn states that the first goal of advertising is to achieve a direct link between a product and a particular brand name, the so-called *Sach-Name-Assoziation*. In reference to Harry D. Kitson's *The Mind of the Buyer* (1923), Hahn names size, colour and movement as the most important means for composing a striking advertisement, and lists a colour table to demonstrate what types of colour can be defined as pleasure-oriented. Red, blue and violet seemed to be the most popular.[47]

During the 1920s, colour and its positive effect on the viewer (and consumer) became an important subject in artistic as well as in economic circles, and peaked at the beginning of the 1930s. The orchestration of colour in drawn animation became automated, when, in 1932, chemist Béla Gáspár applied for a patent for the first Central European colour system Gasparcolor.[48] In his advertisement for the ad agency Tolirag – *Circles* (1933) – animation artist Oskar Fischinger used Gáspár's subtractive three-colour system for the first time. The animator had to shoot one single black-and-white frame (e.g. with a beam-splitter camera) three times by including a red, blue and green filter, each leaking one third of the colour spectrum. Eventually, these three coloured single images were unified into one multicoloured frame. Since Gasparcolor required a single frame-shooting process, it was mostly used in animated film.[49]

GASPARCOLOR ON CANVAS(ES)

One year after Fischinger's Gasparcolor films were shown to industry insiders in the Capitol movie theatre in Berlin, the first public screening organised by the Gasparcolor Association took place at the Nollendorfpalast on 8 December 1935. At this screening about fourteen coloured animated advertisements were projected, including two puppet animations by George Pàl for the Dutch company Philips, *Aethership* (1934) and *De Tooveratlas* (1935). According to an audience survey held at the screening, these two ads were the most popular. Later, they were successfully distributed in seventeen countries. After heading the animation department of the Ufa with animator Wolfgang Kaskeline and businessman Paul Wittke, Pàl launched his own company in 1932 in Berlin, where he anchored puppet animations in the advertising field.[50] Due to the well-received Gasparcolor ads by Fischinger and Pàl, the colour system was widely used and discussed until the beginning of the 1940s.[51] While working for Tolirag, Fischinger is said to have confessed that, from that moment on, he could 'only think in colour or, to be precise, only in coloured spaces'.[52] In *Circles* he channelled sound in an animation schedule, which was sorted by numbered sequences. The timbres therefore became visually readable, resulting in a rhythmically organised 'synchronisation of sound and vision'.[53] The rhythms of Richard Wagner's *Tannhäuser* (1845) and Edvard Grieg's *Sigurd Jorsalfar* (1872/92) were transformed into their visual counterparts and vice versa: visual and sound rhythms refigured each other. The German version ends with the advertising message (and the film's subtitle) *Alle Kreise erfasst Tolirag* (*Tolirag Reaches All Circles*), literally recurring to the psychedelically and hypnotically arranged circles.

> Colour begets happiness and herein lies the secret of the colour advertising film's impact on the audience. Yet colour alone, colour that is well chosen according to the principles of modern psychotechnics, is able to create an atmosphere of cheerful and sympathetic attention that is significant for the success of advertising.[54]

Former Tolirag employee Emil Guckes discusses the merits of colour in focusing on filmic advertising. He notes that it was not until the invention of Gasparcolor that the German advertising film industry integrated colour film into its standard production programme.

Gasparcolor films produced by Tolirag had convinced the industry of the usefulness and the extraordinary effectiveness of colour for advertising. Fischinger's abstract plays on colour were a best-seller in advertising. As a result, the film appeared with several differing closing titles. Its Dutch version, promoting Van Houten chocolate in 1937, was well received: 'The film is a successful combination of art and advertising.'[55]

Submitted by Hans Böhm in 1936, *Circles* reappeared on Viennese censorship lists once again.[56] In one of his last efforts to promote film and colour for advertising purposes, Böhm writes: 'Not only does colour obviously draw the viewer's attention to a much closer degree than a depiction in black and white, colour has also exponentially increased the means of expression for the creative artist.'[57] As he relates to advertising in general, he further states that colour 'opens up a tremendous field of vision for the faithful reproduction of well-known brand packaging, familiar posters, etc.'.[58] For him, the efficacy of the advertising message benefits from colour and its natural and realistic form of expression in general and, especially, from the use of Gasparcolor in animated advertising film. He also mentions the widespread distribution of the only European, industrially useable technique in countries such as Germany, the UK, France, Norway and Austria. However, he noticed that the majority of film producers still do not fully recognise the advantages of colour film. By adding sample strips of actual Gasparcolor films as a supplement to the *Österreichische Reklame-Praxis*, he intended to change that.

In 'The Hidden Network of the Avant-Garde' Márton Orosz describes the well-connected Gasparcolor branch in Europe, including film producers and ad agents, as well as the mentioned artists Pàl, Fischinger, Moholy-Nagy, Fischerkoesen and the Austrians Bruno Wozak and Karl Thomas. In Vienna, Wozak and Thomas worked together in their own animation studio from about 1935 until 1941 and made several animated advertisements, such as *Die Sphinx bei der Morgentoilette* (1934), *Der Radio-Automat* (1936), *Ein Orientalisches Wunder* (1937) and the combination of live-action and animated images *Hammerbrot Schlaraffenland* (1937).[59] Exemplifying an animation style which was commonly used in the 1930s – branded today as *Disney-Kopismus* – their cartoons expanded (to a certain degree) Peter Eng's graphic simplification by adapting Disney's round body shapes and minimalist facial features.[60] Hired by Gasparcolor distributor Dezső Grósz, Wozak and Thomas made their first Gasparcolor ad *Tider Krever* (1936) for the Norwegian Tiedmanns Tobaksfabrik.[61]

LAUNCHING SORELA

One year earlier, in 1935, *Morgenstunde* was produced and distributed by Hans Böhm and, to date, it seems to be the first preserved Austrian Gasparcolor ad. Upon first viewing, the simplified facial features of *Morgenstunde*'s characters point to an animation style generally resembling Wozak and Thomas's *Disney-Kopismus*. Although the two animators had collaborated with Böhm – he had produced and submitted their advertisements *Die Sphinx bei der Morgentoilette* and *Der Radio-Automat* – we cannot confirm that they actually contributed the animation for the Sorela commercial. In a search for further information on the visual credits, we looked for iconic features in the broader Sorela advertising campaign.

Promoted in *Morgenstunde* and labelled 'hair food', the Sorela shampoo was distributed in Austria by the perfumery A. Motsch & Co. It was not possible to determine the producer of Sorela; however, given that it was referred to as an American shampoo in neighbouring countries Czechoslovakia and Yugoslavia, we assume that it was a foreign brand. In Czechoslovakia, for instance, the trademark was registered in 1934 and the product was soon after promoted through voucher coupons, as well as through a film advertisement.[62] The latter, entitled *Životní Povinnost* (1935), was produced by the Czech company IRE-Film and directed by the well-known animator couple Karel and Iréna Dodal. The Dodals used the Gasparcolor colour system intensively and created abstract animated advertisements such as *Hra Bublinek* (1936), which was actually inspired by Fischinger's *Circles*. The Sorela commercial was animated by their co-worker Hermína Týrlová. At the request of the advertising company, the film was shortened and the title was changed to *The Duties of Life*.[63]

During the same year the Czech and the Austrian commercials were screened, ads for the shampoo appeared in various Austrian print media. *Neue Wiener Friseur Zeitung*, a trade paper for hairdressers, barbers and perfumers, promoted Sorela's high-quality merchandise of good repute. With a different subject for each ad, the product was recommended as a must-have item for all members of the trade. Concentrating on sales arguments, the ads are text-heavy and light on images.[64] However, Sorela ads in the illustrated magazine *Das interessante Blatt* followed a different path. In two full-page advertisements, popular actors testify to the quality of the product, either through a step-by-step instruction guide on the use of the shampoo or, in the second

Sorela in press advertising, 1935

ad, by simply confirming their satisfaction with the hair paste.[65] In the latter ad, photographs of four well-known actors appear with additional endorsements by dermatologists and feature a large picture of the Sorela tube revealing the brand name, with additional information in English.[66] In contrast to these large-size advertisements, much smaller and simpler graphical representations were the preferred advertising presence in the women's journal *Das kleine Frauenblatt*. The shampoo tube and the presenter are drawn, not photographed. In the first ad, the availability of Sorela samples is announced with the tagline 'now available in Austria'. The second ad acts as a coupon for a free mail-order sample. Before redeeming the coupon at the perfumery the consumer is asked to choose the condition that is most applicable for the Sorela remedy: dandruff, alopecia, baldness, or other.[67]

In *Werbe-Winke*, a short-lived Viennese gazette of advertising clubs and the institute of advertising and sales, the Sorela campaign is mentioned in the column 'How They See It'.[68] The section surveys the readers on which advertisement recently caught their attention and what they thought about it. A thirty-year-old woman reports: 'I noticed a new product on a poster for Sorela shampoo. The poster is very beautiful and the product seems interesting.' In parentheses, the editors of the gazette add that she is obviously unaware of the extensive press advertising. The poster in question was created by Atelier Hans Neumann, one of the largest graphic design studios in the German-speaking regions.[69] The well-designed bill is divided into two parts. The upper left half shows the head of a smiling woman with her hair covered in foam, set against a dark background. The bottom right half shows the pale pink Sorela tube set against a golden background. The two-fold message of the campaign 'Sorela washes the hair without soap' and 'alkali-free' is positioned at the bottom of the poster.

While the sales arguments 'alkali-free' and 'soapless' connect the different media promoting Sorela – print, poster and film – in terms of content, the unity in visual form is less obvious. Although the different forms of advertising implement the Sorela tube trademark in one way or another, the graphic design of the tube varies from medium to medium. In press advertising, the tube sometimes figures as plain text, listing the shampoo's features and highlighting the brand name, other times as a photograph, showing the actual product packaging. However, the latter already indicates the aim for more unity in visual design to foster a higher value of brand recognition – in other words, to fuse the visual with the brand – acting as a trigger. Once Sorela is illustrated in its real packaging, the consumer is more likely to remember it when shopping. By depicting the tube not only in its actual shape, but also in its real colour (pale pink), the branding effect is intensified in the poster advertising, as well as in its filmed 'incarnation' in *Morgenstunde*. In the film, the Sorela tube is staged as the main protagonist and thus serves as the uniform animated character, in the same manner as suggested by ad expert Fritz Pauli.

The positive impact of colour for advertising purposes, long discussed among psychologists, advertisers and artists alike, was, if nothing else, the decisive factor regarding Böhm's enthusiasm for the 'coloured advertising sound film'. While Gasparcolor offered Böhm an entirely new visual form of expression, he further deployed sound in an elaborate way: by adding a soundscape, consisting of different noises and cheerful musical interludes, to the commonly used narrative voiceover, Böhm's ad innovatively demonstrates the technology's features. For him, sound,

Hans Neumann's Sorela poster (Courtesy of the Vienna City Library) and *Morgenstunde* (1935)

colour and animation were not only inexhaustible technological achievements; they also exceeded established film forms and narratives. With its combination of highly effective advertising factors, such as short length, humour, cartoon, colour and sound, *Morgenstunde* represents a dense realisation of contemporary advertising guidelines as well as state-of-the-art film-making. Even though the implementation of corporate design is not fully evolved in the overall Sorela campaign, Böhm recognised the value of film as a medium for advertising. He makes use of the film's extensive range of stylistic elements to tie in every possible aspect advertisers and psychologists proposed for effective and successful advertising. *Morgenstunde* delivers what the opening titles promise. Beyond its purpose as product advertising, it serves as textbook example for a 'new branch of production' and showcases cartoon animation as well as Gasparcolor as the best means for filmic advertisements overall.

NOTES

1. Hans Ludwig Böhm, 'Der Farbentonfilm. Das modernste Werbemittel', *Österreichische Reklame-Praxis. Zeitschrift für Werbung, Wirtschaft und Verkauf* vol. 3 no. 2 (1934), p. 13. All foreign-language quotations were translated by the authors.
2. *Morgenstunde* (1935); nitrate, 35 mm, sound, colour. Producer: Werbe- und Filmdienst Dr H. L. Böhm; sound system: Selenophon; colour system: Gasparcolor. Collection of the Austrian Film Museum. In the Viennese Film Censorship Lists *Morgenstunde* is mentioned as an advertising film, suitable for minors, of 25m length and submitted by Werbe- und Filmdienst Dr Böhm. Decision date: March 1935. Thomas Ballhausen and Paolo Caneppele (ed.), 'Entscheidungen der Wiener Filmzensur 1934–1938', in *Materialien zur österreichischen Filmgeschichte 11* (Vienna: Filmarchiv Austria, 2009), p. 90.
3. The emphasised phrases in this paragraph are voiceover quotations.
4. See, for example, Michael Cowan, 'Fidelity, Capture and the Sound Advertisement: Julius Pinschewer and Rudi Klemm's *Die Chinesische Nachtigall*', in *Zeitgeschichte* vol. 41 no. 2 (2014), pp. 77–88. Cf. also Cowan's chapter in this book.
5. Steering Committee of the Association of Austrian Advertising Agents, 'Wir arbeiten!', *Österreichische Reklame* vol. 1 no. 1 (1926), p. 3. *Österreichische Reklame* was one of two trade journals on advertising, both first published in the same year (1926). *Österreichische Reklame* was the organ of the Verband österreichischer Reklamefachleute (Association of Austrian Advertising Agents). The second journal was called *Kontakt* (Contact) and was the organ of the Schutzverband der Reklametreibenden Österreichs (Austrian Advertising Protection Association).
6. Erwin Paneth, 'Der Aufstieg der Reklame vom Pfuschertum zur Wissenschaft', *Österreichische Reklame* vol. 1 no. 1 (1926), p. 4.
7. Hanns F. J. Kropff was a successful and influential Austrian adman, advertising theorist and motivational researcher. As head of the Zentral-Reklame-Abteilung he worked for various companies. Many of these companies would later become part of Unilever. See Hanns F. J. Kropff, *Wie werde ich Reklame-Chef?* (Vienna/Essen/Leipzig: Barth, 1926).
8. See Karl Hackl, 'Psychotechnik und Reklame. Zwei Hilfsmittel der Wirtschaft und ihre Beziehung zueinander', *Österreichische Reklame* vol. 3 no. 2 (1929), pp. 15–16.
9. See Alois Wacker, 'Marie Jahoda und die Österreichische Wirtschaftspsychologische

Forschungsstelle zur Idee einer nicht-reduktionistischen Sozialpsychologie', in *Psychologie und Geschichte* vol. 8 no. 1–2 (1998), p. 126. For further information on the research unit, see Gerhard Benetka, *Psychologie in Wien. Sozial- und Theoriegeschichte des Wiener Psychologischen Instituts 1922–1938* (Wien: WUV, 1995).

10. Hanns F. J. Kropff and Bruno W. Randolph, *Marktanalyse. Untersuchung des Marktes und Vorbereitung der Reklame* (Munich/Berlin: R. Oldenbourg, 1928), pp. 290–2.
11. Käthe Kurtzig, 'Wo und wie wirkt der Werbefilm?', *Industrielle Psychotechnik* vol. 5 no. 1 (1928), pp. 367–9.
12. Käthe Kurtzig, 'Werbefilm und Volkswirtschaft', *Die Reklame. Zeitschrift des Verbandes Deutscher Reklamefachleute* vol. 20 no. 12 (1927), p. 419.
13. Käthe Kurtzig, 'Die Arten des Werbefilms', *Industrielle Psychotechnik* vol. 3 no. 1 (1926), p. 313.
14. A. Prox, 'Das Werbewesen in der Deutschen Glühlampenindustrie', *Industrielle Psychotechnik* vol. 4 no. 12 (1927), pp. 353–8.
15. Niels Cederborg, 'Traum und Wirklichkeit', *Österreichische Reklame* vol. 3 no. 7 (1928), pp. 19–20.
16. Christian Adt. Kupferberg, 'Der Werbefilm vom Standpunkt des Verbrauchers', *Die Reklame* vol. 20 no. 12 (1927), pp. 412–15.
17. Hans Ludwig Böhm, 'Filmwerbung und Werbefilm', *Reklame-Presse. Werkblatt des Werbers* vol. 1 no. 2 (1936), p. 2.
18. 'Dr Hans Böhm in Berlin', *Österreichische Film-Zeitung* vol. 5 no. 8 (1931), p. 2; for more information on his biography, see http://sammlungenonline.albertina.at
19. Hans Böhm, 'Der Tonfilm', *Photographische Korrespondenz* vol. 63 no. 3 (1927), pp. 78–80; Hans Böhm, 'Fortschritte im Tonfilmwesen. Über das Triergonverfahren von Massolle, Vogt und Engl', *Photographische Korrespondenz* vol. 63 no. 11 (1927), pp. 337–9.
20. See Hans Richter, *Filmgegner von heute – Filmfreunde von morgen* (Berlin: Reckendorf, 1929).
21. Böhm, 'Der Tonfilm', p. 80.
22. László Moholy-Nagy, 'Photographie und Reklame', *Photographische Korrespondenz* vol. 63 no. 9 (1927), p. 257.
23. Ibid., p. 258.
24. See, for example, his advertising film screenings in December 1933 in the context of the exhibition *Reklame, historisch und modern (Advertisement, Now and Then)*.
25. See Thomas Ballhausen and Paolo Caneppele (ed.), 'Entscheidungen der Wiener Filmzensur 1929–1933', in *Materialien zur österreichischen Filmgeschichte 10* (Vienna: Filmarchiv Austria, 2003); Ballhausen and Caneppele, 'Entscheidungen der Wiener Filmzensur 1934–1938'.
26. Lintas was responsible for Unilever Austria, still referred to by Böhm as the Schicht-Kunerol-Sarg-Sunlight corporation. Hans Ludwig Böhm, 'Werbung durch den Film', *Contact* vol. 8 no. 12 (1933), pp. 16–19.
27. On the role of the Ufa within advertising film production, see Ralf Forster, *Ufa und die Nordmark. Zwei Firmengeschichten und der deutsche Werbefilm 1919–1945* (Trier: Wissenschaftlicher Verlag Trier, 2005).
28. The director of the lost four minutes forty seconds-long film advertisement for the company Indanthrenhaus (IG Farben) is unknown. See Ballhausen and Caneppele, 'Entscheidungen der Wiener Filmzensur 1929–1933', p. 449.
29. The films are listed in *Österreichische Film-Zeitung* vol. 7 no. 49 (1933), p. 4.
30. See Böhm, 'Der Farbentonfilm', p. 12.

Films That Sell

31. Hans Richter, *Der Kampf um den Film. Für einen gesellschaftlich verantwortlichen Film* (Munich/Vienna: Carl Hanser, 1976), p. 139 (original emphasis). The manuscript was originally written by Richter between 1934 and 1939 during his exile in Switzerland.

32. Esther Leslie, *Hollywood Flatlands: Animation, Critical Theory and the Avant-Garde* (London: Verso, 2002).

33. Ibid., p. 29.

34. Ibid., p. 19.

35. Leslie mentions a British animated film commercial by Arthur Melbourne Cooper for Bird's Custard Powder in 1897. Ibid., p. 9.

36. Thomas Renoldner, 'Animation in Österreich – 1832 bis heute', in Christian Dewald *et al.* (eds), *Die Kunst des Einzelbilds. Animation in Österreich – 1832 bis heute* (Vienna: Filmarchiv Austria, 2010), pp. 41–154, 55.

37. See Peter Eng, 'Der Trickfilm', *Die Filmwelt* vol. 2 no. 35 (1920), pp. 5–8.

38. See N. N., 'Der Trickfilm Pavillon', *Die Filmwelt* vol. 3 no. 20 (1921), p. 9.

39. *Lerne Schwimmen!* was recently discovered. To watch excerpts of *Lerne Schwimmen!* online, see the open access platform *FilmStadtWien*: http://stadtfilm-wien.at/film/139

40. An example for such absurd moments is a scene in *Die Entdeckung Wiens am Nordpol*, in which a whale lays an egg, from which a chicken emerges. See Renoldner, 'Animation', p. 83.

41. See Hans Richter's film studies *Rhythmus 21–25* (1921–5) and Viking Eggeling's *Diagonal Symphonie* (1925); see also Thomas Mank, 'Die Kunst des Absoluten Films', in Herbert Gehr (ed.), *Sound and Vision – Musikvideo und Filmkunst* (Frankfurt am Main: Deutsches Filmmuseum, 1993), pp. 73–87; Lydia Nsiah, '"Es lebe die elementare Gestaltung" – der beseelte Werbefilm', in Karin Fest, Sabrina Rahman and Marie-Noëlle Yazdanpanah (eds), *Mies van der Rohe, Richter, Graeff & Co.: Alltag und Design in der Avantgardezeitschrift G* (Vienna/Berlin: Turia+Kant, 2014), pp. 161–8.

42. Kurtzig, 'Die Arten des Werbefilms', p. 314.

43. See Guido Seeber, *Der Trickfilm in seinen grundsätzlichen Möglichkeiten. Eine praktische und theoretische Darstellung der photographischen Filmtricks* (Berlin: Lichtbildbühne, 1927), p. 240.

44. See Lydia Nsiah, '"Wir montieren!" Hans Richters Arbeit an Form und Funktion von Bewegung', in Werner Michael Schwarz and Ingo Zechner (eds), *Die helle und die dunkle Seite der Moderne. Festschrift für Siegfried Mattl zum 60. Geburtstag* (Vienna: Turia+Kant, 2014), pp. 309–17.

45. See Michael Cowan, 'Absolute Advertising: Walter Ruttmann and the Weimar Advertising Film', *Cinema Journal* vol. 52 no. 4 (2013), pp. 49–73.

46. See *Verlautbarungen des Volksbildungshauses Wiener Urania* vol. 7 no. 43 (1924), p. 9; C. F. P., 'Filmkunst', *Die Filmwelt* vol. 6 no. 33 (1924), p. 8; Ballhausen and Caneppele, 'Entscheidungen der Wiener Filmzensur 1929–1933', p. 105.

47. Hans Hahn, 'Amerikanische Reklamepsychologie', *Industrielle Psychotechnik* vol. 2 no. 2 (1925), pp. 33–42. The colour table was originally published in Harry Hollingworth, *Advertising and Selling* (London and New York: D. Appleton and Company, 1924), p. 101.

48. Márton Orosz, '"The Hidden Network of the Avant-Garde": der farbige Werbefilm als eine zentraleuropäische Erfindung?', in Sascha Bru *et al.* (eds), *Regarding the Popular. Modernism, the Avant-Garde and High and Low Culture* (Berlin/Boston: De Gruyter, 2012), pp. 338–60, p. 341.

49. See Béla Gáspár, 'Neuere Verfahren zur Herstellung von subtraktiven Mehrfarbenbildern (Gasparcolor-Verfahren)', *Zeitschrift für wissenschaftliche Photographie, Photophysik und Photochemie* no. 34 (1935), pp. 119–24.

50. See Orosz, 'The Hidden Network', pp. 342–9.

51. For example, Fischinger's Gasparcolor film *Komposition in Blau* (1935) was used for seventeen international ad campaigns. Andreas Riessland, 'Der abstrakte Trickfilm in der deutschen Werbung der 20er und 30er Jahre', in *Hiyoshi Studien zur Germanistik* no. 35 (2003), p. 114.

52. Emil Guckes, 'Der Tonfilm als Werbemittel in Deutschland' (PhD thesis, University of Innsbruck, 1937), p. 60.

53. Helmut Herbst, 'Mit der Technik denken, Konstruktion einer Augenmusik', in *Sound and Vision. Musikvideo und Filmkunst* (Frankfurt am Main: Deutsches Filmmuseum, 1993), p. 41.

54. Guckes, 'Der Tonfilm', p. 63.

55. N. N., 'Reclamefilm Van Houten', *Nieuwsblad van het Noorden*, 15 February 1937.

56. Ballhausen and Caneppele, 'Entscheidungen der Wiener Filmzensur 1934–1938', p. 238.

57. Böhm, 'Der Farbentonfilm', p. 12.

58. Ibid.

59. Ballhausen and Caneppele, 'Entscheidungen der Wiener Filmzensur 1934–1938', pp. 72, 268.

60. Renoldner, 'Animation', p. 84.

61. Born in Budapest, Dezső Grósz spread the Gasparcolor system within the European artistic and advertising circles. In 1933 he launched his own film company in Prague and was closely related to the Czech animator couple Irene and Karel Dodal. Orosz, 'The Hidden', pp. 353–4; for more on Grósz and *Tider Krever*, see Gunnar Strom, 'Desidier Gross and Gasparcolor in a Norwegian Perspective, Part 2', *Animation Journal* vol. 8 no. 2 (2000), pp. 44–55.

62. Sorela's Yugoslavian headquarters was located in Zagreb and, according to the print campaign, the shampoo was 'available in all pharmacies, drugstores, perfumeries and best hair salons'. See *Slovenec*, 30 June 1935, p. 8; *Slovenec*, 21 July 1935, p. 16, as well as the Slovenian women's magazine *Žena in dom*, September 1935, p. 339.

63. Michaela Mertová, Vladimír Opěla and Eva Urbanová, *Český Animovaný Film (1920–1945) /Czech Animated Film (1920–1945)* (Prague: Národní Filmový Archiv, 2012), p. 98.

64. Ads found in the following issues of *Neue Wiener Friseur Zeitung*: vol. 52 no. 5 (1935), p. 7; vol. 52 no. 7 (1935), p. 9; vol. 52 no. 9 (1935), p. 13; vol. 52 no. 20 (1935), p. 13.

65. In eight pictures actress Etha von Storm demonstrates the correct application of the product. *Das Interessante Blatt 10*, 7 March 1935, p. 9.

66. With Hermann Thimig, Luise Ullrich, Romy Schneider's mother Magda Schneider and Heinz Rühmann depicted, the brand is promoted by some of the most popular artists of German-speaking cinema at the time. The English information on the tube reads: 'Hair Food. Sorela. Contains no soap or harmfull [sic] alkali (,) rejuvenates hair and promotes growth. Hair Food. Wien. Prag. Paris.' *Das Interessante Blatt*, 2 May 1935, p. 9.

67. *Das kleine Frauenblatt* no. 9, 3 March 1935, p. 13; *Das kleine Frauenblatt* no. 14, 7 April 1935, p. 8.

68. N. N., 'Wie sie es sehen', *Werbe-Winke. Zs. d. Inst. f. Werbung u. Verkauf in Wien u. d. österr. Werbeklubs in Wien*, 1935, p. 16. The journal was edited by the advertising expert and head of the institute for sales and advertising Alfred Oskar Mendel. Aforementioned Ernst Dichter and Peter Eng were among the guest lecturers of the course.

69. Cp. Peter Noever, *Hans Neumann – Pionier der Werbeagenturen* (Vienna: MAK, 2009).

8

Dream-Work: Pan Am's *New Horizons* in Holland

Nico de Klerk

Between 1960 and 1970, US commercial airline Pan American World Airways sponsored a series of short promotional films. *New Horizons*, as this series was called, advertised Pan Am's intercontinental holiday destinations in Latin America, the Pacific, Asia, Africa and Europe, as well as tourist attractions in the USA itself. What occasioned this chapter are seven distribution prints from this series in the archive of EYE (formerly the Nederlands Filmmuseum), in Amsterdam, that I inspected as part of a de-accessioning project of American nonfiction films produced between 1940 and 1980. In evaluating these prints I focused on their 'resonance', as they clearly had functioned less as aesthetic objects than as useful cinema.[1] As a search in Pan Am's archives, at the University of Miami Libraries, was not practicable within the context of this project, I undertook to relate the company's marketing strategy and positioning of this set of films to other Pan Am campaign materials, to its distribution channels and to the economic and political environments in which the company wanted to show these films and eventually sell the products and experiences they advertised. I considered this approach, despite its practical handicaps, appropriate and necessary, because the circumstances in which these films were released in Holland seemed to make their timing hopelessly wrong and their content glaringly irrelevant.

This set of 16mm prints, with a running time of between ten and fifteen minutes, was deposited by a company named International Film Services (IFS). IFS, founded in 1962 as the privatised Film Department of the American embassy in The Hague, was a distributor of small-gauge documentary, information and promotional films in the Netherlands for screenings in schools, businesses, clubs and other non-theatrical venues. After discontinuing its distribution activities, IFS divested its films: in 1992, the company deposited 728 prints at the Amsterdam archive, followed by a batch of 184 prints the next year, amounting to 599 (predominantly American) titles.[2] At the time of their inspection, between late 2009 and early 2011, the *New Horizons* prints were in pretty good shape, except for some mild wear and tear resulting from projection; in some the Technicolor hues have slightly faded, in others they still look fresh; and they are complete – a few even came with animated lead-ins and concluding panels prompting spectators to see their travel agent.

These prints – all contemporary, judging from their edgemarks[3] – were apparently released in the Netherlands to introduce audiences to the notion of intercontinental jet travel. But what I find intriguing is that this occurred at a time, the early to mid-1960s, when such a notion was far from most people's minds (in Holland as well as,

I assume, elsewhere in post-war Europe). I will try to argue, therefore, why it nevertheless made sense for Pan Am to promote its services before their need was widely felt or affordable and venture that these films laid the groundwork for the idea, and anticipated the desire, of vacationing by plane and visiting the countries that the films advertised: India (1960), Japan (1960), Pakistan (1960), Argentina (1965), Uruguay (1965) and Hawaii, the subject of two films: *The Hawaiian Islands* (1960) and *Hawaii* (1963).[4]

Although the term 'intercontinental' suggests a focus on the American market, different language versions make clear that these films were part of an international campaign, aimed at a number of foreign markets. Pan Am had versions made in a number of standard languages – French, German, Italian, Japanese, Portuguese, Spanish, even British English – examples of which can be downloaded from the websites mentioned in note 4. As a series, then, *New Horizons* evinces a largely Occidental-centric point of view in which the rest of the world is shown as being ready for discovery – and fitted out accordingly: 'It's there and waiting for the traveller,' says the voiceover of *Thailand*. This point of view is borne out, moreover, by the language varieties spoken: the Portuguese or French narrations locate their prints' outlook unequivocally in Portugal and France, not in, say, Brazil or Senegal. In fact, the translations, being the only way in which these films were adapted to foreign audiences, appear to be merely literal renderings of the original American narrations, as they follow the routes American tourists would have taken – that much is clear from the German narration of *The Philippines*, which locates the opening scene 'high over the Pacific' when 'suddenly, … Manila rises out of the boundless sea'.[5] Furthermore, none of the available films contain alternate shots made for locally screened versions: no Japanese tourists people the Japanese spoken films.[6] In other words, adaptation of the films was predetermined, not the result of appropriation – that is, measures taken locally, and often indepen-dently, to bring a foreign commercial and/or cultural artefact into line with domestic laws, languages, markets, manners, or *dispositif*, thereby creating local meanings and appreciations.[7] Consider also three additional facts: first, that the prints in the Amsterdam archive not only retain their American voiceover but also lack subtitling;[8] second, that the specific selection of films released in Holland featured unrealistically faraway countries rather than ones nearby (such as Austria or Ireland); and, finally, that these prints were meant for *non-theatrical* release and were not theatrically distributed as commercials. All this suggests indeed that *New Horizons*, insofar as the series was screened outside the USA, more particularly in countries recovering from the setbacks of the war, rather accustomed audiences to jet plane travel and its associated luxury as such. In fact, the panels in the Amsterdam prints telling spectators to see 'your travel agent' – which, in the contemporary Dutch context, was quite an anachronistic expression – support this idea: these prints were simply and indiscriminately added to IFS's catalogue, not carefully marketed and targeted.

PRINTED MATERIALS

Over the years Pan Am produced for those who would consider jet plane travel a series of print materials, also titled *New Horizons* – some of the films explicated this tie-in by opening with a panel showing a book. These complementary series consisted of various types of publications, some of which were also translated into a number of world languages. The most long-lasting publication was the *World Guide*. Originally published in 1951, this continually revised and updated handbook contained so-called travel facts, which allowed travellers and tourists to anchor themselves quickly: currency, language, electric current, opening hours and calendar of holidays, sites, museums, restaurants, night clubs, etc.[9] With each new edition the number of countries thus glossed shot up: for instance, the 576-page 1958 edition contained travel facts on eighty-nine countries, while the 1970 *World Guide* crammed no less than 138 countries into its 800-plus pages.

However, *New Horizons*' maps and guides were just a part of the small avalanche of print publications in various other series that the airline consistently produced for decades. Many of these publications were for potential target groups of customers, not just tourists. Besides travel and reference guides on specific regions or countries, there were special interest books, such as *Ski New Horizons – A Guide to Skiing around the World* (1961) or *Pan Am's Guide to Golf Courses round the World* (1966); the many European emigrants of the post-war era might have been interested in Pan Am's educational or instructional publications on living or studying abroad, such as *Pan American's Guide to Living Conditions in 88 Countries* (1961) or *Pan American's Guide to Schools and Universities Abroad* (1966); and there were materials targeted at professional groups: for example, *Understanding Latin America* addressed itself primarily to teachers. The introductory 'Note to teachers' states:

> The ever-shrinking world of the Air Age and its parallel ever-increasing tempo of life present a challenge to educators. ... This accelerated and more complex pace makes it exceedingly difficult for teachers to fulfill one of their most important obligations – presenting the most up-to-date material to their students in order to increase their understanding of the world about them.[10]

The book's compressed materials are recommended for their easy integration into the curriculum along with suggestions for study units, examples of which are included in the book together with a list of audiovisual aids that could be ordered additionally. But the tourist, too, was invited to brush up on his knowledge with the help of 'capsule glimpses' of his destination of choice.

The reference to the accelerated pace of the modern world and the reduced sense of distance was, of course, the rationale for *New Horizons*' multimedia campaign: besides the technologically futuristic connotations of the 'Air Age' and the Space Age that clung to so many American media products in the 1950s and 60s, the term was also meant to capture the excitement of the so-called jet age in American civilian aviation. Even though Pan Am's traditional, propeller-driven aircraft had operated nonstop transatlantic services since 1955, the booming American domestic tourist industry led to a scramble for a share of the intercontinental market; airlines engaged American aircraft builders such as Boeing and Douglas for the design of bigger, faster, jet-propelled planes with greater flight range. After the first passenger jet services of the early 1950s, based on British technology, were interrupted by a series of crashes (a result of design flaws that had caused metal fatigue[11]), the new horizons were opened up more successfully by the American-built fleet of long-range jetliners. Pan Am, first past the post in the USA, celebrated the official launch of the jet age on 26 October 1958 with a so-called nonstop flight from New York to Paris in its new Boeing 707.[12]

The jet age allowed Pan Am to forcefully expand its pre-war and wartime international network of destinations and company-owned hotels (from the late 1920s through World War II, Pan Am, with the active assistance of successive US governments, had a de facto monopoly on international commercial services).[13] To attract the tourist trade, *New Horizons* advertised these intercontinental services to ever more faraway destinations worldwide as adventures waiting around the corner. A trip to Morocco, for instance, is recommended as a flight 'from the normality of home to the unexpected wonders of this not so distant land'; Argentina, although 'deep in the southern hemisphere', is 'now, in the jet age, only hours away'; while Thailand is 'just one day away by Jet Clipper'. No wonder that Pan Am, in its 1960 annual report, touted its accomplishments with the phrase, 'The free world has become a neighborhood'.[14]

The term 'free world', of course, was a sign of the times – the Cold War – and betrayed a political stance which informed not just Pan Am's in-house communication, but its publicity as well. Thus, in the films, Thailand is not just 'modern' and 'freedom-loving', the country's very name means 'land of the free'; the 'pace of progress' has made the Philippines a 'showcase of democracy'; and Uruguay is 'one of the world's purest democracies', with its presidency divided over 'a committee of nine executives'. Symbols of government in the shape of houses of parliament or of law and order in the shape of traffic wardens supported this upbeat impression of things. (The downsides of such superficially reassuring statements and images were glossed over. For instance, Uruguay's plural executive power, which always included three seats for the opposition in the country's two-party system – called 'multi-party system' in the film – was in reality the cause of serious popular resentment and political stasis.) In contrast, no promotional film seems to have been made of Pan Am's New York to Moscow service, which opened in 1968.

The *New Horizons* guide books, however, did include travel information about the 'unfree' world. The 1969 edition of the *World Guide*, for instance, with 'travel facts about 131 countries', lists Bulgaria, Czechoslovakia, Hungary, Poland, Romania, the USSR and Cuba (China and Albania have no entries, and 'Korea' only deals with the territory south of the thirty-eighth parallel). However, references to social and political realities were camouflaged or simply skirted: 'In the last few years with typical Romanian energy and imagination, the people have created resorts for winter and summer in the mountains and along the Black Sea coast,' while its northern neighbour 'abounds in sumptuous palaces, picturesque villages and music everywhere. The girls are beautiful, the men gallant, and you're sure to have fun in Hungary.' More astonishing is that in its entries on areas of armed conflict this edition persisted in presenting an airbrushed picture, with no warning of potential dangers, notwithstanding the assurance that the guide 'does not deal with "impressions" but rather with useful facts'. Its descriptions of Cambodia and South Vietnam prefer to paint out the bloody reality: 'Cambodia is an exotic, picturesque country of rice paddies, sugar and rubber plantations, set against a background of ancient temples and monuments that are wondrously ornate.' And of South Vietnam it says, 'On the surface, Saigon is still the same pretty city, although somewhat pockmarked and cluttered with sandbagged control points.' One assumes that the focus on Saigon implicitly ruled out the Vietnamese countryside as a safe place to visit. But even within these limits this description omits much when compared to what long-time Vietnam correspondent Stanley Karnow had observed:

> At the height of the war, the town stunk of decay. Its bars were drug marts, its hotels bordellos, its boulevards a black market hawking everything from rifles to hair spray ... Soldiers ... their pockets bulging with cash, strolled the streets crowded with prostitutes, beggars, cripples and other war victims.[15]

Moreover, in 1969, when American popular opinion had begun to slowly turn against the war in Vietnam and when the war and its escalations were daily topics in newspaper and TV reports in countries all over the world, such blithe disingenuousness was a political statement by omission.[16]

Taken together, then, the *New Horizons* films and printed materials focused the future tourist's attention on the beauty, fun and joys waiting at the destinations advertised. In the films, the suggestion that these were all within easy reach was reinforced by opening shots showing a Pan Am plane's touchdown; departure was implicitly assumed. That was typical for a certain immersive quality, which was sustained in the films' editing pace, hopping from one locale to another, alternating local highlights, both natural and cultural, and comfortable stopping places. And as they steered clear of politically charged idiom, the world was presented as a carefree, sunny place, 'all fashioned to the requirements of your dreams', to quote the narration of *Fiji, New Caledonia*. These are, indeed, highly contrived 'dream worlds', in Rosalind Williams's sense of the term: all the elements that went into their realisation – production processes, labour relations, ownership structures, political and economic dependencies, etc. – have been elided.[17] Pan Am solidly anchored a destination's excitement and exoticism – preconditions for spending one's money on a holiday far away – to a familiar environment of luxury hotels, fancy and/or 'authentic' restaurants, shopping arcades, or beach resorts. The phrase 'a blend of ancient and modern', in the narration's description of Morocco, typifies the series' approach. Yet such a blend should be seen less as a mixture than as the co-existence of two separate worlds. The quoted phrase, in fact, echoes the entry on Morocco in the *World Guide*: 'Except for the modern cities ... much of the country has remained unchanged for centuries.'[18] Any other than this twofold conception would surely have undermined the enticement of a place and the alleged picturesque nature of its people. Thus, *New Horizons* purposefully inserted itself in the travelogue genre, but with one crucial distinction: whereas the attraction of the travelogue in its heyday – the early twentieth century – was that it showed places its spectators would *not* visit, now the modern conveniences displayed in Pan Am's films assured potential customers that their *own* trip was to be as untroubled as the series' vicarious journeys. In other words, a holiday destination was meant to be different while at the same time it should make the vacationer feel at home. Small wonder, then, that in the films – as well in Pan Am's artwork – a country's allure often took the form of tourist art: leather gaucho wear and accessories in Buenos Aires souvenir stores, hula dancers in Hawaii, etc.

This was a predictable if not inevitable outcome. The guidebooks to golfing or skiing surely were symptomatic of Pan Am's positioning itself as a jet-settish airline of sophistication and style, an approach that may have attracted a trendsetting clientele. But the expected mass-tourism boom was what really justified the company's investments in its new fleet of jet planes and tourist industry infrastructure. In fact, as early as 1948, Pan Am seized the opportunity to introduce the cheaper tourist-class fares on international routes; the more compact designs and bigger aircraft of the post-war era accommodated unprecedented numbers of passengers, generating the funds the company needed.[19] Pan Am, as one of its commercials stated, promised 'fares and schedules [that] make it possible for the average person with a two-week holiday to go anywhere in the world'. What, in the end, the airline offered were, indeed, safe and easily attainable impressions: 'capsule glimpses', readymade experiences and souvenirs, including the characteristic and often product-placed, petrol blue Pan Am bag.

POST-WAR HOLLAND

Traditionally, we can distinguish two basic purposes in commercial advertising: announcing and reminding. In the first case, advertising is meant to nudge people to change brands or try a new one, often by giving shape to real or perceived trends and desires.[20] In the second, it is meant to reinforce behaviour or opinions (for example, by appealing to customers' sense of brand loyalty, whether to a product or to, say, a political candidate or by stressing a business's or organisation's track record). Here, advertising campaigns reinforce a brand or company's continued presence and image (as in those commercials where Coca-Cola keeps on uniting the world). In long-term advertising campaigns, such as *New Horizons*, these purposes are often combined: with every film a new destination is suggested while reminding spectators of the same trusted carrier. However, as far as the Pan Am films for the Dutch market are concerned, none of the above-mentioned considerations could have been felt to be urgent: indeed, there were so few customers for jet travel that the market for their product was virtually nonexistent.

The films deposited at the Amsterdam film archive had been released in a country in which going on holiday abroad, *by car*, had barely become mainstream; in 1960, only 25 per cent of the Dutch population spent its holidays outside Holland's borders.[21] And while charter flights to holiday destinations, notably the beaches of the Mediterranean, had not been unheard of, these were the privilege of the adventurous, happy few only. (Dutch charter company Martinair, founded in 1958, opened a service to Palma de Mallorca with its propeller-driven De Havilland DH 104 Dove that seated only a few dozen passengers.) Intercontinental jet travel must have seemed light years away, and not just for vacationers. Between the late 1940s and early 60s, hundreds of thousands of Dutch emigrants left for destinations that were literally overseas; they largely travelled by boat rather than by plane.[22]

By the early 1960s, after the reconstruction of the war-ravaged country and after more than a decade of economic policies that favoured controlled wages and investment in infrastructure and industrialisation, Dutch society was just about to turn the corner to prosperity. Slowly but steadily, from the early 1950s onward, Holland experienced 'an economic miracle': between 1951 and 1973 the economy grew uninterruptedly; real national income tripled while per capita income doubled (although there was no real wage increase between 1948 and 1954); and full employment prevailed, notwithstanding a rapidly expanding population. Growing affluence, though, was signalled only from the early 1960s onwards, when imports of consumer goods showed a greater increase than imports of raw materials. Consumers, long restrained by a spirit of frugality and soberness, finally felt able to spend: the early 1960s saw annual wage increases of around 10 per cent.[23] But while consumer goods came increasingly within Dutch households' purchasing power, a pleasure trip to Latin America or Asia was decidedly not widely affordable. In fact, a fledgling leisure industry just began to flourish after the phasing out, in December 1960, of the working Saturday for many occupational groups (others followed quickly over the next few years). So, why did Pan Am go through the trouble of having its films released in Holland – as well as in countries, such as France or Portugal, in similar or even worse economic circumstances – a decade or so too early?

A useful starting point is provided by historian Tony Judt's remark that, in the late 1950s and early 60s, '[f]or many people, the world as depicted in advertisements was still beyond their reach'. 'Many people' were in actual fact young respondents to an opinion poll in France. But, Judt continues, the respondents didn't just complain 'that they lacked access to entertainment of their choice, the vacation of their imaginings, a means of transport of their own', it was 'symptomatic that those polled already regarded these goods and services as rights of which they were deprived, rather than fantasies to which they could never aspire'.[24] It was symptomatic, in other words, of a change in mentality that had in no small measure been determined by the way America – asserting itself as the leading military, political and economic world power in the post-war years – was being regarded. The resulting image, if not quite imaginary, was based on Hollywood features or magazines, rather than on first-hand experience or more informed opinions. After all, for many people at that time, America itself was practically and financially unattainable, what with weak national European currencies against the US dollar.[25]

In making America a measuring stick for Europeans' definitions of economic progress, security and welfare the Truman administration had played an active role in steering these changes and bringing these goods within Europe's horizon of expectations. It launched a vision of a new, post-war world order, in which:

> economic growth was presented as the material condition for military security and political stability. ... The American vision of an economic order based on free trade, free enterprise, and stable exchange rates as well as the emergence of the modern welfare state in Western Europe succeeded primarily because of two factors: first, the development of technology was unprecedented in scale, volume, and complexity; and second, there was a subsequent, systematic buildup of a modern industrial mentality (with American ideas of efficiency, company organization, management theories, and new ways of distribution).[26]

For the Netherlands, the most immediately relevant context in this respect was, of course, the European Recovery Program (ERP) (1947–52), drawn up by the countries receiving Marshall Aid. It was through ERP that acceptance of this American concept and the implementation of policies towards reinforcing the interconnectedness of economic growth, political stability and military security had been achieved – often, in fact, forced.[27] Incidentally, extensive publicity campaigns camouflaged the fact that ERP, despite its name, was less crucial for economic recovery than it was for preventing a slowdown of economic growth (huge imports from the USA to support its ongoing recovery threatened to deplete Europe's dollar supply, threatening the American economy in its turn) and providing a model for political and economic orientation.[28] But because Marshall Aid administrators stipulated that the benefiting countries were responsible for the way aid was implemented (although funds were administered by American advisors), each country adapted this model to its own traditions and circumstances.[29] One result of this was that American ideas and products were not adopted wholesale. In the Netherlands, there were scattered, private Americanising initiatives, such as the faltering introduction of self-service stores in the late 1940s and the slow spread of supermarket chains during the 50s. And throughout the 1950s and early 60s the time-honoured structure of separate togetherness of Dutch public and semi-public institutions – education, health care, public housing, trade unions, emigration, newspapers and broadcasting were vertically organised into ideological pillars (Protestant, Catholic, social-democratic, liberal, etc.) – proved resilient to the American way, not least because of the concomitant tradition of coalition governments that provided the pillars with a collective roof. Yet subsequent Dutch governments in those years planted the seeds of change that would result in legislation that created, between the mid-1950s and the late 60s, an across-the-board welfare state that provided a modern (i.e. centralised, non-ideological) system of pensions and other collective insurances, financed by the ever-expanding economy.[30] (This new system, in fact, resembled the Nordic model of a social safety net more than anything American.) The delayed impact of Americanisation was also a generational matter: the post-war era, with its demographic explosion and its shift to a more urban culture, saw the birth of the teenager. The young and the post-war baby-boomers personified the rift most visibly: they identified, and were identified, with the most conspicuous aspects of American culture – notably through their tastes in entertainment, fashion, music and, once they had money to spend, through a more consumerist lifestyle.[31]

There were also a number American-led initiatives aimed at orienting specific segments of the Dutch population more favourably towards the USA. The State Department's Fulbright Program, established in 1946, promoted public relations and first-hand experience by targeting its activities, particularly its exchange programmes, at students, scholars, scientists and artists. From a military-strategic viewpoint the Netherlands was, in fact, one of the programme's key countries, because of its achievements in atomic physics, mathematics, aviation, astronomy and agricultural science.[32] In addition, ERP funds were allocated to learning tours and productivity missions that enabled European professionals to travel to the USA and acquaint themselves with business and managerial practices on-site. One published case study concerns the reports written between 1949 and 1956 by Dutch participants of such tours, during which they were introduced to – often highly selective – aspects of American business and culture (farms, factories, laboratories, universities). It was, therefore, not really surprising that in these reports America is held up as an example for emulation: a country of unlimited possibilities with a standard of living much higher than in Holland; with more leisure time (in the USA, the working Saturday was abolished in 1954); and much more disposable income, so that even workers owned their home and stocked it with expensive objects: cars, refrigerators and other large appliances, smaller household appliances, radio and TV sets, etc. America, in contemporary Dutch eyes, was a country where luxury had been 'democratised'.[33]

Much of what these Dutch participants admired could have been copied straight from the pages of the *Saturday Evening Post* or, for that matter, from largely pro-American Dutch newspapers and magazines, as well as from the materials distributed by the US Information Agency (USIA), an organisation created by the Eisenhower administration in 1953 as the clearing-house for America's cultural diplomacy. USIA provided library services, distributed books and pamphlets and mounted exhibitions and trade fairs. (One such fair, the American National Exhibition in Moscow, in 1959, was the occasion for the famous kitchen debate, staged for TV, between American Vice-President Nixon and Soviet leader Khrushchev. Closer to home, the American house and kitchen featured prominently at the 1958 World's Fair in Brussels – visited by almost 42 million people, including approximately 1 million Dutch[34] – and the International Horticultural Exposition Floriade in Rotterdam in 1960, doubtlessly influencing the desires of many a homemaker.) And, of course, the media – cinema, broadcasting and the press – were instrumental in realising USIA's information offensive, either by supplying materials or by direct broadcasting and distribution. Surely, with the Cold War at freezing point in the 1950s, the agency produced, sponsored, or picked up films and programmes concerning US foreign policy, but its catalogue actually covered a wide range of topics promoting American culture and way of life.[35]

No quantified data on the effects of these initiatives are available. Certainly the exchange programmes and productivity missions, aimed at specific, limited target groups, make it hard to gauge to what extent these groups' experiences and opinions percolated through society at large.[36] Of the 600 or so USIA film titles that circulated in the Netherlands it has been said that they were much in demand, but here, too, hard figures are lacking.[37] What's more, over time official information and propaganda were seriously challenged by issues that had not been (sufficiently) critically addressed – notably the Civil Rights movement, galvanised by extensive domestic press coverage, and the war in Vietnam. Nevertheless, in the Netherlands, the above-mentioned initiatives coincided with the unmistakable success of economic growth and mass production that took off in the 1960s and led to the rise of a full-fledged consumer society.

CONCLUSION

These were the local political and economic contexts in which Pan Am released its *New Horizons* series. At the same time, it may well have kept a watchful eye on the performance of the Dutch national airline. It didn't have to compete with similar advertising from the Dutch national carrier: in the same year that Pan Am launched its intercontinental jet service, 1958, KLM opened its first, *propeller*-plane service to Tokyo, now 'only thirty hours away'.[38] But in the post-war years, KLM increasingly operated beyond its domestic market, using its home port, Schiphol, to connect flights among multiple foreign countries – the so-called sixth freedom of the air – particularly on intercontinental routes.[39] And, of course, in the late 1950s and early 60s most Western European airlines began to replace or expand their fleets with jet planes, too.

Unfortunately, though, the *New Horizons* film series have left no significant paper trail in Holland. Unlike the films, IFS's company papers have not survived.[40] And because the films were distributed non-theatrically, they do not show up in published censorship records either. These records, which at the time were included in *Film*, the bi-monthly newsletter of the Dutch Association of Cinema Theatres, only listed films screened by the association's members; in its annually published, updated membership list the name of IFS does not occur nor do the venues it rented its prints to.[41] (I assume that the voluntary submission of films for censorship by non-members, such as the Department of Agriculture or Shell, reflect a wish for the widest possible range of exhibition venues, both non-theatrical *and* theatrical.)

In fact, only one *New Horizons* film, *Ski* (1961), was put to the censorship committee. Submitted by the Netherlands Fox Film Corporation, the Dutch office of 20th Century-Fox in January 1962, the film was apparently distributed through the company's regular, commercial channels, considering that this episode, unlike the IFS prints in the Amsterdam archive, was listed under a translated title.[42] And although the censorship record does not indicate – as it normally would – that this was a 16mm reduction print, the common gauge for non-theatrical screenings, Fox must have held 16mm prints of this title or at least the rights to such prints: a 1935 resolution of the Association of Cinema Theatres, reaffirmed in 1958, stipulated that any member distributor that acquired the rights for 35mm prints of a film was obliged to also secure the rights for small-gauge prints of that title.[43] But the censorship records mention no other *New Horizons* titles, although in mid-1968 the lists ceased to be exhaustive and were dropped altogether in early 1970.

By making most of its films available through the same channel – IFS – that distributed official American information films, Pan Am may have aimed at a deeper, certainly longer penetration of the Dutch market than a regular theatrical distribution might have accomplished; in fact, IFS rented its films many years after their initial release.[44] Moreover, the series' association with American ideas and ideology may have been strengthened through the contingencies of programming of IFS's predominantly American catalogue. The ever-widening horizon of expectations thus propagated allowed Pan Am to invite the Dutch to slowly but steadily close the time-gap of a decade or so in prosperity. In that sense, the *New Horizons* promotional campaign can be seen as part of a long-term *anticipatory* business strategy. With a firm base in an affluent and expanding domestic market for jet travel, the airline had the leverage to patiently work the developing post-war, western markets. Readying itself for a cut of sure-fire future profits, Pan Am targeted Dutch (and other non-American) audiences by showing the splendour of things to come. So, with each screening of its *New Horizons* films, the airline essentially suggested a legitimate reward for an expanding economy and made a promise to Dutch stragglers: work hard and your dreams will come true.

NOTES

I thank Hans Schoots and Marja Roholl for their very helpful comments.

1. I borrow the term 'resonance' from Stephen Greenblatt's essay 'Resonance and Wonder', in Ivan Karp and Steven D. Lavine (eds), *Exhibiting Cultures: The Poetics and Politics of Museum Display* (Washington, DC, and London: Smithsonian Institution Press, 1991), pp. 42–57. Greenblatt defines resonance as 'the power of the ... object to reach out beyond its formal boundaries to a larger world, to evoke ... the complex, dynamic cultural forces from which it has emerged' and contrasts it with the notion of wonder, 'the power ... to ... convey an arresting sense of uniqueness, to evoke exalted attention'. Although his paper was originally presented at a conference on museum exhibitions, Greenblatt states that these terms were developed for the interpretation of texts.

   'Useful cinema' is an umbrella term for non-commercially distributed films and their non-theatrical venues of exhibition, where they are largely shown for their persuasive or educational rather than entertaining qualities.

2. Currently called IFS Audiovisueel, the company focuses on audiovisual production and presentation techniques: http://www.ifsaudiovisueel.nl/

   At the time, the privatisation of the American embassy's Film Department in Holland may have been welcomed, perhaps even suggested, by the US Information Agency (USIA), which was responsible for foreign information and cultural programmes, usually channelled through American embassies. In the early 1960s, USIA was expanding its programmes in Asia and Africa, while scaling back its activities in western countries; see Wilson P. Dizard Jr, *Inventing Public Diplomacy: The Story of the US Information Agency* (Boulder, CO, and London: Lynne Rienner, 2004), pp. 84, 92, 103.

3. An edgemark – or date code – is an identification code printed along the edge of a reel of film by film stock manufacturers at the moment raw sheets of film were cut and perforated.

4. Other *New Horizons* films can be accessed at YouTube.com, travelfilmarchive.com, britishpathe.com and periscopefilm.com: *Thailand* (1960); *The Philippines* (1960); *Australia and New Zealand* (1961); *Ireland* (1962); *Fiji, New Caledonia* (1960s); *New York* (1967); *National Parks* (1968); *New Zealand* (1969); *Morocco and Kenya* (1970); and *California* (197?); *India, Pakistan* and *Hawaii* can be found online as well. In addition, the BFI Film & TV Database lists *Austria* (1968) and *Brazil* (1968). And a Pan Am list captioned 'Active film library', dated 14 June 1962, mentions *Hong Kong, Singapore* (1961), *Turkey* (1961) and a thematic episode, *Ski* (1961); the Active film library can be found at the Pan American World Airways Papers, Accession II, Box 532, Folder 11, Special Collections, University of Miami Libraries. I thank librarian Laura Capell for providing this document.

   With no filmography available, I cannot tell whether the titles mentioned here and in the main body of the text exhaust the series' output. The films released in 1960–1 were produced by 20th Century-Fox's Movietonews; later titles identify Film Authors or the British firms mentioned in note 6 as production companies.

5. The German narration runs, respectively: 'Hoch über dem Pazifischen Ozean' and 'Plötzlich steigt aus dem unendlichen Meer ... Manila.' During the Cold War, civilian flights from Europe to East Asia either connected through Alaska or used the Middle East route.

6. The production credits for *New Zealand* and for *Morocco and Kenya* – Associated British Pathé in association with Film Services, London, and JTE/Intercine Production in association with

Film Services, London, respectively – suggest, nevertheless, that the production of the series at one time or another was farmed out to foreign companies (not an uncommon strategy for Pan Am; some films in its series *Wings to ...* were foreign produced as well). Another possibility, suggested by the narration of *California*, is that by the end of the decade Pan Am ceased making these films for American audiences: over the image of a Pan Am plane landing at Los Angeles airport, the British voiceover says that it has arrived 'from Europe'.

7. Such measures include, besides translation: censorship, marketing, publicity and presentation. See Nico de Klerk, 'The Transport of Audiences', in Richard Abel, Giorgio Bertellini and Rob King (eds), *Early Cinema and the 'National'* (New Barnet: John Libbey, 2008), p. 107.

   Translation and censorship are invasive measures, as they physically alter a local release print compared to its domestic counterpart. Marketing, publicity and presentation can be called contextual measures, although presentation can also involve invasive measures, such as cuts to allow intermissions (until the late 1990s a widespread practice in Dutch commercial cinemas) or the removal of scenes, particularly in overly long films, to allow the usual amount of daily shows. Paratextual elements, such as local distributors' logos, physically affect a print as well.

8. IFS may have presumed, perhaps self-servingly, a sufficient command of English and saved money accordingly. Moreover, besides Dutch promotional films, IFS distributed many other films in its catalogue on behalf of embassies, foreign organisations and companies; possibly too many for too small a market to profitably allow systematic translation.

9. This was based on a model of practical information introduced by British publisher John Murray in 1836, in a series of handbooks for travellers that were published under Murray's name until 1915 and covered countries on four continents. For an impression of the contents of the sixth edition of *Handbook for Travellers in Japan*, published in 1901, see http://archive.org/stream/ahandbookfortra04firgoog#page/n11/mode/2up

10. Lou A. Phillips, *Understanding Latin America* (New York: Pan American Airways, 1965), unpaginated.

11. Marc Dierikx, *Luchtspiegelingen: Cultuurgeschiedenis van de Luchtvaart* [*Mirages: A Cultural History of Aviation*] (Amsterdam: Boom, 2008), pp. 69–70.

12. In actual fact, a stop had to be made in Newfoundland, as no long-range Boeing 707 jet was yet available for this flight, only a domestic version; see Carl Solberg, *Conquest of the Skies: A History of Commercial Aviation in America* (Boston and Toronto: Little, Brown and Company, 1979), pp. 396–7. See also ibid., pp. 354–60, 371; George E. Burns, 'The Jet Age Arrives', http://www.panam.org/online-archives/chronicles/216-jet-age-arrives.html

   A stand-alone Pan Am promotional film celebrating the arrival of the jet age is *6½ Magic Hours* (1958), about a nonstop flight to London; see http://www.youtube.com/watch?v=Uvkxa1O7Mec&feature=related

13. Emily S. Rosenberg, *Spreading the American Dream: American Economic and Cultural Expansion 1890–1945* (New York: Hill and Wang, 1982), pp. 105–7, 198–9; Solberg, *Conquest of the Skies*, pp. 348–9, 225–48, 259–71.

14. Burns, 'The Jet Age Arrives'.

15. Stanley Karnow, *Vietnam: A History* (New York: Penguin, 1997 [1983]), p. 45.

16. Gerald W. Whitted, *New Horizons World Guide: Pan American's Travel Facts about 131 Countries*, 16th revised edition (New York: Pan American Airways, 1969 [1951]), pp. [5], [6–7], 139, 216, 357, 685, 719, 742 (page numbers inbetween [ ] are actually unpaginated).

17. Rosalind H. Williams, *Dream Worlds: Mass Consumption in Late Nineteenth-Century France* (Berkeley, Los Angeles and Oxford: University of California Press, 1991 [1982]), pp. 62–4, 89.
18. Whitted, *New Horizons World Guide*, p. 646.
19. Solberg, *Conquest of the Skies*, pp. 345–8; http://www.everythingpanam.com/1946_-_1960.html; http://www.boeing.com/news/frontiers/archive/2008/july/i_history.pdf
20. Michael Schudson, *Advertising, the Uneasy Persuasion: Its Dubious Impact on American Society* (London: Routledge, 1993 [1984]), p. 9.
21. Kees Schuyt and Ed Taverne, *1950: Prosperity and Welfare* (Assen and Basingstoke: Van Gorcum/Palgrave Macmillan, 2004), pp. 154–5, 256–7. Dutch Culture in a European Perspective, vol. 4.
22. It was only late into this emigration wave that the balance began to shift. With respect to travel to North America, where Canada was many an emigrant's destination, aviation historian Marc Dierikx writes: 'On the North Atlantic route the economy class was introduced as a new and cheaper travel option. The price of economy class tickets was another 20 per cent lower than those of the tourist class. In competing with the shipping trade, the traditional transport of the well-to-do and of the poor emigrant, the airline companies' economy class dealt the decisive blow. In 1958, for the first time more people travelled across the ocean by aeroplane than by ship' [my translation]. See his *Blauw in de Lucht: Koninklijke Luchtvaart Maatschappij 1919–1999* [*Blue in the Sky: KLM 1919–1999*] (Den Haag: Sdu, 1999), p. 180; see also Dierikx, *Luchtspiegelingen*, pp. 101–2; Marja Roholl, 'Uncle Sam: An Example for All? The Dutch Orientation towards America in the Social and Cultural Field, 1945–1965', in Hans Loeber (ed.), *Dutch–American Relations 1945–1969: A Partnership. Illusions and Facts* (Assen and Maastricht: Van Gorcum, 1992), p. 118.
23. Schuyt and Taverne, *1950*, pp. 37–42, 64–8, 250–7.
24. Tony Judt, *Postwar: A History of Europe since 1945* (London: Vintage, 2010 [2005]), pp. 349–50.
25. Ibid., p. 350. Practical obstacles had not least been raised by restrictive US immigration policies; see Roholl, 'Uncle Sam', pp. 117–18.
26. Schuyt and Taverne, *1950*, p. 57.
27. Pierre van der Eng, *De Marshall-hulp: Een Perspectief voor Nederland: 1947–1953* [*Marshall Aid: A Perspective for the Netherlands: 1947–1953*] (Houten: De Haan/Unieboek, 1987), p. 10.
28. In fact, these goals were explicitly and purposefully mentioned in the first public statement about European aid, on 5 June 1947; see George C. Marshall, 'Speech at Harvard University', in Ted Widmer (ed.), *American Speeches: Political Oratory from Abraham Lincoln to Bill Clinton* (New York: The Library of America, 2006), pp. 472–5.
    Indicative of how the myth of Marshall Aid's importance for economic recovery was able to settle itself in the popular mind is the 1950 film series *ERP in Action*, a monthly overview in magazine format in various language versions that showed the progress made in Europe's recovery by focusing almost exclusively on increased productivity in industry and agriculture, as well as the reconstruction of infrastructure; see, for content descriptions, http://www.marshallfilms.org/mpf.asp
    For ERP public relations campaigns in the Netherlands, see van der Eng, *De Marshall-hulp*, pp. 109–32.
29. Ibid., pp. 12–17, 245–6; Judt, *Postwar*, pp. 91–3.
30. Schuyt and Taverne, *1950*, pp. 262–75.
31. Judt, *Postwar*, pp. 327–31; Roholl, 'Uncle Sam', pp. 132–44.

32. Schuyt and Taverne, *1950*, p. 69.

33. Frank Inklaar, *Van Amerika Geleerd: Marshall-hulp en Kennisimport in Nederland* [*Learned from America: Marshall Aid and Knowledge Import in the Netherlands*] (Den Haag: Sdu, 1997), pp. 83–104, 129–30.

35. Marja Roholl, '"We'll Go on Trial at the Fair": het Amerikaanse paviljoen op de EXPO '58 in Brussel', *Groniek* no. 146 (October 1999), p. 33.

35. This wide range echoed President Truman's 1945 statement that foreign information programmes present 'a full and fair picture of American life and of the aims and policies of the United States government'; quoted in Richard Dyer MacCann, *The People's Films: A Political History of US Government Motion Pictures* (New York: Hastings House, 1973), p. 175.

36. Schuyt and Taverne, *1950*, pp. 70–1; Inklaar, *Van Amerika Geleerd*, pp. 341–5.

37. Roholl, 'Uncle Sam', pp. 146–9. Dizard even anticipates that USIA's activities 'will be forever unmeasurable' (*Inventing Public Diplomacy*, p. 5).

38. See *Amsterdam to Tokyo* (1958) at https://www.youtube.com/watch?v=T6Dwkq1kjx8. This promotional film, although similar in editing style to the *New Horizons* films, differed in image 'idiom' as it didn't skirt the downsides of life in the Japanese capital.

39. Dierikx, *Blauw in de Lucht*, p. 154. In 1962, a regional Dutch newspaper reported that Pan Am's in-flight *Clipper Magazine* listed KLM as the airline with the third-longest network, longer than that of Pan Am and TWA combined; see *Leeuwarder Courant*, 28 December 1962 http://www.dekrantvantoen.nl/vw/article.do?id=LC-19621228-15007&vw=org&lm=klm %2Cluchtlijn%2Clengt%2CLC. Although the news item admitted that the significance was promotional rather than anything else, it does indicate the success of KLM's exploitation of the right to carry passengers or cargo from second to third countries through Amsterdam.

40. Telephone interview with IFS director Erik Padding, December 2010.

41. For membership lists in this period, see NBB Archief [Papers of the Dutch Association of Cinema Theatres], Box #626, Folders 366–71 and Box #627, Folders 372–7, EYE-Nederlands Film Instituut, Amsterdam. Non-theatrical venues were prevented from becoming members, as they couldn't be expected to conform to the association's regulatory stipulation of showing films between a minimum of fifty-two and a maximum of 124 days a year; see: *Algemeen Bedrijfsreglement* [*General Company Regulations*] (Amsterdam: Nederlandsche Bioscoop-Bond, January 1960), pp. 4–5, NBB Archief, Box #624, Folder 311b. Throughout the 1960s, this stipulation was reaffirmed in the regulations' reprints of August 1961 (pp. 4–5) and March 1967 (pp. 4–5), ibid., Folders 311c and 311d.

42. *Film: Orgaan van de Nederlandse Bioscoopbond* [*Organ of the Dutch Association of Cinema Theatres*] vol. 24 no. 227 (March–April, 1962), p. 288.

43. *Bedrijfsbesluit in zake Zogenaamde Smalfilms* [*Company Ruling in the Matter of So-Called Small-Gauge Films*] (Amsterdam: Nederlandsche Bioscoop-Bond, August 1958), p. 3, NBB Archief, Box #625, Folder 339.

44. Telephone interview with IFS director Erik Padding, December 2010.

9

The Five Year Plan on Display: Czechoslovakian Film Advertising

Lucy Česálková

The economic and political situation in Czechoslovakia during the first decade after World War II pushed the advertising of consumer goods out of public discourse. In the early years after the war, models of supply and organisation of services were restored. Giving priority to the production side of the national economy, the Communist Party that ascended to power in 1948 suppressed the significance of consumption as a factor in the standard of living. Socialist consumer culture in Czechoslovakia thus began to develop at the end of the 1950s and in the early 60s in the context of political liberalisation. This early phase, the phase of alignment of the socialist practice of advertising, is very important for several reasons: it established the basic models of organisation and several practices typical of socialist advertising in the coming years; it allowed specialisation in certain sectors of short film production, mainly to distinguish popular-scientific and educational film from advertising; it also created a space for the experimental practice of authors of the later, visually attractive genre features of the 1960s (mainly musicals). A key factor fundamentally affecting advertising in Czechoslovakia during the entire socialist period from 1948–89 was the existence of a market in which there was no competition. Thus, instead of promoting brands, advertising promoted commodities. The study of socialist advertising is, therefore, not possible without taking into account connections between the advertising industry, the national economy and domestic trade, as well as considering the impact of ideological concepts of a (healthy) lifestyle on socialist consumer culture.

The magazine *Reklama* (*Advertising*), the official journal defining key concepts and practices of advertising in Czechoslovakia during the second half of the 1950s, worked with a specific format of adverts for advertising media. These advertisements showed state enterprises how and why it was possible to advertise goods and services and demonstrated the role and functions assigned to a particular media in comparison with others. One of the advertisements on advertising film showed a flute player abandoned in an orchestra and ran with the following copy:

> He cannot perform a symphony alone. This requires strings, brass instruments, drums and a perfectly harmonious orchestra. It is likewise with advertising. Only a perfect promotional campaign will produce the results and the effects. The reliable axis of any well thought-out campaign, its impressive solo part, is an advertising film.

'He cannot perform a symphony alone': advertisement on advertising film (1956)

The orchestra metaphor for advertising was a good illustration of the situation in socialist Czechoslovakia and reflects the key aspects of socialist advertising: its central organisation in the coordination of state, state enterprises and producers of promotional materials, as well as the need for the differentiation and interplay of particular tools and instruments in broader advertising campaigns. The orchestra is a traditional, familiar cultural element and advertising tools should, in the socialist trade, be naturalised and have specific functions, forms and mutual relations. The orchestra is also based on interplay according to a prescribed score: it assumes the central management and coordination of particular instruments. Following this metaphor, in this chapter I will introduce the organisational model of advertising film production in Czechoslovakia at the level of institutional relations while also showing how film functioned in relation to other means of advertising. I will, furthermore, present the style of contemporary advertising and explain the reasons why the first advertisements in the 1950s were very similar to popular-scientific films and point out in which ways they began to differ in the early 1960s. I will also use a specific example to analyse joint advertising campaigns as model types of socialist advertising.

ADVERTISING IN A PLANNED ECONOMY

Czechoslovakian socialist film advertising – and the ways it changed during the centrally controlled system of planned production of the 1950s – was significantly influenced by the requirements of state ideologues who strived to regulate the market movements of goods and services and, in connection with production planning, to plan consumption as well: 'The business plan adapts to trade production needs and the production plan, on the other hand, adapts to the business plan.'[1] The Five Year Plan functioned in socialist Czechoslovakia as the doctrine of production and consumption, expecting cooperation between individual economic components: 'The specific structure of socialist society allows the plan to be instrumental in the coordinated campaigns of economic entities, the alignment of their interests, and the determination of a preferential scale of objectives in the form of their hierarchical structure.'[2] Plans for advertising activities also originated in direct correlation with production planning and market-movement predictions. The relation between advertising and the Five Year Plan was, figuratively speaking, that between master and servant – advertising should:

> influence sales of goods according to strict directives of the national economic plan, exercise active influence on the development of consumer demand, contribute to the transformation of obsolete patterns of consumption and the creation of new ones, and effectively assist in the rapid introduction of new types of consumer goods.[3]

From a critical historical perspective, it is thus possible to understand socialist advertising as a visualisation of the economic plan priorities accompanied by their verbal condensation into a punchline.

Until 1955, an average of roughly twenty-five advertising films a year originated in Czechoslovakia,[4] and the reason for this and also for the significant increase in the years to follow had much to do with the organisation of state trade during that period. Long after the end of World War II, domestic trade still suffered from an immense lack of domestic market goods. Both the demand and purchasing power of the population exceeded the possibilities of production, limited by small stocks of raw materials and the country's labour force. Therefore, the market operated on a basis of regulated rations. In parallel with the ration (ticket) economy of the tied market, a free market also existed where purchase of more expensive products for the state-set unified prices was allowed.[5] This is why all advertising produced under these conditions in Czechoslovakia was, in fact, intended for export only – promoting export goods to customers abroad.

The need for domestic advertising began to rise after 1953, when the rationing system was removed as part of fiscal reform. Persistent supply problems became partially solved by the supervision of pricing, which enabled the state to modify the availability of certain kinds of goods, and therefore the demand for them. From 1953 until the end of the first Five Year Plan in 1955 and during the announcement of the second Five Year Plan (which, due to the events of 1956, took place in 1958),[6] the importance of advertising increased in tandem with the increasing volume of goods stocks as well as wages. Consumer demand trends were changing too – both spending on paid services and the value of deposits in savings banks were rising.[7] Given the fairly low quality of household goods, advertising proved to be quite an effective means of directing consumer demand to specific commodities. Even at relatively low costs of advertising, sales showed increases of up to 15 per cent between six-month periods.[8]

In terms of the Czechoslovakian economy and advertising, 1957 was a groundbreaking year as it started the reform of the centrally controlled economic structure by redistributing the decision-making powers from state ministries to state companies, thus transforming them into independent economic entities.[9]

The significance of this action for advertising was mainly in giving greater authority to an umbrella body in the form of the Reklamní podnik (State Advertising Company). The purchasing power of the population and the rising quality of household goods as factors that strongly differentiated consumer interests of individual social classes, however, continued to play an important role during that era.

The contracting authority for marketing in socialist Czechoslovakia was not a private enterprise, but, at the lowest level, the Reklamní podnik, or Reklama obchodu (Business Advertisement Company), which typically represented state-owned enterprises (e.g. the Food Trade Association, National Insurance Company, Association of Oil Industry, etc.) or research institutions (e.g. the Institute of Health Education). These institutions further derived their orders from national plans of goods and services promotion produced in cooperation with production planning and market regulation at the level of ministries – for instance, the Ministry of Food Industry, Ministry of Light Industry, the Ministry of Internal Trade, Ministry of Foreign Trade, etc. The responsibility for this task belonged to the Inter-Ministerial Coordination Committee for the Management of Promotional Activity.[10]

The producer of an advert was usually the Advertising or Promotional Department of constituent state media institutions – Publishing Trade, Czechoslovak Radio, Czechoslovak Film and Czechoslovak Television. Advertising films were produced by the Short Film Company, an institution focusing on short film production (including newsreels), which was part of Czechoslovak (State) Film (controlled by the Ministry of Information until 1953, and later by the Ministry of Education).[11] Advertising films were, from the point of view of Short Film, understood to be custom-made productions, created at the instigation of, and in communication with, the contracting authority (the Advertising Company or other institutions) while the funding was provided not by Short Film but rather by the contracting entity. The Advertising Company itself functioned as an intermediary. It worked in response to the thematic, promotional plans coming from the different ministries (or the Inter-Ministerial Coordination Committee) – which were, in the words of the trade, the Company's customers. And since it was financially demanding, film was definitely not the most sought-after means of advertising – and there were doubts, moreover, about any actual impact on consumers of advertisements screened in cinemas (with their ever-declining attendance).[12]

The goal of an advertisement in a system with no competition between different brands or companies was not to increase profits. Production in individual economic sectors, carried out by specialised state-owned enterprises (dairies, canneries, soda factories, etc.), was subordinated to central state planning. Advertising, then, was envisaged primarily as a means of stimulating interest in the goods, which, furthermore, had a scheduled sales priority. At the same time, the advertisement should, by targeting a particular type of good, cover the shortage of another type of good on the market. As such, it functioned as an educational regulator and took over responsibility for shaping consumer behaviour – first and foremost, the taste and lifestyle priorities of Czechoslovakian society of the late 1950s and early 60s.

Hence, in the spirit of educational imperative, ideal advertising should not focus solely on the products or services themselves, but set them in a wider cultural and social framework and take into account, for instance, their importance for health and hygiene, working conditions and so forth. In the eyes of the socialist ideologues of advertising, non-economic factors influencing consumer behaviour appeared particularly problematic. These ideologues were especially allergic to 'fashion trends' that could threaten Czechoslovakian consumption from abroad. They therefore strove to balance such an impact with advertising campaigns in which they directly set not only the parameters of good nutrition, but also of what in the noble educational spirit was called the 'culture of living' or 'culture of clothing'.

Introducing new products to the Czechoslovakian market happened in direct conjunction with plans to increase the level of material culture and public facilities. Advertising, therefore, focused on just those kinds of goods and products which were permanently abundant, as 'the promotion of goods which are scarce on the market causes more political harm than good'.[13] For example, due to the lack of fresh food, a result of fluctuations in agricultural production and supply, food advertising was supposed to focus on durable goods: fruit juices and syrups, baby food, dairy products, pasta, frozen and canned products (such as fruit and meat) and convenience foods (soups, etc.). Outside the food sector, industries focused on goods for female consumers, and one of its priorities became the promotion of products that facilitated housework for employed women.[14] These mostly comprised various types of domestic equipment which facilitated the processing of raw food (such as blenders), the storage of groceries in the home (refrigerators and freezers) and other electrical household appliances, which had just begun to appear on the Czechoslovakian market of the late 1950s. The advertising plan in this regard fully replicated the production plan with the aim to support product introduction on the market.

Film advertising was rather specific in this respect. Considering the costs and time requirements of its production, a film advertisement (which had to undergo a multiple-phase approval process) was not always completed within the expected schedule in order to promote the goods in question – this often influenced the market in 'unplanned' ways. An example of such an incompatibility of film advertising with planned economy forecasts was the role of film to support the sale of Loden coats. Around 1954, while wholesale warehouses were filled with plenty of Loden coats that did not sell for the next two years, the advertising film *Pro každou příležitost* (*For Every Opportunity*, 1954), managed to increase the coats' marketability in a very short time and in such a way that some varieties and sizes of the coat became virtually impossible to obtain, with customers looking for them long after the warehouses had been emptied. Hence a legitimate question often resounded from the mouths of consumers: 'Why do they offer it, then, if they don't have it?'[15] This paradoxical case of film advertising, whose unexpected success surprised the planned economy and changed the market situation, aptly illustrates the lack of coordination in planning, advertising and consumption. Advertising efforts in the end worked against the manufacturer, who, in turn, was confronted by disgruntled consumers.

EDUCATIONAL TRAINING OR ADVERTISING?

For its interconnection with the national economic plan regulations, socialist advertising resembled state propaganda rather than commercial advertising in free-market economies. Although similar devices of visual and verbal persuasion were employed, it was nonetheless the result of a complicated hierarchical planning structure in which the commission and its funding were conducted by state authorities and the government budget, respectively. Contemporary discourse, then, defined 'socialist promotion' in contrast to 'capitalist advertising' in the sense that the socialist model is rationalised; customers are neither deliberately deceived nor left unaware of the important facts, and, most importantly, it is not about profit.[16]

However, the dissociation of the term 'advertising' and its replacement by 'socialist promotion' in contemporary discourse was mainly a rhetorical ploy of the communist idiom. The need to distinguish between advertising and promotion became noticeable in 1961. This rather vague transformation was apparently related to the need to postulate new ideological concepts for the third Five Year Plan (1961–5), which tried to distinguish itself from the previous, economically unsuccessful phase, by establishing radical 'new' trends. In the case of promotional activities that was meant as a 'transition from commercial advertising to informing and educating consumers',[18] although the educational aspect of promotion had already been emphasised in the previous period.

'Socialist promotion' was supposed to be 'serious and true, and unlike its capitalist counterpart should not target instincts and desires'.[19] Its essential features should include 'ideology, truthfulness, concreteness, deliberateness and planning'[20] and together with campaigning it was supposed to be one of the key means of 'mass political work'. However, while promotion was meant as an activity to popularise a certain topic so that recipients were better informed (with the help of facts and information based on science), campaigning was seen as an activity conducted in order to win the masses by persuasion, using illustrative examples from life, and not through factual data.[21]

Still, promotion and agitation used similar means of mass political work, be they posters, stickers, picture boards, band slogans, charts, displays, picture books, thematic corners, photographs, slides, slide films, radio programmes, films, TV, or theatre shows.[22] Both forms were subject to governmental control, and therefore the activities of promotional as well as campaigning bodies were heavily politicised. The concept of consumer education, however, did not serve only as a rhetorical differentiation of capitalist and socialist practices; it also, in the case of advertising film, fundamentally predetermined its early institutional integration and, with it, also its form.

Advertising film as an activity within the umbrella production company Short Film went through several phases in the late 1950s and early 60s. Until 1957, the production of these films was provided by the Studio of Popular Scientific and Educational Films. An independent studio, Propagfilm, specialising in 'advertising, promotional and instructional films',[23] did not become operational until 1 July 1957. However, the final organisational independence of advertising film came as late as 1964, when the original Propagfilm was subdivided into two separate departments: Promotional Film and Educational Film.[24] Thus, until 1957 advertising films were produced as an offshoot of the popular-scientific and educational genre; even after the establishment of Propagfilm, production of advertising film was still not fully separated from that of instructional films on workplace safety, fire protection, or sport, or of recruitment films inciting citizens to settle in the borderlands and lecturing about the mission of industry, agriculture, health care, etc. This organis-ational background corresponded to the prevailing concept of advertising as a tool for the education of citizens, yet it significantly influenced both the thematic focus and the stylistic rendition and rhetoric of advertising films.

Moreover, this gradual detachment of advertising film from scientific and educational films was not accompanied by changes in personnel. On the contrary, directors of advertising films were in most cases the same people who had also directed popular science films or propaganda pieces in the Popular Scientific and Educational Films Studio. One of the most productive advertising film-makers of the early 1960s, Milan Tichý, had worked for Short Film since 1952 and his filmography prior to the establishment of Propagfilm had included educational propaganda[25] and propagandist reportages.[26] Ladislav Rychman had made, before 1957, such films as *Umělé osvětlování pracovišť* (*Artificial Lighting of Workplaces*, 1951) and *Nové využití propanu-butanu* (*New Use of Propane-Butane*, 1952); Oldřich Mirad had directed *Konservování ovoce a zeleniny I–IV* (*Canning of Meat and Vegetables I–IV*, 1951), *Stavíme z oceli* (*Building with Steel*, 1954) and *Dechové hudební nástroje* (*Wind Instruments*, 1955). Likewise, the creators of animated films prior to their engagement in promoting goods had focused on the public awareness of educational concepts – Václav Bedřich had filmed with Jaroslav Možíš the medical and educational shorts *Kašlání a kýchání* (*Coughing and Sneezing*), *Mouchy* (*Flies*) or *Neviditelní nepřátelé* (*Invisible Enemies* [about germs]) (all 1951), before he made award-winning advertising films such as *Sedací nábytek* (*Seating Furniture*, 1959), *Skříňový nábytek* (*Cabinet Furniture*, 1959), *Kovolesk Druchema* (*Metal Polish Druchema*, 1960), etc.

The indistinctiveness of the advertising genre and its links with educational films were clearly factors that directly influenced its form. The persisting tendencies were towards a presentational/informational mode of communication, documentary production interludes and a product parade at the end of the film. An advertisement for nylon goods (*Silon/Nylon*, 1954) is thus framed by examples of stockings shown on a model looking at herself in the mirror. After a poetic introduction describing nylon as 'the fairytale reality of today' and a wonder 'cracked from Cinderella's nut', the short switches to practical and descriptive comments on scenes from a shop and the factory, demonstrating various ways of washing and drying nylons, and a warning that nylon goods should not be ironed. Only at the end does the short return from its documentary instruction to its advertising message and, with the model as the central figure, the key slogan, 'Light as a breath, soft as a breeze' appears in the frame.

In *Nylon*, just like in the film *Svět o nás ví* (*The World Does Know about Us*, 1960; an advertising short about JAWA motorcycles), advertising merely constitutes the framework of the film. *The World Does Know about Us* combines not only sports coverage of motor racing and industrial footage about the production of motorcycles, their testing etc., but also the practical application (their use by a mailman or a housewife taking home her purchases from the local shop). The advertising role here is basically limited to slogans only ('Elegance – Speed – Reliability – Made in Czechoslovakia') and examples of the product's easy manoeuvrability and usefulness for the masses.

The number of rhetorical modes combined in the films was related to the original idea of the widest possible spectrum of applicability, in the spirit of which Short Film produced its films until 1957. This broad category was exemplified in the production of the Popular Scientific and Educational Films Studio, where even advertisements employed a scientific rhetoric and were primarily designed to transmit accurate information about the advertised product. The reason why the product was popularised, or why it was this particular product and not any other, was related to whichever kind of market supply was taken into account by the economic plan and what the expected consumption in a given region was. The main function of the film, however, was to inform viewers about the existence of the goods and their properties.

Still, the contemporary ideologues of advertising hoped for success in portraying the educational intention of the advertisement in an original way, at the same time hoping that the experimental aspect would not impede comprehensibility. Many films from the 1950s and early 60s were, nevertheless, retrospectively criticised as being too simplistic, unimaginative with regard to the possibilities of innovative practices and techniques and devoid of the possibilities of film advertising shortcuts or anecdotes. In contrast to this, films combining feature footage and animation, working with split-screen techniques or with artistically elaborate scenes, or films rhythmically synchronising the footage with music were all highly valued.

The lack of communication between film professionals and contracting authorities also remained a long-term problem. One historical joke about the allegedly typical manner of formulating the order was, 'Sit down here and bring me a nice idea about how to advertise watches tomorrow.'[27] Because of such attitudes, advertising film production failed to be properly aligned either with the ideas of the Advertising Company and individual ministries or with economic interests. This failure is further demonstrated by the fact that we could search the production of the Popular Scientific and Educational Films Studio or the later Propagfilm in vain to find any emphasis on the key promotional priorities, which were, as mentioned above, the campaigns for the sale of Loden coats, hats, syrups and juices, dairy products, pasta, rice, coffee and tea. Films with these topics did exist, but only in limited quantities – say, two to three per subject. At the same time Propagfilm, in the years between 1957 and 1963, produced about seventy-five advertising films a year[28] and, outside the focal sector, it was intensely engaged in the promotion of industrial and chemical goods (tools, equipment and chemical cleaners), cosmetics, motorcycles and cars, dry cleaning services, insurance and repairs of clothing and appliances and, despite a nationwide campaign to combat alcoholism, filmed advertisements stating that only beer can quench thirst (for example, *Pilsner Urquell* [1961] by director Karel Pechánek).[29]

Contracting authorities also complained that films often did not contain the information that the film-makers were supplied with and that the films did not lead viewers towards proper consumption or to the right way of life.[30] This problem began to be resolved in 1961, when a more sophisticated control of promotional materials in all media through a new body, the Inter-Ministerial Committee for the Management of Promotional and Advertising Activities in the Field of Production and Sale of Consumer Goods and Services, was installed.[31] Definition of the main tasks of the Committee, however, did not differ much from the mission of its predecessors: it should be a central, coordinating body that would map out prospective promotion plans in relation to the priorities of the economy and education in new ways of living. The only change in approach was a stronger emphasis on determining and coordinating the distribution of responsibilities and the financial involvement of the individual participants in a promotional campaign – or, in contemporary parlance, 'promotional action'.

From 1961, films began to be categorised not with regard to their length and adaptation techniques (fiction, cartoons, puppetry), but according to economic sector. Altogether, there were eight of these categories: industrial goods, food products, textiles, tourism, eating, cosmetics, services and propaganda – the latter differed from the others in that films included in this category were not intended to encourage proper consumer habits, but other socially beneficial routines (collection of paper, or the planting of various crops, herbs, etc.).[32]

To justify the changes in the categorisation the organisers stated that the previous system was taken from international competitions and festivals and their considerations of film as an art object abroad. Yet, rather than attracting foreign festival juries films should be functionally incorporated into promotional campaigns, whether for the domestic or the foreign product market.

This categorisation deprived Czechoslovakian film advertising in the late 1950s and early 60s, both rhetorically and officially, of a place in film discourse and assigned advertising film to the role of a mere assistant in the complex system of economic plan implementation. Its effect within individual campaigns was to become the main priority of supervision. Only from this experience should any lessons about what means of expression to choose from for specific kinds of goods and corresponding methods of promotion be derived. Hence, it could be said that the specifics of the Czechoslovakian film advertising genre within the socialist economy started to be delineated only in the first half of the 1960s, based on a more sophisticated control of real relationships between promotion and trade. This system in turn fostered a specific mode of production in which the film topic was defined by planned instructions and the style of execution determined by market research and public opinion. It was specific only to a certain extent, of course. Naturally, the aesthetic was driven by economic imperatives.

The organisation of advertising and ideology of promotion remained exclusively socialist, even when Czechoslovakia at least partially rationalised the methods of production of advertising films by their separation into an independent production department (studio). The state remained the contracting authority, its objective to direct consumer behaviour in order to meet the plan of escalating production without causing excess or shortage of goods on the market. Advertisement funding (albeit coming from constituent ministries, research institutes, or national enterprises) was actually government funding, only through the budgets of institutions applying for funds in accordance with their own plans.

Coordinators of promotional work were aware of the persistent communication problems with the creators of promotional materials and held the insufficient linking means and media campaign effectiveness responsible for consumer confusion. A confused consumer was not desirable for promotional staff – he or she acted unpredictably, and thus threatened the plan. The coordinators set themselves the goal to prevent this type of 'unrestrained' consumption – a term which acquired a pejorative connotation through its frequent use in connection with capitalist practices – and make the market situation clearer for customers by supporting production of complex joint campaigns. This meant not only connecting a large number of mass media resources in order to collectively support one type of goods or services within a single campaign, but also by ideologically consolidating several related campaigns into even larger units, which would present the objects of support from different angles. This included film advertising as well, which, to varying degrees and in different ways, was involved in a number of complex promotional structures.

FILM IN A COMPLEX JOINT CAMPAIGN: VITAMINS – JUICES – BLENDERS

As indicated by the orchestra metaphor, socialist advertising pushed for the maximum possible harmonisation and mutual support of advertising media. Yet, the conditions of the socialist market, where there was no competition, allowed the creation of complex advertising campaigns based not only on media synergy, but also on the mutual support of two or more products. Hence the Advertising Company – in its press body, the magazine *Reklama* (*Advertising*) – constantly called attention to the need to implement socialist advertising in so-called joint actions.

In practice, this could mean in the simplest case that in the windows of the department store Perla was a display with samples of formal clothing featuring a slogan about the impending peak theatre season, with the background composed of enlarged pictures of theatre actors from the play *Čert nikdy nespí* (*Devil Never Sleeps*), which was currently in the repertoire of the ABC theatre. At the same time, on the theatre boards were recommendations for shopping in Perla. Similar simple synergies were fairly common between department stores, cultural venues and restaurants.[33]

An example of successful advertising harmony was the positively evaluated 1957 campaign promoting fruit cakes and biscuits in which the main motives of the advertising films *Medvěd* (*The Bear*), *Jasnovidka* (*The Clairvoyant*) and *Raketa* (*The Rocket*) were repeated in magazines, printed advertisements, banners, posters and displays. Likewise, this was so with the films *Silona* (*Nylon*), *Melta* and *Express* from the same year.[34] Ideally, motive linking should appear in as many advertising media as possible: in print advertising, film, radio, street advertising, road-side advertising, on surfaces of empty walls, on vehicles, in flyers, or in recruitment letters.[35]

Inter-level linking occurred when advertising was combined with national promotion campaigns, recruitment and persuasive educational campaigns.[36] Hierarchical organisation of promotional campaign goals thus reflected the hierarchical relationships between different advertising means within campaigns. Examples of such 'orchestration' are campaigns on fruit juices and canned and frozen fish – both durable goods heavily promoted as an evidence of sufficiency and variety of food products while actually compensating for a shortage of fresh food on the market.

Posters, billboards and shopping windows, as well as films on fruit juices, shared the same idea of a fruit juice as a healthy non-alcoholic beverage suitable for drivers and athletes, a source of necessary vitamins, refreshing and available through the whole year – bottles of juice were displayed together with apples, cherries, etc. and glasses with a straw. 'The sea of health in fish cans' was a slogan repeated on various canned-fish adverts by various artists in various styles as well as in Emanuel Kaněra's film *Rybí výrobky* (*Fish Products*, 1959). The play with ideas and themes was a tactic to newly inform about the same product as something unique in the market that was unlikely to change too much. This strategy also reminds us that, in the late 1950s, socialist advertising and socialist consumer culture were still quite young – products

'And This is Over': fruit juices poster (1958)

Fruit Juices (Ludvík Hájek, 1959)

did not have their established brands and logos, a lack of competition meant there was no need to innovate and market dynamics were determined mainly by the possibility of internal industry and national authorities to ensure sufficient import of goods. The main tasks of advertisers were to create an impression of a developing consumer culture and to skilfully time particular campaigns to cover up any shortages in supply.

The position of film was significantly influenced by the national long-term availability of the advertised goods. The less predictable the situation on the market for a particular commodity, the lower the willingness of the contracting authorities to purchase an advertising film, despite the fact that its prospective effect was undisputed. Film – 'the advertisement for hundreds of thousands' – and its effects were, in fact, potentially uncontrollable; it might attract attention and provoke demand to soar too high and cause shortages. Moreover, the multipurpose character of films on goods whose consumption was difficult to predict was initially strongly supported by the organisational integration of Advertising within Short Film.

The internal synergic combination of several promotions was always backed by a grand educational concept. A good example is provided by nutritional campaigns, in which foods were treated as an element of the food industry as well as scientific concepts of healthy nutrition. The organisers of these types of campaigns were generally the Central Institute of Health Education, the Ministry of Food Industry and the Food Trade Association. Among the priorities of health promotion in the late 1950s and early 60s were, above all, the campaigns Fighting against Alcoholism, Promotion of Milk and Promotion of Fruit Juices and Syrups.[37] These campaigns could be (and were) interconnected. Juices, for instance, were highlighted as non-alcoholic drinks suitable as substitutes for beer, wine and other alcohol drinks. The connection to a vast number of other smaller campaigns, as well as the close relation to the economic interests of several ministries, enlarged the campaign's scope and enhanced its impact significantly. In many respects, therefore, this campaign can be seen as one of the key instruments of the promotional and educational priorities of the state in

Czechoslovakia in the late 1950s and early 60s, and an example of the workings of promotion at that time.

A key imperative for each element of a 'joint action' was 'to hit at least one-third of families in the nation'.[38] This determined the distribution of assignments to each media resource involved in the campaign. One of the most expensive campaigns of the late 1950s was a campaign focused on promoting shortening. For CSK 500,000, a three-minute film, two short one-minute spots and a slide series were produced as a series of audiovisual tools that travelled cinemas for six weeks. Radio promotion was carried out indirectly through two debates on the show *Discussions for Women*, three types of posters were printed and extensive (although, reportedly, not tightly controlled) advertising was ordered in the local press. As a result, consumption of shortening increased by 1,000 tons per six-month period compared to the corresponding period a year before.[39]

An interplay of multiple media tools also characterised the above-mentioned 'joint action' for Fruit Juices and Syrups, implemented by the Ministry of Food Industry in cooperation with the state enterprise Sodovkárny (Soft Drinks). Print authorities provided several series of posters, banners and placards purposefully placed in indoor and outdoor swimming pools and sports grounds; decoration departments in department stores repeatedly created their own specialised shop window displays; large billboards were also designed for available house walls. Radio was utilised in the campaign through a traditional indirect form of education from health workers within discussion shows and the films *Ovocné šťávy* (*Fruit Juices*, 1959), directed by Ludvík Hájek, and *Nealkoholické nápoje* (*Non-alcoholic Beverages*, 1960), directed by Jan Karpaš, were shot for the campaign. Both films were in colour and used a puppet-animation technique and were quite obviously planned as an outreach – an element that would link the campaign Fruit Juices and Syrups to other campaigns of this complex interrelated joint campaign.

Using the example of three different characters and scenes, Hájek's short advertising fairy tale shows fruit in unconventional seasons or in unusual places. With the magic spell 'Čáry máry fuk' (equivalent to 'Hocus Pocus'), some currants, cherries and an apple appear in a child's room, in a mine next to an apprentice miner and in the snow, as soon as the characters start thinking about them. The film refers to the

Fruit Juices (Ludvík Hájek, 1959)

availability of fruit juices outside the summer months, which is reflected in the slogan, 'Drink fruit juice – drink the sun in a bottle'. The voiceover of the puppet section of the film, which at the same time makes up a playful narrative, is in the form of a simple nursery rhyme spoken by a child. However, after the slogan, both the voice and visual design change – the slogan, announced by an adult voice, is followed by an animation sequence of a 'parade' with colourful bottles and glasses full of juice from which the drink, sucked out by straws, 'magically' disappears. Hence, while the film's playfulness, through association with fairy-tale childhood, activates a rather emotional experience, the revue part of the film comes with rational information as an incentive to purchase the products.

Fruit Juices and its message aligned with films that, outside the campaign Fruit Juices and Syrups itself, were part of a broader promotion campaign on fruit substitutes as compensation for scarce fresh fruit; their consumption was simultaneously promoted within the campaign on the benefits of vitamin C,[40] related to the Asian influenza pandemic in 1957 and 1958. The vitamin C campaign was in turn linked with campaigns promoting other fruit products such as jams, marmalades and frozen fruit, as well as campaigns promoting other foods that were considered a suitable source of vitamin C.

Fruit in Czechoslovakia had for a long time been in short supply, and so the requirement of health education directed at the promotion of vitamin C as a means of protection against the Asian influenza collided head-on with the possibilities of internal trade. The fact that the Department of Health Education ordered the publication of promotional materials without consultation with economic experts was sharply criticised with regard to the possibility of scaremongering among consumers. Quite justifiably, consumers demanded the promoted yet scarce goods. Given the market situation, watching movies promoting fruit even allegedly provoked fits of laughter in the audience, and therefore the production of such films was perceived as wasting money on ineffective or even harmful projects.[41]

Moreover, consumer frustration and unfulfilled expectations caused by a scarcity of fruit on the market were further aggravated by a parallel promotional campaign for Pragomix blenders, which initially gave the impression of an anti-campaign in relation to Fruit Juices and Syrups. Pragomix had long been promoted without any demonstrations of its usage. Therefore, the number of sales had not initially matched the plan. It was only after it began to be promoted as a device that processed fruits and vegetables (most often in combination with milk), both in film and in cookery shows, that it started to sell more (see cover image of a recipe book for cooking with Pragomix). The blender was recommended for making fruit and vegetable purees as well as domestic fruit and vegetable juices. The improved marketing of Pragomix was,

Pragomix advertisement

however, accompanied by an increased demand for dairy products, fruits and vegetables – a turn appreciated by the national enterprise dairies, but not so much by the institutions responsible for the supply of fruit.

So, the promotion of Pragomix consequently heightened the need to promote not only juices, but also frozen or canned substitutes of fresh fruit. Generally speaking, however, advertising film-making applied the principle of not producing any films about scarce goods or goods which were subject to frequent change, considering the uncertain applicability of the shorts and their high costs. Furthermore, films were not allowed to connect advertising of several types of goods, since there was a fear that the consumer would not remember extensive messages, or alternatively that one type of good would suddenly become scarce while the other one would need further promotion.[42] Fresh fruit substitutes were therefore promoted in separate 'single-type' shorts *Ovocné nátierky* (*Fruit Spreads*, 1962) (promotion of marmalades and jams) and *Mražené ovoce a zelenina* (*Frozen Fruits and Vegetables*, 1960).

In contrast, the campaign Fruit Juices and Syrups (besides its connection to the problematic promotion campaign for consumption of vitamin C because of the Asian flu) served to complement a campaign to combat alcoholism, or a promotion of temperance, respectively. The drinking of fruit juices was also presented in the film *Non-alcoholic Beverages*, which simultaneously was an indirect warning against the risks of alcohol behind the wheel. In addition to film, the fight against alcoholism also used posters and leaflets. For this, there were two types of poster. The first type often had a bottle of juice as the central motif of the image, usually surrounded by stationery and the figure of a man. Posters of this type presented juice as a means of guaranteeing the refreshing of tired minds and supporting 'alcohol-free' creativity with the slogan 'Good ideas emerge only in a clear head'. The second type of poster focused on disciplined, safe driving, showing a glass of juice in the hands of drivers of cars, as well as tractors, combine harvesters and trucks. Here the slogan was, 'I wonder, if you can understand why they don't have accidents!'

A specific synergy that was not reflected in the film, however, was the connection of the action Fruit Juices and Syrups with the promotion of the cycling Peace Race/Závod míru (sometimes also called the Berlin–Prague–Warsaw race). Instead of drivers, in the photographic posters (which were placed mostly in shop windows with bottles of juice and soft drinks lined up around a decoration showing a glass full of various fruits), athletes, especially cyclists, were shown drinking juice. The fruity soda Pribinka was therefore known as the 'drink of athletes'.[43]

The promotion of food products was intended to be organised in accordance with health education, but it was also related to promoting awareness of traffic safety, or, in other cases, to the promotion of consumer goods used by housewives in the kitchen. The multi-level synergy of several branches strongly converged advertising with propaganda work, as through advertising the socialist promotion logic equalled promotion of goods and services with education. This formulated project of socialist advertising was driven by the idea that political power can claim a right to direct and control the behaviour of individuals at various levels of daily life, identifying this practice with noble goals of education. Within such a model, business operated as a mechanism of education, and advertising as a business tool became an educational tool. Through advertising the state claimed a monopoly on the determination of proper taste, but not simply because of economic profit. Whatever the state offered would actually have to be ideologically right to consume, since it was a product originating from the plan of production. The point was not to consume certain goods more and others less, but to consume goods prioritised by the state economy.

CONCLUSION

Advertising allowed the state to educate citizens and regulate their conduct – in the words of contemporary advertising ideologue Milan Weiner, 'to give them insight into the correct way of life'.[44] The example of Czechoslovakian film advertising in the late 1950s and early 60s, however, draws attention to the substantial discrepancy between theory and practice of socialist advertising. Although organisationally and ideologically fully wedged in the structures of economic planning, the production of advertising films did not always manage to avoid problematic economic impacts. The key reason for these difficulties was the lack of communication between the planning (ideological) and production (executive) component of the national economy. The problem of 'unrestrained consumption', as it was called in contemporary discourse, was its incompatibility with a planned economy. Consumer dissatisfaction, despite the promotional efforts, remained a persistent problem.

The practice of advertising film production at end of the 1950s was crucial for establishing key institutional and formal patterns for its future development. In many respects it prepared a typical template for the following years, even though many of its practices proved to be unsustainable. A long-term continuity can be seen at the organisational level: towards the end of the 1980s the socialist economy ensured advertisements in communication between the state (represented by the Ministry of Commerce and other entities), the State Advertising Company and other particular media agents. However, even in the 1960s, the calls for television advertising grew louder. Hence, the dominant manufacturer of audiovisual advertisements in Czechoslovakia after 1968 became Czechoslovak Television. Nevertheless, what transformed most intensely was the concept of educational aspects in an advertisement, together with the concept of complex joint campaigns. The strategy of joint campaigns was a significant tool of socialist advertising for a number of reasons. In the centralised socialist economy it not only allowed a synergy of different manufacturing (consumer) sectors, but also a link between economical and ideological objectives. Joint campaigns could promote two or more commodities together (food with electrical appliances, clothing with cars), as well as promote a commodity together with an event (ideological, cultural, sport, etc.). The consumption of goods and services thus ceased to be programmatically associated with civic educational concepts and crystallised into a distinctive and individualised social practice.

NOTES

1. Jana Kalinová, *Charakter a poslání propagace v socialistickém státě* [*The Nature and the Mission of Promotion in the Socialist State*] (Praha: Čs. obchodní komora, 1959), p. 8.

2. Karel Kouba, *Plán a trh za socialismu* [*The Plan and the Market under Socialism*] (Praha: Ekonomický ústav ČSAV, 1967), p. 40.

3. Quoted from a speech of František Krajčír, minister of internal trade at the International Conference of Advertising Companies. The speech was published in the magazine *Reklama* after the conference. František Krajčír, 'Úvodní projev Mezinárodní konference reklamních pracovníků' ['The Introductory Speech at an International Conference of Workers in Advertising'], *Reklama* vol. 4 no. 1 (1958), pp. 1–2.

4. Data calculated from figures in publications: Jiří Havelka, *Čs. filmové hospodářství 1945–1950* [*Czechoslovak Film Economy 1945–1950*] (Praha: Český filmový ústav, 1970). Jiří Havelka, *Čs. filmové hospodářství 1951–1955* [*Czechoslovak Film Economy 1951–1955*] (Praha: Český filmový ústav, 1972).

5. Miroslav Tuček, 'Měnová reforma 1953 a některé širší souvislosti' ['Currency Reform 1953 and a Broader Context'], *Revue politika* vol. 1 no. 6 (2003), pp. 24–6. Compare with Karel Kaplan, *Sociální souvislosti krizí komunistického režimu v letech 1953–1957 and 1968–1975* [*Social Connections of Crises during the Communist Regime*] (Praha: Ústav pro soudobé dějiny AVČR,1993).

6. Khrushchev's 'secret' speech at the XX Congress of the CPSU in 1956 raised a wave of concerns in the Eastern Bloc. The revelation of Stalin's crimes and repressions shocked the leadership of the Communist Party of Czechoslovakia. Unlike Poland or Hungary, Czechoslovakia had an incomparably better economic situation. Thus, the social discontent was not so closely linked to political discontent. Although the reaction in Czechoslovakia was rather passive and cautious, the events of 1956 meant the inevitable reassessment of existing political practices.

7. Miroslav Hiršl, *Rozsah a struktura společenské spotřeby obyvatelstva v ČSSR v letech 1945–1970* [*The Range and the Structure of Social Consumption of the Czechoslovakian Population 1945–1970*] (Praha: Výzkumný ústav sociálního zabezpečení, 1974).

8. Jaromír Balák, *Zásady propagace* [*Basics of Promotion*] (Praha: Vydavatelství obchodu, 1963), p. 10.

9. Josef Růžička, *Efektivnost československého obchodu* [*The Effectiveness of Czechoslovakian Trade*] (Praha: Státní úřad statistický, 1958), p. 5.

10. This institution (in full, Meziresortní koordinační výbor pro řízení propagační a reklamní činnosti v oboru výroby a prodeje spotřebního zboží a služeb [Inter-Ministerial Coordination Committee for the Management of Promotional and Advertising Activity in the Field of Production and Sales of Consumer Products and Services]) in 1961 became the assisting body of the State Plan Bureau which had engaged in this activity until then. Jaromír Balák, 'Z jednoho místa' ['From One Place'], *Propagace* vol. 7 no. 12 (1961), pp. 265–6. Balák, *Zásady propagace*, p. 14.

11. NA (National Archive), Praha, f. Ministerstvo informací (1945–1953) – Inventář, box 197, Organizace V. odboru (Materials of the Ministry of Information).

12. Ibid.

13. Josef Řeháček, 'Výroba a reklama potřetí' ['Production and Advertising for the Third Time'], *Reklama* vol. 4 no. 3 (1958), p. 69.

14. Krajčír, 'Úvodní projev Mezinárodní konference reklamních pracovníků', pp. 1–2.
15. Antonín Navrátil, 'Filmová reklama' ['Film Advertising'], *Kultura* vol. 2 no. 51 (1958), p. 3.
16. Ibid.
17. This is best demonstrated by the change of the magazine *Reklama* (*Advertising*) into *Propagace* (*Promotion*). The cover of the last, twelfth issue of the monthly *Reklama* from 1961 read 'magazine *Reklama/Propagace*'. From January 1962 the name was changed to *Propagace*, yet both the publisher Reklamní podnik (Advertising Company) and all editors remained the same.
18. Milan Weiner, 'Staré hranice' ['Old Borders'], *Propagace* vol. 8 no. 1 (1962), p. 17.
19. Kalinová, *Charakter a poslání propagace v socialistickém státě*, p. 29.
20. Bohuš Häckl, *Propagační prostředky. Jak je vytvářet, posuzovat a používat* [*Promotional Tools. How to Create, Evaluate and Use Them*] (Praha: Vydavatelství obchodu, 1962), p. 11.
21. Klement Guth, *Názorná propagace a agitace* [*Illustrative Promotion and Agitation*] (Praha: Státní zdravotnické nakladatelství, 1958), pp. 5–6.
22. Ibid., p. 11.
23. Jiří Havelka, *Čs. filmové hospodářství 1956–1960* (Praha: Čs. filmový ústav, 1974), p. 137.
24. Jiří Havelka, *Čs. filmové hospodářství 1961–1965* (Praha: Čs. filmový ústav, 1975), pp. 188–9.
25. See, for example *Umění nového života* (*Art of New Life*, 1954), *Třetí snížení cen* (*Third Price Cut*, 1954), *Poselství přátelství a míru* (*Message of Friendship and Peace*, 1955).
26. For example, *Pohřeb Marty Gottwaldové* (*Funeral of Marta Gottwaldová*, 1953).
27. Commentary of the deputy director of Short Film, R. Gráf, at a meeting of the section Propagace tiskem, televizí, rozhlasem a filmem (Print, Television, Radio and Film Promotion) at a national conference of promotional workers in Brno in 1963. Kolektiv, *Sborník celostátní konference propagačních pracovníků* [*An Anthology of the National Conference of Promotional Workers*] (Praha: Vydavatelství obchodu, 1964), p. 209.
28. The total volume of production of Propagfilm in those years was naturally much higher, but the rest of the films were predominantly instructional. The number of advertisements is taken from data available to the committee of the annual festival of advertising films and economic statistics. Pavol Bauma, *Ekonomika čs. státního filmu* [*Economics of Czechoslovak State Film*] (Bratislava: Slovenské vydavatelstvo technickej literatury, 1965), p. 92.
29. According to the produced films overview by Jiří Havelka: Havelka, *Čs. filmové hospodářství 1956–1960*, pp. 138–46. Havelka, *Čs. filmové hospodářství 1961–1965*, pp. 189–95.
30. Commentary of a worker of Ústřední správa nákupu (Central Purchasing Management), M. Weiner, at the meeting of the section Propagace tiskem, televizí, rozhlasem a filmem at a national conference of promotional workers in Brno in 1963. Kolektiv, *Sborník celostátní konference propagačních pracovníků*, p. 214.
31. The chair of the new committee was the minister of internal trade. Other members were representatives of ministries of Internal Trade, Food Industry, Consumer Industry, General Mechanical Engineering, Chemical Industry, Finance, Education and Culture, and Health Care; vice-chairmen of the Ústřední svaz spotřebních družstev (Central Union of Consumer Cooperatives) and Ústřední svaz výrobních družstev (Central Union of Production Cooperatives); and Deputy General Directors of Čs. rozhlas, Čs. televise and Krátký film (Czechoslovak Radio, Czechoslovak Television and Short Film).
32. Otto Jirák, 'VI. přehlídka reklamních filmů' ['6th Festival of Advertising Films'], *Reklama* vol. 7 no. 4 (1961), pp. 74–6.

33. Helena Bohunová, 'Výlohy s divadelními náměty v obchodním domě Perla v Praze' ['Shopping Windows with Theatre Motifs in Department Store Perla'], *Reklama* vol. 4 no. 3 (1958), pp. 90–1.

34. Karel Purkyrt from the Ministry of Food Industry in a Survey about the Exhibition of Advertising films in 1958. *Reklama* vol. 4 no. 4 (1958), p. 75.

35. Jaromír Balák, 'Reklama v socialistickém hospodářství' ['Advertising in the Socialist Economy'], *Reklama* vol. 1 no. 1 (1955), pp. 1–9.

36. Ibid.

37. Balák, *Zásady propagace*, p. 14.

38. Ibid., p. 57.

39. Ibid.

40. Miroslav Písařovič, 'Pomůcka pro reklamu v potravinářském obchodě' ['Advertising Tool for a Grocery'], *Reklama* vol. 4 no. 1 (1958), p. 8.

41. Kolektiv, *Sborník celostátní konference propagačních pracovníků*, p. 205.

42. Häckl, *Propagační prostředky*, pp. 80–1.

43. *Reklama* vol. 4 (1958).

44. Kolektiv, *Sborník celostátní konference propagačních pracovníků*, p. 198.

10

Advertising Form, Technological Change and Screen Practices in the USA

William Boddy

In 1939 RCA sponsored a ten-minute industrial film, entitled simply *Television*, to introduce the new medium to the American public. Most extant prints of the film include a ninety-second prologue situating the company's plans for television within its existing activities in radio, theatrical film and the growing market of 16mm non-theatrical exhibition. The exceedingly modest prologue nevertheless evokes a number of important issues regarding industry continuity, technological innovation, and medium specificity in advertising practices across twentieth-century electronic and visual media in the USA. RCA's reflexive prologue offers a more prosaic, if equally reflexive echo of Dziga Vertov's 1929 modernist classic *Man with a Movie Camera*, echoing Vertov's striking cut from the illusionistic cinematic image to the static physical film strip (here addressing the film's optically recorded soundtrack) and offering a more sedate rotating projector in the place of Vertov's pixilated dancing tripod. The brief prologue, promoting RCA's 16mm non-theatrical projection equipment, which was likely bringing these very images to viewers from the back of the classroom or meeting hall, takes pains to link the device and its manufacturer to the scale and prestige of large-scale theatrical film-making and exhibition (citing Radio City Music Hall, the world's largest public cinema, along with 6,000 other theatrical venues in the USA and abroad). At the same time, the film's narrator identifies RCA as 'the largest sound organisation in the world', and the company's very name signals its 1919 origins as a patent pool designed to dominate point-to-point wireless communication shortly before the unexpected application of broadcasting, the 'surprise party of radio', as a former RCA president described it in 1929.[1] The prologue's foregrounding of RCA's leadership in sound engineering also evokes the critically fraught expressive relations between sound and image in motion-picture history, an aesthetic controversy that would be restaged along the more instrumental grounds of advertising efficacy in the medium of television, itself the subject of the ten-minute promotional film which follows the prologue.

Commercial television's competing aesthetic debts to earlier visual and aural media, including the public billboard, radio and the theatrical and non-theatrical motion picture, formed the axis around which the essential nature and mission of the new domestic medium were debated. Perhaps surprisingly, such aesthetic disputes were as vigorously contested in the context of the television commercial as in the realm of dramatic programming. If the question of the new medium's formal debts to earlier advertising forms was raised by RCA's 1939 film, the formal strategies of its prologue invite speculation about the film's specific goals and intended audiences (Motion-picture exhibitors? Business leaders? Technophillic students? Home movie-makers?), especially from its concluding narration: 'Whenever you need any motion-picture sound, projection, or recording equipment, look to RCA, the largest sound organisation in the world.'

The 1939 film's invocation of the disparate non-theatrical uses of 16mm projectors in education, industry and the home underscores Thomas Elsaesser's reminder that 'there are many histories of the moving image, only some of which belong to the movies'.[2] Haidee Wasson estimates that, by the 1950s, portable 16mm projectors like those featured in RCA's film outnumbered theatrical cinema venues by a factor of 370:1, and a 1954 Association of National Advertisers monograph estimated that there was one 16mm projector for every 320 US residents. Wasson argues that such portable projectors provide a bridge between the pre-cinematic philosophical toys of the nineteenth century and the contemporary digital screens of tablets and mobile phones, suggesting an alternative historiographic genealogy for the moving image.[3]

Indeed, a chorus of contemporary scholars has urged expanding cinema's traditional research field to encompass various forms of non-theatrical film, part of a wider project of media archaeology, though there is less certainty about the critical methods best suited to these new objects of study. If traditional film history's teleological unfolding of film genres, movements and auteurs seems inappropriate to the expanded field, we might take up Thomas Elsaesser's suggestion to interrogate client, occasion, and target in the industrial film in exploring the narrower context of the advertising film. The question of which cultural forms are granted the status of fully authored works has historically agitated the advertising community, evidenced in its proclivity for award ceremonies and creative honours; it is also apparent in popular culture references such as fictitious director Marty DiBergi's (Rob Reiner) prideful boast about his dog food commercial in his on-camera introduction to the mock-doc *This Is Spinal Tap* (1984) or Don Draper's triumph as creative author of a 1950s Glo-Coat commercial on television's *Mad Men*. American media texts and producers have long been assigned cultural prestige according to their relative dependence upon commercial sponsorship, with novels and feature films at one extreme and broadcast programming and TV commercials themselves at the other.[4] Indeed, it is no accident that perhaps the most universally denigrated cultural form in mid-twentieth-century America, the female-centred day-time radio soap opera, was identified in its scornful label precisely by its too-intimate link to its sponsor, at a time when advertiser-supplied programmes dominated many other broadcast genres as well.

If contemporary film historians face the challenge of confronting a vast and obscure body of non-theatrical texts and reception contexts, I would argue that the study of these new film texts necessitates a corresponding expansion of the traditional sources for critical commentary and exegesis. In 1950s American television, for example, the one-off plays of live anthology drama series received disproportionate critical commentary in the quality press, and when such programming virtually disappeared by the end of the decade, one prominent New York-based critic confessed that 'after the first show, I don't know what to say about a western or quiz show, and I don't know anybody else who does either'.[5] Not surprisingly, American television's interstitial marginalia of commercials and network and station promos have received little sustained critical scrutiny at any point in TV history.

If the organs of official criticism were largely mute in the face of the ubiquitous TV commercial, there were other venues where their appropriate aesthetic forms were vigorously debated, including a variety of advertising and broadcast trade journals and practical handbooks for industry professionals. The typical critical writing in such industry venues was not shy about offering clear and highly prescriptive pronouncements about the ontological givens of a specific advertising medium, the constituent models of human perception and psychology and the rationale for the social and economic importance of advertising generally. Sensitive to advertising's oversize role in the US economy relative to other advanced nations and to its dominance of American broadcasting, many mid-century commentators in the USA offered variations of national exceptionalism in defending what was, by the end of the 1920s, already called 'the American system of broadcasting'. For example, veteran ad executive Leo Burnett wrote the introduction to Henry Wayne McMahan's 1957 *The Television Commercial: How to Create and Produce Effective TV Advertising*; in it he spoke of Burnett's hope that the book would lead 'maybe even to an improved commercial culture in this vital country of ours where selling things and services and ideas to each other is part and parcel of our accepted, respected and dynamic way of life'.[6] The status of advertising in the broadcast media was especially fraught, where spectrum scarcity and advertising intrusiveness (long seen as violating Victorian notions of the home as refuge from business concerns) provided a unique rationale for federal oversight, notably under President Franklin D. Roosevelt's reformist Federal Communications Commission. One emphatic industry defence came in a series of talks to the Dallas Advertising League by advertising executive Stanley Campbell, published in 1939 under the title *Because of These Things Advertising Pays*. The author, after warning of secret government broadcasting facilities hidden in Washington, DC, penthouses, exhorts his readers:

> The power of radio has been demonstrated. The power of the press is known to all of us. Both are in grave danger ... NOW ... not maybe ... not later ... not merely if things continue as they are ... but NOW. A danger which can ... and will, unless checked ... destroy the value of those media for advertising and as public safeguards. It is time we did some thinking and acting about our America while we struggle with our problems of advertising, because the two are definitely related.[7]

Historical periods of rapid technological change, like those marking the growth of radio broadcasting in the 1920s and television in the late 40s and early 50s, often bring heightened stakes and sharpened aesthetic distinctions between competing advertising media. Advertising's quick penetration of the new electronic media provoked resistance from amateur radio operators, the print press and members of the public in the early 1920s, and even a sympathetic TV advertising handbook in 1958 reported that a majority of 450 surveyed industry leaders believed that the television medium was over-commercialised.[8] Both periods were also marked by striking dystopian scenarios in popular fiction and film of media-linked interpersonal alienation and social coercion, anxieties that echoed longstanding associations of electronic media with the uncanny.[9] Much of the trade press writing addressing twentieth-century advertising practices is frankly defensive in tone, responding to public and elite objections that advertisers 'have gone about as far as they can go', popular complaints which, as Raymond Williams pointed out, go back to the late eighteenth century.[10]

Philosophical and aesthetic debates within the ad industry drew upon shifting models of human nature, advertising objectives and presumed hierarchies of human senses; business historian Merle Curti surveyed eighty years of the trade journal *Printers' Ink* and described an unsteady movement from more static, monolithic and rationalist notions of human nature to ones which privileged more dynamic, complex and non-rational processes. Simultaneous with the shifting and competing notions of mental life across the period, however, was a growing confidence among industry practitioners about the power of advertisers to discern and control mental activity and behaviour through advertising.[11]

Advertising industry debates over the aesthetic norms of film and television advertising often argued deductively from the putative formal qualities of the medium and its essential conditions of reception. Via such instrumental notions of media specificity, twentieth-century electronic advertising media were theorised in dialogue with a range of other advertising forms, including outdoor advertising, window displays, and store design. I have argued elsewhere for the common roots of both cinema and broadcasting in the nineteenth-century cultures of the scientific demonstration, world's fair and the so-called 'spectacular' displays of outdoor electrical advertising.[12] As many historians of early cinema have noted, the new medium grew up alongside the informing contexts of the railway journey, the assembly line and the glass and cast iron architecture of the department store, office skyscraper and urban shopping arcade. Elaborate rehearsals of technological spectacle staged within public urban space began in the pre-cinematic era and continue to be a staple of the promotion of new screen devices and services. The public career of Serbian inventor Nikola Tesla, with his own glowing and lightning bolt-emitting body, dazzled scientific and amateur audiences alike, including those at the Westinghouse pavilion he designed at the 1893 Chicago Columbia Exposition – a single venue that employed more electric light bulbs than any city in America at the time.[13] Tesla's Westinghouse exhibit in Chicago featured an 18-foot darkened public chamber situated between two massive high-frequency emitting plates, where visitors were invited to pick up and handle an assortment of free-standing glowing phosphorescent tubes which spelled out the names of electrical inventors and Serbian poets.[14]

Likewise, the career of Douglas Leigh, the Depression-era builder of spectacular Times Square billboards, suggests the phenomenological intersections of the electric billboard, the cinema, and television as advertising media. Arising, like early cinema, from the context of late nineteenth-century scientific expositions and world's fairs, outdoor advertising's so-called 'spectacular' display had its origins in the twenty-four-sheet billboards at the turn-of-the-century Paris and Chicago World's Fairs; by the end of the first decade of the twentieth century, the advertising 'spectacular' described large-scale animated incandescent and neon displays in central business districts. At a time when only 5 per cent of US homes had electricity, Broadway was already known as the Great White Way.[15] Douglas Leigh, the industry figure most associated with the twentieth-century outdoor advertising spectacular, was called the Boy Sign King of Broadway (in 1955 *The New Yorker* called Leigh 'the ageless boy wonder of electric spectaculars'), whose massive mid-century displays included a 25-foot tall steaming coffee cup, an animated detergent billboard with 3,000 blinking incandescent soap bubbles, a giant billboard Camel smoker continuously exhaling perfect 5-foot smoke rings for twenty-seven years (a display replicated in twenty-two other US cities), a 120 foot-wide Pepsi waterfall which circulated 50,000 gallons of water a minute (the sign featured 3,000 bulbs, 492 miles of wiring, consumed a million watts of electricity and burned out an average of 580 bulbs and sixty floodlights a month).[16] By 1937 Leigh had created twenty-five spectaculars between New York's Times Square and Columbus Circle, serviced by two full-time crews that cruised the neighbourhood's night-time streets continuously in search of malfunctions.[17] Leigh also designed spectaculars for the 1939 World's Fair for Bromo Seltzer, and served as one of the fifteen original directors of the 1964 World's Fair.[18] His many unrealised projects included painting the Rock of Gibraltar with the Prudential Insurance Company logo, erecting a crown on the top of the Empire State Building for RC Cola and towing decommissioned floating grain elevators with illuminated advertising messages in New York's East River.[19]

In 1937 Leigh bought rights to the EPOK display system, which projected 16mm film onto 4,104 photocells that controlled an equivalent number of made-to-order 6-watt light bulbs connected by 200,000 miles of wiring and 15,122 soldered joints in a 24 x 30-foot proto-digital display opposite the Astor Theatre in Times Square.[20] Leigh employed Felix the Cat animator Otto Messmer for thirty-seven years to design brief animations (the longest was seven minutes), sometimes employing clips from new Hollywood releases, to programme the display.[21] In addition to these brief out-of-home advertising movies, Leigh claimed to have produced the first animated TV commercial during the medium's semi-commercial launch in 1940.

Beginning in 1936 Leigh was the subject of several *New Yorker* 'Talk of the Town' pieces over the ensuing decades, profiles that combined enraptured tributes to the technological scale and engineering complexity with the condescending tone familiar to mid-twentieth-century elite attitudes towards television. E. J. Kahn's 1941 *New Yorker* profile suggested that 'Leigh thinks of his creations as works of art, which is probably the way postcard men feel about postcards,' reporting that:

> Leigh says he feels deeply moved whenever he glances at the girl's face hovering over a steaming coffee cup – one of his favorite motifs – in a spectacular he recently completed for Silex. The face has bright-red neon lips, under which the words 'Yum Yum' appear from time to time. 'Look at that mouth', Leigh says, with all the fervor of a Cezanne contemplating one of his apples.[22]

Leigh's post-war projects included airborne illuminated surplus World War II airships (involving several 360-foot dirigibles, each with 14,000–16,000 animated lights), elaborate lighting schemes for individual buildings (including the bicentennial designs for the Empire State Building in 1976) and lighting designs for entire city centres. In response to the threat of blackouts during World War II, Leigh also pioneered the networked or remotely controlled billboard, enabling all of his Times Square spectaculars to be shut down from his Rockefeller Center offices.[23]

If Douglas Leigh promised (or threatened) to turn the outdoor spectacular display into a new kind of public cinema, many early commentators on radio advertising worried about the relationship of the new audio advertising medium to established media of persuasion. Historian Merle Curti notes that, as early as 1898, a minority within the advertising community argued that consumers were especially susceptible to appeals to emotion and sentiment, particularly through the use of illustration; 'a picture appeals to all classes, races, and languages, irrespective of culture or intellect', a turn-of-the-century advertising executive wrote in *Printers' Ink*.[24] In his 1939 book, *Because of These Things Advertising Pays*, Stanley Campbell warned advertisers that because 87 per cent of mental impressions come through the eyes, radio advertising should strive to call attention to things that have been seen or can be seen.[25] Nearly two decades later an advertising textbook offered different, though equally precise calculations (quoting a psychologist) that 65 per cent of human knowledge is gained through the sense of sight, 25 per cent through sound and 10 per cent through taste, smell and touch.[26] Furthermore, the early radio industry's model of the distracted housewife as listener had implications for the design of broadcast programming. Commercial broadcasters were advised to keep programmes simple, since the attention of listeners in the home was likely to be divided; 'besides', one industry executive argued, 'the average woman listener is neither cosmopolitan nor sophisticated. Nor does she have much imagination.'[27] However, as another early radio advertising executive noted optimistically, 'literacy does not figure. Mental effort is reduced to that involved in the reception of the oral message.'[28] Informed by such assumptions about their imagined domestic audience, by the end of the 1920s, commercial radio broadcasters rarely designed programming to elicit or repay full attention. Instead, as the author of the monograph *Women and Radio Music* argued, radio, like furniture or wallpaper, 'creates an atmosphere'.[29]

Not surprisingly, with television's arrival, many in the advertising community were eager to see the new medium fulfil the promise of visual persuasion that remained out of radio's reach. Henry Wayne McMahan, in 1957, offered this syllogistic calculation adding the appeal of the billboard to the power of radio advertising and the moving picture:

> The sense of sight and the sense of sound have both long worked their independent ways to do effective selling. The billboard is effective. Radio is effective. It follows that television, with both sight and sound, should be more effective. Plus this fact: The sight is *sight-in-motion*.[30]

Drawing upon a typical mixture of appeals to psychological study, advertising practice and amateur anthropology, McMahan argued that: 'generally, the visual is more important because it is our most believing sense – and we are selling belief. And pictures are more emotional, probe deeper psychologically, than words. "Don't tell me, *show* me", say the Chinese.'[31]

For Clark M. Agnew and Neil O'Brien writing in 1958, such deductive claims for the primacy of the visual in the TV commercial were confirmed by the economic practices of the television networks, whose business policy was to refund sponsors 25 per cent of advertising fees in the case of the loss of an audio signal, but 75 per cent for the loss of the image; 'with this argument from finance rather than from academic research, we will leave this phase of the subject for the present', they confidently concluded.[32]

However, before the power of television advertising was indisputably established in the 1950s, the anticipated new perceptual demands of television worried many in the industry. In 1935, RCA Chairman David Sarnoff pointed out,

> Television reception is not like, cannot be like, sound reception. Today, radio is used as a background for other entertainment, or by the housewife who ... listens to the music, while she goes on with her work. Television can never be like that, because not only will it require close attention on the part of the onlooker, but it will also be necessary for the room to be somewhat darkened ... [L]isteners ... instead of roaming around as they do now while enjoying a programme, will have to sit tight and pay close attention to whatever is being thrown on their screen. But will they want to do this? ... I don't know.[33]

Veteran cultural critic Gilbert Seldes wrote of television in 1937: 'The thing moves, it requires complete attention. You cannot walk away from it, you cannot turn your back on it, and you cannot do anything else except listen while you are looking.'[34] Other commentators pointed to the relative failure of attempts by advertisers to reach motion-picture audiences through screen advertising; one 1942 book warned that 'the eye, trained by motion pictures, might not tolerate advertising on the screen'.[35] Philip Kerby, in his 1939 book, *The Victory of Television*, cautioned potential television advertisers that 'experience gained through radio will be of little avail ... In television, it is doubtful if the audience sitting in a semi-darkened room and giving its undivided attention to the screen will tolerate interruptions in the program.'[36]

To a degree, the industry anxiety about the perceptual demands of the new television medium reflected the legacies of the gendered split in the early 1920s radio set market as it moved from one largely consisting of electronic parts sold to male hobbyists to one consisting of AC-powered and loudspeaker-equipped receivers in fine cabinetry sold largely to women. Early efforts by TV-set manufacturers to address both the male electronics enthusiast and the non-technical-minded housewife and husband evoke some of the gendered micro-battles over installing the set in the domestic space. The central problem, according to one industry executive in 1945, was 'the degree to which housewives would drop their housework to watch television during the daytime'.[37]

Writing in 1958, Agnew and O'Brien reaffirmed the importance of the distinct reception demands of radio and television and argued that the lack of extensive industry experience in cinema advertising left both film producers and advertising agency personnel unprepared for what the authors foresaw as 'the avalanche of film commercials demanded by television'.[38] They argued (anticipating Thomas Elsaesser's concern with issues of client, occasion and target) that feature films and TV programmes, unlike commercials, are designed for entertainment,

> so, in some respects, production techniques applicable to them do not apply to television advertising. Since the purpose of advertising is to persuade or to induce action, it appears that, in its nature, television advertising is perhaps closer to educational motion pictures ... than to entertainment programs. The aim of visual aids in education is to impart information convincingly in such a way that it will be remembered as long as possible. The information and memory elements apply also to television advertising.[39]

For Agnew and O'Brien, the compelling analogue to the new art of the TV commercial was not the theatrical feature film, but the classroom educational film, although they admitted the distinct reception contexts of the TV commercial versus the educational film, where films 'are considered a treat, a diversion from usual classroom methods ... it is safe to say that initial reception of an educational film is almost always more favorable than of a television commercial'.[40]

A final link between early TV advertising writing and contemporary industry practices concerns product placement and the digital insertion of virtual logos, advertising copy and branded products in the electronic image. Agnew and O'Brien, like many other industry observers by the late 1950s, lamented the tendency of television viewers to use commercial breaks as an opportunity to withdraw their attention from the television screen, which, they argued, induced advertisers to respond by devising audio-driven commercials to capture a distracted audience, a tactic that reflected 'a somewhat defeatist attitude', in their view.[41] A better strategy, they argued, might be to integrate commercials into the programme, 'weav[ing] them into the fabric of the show so there is no clear dividing line between commercial and noncommercial content'.[42] However, at the moment that Agnew and O'Brien were advocating the integration of advertising into programme content, a common practice in early 1950s US television, American primetime television was undergoing a permanent shift away from single sponsorship towards participating sponsorship formats, fuelled by growing network control over programme licensing and scheduling and shifts in the composition and strategies of television advertisers.

It was only after decades of accelerating erosion of the power of the traditional TV commercial at the hands of the accumulated assaults of the remote control, multi-channel cable channel surfing, VCR time-shifting and the digital video recorder that new countermeasures in the form of virtual advertising and virtual product placement arose in the late 1990s.[43]

This highly selective survey of twentieth-century advertising discourses in the USA underscores advertising's historically variable, national- and medium-specific and culturally contested relationship to American communications media, old and new. As the overall US advertising sector steadily grew as a proportion of overall economic activity over the past century, complaints from advertising executives about recalcitrant consumers, sometimes couched in gentler language about the perennial 'increasingly sophisticated viewer', have inspired ever-increasing efforts to insert advertising messages into new venues and activities of everyday life. Scholars of the moving image must continue to address the relentless efforts of advertisers and media firms to pursue consumers onto new screen platforms and settings. Haidee Wasson and Charles Acland point out that, while the current proliferation of digital screens challenge traditional film history's near-exclusive focus on theatrical film-making, cinema has historically always exceeded the theatrical context. In the current media environment of proliferating screens, platforms and economic models, it is imperative for film and media scholars to move beyond the monolithic models of cinema and television as technological apparatuses and cultural forms. Coming to terms with the diversity and instability of screen culture requires sustained attention to the heretofore marginal critical and production practices excluded from traditional histories of cinema.[44]

NOTES

1. J. G. Harbord, 'Commercial Uses of Radio', *Annals of the American Academy of Political and Social Science* no. 142 (March 1929), p. 57.

2. Thomas Elsaesser, 'Archive and Archaelogies: The Place of Non-Fiction Film in Contemporary Media', in Vinzenz Hediger and Patrick Vonderau (eds), *Films that Work: Industrial Films and the Productivity of Media* (Amsterdam: University of Amsterdam Press, 2009), p. 19.

3. Haidee Wasson, 'Suitcase Cinema', *Cinema Journal* vol. 51 no. 2 (Winter 2012), p. 152.

4. This traditional opposition has recently been explored and contested in Lynn Spigel, *TV by Design: Modern Art and the Rise of Network Television* (Chicago and London: University of Chicago Press, 2009); see especially Chapter 6, 'One Minute Movies: Art Cinema, Youth Culture, and TV Commercials in the 1960s'.

5. John Crosby, *New York Herald-Tribune*, 6 July 1958; cited in Frank Henry Jakes, 'A Study of Standards Imposed by Four Leading Television Critics With Respect to Live Television Drama' (PhD dissertation, Ohio State University, 1960), p. 72.

6. Harry Wayne McMahan, *The Television Commercial: How to Create and Produce Effective TV Advertising*, revised edition (New York: Hastings House, 1957), p. 7.

7. Stanley Campbell, *Because of These Things Advertising Pays* (Dallas: Jagger-Chiles-Stovall, 1939), p. 35. Ellipses and emphasis in original.

8. Clark M. Agnew and Neil O'Brien, *Television Advertising* (New York: McGraw-Hill, 1958), p. 17.

9. Jeffrey Sconce, *Haunted Media: Electronic Presence from Telegraphy to Television* (Durham, NC: Duke University Press, 2000); Charles R. Acland, *Fast Viewing: The Popular Life of Subliminal Influence* (Durham, NC: Duke University Press, 2011).

10. Raymond Williams, 'Advertising: The Magic System', in Williams, *Problems in Materialism and Culture* (London: Verso, 1980), p. 172.

11. Merle Curti, 'The Changing Concept of Human Nature in the Literature of American Advertising', *The Business History Review* vol. 41 no. 4 (Winter 1967), pp. 335–57.

12. William Boddy, 'Early Cinema and Radio Technology in Turn of the Century Popular Imagination', in André Gaudreault, Catherine Russell and Pierre Véronneau (eds), *The Cinema: A New Technology for the Twentieth Century* (Lausanne: Payot, 2004), pp. 285–94.

13. David E. Nye, *Electrifying America: Social Meanings of a New Technology, 1880–1940* (Cambridge, MA: MIT Press, 1990), p. 149.

14. 'Mr Tesla's Personal Exhibit at the World's Fair', in Thomas Commerford Martin (ed.), *The Inventions, Researches and Writings of Nikola Tesla*, 2nd edition (New York: Barnes and Noble, 1992 [1893]), n.p.; see also Nye, *Electrifying America*, pp. 382–3, and Carolyn Marvin, *When Old Technologies Were New: Thinking About Electric Communication in the Late Nineteenth Century* (New York: Oxford University Press, 1988), p. 48.

15. Nye, *Electrifying America*, p. 383.

16. 'Cooling and Light', *The New Yorker*, 16 July 1955, p. 16.

17. 'Spectacular Service', *The New Yorker*, 18 April 1936, p. 15.

18. 'Additional Projects by Douglas Leigh' clipping file, Douglas Leigh Papers, Archives of American Art, Smithsonian Institution, Reel 5843.

19. Ibid.

20. 'Leigh's Biggest', *The New Yorker*, 7 August 1937, p. 10.

21. Robert Sellmer, 'Douglas Leigh: The Man Whose Gadgets Lighted up Broadway now Turns to Main Street', *Life*, 1 April 1946, pp. 47–51; also see John Canemaker, 'The Electric Felix Man', *AnimationWorld Magazine* vol. 1 no. 8 (December 1996), http://www.awn.com/mag/issue1.8/articles/canemaker1.8.html

22. E. J. Kahn, 'Lights, Lights, Lights', *The New Yorker*, 7 June 1941, pp. 24–5.

23. 'Aglow', *The New Yorker*, 19 May 1945, p. 20.

24. J. H. Phinney, 'A "Cut" Argument', *Printers' Ink* XXIII (15 June 1898), p. 3; quoted in Curti, 'The Changing Concept of Human Nature', p. 342.

25. Campbell, *Because of These Things Advertising Pays*, p. 33.

26. Agnew and O'Brien, *Television Advertising*, p. 6.

27. Mary Loomis Cook, 'Programs for Women', in Neville O'Neill (ed.), *The Advertising Agency Looks at Radio* (New York: D. Appleton, 1932), p. 136.

28. Frank Presbrey, *The History and Development of Advertising* (New York: Doubleday, 1929), p. 581.

29. Peter W. Dykema, *Women and Radio Music* (New York: Radio Institute for the Audible Art, n.d. [1928?]), n.p.

30. McMahan, *The Television Commercial*, p. 17.

31. Ibid., p. 19.

32. Ibid.; Agnew and O'Brien, *Television Advertising*, p. 7.

33. Owen P. White, 'What's Delaying Television?', *Colliers*, 30 November 1935, p. 11.

34. Gilbert Seldes, 'The "Errors" of Television', *Atlantic*, May 1937, p. 535.

35. Orrin E. Dunlap, Jr, *The Future of Television* (New York: Harper and Brothers, 1942), p. 12.

36. Philip Kerby, *The Victory of Television* (New York: Harper and Brothers, 1939), p. 84.

37. Lyndon O. Brown, 'What the Public Expects of Television', in John Gray Peatman (ed.), *Radio and Business 1945: Proceedings of the First Annual Conference on Radio and Business* (New York: City College of New York, 1945), pp. 139, 137.

38. Agnew and O'Brien, *Television Advertising*, p. 1.

39. Ibid., p. 12.

40. Ibid. While the advertising industry was debating the issues of formal specificity and reception conditions in the new TV medium, similar issues were being evaluated in the non-theatrical advertising film. See the mid-1950s survey of the industrial film in a monograph of the Film Steering Committee of the Association of National Advertisers, *The Dollars and Sense of Business Films: A Study of 157 Business Films* (New York: Association of National Advertisers, 1954).

41. Agnew and O'Brien, *Television Advertising*, p. 5.

42. Ibid.

43. See chapter 8, 'Marketers Strike Back: Virtual Advertising', in William Boddy, *New Media and Popular Imagination: Launching Radio, Television, and Digital Media in the United States* (Oxford: Oxford University Press, 2004).

44. Charles R. Acland and Haidee Wasson (eds), *Useful Cinema* (Durham, NC, and London: Duke University Press, 2011), p. 2.; Haidee Wasson, 'Introduction: In Focus: Screen Technologies', *Cinema Journal* vol. 51 no. 2 (Winter 2012), p. 142.

11

The Best Thing on TV: 1960s US Television Commercials

Cynthia B. Meyers

The 1960s was a transitional decade for American commercial television and the advertising industry that sustained it. The television industry completed its shift from the radio-era business model of single sponsorship, in which advertisers financed and controlled programming, to the network-era model, in which advertisers purchased interstitial minutes for commercials and ceded programme control almost entirely to networks. At the beginning of the 1960s, advertising executives were worrying about a crisis of creativity and consumer cynicism.[1] By the end of the 1960s, the advertising industry's 'Creative Revolution' had permanently replaced the rational and product-centred hard sell with the emotional and user-centred soft sell. In late 1960s 'hip' advertising, 'the idea became mightier than the marketing'.[2] The advertising industry was reorganised to accommodate this change. Whereas, before the 1960s, account executives often directed copywriters' work and controlled the agency's relationship with advertisers, and copywriting was often shaped by quantitative research, by the end of the 1960s, a 'creative department', staffed by pairs of copywriters and art directors, conceived ideas independently and played a strong role selecting them. Advertising became an intuitive process of finding images and ideas that would resonate with audiences and disarm their resistance.

Consequently, late 1960s 'hip' television commercials differ strikingly from the demonstrations of product attributes that prevailed earlier in the decade. By the 1970s one observer, Jonathan Price, claimed commercials were 'the best thing on TV':

> Financially, commercials represent the pinnacle of our popular culture's artistic expression. More money per second goes into their making, more cash flows from their impact, more business thinking goes into each word than in any movie, opera, stage play, painting, or videotape.[3]

Commercials, as measured by production budgets, were the most elaborately and expensively produced artefacts of mid-century American culture. If not 'art', they had attained a kind of cultural legitimacy unimaginable a decade before.

To contextualise the changing strategies and aesthetics of American television commercials during the 1960s, I begin with an overview of industrial shifts, first in the broadcasting industry and then in the advertising industry. Then I review the debates over the shifting commercial strategies of the period. What, in retrospect, appears to be a clear demarcation between the early and late 1960s is actually, on closer examination, a conflicted evolution of business models, advertising strategies, and aesthetic values. While the outcome – the dominance of the television network business model and the prominence of hip advertising – seems obvious in retrospect, it was not so obvious at the time.

CHANGING RELATIONS AMONG BROADCAST NETWORKS, ADVERTISERS, AND ADVERTISING AGENCIES

During the 1930s and 40s the national radio broadcast networks NBC and CBS simply rented a block of airtime to an advertiser, which then produced and paid for the programming. Each advertiser, whether a manufacturer of cars or coffee or soap, hoped that audiences would be inspired by this 'free' entertainment to feel 'gratitude' and 'good will', and so buy its products.[4] To help ensure this result, advertisers hired advertising agencies to oversee the entertainment as well as the advertising. With the aim of achieving 'sponsor identification', of associating a brand with a star or a programme, advertising agencies produced most national radio entertainment programmes.[5] As broadcast advertising, 'single sponsorship' had several drawbacks.[6] The advertiser could reach audiences only on its own programme. Moreover, in closely integrating a product with a programme, the advertiser made the product's reputation vulnerable to any flaw in the reputation of the programme or its star. Meanwhile, mass culture critics and consumer advocates attacked single sponsorship as promoting blandness, censorship, and blacklisting.[7]

Because of these problems, some in the advertising industry proposed broadcasters institute a 'magazine plan' of advertising: the networks, like magazine editors, might select the programming and then sell interstitial airtime to advertisers.[8] Advertisers would then be able to reach various audiences at various times; they might avoid dangerously close association with one programme or star; and networks could shape the broadcast schedule to serve audiences overall rather than the narrow interests of separate advertisers. Others opposed this plan on the grounds that broadcast advertising depended on a tight association between a programme and the sponsor. The advent of television, however, forced the issue: the exponentially higher production costs made single-programme sponsorship financially unfeasible for many advertisers.[9]

Throughout much of the 1950s, networks moved aggressively to seize programme control.[10] Programme packagers and Hollywood studios replaced advertising agencies as programme suppliers.[11] To spread costs, networks began selling 'participating' sponsorship, in which more than one advertiser sponsored the programme, and 'alternating' sponsorship, in which two advertisers alternated episodes. The number of single-sponsored programmes on prime time dropped from seventy-five in 1955 to forty in 1959, and to twelve in 1964.[12] The percentage of network programmes sold as 'participating' or 'co-sponsored' increased from about 11 per cent in 1953 to 84 per cent in 1963.[13]

Network control was supposed to improve the quality of television programming because, presumably, programme decisions would be determined by audience demand rather than advertisers' tastes. To measure such demand, networks used ratings, such as Nielsen's audience sample, and they quickly cancelled programmes not meeting ratings expectations, even if those programmes had sponsors willing to pay. Lee Rich, an executive at the agency Benton & Bowles (B&B), noted that 'what bothers tv advertisers so much today is that, while making substantial investments in tv, very few of them are controlling their own destinies. It's all in the hands of the networks.'[14] The networks' separation of programming from advertising 'may be the worst thing that ever happened to tv', according to one ad executive, because the networks favoured programmes with mass audiences, as measured by ratings companies, that would cater to the lowest tastes.[15]

The magazine plan was blamed for creating more 'clutter' and interruptions. During the radio era, commercials were often textually integrated into the programme, sometimes featuring cast members, and usually only one product brand was advertised per programme.[16] On television, the magazine plan featured separate advertisements adjacent to programme content; networks, rather than advertisers or their agencies, selected the position of the commercial within the programme. Advertisers, having abdicated control of programmes, focused on commercials, little caring how they affected programmes.[17] 'Participating' sponsors began to insert two thirty-second commercials for two different products in their sixty-second slots. They defended these 'piggybacks', heavily used by packaged-goods companies advertising multiple brands, as a rational, economic, and efficient use of airtime.[18] Thus, the amount of *airtime* devoted to advertising did not increase but the *number of commercials* did.[19]

Advertisers' goal for television advertising gradually shifted: rather than an 'identification' medium, in which audiences make a close association between programme and advertiser, television would be a 'dispersion' medium, in which advertisers try to reach as many homes as possible, their advertising 'scattered' across multiple programmes.[20] Commercials, dispersed among many time slots and programmes, could spread the message with 'volume' instead of 'intensity', or, as one observer put it, advertisers changed their targeting of consumers from a 'William Tell' to a 'Machine Gun Kelly' approach.[21]

At length, as the magazine plan became more settled, the advertising industry reached widespread agreement about its advantages. Television, according to a BBDO executive, had become more efficient at reaching large audiences and more flexible for advertisers, who were not only freed from season-long time buys, but also 'unburdened of program-development risks'.[22] Agencies soon realised the many advantages of ceding programme control: they could blame the network or producer or star if a programme failed; they could claim better objectivity in advising their clients since they were no longer financially and emotionally invested in any particular programme; and they no longer had to risk their own profit margins on programming success.[23]

Thus, during the 1960s, advertisers and their agencies almost completely abandoned a once strongly held belief about broadcast advertising. In the early 60s, according to advertising executive Fairfax Cone, 'Sponsor identification was still an important measurement of value, and this held down interest in commercials.' To sponsors, the programmes were more important than the advertising, so 'little thought' was put into commercials.[24] However, by 1969, Cone notes that the situation had reversed: 'Now the commercial became important, and new attention was paid to each one. ... Commercials that might appear anywhere there was a time spot for sale had to stand on their own.'[25] Rather than focus on developing programmes with which to associate their brands, advertisers began focusing instead on creating commercials that would keep audiences attentive.

THE CREATIVE REVOLUTION IN THE ADVERTISING INDUSTRY

While the broadcasting industry was completing its transition away from sponsorship, the advertising industry was itself undergoing a significant change. Ad-makers have tended to identify themselves with one of two schools of thought: the hard sell or the soft sell.[26] On the one hand, early theorists of hard-sell advertising, such as Claude Hopkins and Albert Lasker, conceive it as 'salesmanship in print'.[27] Their ads supply product information and multiple 'reasons why' to buy it. Often they lack faith in their audience's attention or intelligence, and so will describe the product repetitiously, as in the 1952 Ford advertisement that centres on the product: 'Any way you measure, it's America's ablest car!' The product-centred strategy is evident in the descriptions of the automobile's mileage, design, efficiency, engine power, and cost. Proponents of the soft sell, on the other hand, following such rival theorists as Theodore MacManus, appeal to the consumers' emotional needs.[28] They juxtapose a soap with an illustration of a woman embraced by her husband, implying that the soap creates the 'skin you love to touch'. They attract the consumer with clever concepts, puns, humour, and visually arresting imagery.

During the 1950s, the hard sell reigned and agencies attempted to develop advertising as a set of codified techniques, analysed and confirmed by scientific methods.[29] Social scientists such as Daniel Starch and Ernest Dichter dominated advertising 'research' into consumer behaviour and attitudes, and they were sometimes accused of attempting to manipulate consumers in new devious ways.[30] Meanwhile, account executives, stereotyped and parodied in Hollywood movies as

'It's America's Ablest Car!' (1952)

Films That Sell

martini-swilling grey-suited men, tyrannised over the 'creative department' where the advertisements actually got made.[31] They instructed copywriters on the proper copy 'slant'; then gave the copy to art directors to design appropriate visuals; and then chose what to bring to clients for approval.[32] In this traditional system, copywriters, also called 'creatives', were 'cautioned against' being too creative, as copywriter (and then-CEO of BBDO) Charles Brower recalled: 'I remember clients and older men telling me many times that if I were ever pleased with an idea ... I had better start over.'[33] Advertisers suspected the 'creatives' of being more concerned with the aesthetics than the selling power of their advertisements.[34] Copywriters were encouraged to think of their work as a craft practised anonymously in teams and within accepted conventions. As one advertising textbook recommended, 'Like a tennis player, [the copywriter] must ... put the ball inside the court lines; but he may choose his own strokes, he may hit hard or softly, he may play near the net or back court.'[35]

Yet many in the advertising industry worried there was a creativity 'problem' and that dull, repetitive, predictable, hard-sell advertising, along with indistinguishable parity products (such as soaps), were alienating consumers.[36] Hard-sell copy often employed half-truths, implying that a brand provided an exclusive benefit that in actuality all brands provided. One of the top copywriters of the 1950s, Rosser Reeves, an acolyte of Claude Hopkins, boasted thus of his 'Unique Selling Proposition' technique: '[We] gave [Colgate] "cleans your breath while it cleans your teeth". Now, every dentifrice cleans your breath while it cleans your teeth – *but nobody had ever put a breath claim on a toothpaste before.*'[37] If it were true that Colgate could clean breath, it was also true that every other toothpaste brand could clean breath. Since no other brand had made this claim, Reeves argued it was a 'unique selling proposition'. Advertising critics pounced on such sleight-of-hand product claims as evidence of advertising's lack of credibility.

In the late 1950s, the agency Doyle Dane Bernbach (DDB) designed an ad campaign since mythologised as the launch pad for the Creative Revolution.[38] In one print ad, a black-and-white photograph of a Volkswagen Beetle the size of a coin appeared on a page of mostly white space, with the headline 'Think Small'. The ad copy noted the advantages of 'small' insurance and 'small' repair bills and of being able to squeeze into 'small' parking spaces, implicitly mocking the excessive blustering of hard-sell claims of 'bigger, better'.[39] In another ad headlined 'Lemon' and featuring a photo of a normal-looking VW, the copy explains that an inspector noted a 'chrome strip' is 'blemished' and must be replaced; 'Chances are you wouldn't have noticed it. Inspector Kurt Kroner did.' Concluding that 'we pluck the lemons, you get the plums', the ad turns an apparent admission of imperfection into a claim for perfection. Designed to counter consumer cynicism with honesty, understatement, and tongue-in-cheek humour, DDB's Volkswagen campaign was hailed as an 'artistic innovation' on par with 'pop art or the frug'.[40]

Bill Bernbach, the creative leader of DDB, sought to elevate the status of 'creatives' in advertising and ease advertisers' suspicions: 'It is ironic that the very thing that is most suspected by business, that intangible thing called artistry, turns out to be the most practical tool available to it.'[41] Bernbach put the copywriters and art directors together in teams, instructing them to collaborate on an ad's conceptual, textual, and visual elements. Former DDB art director George Lois claimed that Bernbach 'revolutionized the creative process in advertising by encouraging his artists and writers to work together without

'VW: Think small' (1959)

Think small.

account men jamming fortune cookie copy into the blend'.[42] The creatives at DDB rose in status above the account executives. Although Lois claimed Bernbach 'treated advertising as an art',[43] Bernbach believed advertising to be a craft in the service of a specific goal: 'Properly practised creativity *must* result in greater sales more economically achieved.'[44] Bernbach's emphasis on the creative idea ignited a wave of new advertising that, according to Thomas Frank, 'pandered to public distrust of advertising and dislike of admen' through a new style of 'hip' advertisements.[45] Frank describes hip advertising as using minimalist graphics (with sans serif fonts and lots of 'white space'), flippant language about products that mocks consumer culture, and references to escape, defiance, rebellion, or nonconformity. Sampling print magazines, Frank finds that this DDB-influenced style became predominant in print ads by about 1965.[46]

The rise of hip advertising pre-dated the explosion of the counterculture, but the counterculture soon influenced agencies, particularly the creative departments.[47] By 1967, the style of youth culture had taken hold in agency creative departments anxious to demonstrate their connection to the zeitgeist: 'Agency Swingers Flourish Their Mini-Skirts', boasts a headline in the venerable trade magazine *Printers' Ink*.[48] Agency head Jerry Della Femina noted that agencies often gave clients tours to show off their eccentric creatives: 'It's like an arms race. ... Our nuts are nuttier than anyone else's. We have more madmen per square inch than any other agency. Therefore we are creative.'[49] The countercultural creative abjured market research and social science behaviourism, blaming them for the crisis in advertising creativity.[50] Seeking a more authentic and honest form of advertising, they experimented with humanistic psychologies, such as encounter groups and self-actualisation, and drugs such as hallucinogens and marijuana.[51] Some, such as the 'ad-man head', claimed that using marijuana qualified him to 'talk to the youth market'.[52]

DDB creatives spun off to found their own agencies. Lois boasted that these agencies

Films That Sell

were 'a hundred creative nonconformists with common roots and a separate language from the oily mainstream of American advertising'.[53] Agencies, such as Papert Koenig Lois, Jack Tinker & Partners, and Wells Rich Greene, became known as 'boutique' creative agencies because they did not supply a traditional agency's full range of services. Instead, through word play, humour, appeals to consumers' self-image, and direct critiques of the conventional, they aimed to disarm consumers' practised defences to advertising long enough to deliver the advertising message. Copywriter Mary Wells Lawrence's Braniff airlines print campaign features images of flight attendants changing uniforms mid-flight under the headline, 'Introducing the Air Strip'.[54] Art director George Lois's Maypo hot cereal ad features strong male athletes crying like spoiled children, 'I want my Maypo! I want it!'[55] DDB's ad for the whiskey Chivas Regal, under the provocative headline, 'Does Chivas Regal embarrass you?' continues:

> If it does, it's all our fault. ... It's possible we left you with the notion that you have to be a special kind of person to be at home with it ... You're that kind of person. You want nothing but the best.[56]

The ad copy cleverly shifts from what appears to be frank honesty to shameless flattery. Like most such ads, it is about the consumer, not the product.

Traditional agencies fought back. An executive at Ogilvy & Mather criticised this 'cult of meaningless advertising called Creativity' as having 'practically nothing to do with consumers'.[57] BBDO CEO Tom Dillon complained, in a speech titled, 'The Triumph of Creativity over Communication', that 'creativity' is a 'Humpty Dumpty word', in other words, meaningless: 'Humpty Dumpty ... is the egg who stated that the meaning of a word was whatever he intended it to be – no more nor less.'[58] In 1968 Dillon criticised hip advertising: 'Advertising which has had dramatic form but no content has not proven itself in the marketplace. The problem is an age-old one – it is easy enough to make advertising exciting if you don't say anything.'[59] Arguing that the Creative Revolutionaries misunderstood the aim of advertising, hard-sell proponent Rosser Reeves insisted that 'the agency must make the *product* interesting, and not just the advertisement itself'.[60] And Fairfax Cone, concerned that 'advertisers are going headlong down a primrose path' towards arty advertising that is not 'intelligible insofar as advertising is concerned', insisted that 'Advertising is a business ... it is not an art.'[61]

Thomas Frank argues that the rise of hip advertising and the Creative Revolution was not just a response to the youth market or the rise of market segmentation; neither was it an effort to destroy or reject consumer culture. The business world, he argues, shared the counterculture's critiques of mass culture as a system of conformity and therefore welcomed the changes brought by the counterculture as a way to 'revitalize American business and the consumer order generally'.[62] Hip advertising and the Creative Revolution thus solved the crisis of creativity and rejuvenated the ad industry when consumer cynicism, increased regulation, and saturated markets had threatened it. The rise of the countercultural creatives and the proliferation of advertising awards for 'creativity' also helped legitimate advertising as a cultural form.[63] Rather than technicians or craftsmen, many advertising creatives viewed themselves as artists.[64] Some would compare themselves to Michelangelo working for his 'client', the Pope, a romantic ideal of patron and artist.[65]

CHANGING TELEVISION COMMERCIAL STRATEGIES

These changes in both the television and advertising industries had a strong impact on how commercials were conceived and produced. In the early 1960s, advertising agencies were still relying on traditional, hard-selling techniques long established in radio and print. Sponsorship and the integration of programme and stars into advertising were still common until the mid-1960s. Continuing their work in radio and live television, many advertising agencies still oversaw the production of television programmes for their clients. B&B oversaw *Ben Casey*, *Gunsmoke*, and the Danny Thomas, Andy Griffith, and Dick van Dyke programmes.[66] BBDO oversaw sponsored programmes for clients Du Pont, Armstrong Cork, Pepsi, Liberty Mutual and US Steel – many of whom had been active corporate-image sponsors on radio.[67] Young & Rubicam (Y&R) became executive producer for Procter & Gamble's soap opera *Another World* and Gulf Oil's sponsored news specials.[68]

Many advertisers assumed that television's great advantage over radio or print was its ability to demonstrate products, so initially they conceived commercials as a form of 'show and tell', most famously in live demonstrations of Westinghouse appliances.[69] As in radio, announcers, either on screen or in voiceover, would instruct and explain the product. In a 1962 BBDO commercial for Dristan, a cold medicine, over close-ups of a woman suffering from congestion, an announcer describes cold symptoms before explaining, 'What you need is Dristan ... Today's Dristan has this exact formula with the one decongestant most prescribed by doctors to swiftly help ... restore you to free breathing.' Graphic triangle shapes point to the location of the woman's sinuses, before the announcer concludes, 'Don't let cold symptoms hang on and hurt. ... Get Dristan. Today's Dristan works where it hurts.'[70] The commercial makes its point in

'Dristan: Say When' (1962)

Joy dishwasing liquid (no date)

the copy rather than in the visuals, which were added afterward to illustrate the words. Industrial film producers, specialists in instructional film-making for corporate clients, often shot such commercials, which 'sounded like a print ad being read aloud'.[71]

Early 1960s commercials also often used traditional hard-sell strategies such as presenting the product as the solution to a problem, like dirty laundry or bad breath. In a 1963 Y&R commercial for Excedrin pain reliever, a housewife is 'overheard' on a 'hidden camera' describing her headaches, which she learns can be eliminated by using Excedrin.[72] Either an announcer would then instruct audiences in these solutions or the housewife herself would encounter them in 'slice of life' scenes about making better coffee or washing whiter laundry. Folger's coffee, for example, ran a series of commercials featuring 'Mrs Olson', a motherly expert in coffee preparation, whose advice to housewives would placate unhappy husbands and resolve marital tensions.[73] The 'slice of life' was occasionally enlivened by the fantastic, as when a white knight, representing Ajax laundry detergent, rides a horse down a suburban street to zap laundry whiter with his lance,[74] or when a housewife encounters miniature versions of herself on supermarket shelves explaining the advantages of Joy dishwashing liquid.[75]

Another hard-sell advertising approach popular in early 1960s commercials was the testimonial by either a typical member of the targeted audience or a well-known 'personality' admired by that audience. For example, in a 1962 Y&R commercial for Cheer laundry detergent, an actress playing a housewife testifies to Cheer's superiority: when asked to choose between two piles of laundered towels, she settles on the 'Whiter, a lot brighter' pile, concluding, 'I'll have to try Cheer'.[76] The talk show 'personalities' Arthur Godfrey, Art Linkletter, and Garry Moore endorsed products during their talk shows. A BBDO executive explained that such a personality 'has 1,000 – perhaps 1,000,000 – times more contact with the consumer than … any individual salesman' and so had an outsize impact on brand image.[77] Advertisers believed that the effectiveness of the personality endorsement was predicated on audiences believing that he or she actually used the product.[78] Media personalities, then, could only endorse products they could reasonably be assumed to use and had to avoid publicly using competing brands. Godfrey, whose improvised kidding of products was quite popular with audiences, screened the products of potential sponsors and rejected any he did not like; publicising this likely helped maintain a perception of his integrity.[79]

Stars and celebrities endorsed products in commercials.[80] BBDO had its own casting department, run by Nan Marquand, in which both 'name' and 'no name' talent were booked for BBDO commercials. BBDO hired Jim Backus for General Electric, Fred Gwynne for Armstrong Cork, Celeste Holm for US Steel, and Hermione Gingold for Philco.[81] Film stars Claudette Colbert, Edward G. Robinson, and Barbara Stanwyck were paid up to $100,000 to appear in Maxwell House coffee commercials.[82] Marquand explained that stars who once avoided such appearances were now attracted by 'more sophisticated' commercials and high pay, which helped replace income lost from the decline of live television.[83] Stars had to consider the problem of overexposure and credibility; some actors insisted that too strong an association with an advertiser would prevent their working for other advertisers and preclude acting opportunities.[84]

Some advertisers believed that cast commercials, in which actors appeared in character, would help reduce audience annoyance at commercial interruption. This strategy had been used on 1930s radio when *Show Boat* cast members sipped Maxwell House coffee during 'intermissions' and on 1950s television when Molly Goldberg chatted confidentially about Sanka decaffeinated coffee during *The Goldbergs*.[85] In the early 1960s Y&R produced cast commercials for Jell-O in the *Andy Griffith Show*.[86] The casts of *Dennis the Menace*, *The Beverly Hillbillies,* and *My Favorite Martian* appeared in commercials for Kellogg's cereals.[87] Buddy Ebsen, the lead actor of *The Beverly Hillbillies*, admitted he felt a 'twinge' when he started doing cast commercials, but that 'as the money started coming in, the twinge eased'.[88]

The Beverly Hillbillies cast also appeared in commercials for Winston cigarettes; in one, Ebsen's character 'Jed' offers the character 'Granny' an alternative to her corn cob pipe, Winston cigarettes.[89] As Granny, a country rube unaccustomed to city habits, puts the cigarette into her pipe, she inhales and exclaims, 'By thunder, Jed, that *is* good smoking!' Jed suggests she try smoking the cigarette by inhaling it directly, and Granny exclaims, 'Tastes even better!' She goes on to say she 'may even put away my corn cob'. Jed notes, 'There just ain't no way of saying just how good a Winston is, you gotta smoke one to find out.' Granny replies, 'Well, I can say this, Winston tastes mighty good,' and Jed concludes, 'Like a cigarette should.' During the first take of one Winston

Winston cigarettes cast commercial on *The Beverly Hillbillies* (c. 1965–6)

commercial, Ebsen didn't inhale because inhaled smoke made him dizzy. According to Ebsen, 'the ad agency man was frantic and said 'we would have to do retakes'. Because advertisers expected celebrity endorsers to use their products, Ebsen realised that 'The agencyman feared he would lose his job as a result of the commercial I did.' A month later, however, the 'agencyman' informed Ebsen that Winston was happy with the commercial because it opened up a new market for smokers who did not inhale.[90]

One of the most elaborate cast commercials was a five-minute long Chevrolet commercial in 1964 employing the casts of two different programmes: *Bonanza*, a Western drama, and *Bewitched*, a sitcom about an ad-man and his wife who has magical powers. *Bonanza* cast members introduce different Chevrolet models as they parade down the centre of the *Bonanza* set, or as one character describes it, 'Virginia City, or I guess what we should call Chevrolet City'. Cast members show features of various Chevrolet models, and then stars of *Bewitched* appear to announce that 'part of our new job for Chevrolet this fall is to be very bewitching'; then they 'magically' make a *Bonanza* character and then a Chevrolet appear.[91] These cast commercials were the last gasps of the integration strategy common in the single sponsorship era. By the late 1960s they had largely disappeared. Advertisers had given up on maintaining a tight association with programmes and stars, and some market research had indicated that cast commercials might not be very effective.[92]

By the mid-1960s, some were calling for commercials to be interesting interludes rather than instructional interruptions. An executive from the Television Bureau of Advertising exhorted advertisers to think of television as an 'idea medium', rather than a demonstration tool.[93] Pointing to a Xerox commercial in which a monkey runs a copier to show its ease of use, and to a Hertz commercial, 'Let Hertz put you in the driver's seat', in which actors descend, flying magically through the air, to land in an empty speeding car's driver's seat, he argued television could plant the 'idea' for buying through clever concepts rather than product information or demonstrations.[94]

New aesthetic strategies emerged for commercials that could hold audience attention on their own without integration into a surrounding programme. Hard-sell advertisers had been worried that sixty seconds of airtime gave them fewer opportunities to describe products than a full page of a print ad and so had often insisted on commercials consisting of 'fifty-eight seconds of spoken copy delivered with the staccato accent of a machine gun'.[95] In a reaction to this, and inspired by DDB's approach to print advertising, most famously the Volkswagen ads, some began to use more 'white space' in commercials as well.[96] Agencies began using sound in a more naturalistic way. In one pioneering Cracker Jack snack commercial, no voiceover accompanies shots of a father who searches the family home until he finally finds his son's hidden supply of Cracker Jack snacks.[97]'Showing' supplanted 'showing and telling'. Well-known audio artist Tony Schwartz specialised in creating what he called 'sound photos' for commercials: instead of having an announcer describe a food as 'delicious', Schwartz simply recorded a consumer enjoying it. Schwartz claimed this naturalistic sound and action projected 'a strong feeling of delicious without using the word'.[98]

Probably the most notable aesthetic shift in the mid- to late 1960s was towards a more cinematic visual style, sometimes referred to as the 'New York school of film'. Gordon Webber of B&B described this 'New York Look' as a 'synthesis of intimate, fluid movement and dynamic editing that eventually would find its way into feature film-making'.[99] Agencies began hiring directors who hoped to break into Hollywood film-making, replacing the industrial film-makers trained in didactic techniques, and they showed an increasing interest in close-ups, long shots, location shooting, faster editing, and shorter shots. Directors were often allowed some latitude to try shots not included on a storyboard, and eventually became key collaborators in commercial production.[100] By 1969, Foote, Cone & Belding, traditionally a hard-sell agency, was experimenting with sudden edits, shots of less than a second in length, naturalistic soundtracks, and minimal dialogue.[101] Some of this style came from documentary film-makers, like the Maysles brothers, well-known documentarians who made commercials for Jell-O and for Champion Spark Plugs. As with their documentaries, the Maysles followed subjects around and filmed them for days to get one clip of spontaneous natural dialogue for the commercial.[102] Their handheld camerawork and emphasis on spontaneity signalled authenticity, a kind of authenticity that was necessary for hip commercials to resonate with cynical consumers. At B&B, an interest in cinematic techniques 'became the passion, the religion of the new generation', recalls Webber, such that there were weekly screenings of animated, experimental and avant-garde films – even the account executives began attending the screenings.[103]

This new focus on aesthetics led to a drastic increase in production costs by the late 1960s. In one estimate, such costs increased 72 per cent between 1963 and 1967.[104] As commercials evolved, agencies hired more specialists, such as sound consultants for 'sound logos', music composers for original music, famous photographers such as Irving Penn and commercial actors who received residual payments; raising production quality required more location shoots, more elaborate lighting, and special effects.[105] Airtime costs also rose, as networks charged higher prices for larger audiences. By 1965, all the networks broadcast colour programmes; by 1966, nearly 70 per cent of commercials were also filmed in colour, an additional expense.[106]

Advertising agencies began reorganising their employees to manage the increasing workload of producing commercials. The intensely collaborative process of commercial production led to conflicts over who exactly was in charge. Art directors, who had hitherto only executed copywriters' ideas by drawing storyboards to sell clients on the commercial idea, began to take a larger role in the conceptualisation of commercials.[107] A television art director, 'part director, writer, diplomat and general overseer of the entire commercial project', began to replace the copywriter altogether.[108] These television art directors, as one B&B executive noted, 'dreamed up concepts that sent production budgets soaring like the Red Balloon', as in a United Airlines commercial that cost over $100,000 to produce and looked like a mini Broadway musical, complete with Busby Berkeley-style shots of dancers from above.[109] To contain these costs, agencies began to hire production companies on a cost plus fixed fee basis or they demanded competitive bidding with detailed budgets.[110] Some criticised the trend towards high-budget commercials. One executive noted that 'Commercials can be so loaded with frills that the message becomes buried under the glitter and glamour of a tiny motion picture epic.'[111]

All these changes helped elevate the cultural prestige of the television commercial. Some called the late 1960s 'the golden age of arty commercials'.[112] Advertising, once defended as a rational business practice based on scientific research, was now an art, a cultural form on a par with other cultural forms.[113] The new creatives argued that no idea is too wild: all ideas could be considered, like a party when 'everyone [is] in the pool'.[114] Tony Schwartz advised commercial-makers to leave behind not only the hard sell but the soft sell as well and turn to the 'deep sell'. Instead of 'teaching' the consumer 'the name of the product and hoping he will remember it when he goes to the store', Schwartz suggested commercials create a 'deep attachment to the product in the commercial' so that 'there is no need to depend on their remembering the name of the product' because the sound and imagery would 'resonate with the experiences a person has in relation to a product'.[115] The idea that advertising should be a form of experience that aligns the product with the consumers' emotions would soon become conventional wisdom.

Commercials also began to reflect a critique of traditional advertising from within the ad industry, or what Thomas Frank calls 'anti-advertising': a 'style which harnessed public mistrust of consumerism'.[116] Ad-makers began to view the consumer as well-armed to resist the direct advertising message. As one boutique creative agency claimed, the consumer, 'like an insect that builds up resistance to DDT, is getting harder to fool'.[117] To get past this resistance, hip commercials make product claims visually rather than verbally. For example, a famous 1964 DDB Volkswagen commercial opens with a close-up of a man's boots crunching through snow, close-ups of headlights lighting up as he starts a car, followed by artfully composed shots of the VW Beetle driving through a snowy rural landscape, headlights cutting through the gloom, with only the natural sounds of crunching snow and engine noise, until a voice-over asks, 'Have you ever wondered how the man who drives the snowplough drives *to* the snowplough? This one drives a Volkswagen. So you can stop wondering.'[118] The product claim is implied, while overtly our attention is directed to the cinematic camera angles that ensured this commercial's place in the canon of the Creative Revolution.[119]

Other commercials satirised advertising itself. Like hip print ads, these hip commercials directly critiqued traditional product-centred hard-sell commercials without losing the selling message, appealing to intelligent consumers who could congratulate themselves for getting the joke. In one example, DDB's 1969 commercial for Alka-Seltzer, an indigestion medication, the problem/solution paradigm –

Benson & Hedges 100s (no date)

indigestion solved by Alka-Seltzer – is disguised by satire. The commercial shows an actor at a table, taking bites from a plate of pasta, and repeatedly messing up his line for a putative commercial: 'Mama mia, that's a spicy meatball.' As the unseen director calls 'cut' after every error, we see the actor struggle to repeat the action and line, until 'take 59', when 'Jack' the actor is unable to take another bite. The voiceover explains that 'Sometimes you eat more than you should, and when it's spicy besides, mama mia, do you need Alka-Seltzer.' Revived by Alka-Seltzer, the actor happily performs his part, and then a prop crashes on the set and the unseen director calls 'cut'.[120] Other commercials satirised hard-sell product claims by humorously claiming product disadvantages. Wells Rich Greene made headlines with commercials for Benson & Hedges, an extra-long cigarette, showing vignettes of cigarettes broken by closing elevator doors, helmet visors, juicers, pigeons landing on the cigarette, and opening car boots.[121]

Other commercials overtly incorporated countercultural imagery and language. The J. Walter Thompson agency produced a 1968 campaign for the 7UP soft drink that features animated psychedelic imagery in the style of graphic artist Peter Max and the Beatles' *Yellow Submarine*: 'You can do your own thing' with 'the UnCola, 7UP'.[122] BBDO, one of the most conservative agencies, oversaw commercials for Dodge automobiles that open with a vignette of someone, such as a bullfighter, worrying about how to complete a task when 'Dodge Fever' is around and 'there's just no resisting it'.[123] After an attractive young woman in a mod white miniskirt delineates the car's 'wild new taillights' and other features, the bullfighter is distracted by a passing Dodge and the bull knocks him out because 'Dodge Fever' is 'more forceful than ever'. The commercial encourages viewers to give in to a feverish impulse and purchase a new stylish car.

Hip commercials won awards at the increasing number of advertising awards shows, but traditional agencies, such as BBDO, which produced about 500 commercials a year, remained sceptical.[124] B&B executives worried that hip advertising was trying to become 'as entertaining as the programming' and invented the slogan, 'It's not creative unless it sells.'[125] Another B&B executive attacked 'Filmic fireworks and award winning commercials that didn't sell'.[126] Claimed another contrarian executive, 'If too much of our selling time is devoted to humour just to attract attention, we may not attract the attention we need for the selling message.'[127] The recession of 1970

7UP, the UnCola (c. 1968)

brought a backlash: advertisers began demanding more 'pre-testing' of commercials, anathema to the hip creatives. A trend of 'back to basics', including more product information, ensued and a B&B executive was able to claim, 'The hippie fashionable advertising of the past wasted a tremendous amount of money.'[128] Agencies like B&B rejoiced at emerging at last from the Creative Revolution, 'when all too often the medium was the message, and form dominated content'.[129]

Yet the backlash was temporary; even B&B soon shared the enlarged sense of advertising's mission. In 1972 B&B produced a fifteen-minute documentary, *Stalking the Wild Cranberry*, 'a behind the scenes look' at how commercials are made, designed to improve the public's attitude towards advertising.[130] Showing every step in the making of a Grape-Nuts cereal commercial that featured the celebrity naturalist Euell Gibbons, the film includes re-enactments of the creative process. Hiply dressed ad-men gather in space-age meeting rooms, redesigned to reflect the agency's 'commitment to creative work'.[131] In a creative department meeting, one executive explains that this is a chance to do something 'really fresh and original in the cereal category'. They discuss how their trip to the cereal factory helped them understand how Grape-Nuts is made from natural ingredients, and then the creative partners, the art director and copywriter, sit in front of the Peter Max poster of Bob Dylan, a clear signifier they are members of the Creative Revolution, to discuss potential spokesmen, from bakers to wheat farmers, before settling on Euell Gibbons, author of a book on natural foods including cranberries. One creative cogitates:

> Perhaps we could base our commercial on something like wild cranberries? What if we had a scene in the snow, and he says something like 'I'm gathering part of my breakfast,' and you don't see anything but snow until you get to a close-up of the cranberries. Then we could go to an inside scene where he's putting the cranberries on the Grape-Nuts.

Subsequent scenes show the making of the storyboards, the client meetings, and the production of the commercial in a snowy mountainous location, where technical challenges are laboriously surmounted in multiple takes. The editing process and the

Grape-Nuts: *Stalking the Wild Cranberrry* (1972)

screening of the commercial film for approval by the creative director is the 'moment of truth'. The creative director wants a closer zoom in on the cranberry bush; fortunately, they have such a take, so after re-editing and client approval, the commercial runs. The narrator concludes, 'Finally, an idea that began life in an art director's office more than two months before is transformed by a small army of specialists, a long chain of events, into a television commercial.' This Grape-Nuts commercial then, despite its use of such traditional strategies as a testimonial by a celebrity, product claims ('made from natural ingredients, wholesome wheat and barley'), and the half-truth of Gibbons picking cranberries that likely grow better in summer bogs than winter snow, is presented as an authored creative text, its cinematic documentation legitimating the commercial as a cultural form rather than an irritating interruption of the viewers' pleasure.

CONCLUSION

In this brief overview of television and advertising during the 1960s, I have summarised some of the tremendous changes that reshaped both industries. The television industry in the early 60s was still in transition away from sponsorship and advertiser control of programming and towards separable, mobile commercials textually distinct from programmes. As programme control shifted from sponsors to networks, advertising strategies likewise had to change, away from radio strategies such as cast commercials and product demonstrations and towards the development of new aesthetic styles. The advertising industry, having suffered as the target of many mass-culture critiques, also transitioned from the old hard sell to an updated soft-sell, user-centred, associative approach, culminating in what became known as the Creative Revolution. The 'creative' advertising workers, art directors and copywriters, enjoyed a newly elevated status, replacing the account executives as the glamorous representatives of the advertising industry. The Creative Revolution, while fiercely resisted by many in the ad industry at the time, reshaped basic assumptions and strategies in ways still evident decades later. Advertisers' view of consumers changed: rather than masses receptive to direct education about products, consumers became sophisticated members of segmented markets that needed to be wooed and disarmed. Advertising agencies sought to counter consumer cynicism and revive consumer attention by producing visually, aurally, and conceptually interesting commercials. Breaking from the low resolution and static camera angles of live television predominant in the 1950s, commercials incorporated more cinematic aesthetics, such as a wider variety of shot compositions and faster editing styles. Commercial directing became a stepping-stone to Hollywood careers for some, helping to legitimate television commercials as a proto-cinematic form.[132] As hip commercials critiqued traditional hard-sell advertising, observers could call television commercials the 'best thing on television' without sarcasm. By the 1970s, the new order was established: both traditional and boutique creative agencies had reordered creative work processes to emphasise the cultural relevance and salience of their advertising; and both the networks and the advertising agencies began to enjoy several decades of fat profit margins delivering commercial exposure to audiences accustomed to trading their time for free programming.

NOTES

1. Thomas Frank, *The Conquest of Cool* (Chicago: University of Chicago Press, 1997), p. 22.
2. Ted Morgan, 'New! Improved! Advertising! A Close-up Look at a Successful Agency', in John Wright (ed.), *The Commercial Connection* (New York: Dell, 1979), p. 299.
3. Jonathan Price, *The Best Thing on TV: Commercials* (New York: Penguin, 1978), p. 2.
4. Edgar H. Felix, 'Broadcasting's Place in the Advertising Spectrum', *Advertising & Selling*, 15 December 1926, p. 19.
5. For more, see Cynthia B. Meyers, *A Word from Our Sponsor: Admen, Advertising, and the Golden Age of Radio* (New York: Fordham University Press, 2014).
6. For more on non-network broadcast advertising in this era, see Alexander Russo, *Points on the Dial* (Durham, NC: Duke University Press, 2010).
7. See Kathy M. Newman, *Radio Active* (Berkeley: University of California Press, 2004); James L. Baughman, *Same Time, Same Station* (Baltimore, MD: Johns Hopkins University Press, 2007), chapter 8; William Boddy, *Fifties Television* (Urbana: University of Illinois Press, 1990), chapter 6; and Erik Barnouw, *The Sponsor: Notes on a Modern Potentate* (New York: Oxford University Press, 1978).
8. Cynthia B. Meyers, 'The Problems with Sponsorship in Broadcasting, 1930s–50s: Perspectives from the Advertising Industry', *Historical Journal of Film, Radio and Television* vol. 31 no. 3 (September 2011), pp. 355–72.
9. Michael Mashon, 'NBC, J. Walter Thompson, and the Evolution of Prime-Time Television Programming and Sponsorship, 1946–58' (PhD dissertation, University of Maryland College Park, 1996).
10. Ibid.; William Boddy, 'Operation Frontal Lobes versus the Living Room Toy: The Battle over Programme Control in Early Television', *Media, Culture and Society* vol. 9 (1987), pp. 347–68.
11. Christopher Anderson, *Hollywood TV* (Austin: University of Texas Press, 1994).
12. Boddy, *Fifties Television*, p. 159.
13. 'Co-Sponsorship Stages Strong Network Comeback', *Sponsor*, 1 June 1964, p. 42.
14. 'The Spiral's Got to Stop', *Sponsor*, 1 June 1964, p. 29.
15. John E. McMillin, 'TV's New Non-Influentials', *Sponsor*, 25 September 1961, p. 42.
16. Companies that made multiple brands, like Procter & Gamble or Lever Bros., sponsored multiple programmes, each advertising a separate brand.
17. Les Brown, *Television* (New York: Harcourt Brace Jovanovich, 1971), p. 65.
18. '30–30 or Fight, Agencies Defend Piggybacks', *Sponsor*, 3 February 1964, p. 34.
19. Brown, *Television*, p. 350.
20. 'Net TV – Where Is It Headed?' *Sponsor*, 11 September 1961, pp. 25–8, 46–50.
21. Bob Shanks, 'Network Television: Advertising Agencies and Sponsors', Wright (ed.), *The Commercial Connection*, p. 98.
22. 'As Good a Buy as Ever', *Sponsor*, 1 June 1964, p. 30.
23. Shanks, 'Network Television', p. 98.
24. Fairfax Cone, *With All Its Faults* (Boston: Little, Brown, 1969), p. 298.
25. Ibid., p. 299.
26. Stephen Fox, *The Mirror Makers* (New York: William Morrow, 1984).
27. Claude Hopkins, *Scientific Advertising* (Lincolnwood, IL: NTC Business Books, reprinted 1966); Albert Lasker, *The Lasker Story* (Chicago: Advertising Publications, 1963).
28. Fox, *The Mirror Makers*, pp. 71–5.

29. Fox argues that the advertising industry swung between the hard and soft sell decade by decade. See also Martin Mayer, *Madison Avenue USA* (Lincolnwood, IL: NTC Business Books, 1992 [1958]).

30. Vance Packard, *The Hidden Persuaders* (New York: David McKay Co., 1957).

31. For example, *The Hucksters* (1947), starring Clark Gable, and *Will Success Spoil Rock Hunter?* (1957), starring Tony Randall.

32. 'Copy' refers to the text in the ad as opposed to the illustrations and layout.

33. Charles Brower, 'Who's Having Any Fun?' *Advertising Agency and Advertising & Selling*, June 1954, p. 38.

34. Mayer, *Madison Ave USA*, p. 29.

35. Mark Wiseman, *Advertisements* (New York: Moore-Robbins, 1949), p. 3.

36. Fox, *The Mirror Makers*, p. 180.

37. Quoted in Mayer, *Madison Avenue USA*, p. 49.

38. Larry Dobrow, *When Advertising Tried Harder* (New York: Friendly Press, 1984).

39. Frank Rowsome, Jr, *Think Small* (New York: Ballantine, 1970).

40. Stephen Baker, 'The Cultural Significance of Doyle Dane Bernbach', *Advertising Age*, 1 November 1965, p. 99.

41. Bob Levenson, *Bill Bernbach's Book* (New York: Villard Books, 1987), p. 113.

42. George Lois, with Bill Pitts, *George, Be Careful* (New York: Saturday Review Press, 1972), p. 50.

43. Ibid., p. 64.

44. Levenson, *Bill Bernbach's Book*, p. 25.

45. Frank, *Conquest of Cool*, p. 54.

46. Ibid., p. 238.

47. Ibid., p. 133.

48. 'Agency Swingers Flourish Their Mini-Skirts', *Printers' Ink*, 11 August 1967, p. 12.

49. Jerry Della Femina, *From Those Wonderful Folks Who Gave You Pearl Harbor* (New York: Simon & Schuster, 1970), p. 233.

50. Bernbach argued advertising was not a science. Levenson, *Bill Bernbach's Book*, p. 115.

51. Robin Nelson, 'Harper's Happy Hippies', *Marketing/Communications*, October 1967, pp. 51–8; 'The Touch-Touch Bang-Bang School of Creativity', *Marketing/Communications*, February 1969, pp. 32–4; 'Chat with an Ad-Man Head', *Marketing/Communications*, January 1968, pp. 63–5; Cynthia B. Meyers, 'Psychedelics and the Advertising Man: The 1960s Countercultural Creative on Madison Avenue', *Columbia Journal of American Studies* vol. 4 no. 1 (2000), pp. 114–27.

52. 'Chat with an Ad-Man Head', p. 64.

53. Lois, *George, Be Careful*, p. 226.

54. Mary Wells Lawrence, *A Big Life in Advertising* (New York: Alfred A. Knopf, 2002).

55. 'George Lois: Maypo', available from http://www.georgelois.com/pages/milestones/mile.maypo.html, accessed 11 March 2014.

56. Levenson, *Bill Bernbach's Book*, p. 71.

57. John S. Straiton, 'The Fey Cult of Cutie-Pie Creativity', *Marketing/Communications*, November 1969, p. 64.

58. Tom Dillon, 'The Triumph of Creativity over Communication', speech at Ad Age Creative Workshop, 23 July 1974, BBDO Records, New York.

59. Tom Dillon, 'Remarks', *c.* 1968, BBDO Records.

60. Quoted in Fox, *The Mirror Makers*, p. 271. Italics in original.

61. Fairfax Cone, *The Blue Streak* (Chicago: Crain Communications, 1973), pp. 193, 189.

62. Frank, *Conquest of Cool*, p. 9. For an analysis of 1960s television programming influenced by counterculture style, see Aniko Brodoghkozy, *Groove Tube* (Durham, NC: Duke University Press, 2001).

63. Advertising awards include the Clios, the Golden Lions, and the Addys. Michael Z. Newman and Elana Levine note that the identification of an 'author' of a cultural text, such as a television programme, is a step towards 'cultural legitimation'. *Legitimating Television* (New York: Routledge, 2012), pp. 9, 45.

64. Howard Luck Gossage, *Is There Any Hope for Advertising?* (Urbana: University of Illinois Press, 1986), p. 87.

65. This comparison appears elsewhere, but one later example is Aimee Stern, 'Selling Yourself on Madison Ave', *The New York Times,* 1 October 1989, p. F4.

66. Gordon Webber, *Our Kind of People: The Story of the First 50 Years at Benton & Bowles* (New York: Benton & Bowles, 1979), p. 124.

67. Ed Roberts, 'Television', unpublished manuscript, *c.* 1966, BBDO Records.

68. *Y&R and Broadcasting: Growing up Together* (New York: Museum of Broadcasting, 1988), p. 32.

69. Webber, *Our Kind of People*, p. 87; Lawrence Samuels, *Brought to You By* (Austin: University of Texas Press, 2001), p. 105.

70. 'Say When', Dristan commercial photoscript, 16 October 1962, BBDO Records.

71. Price, *Best Thing on TV*, p. 2.

72. *Y&R and Broadcasting*, p. 61.

73. Benton & Bowles commercial for Folger's coffee, 'Mrs Olson Saves a Hostess', available from https://archive.org/details/dmbb46710, accessed 11 March 2014.

74. Ajax commercial, available from http://www.youtube.com/watch?v=R4trEWzghZM, accessed 11 March 2014.

75. Benton & Bowles commercial for Joy detergent, available from https://archive.org/details/dmbb47038, accessed 11 March 2014.

76. *Y&R and Broadcasting*, p. 60.

77. Arthur Bellaire, *TV Advertising* (New York: Harper, 1959), p. 194.

78. Charles Anthony Wainwright, *The Television Copywriter: How to Create Successful TV Commercials* (New York: Hastings House, 1966), p. 255.

79. Susan Murray, *Hitch Your Antenna to the Stars* (New York: Routledge, 2005), p. 123.

80. Ibid., chapter 5.

81. Wainwright, *The Television Copywriter*, p. 195.

82. 'Specialists on Commercials Mean Cost Increases for Advertisers', *Sponsor*, 15 June 1964, p. 34.

83. Wainwright, *The Television Copywriter*, p. 194.

84. 'Should Stars Plug Products?' *Sponsor*, 13 January 1964, pp. 30–5.

85. An example from *Show Boat* available from http://www.youtube.com/watch?v=dUbvRVcY6qI&feature=youtu.be, accessed 11 March 2014. An example of a commercial from *The Goldbergs* available from https://archive.org/details/theGoldbergs-12September1949, accessed 11 March 2014.

86. *Y&R and Broadcasting*, p. 37.

87. Wainwright, *The Television Copywriter*, p. 256.

88. 'Should Stars Plug Products?', p. 32.

89. Winston commercial, available from http://www.youtube.com/watch?v=xEx44ETP8Ac, accessed 11 March 2014.
90. 'Should Stars Plug Products?', p. 32.
91. Chevrolet commercial, available from https://www.youtube.com/watch?v=_FjPgj_U0gY, accessed 15 January 2016.
92. Samuel, *Brought to You By*, p. 172.
93. W. B. Colvin, 'More than Meets the Eye', *Sponsor,* 23 September 1963, pp. 30–2.
94. Xerox commercial, available from http://www.georgelois.com/pages/milestones/mile.xerox.html#, accessed 11 March 2014. Hertz commercial, available from http://www.youtube.com/watch?v=M30XXrrK3lY, accessed 11 March 2014.
95. G. D. Gudebrod, 'Look Dad, No Words', *Sponsor,* 17 June 1963, p. 18.
96. 'Commercials as Art', *Sponsor,* 23 September 1963, p. 18.
97. Gudebrod, 'Look Dad, No Words', p. 18.
98. 'Sound Shouldn't Be an Afterthought', *Sponsor,* 9 March 1964, p. 51.
99. Webber, *Our Kind of People*, p. 130.
100. Wainwright, *The Television Copywriter*, p. 50.
101. Cone, *With All Its Faults*, p. 319.
102. Price, *Best Thing on TV*, pp. 96–7.
103. Webber, *Our Kind of People*, p. 130.
104. Ibid., p. 131.
105. 'Specialists on Commercials', pp. 34ff.
106. Christopher Sterling and John Kittross, *Stay Tuned* (Belmont, CA: Wadsworth, 1978), pp. 398–9.
107. Wainwright, *The Television Copywriter*, p. 46.
108. Ibid., p. 16; 'The Ad-Producer – A New Breed', *Sponsor,* 4 May 1964, p. 48.
109. Webber, *Our Kind of People*, p. 131. United Airlines commercial, available from http://www.youtube.com/watch?v=uzwPsFbhSqY, accessed 11 March 2014.
110. Webber, *Our Kind of People*, p. 132; Price, *Best Thing on TV*, p. 110.
111. Quoted in Wainwright, *The Television Copywriter*, p. 90.
112. Price, *Best Thing on TV*, p. 4.
113. Wainwright, *The Television Copywriter*, p. 17. See Lynn Spigel, *TV by Design* (Chicago and London: University of Chicago Press, 2009), chapter 6.
114. Morgan, 'New! Improved!', p. 299.
115. Tony Schwartz, *The Responsive Chord* (New York: Doubleday, 1973), pp. 71, 79.
116. Frank, *Conquest of Cool*, p. 55.
117. Morgan, 'New! Improved!', p. 294.
118. 'Snowplow', 1964 DDB Volkswagen commercial, available from https://www.youtube.com/watch?v=ABcckOTVqao, accessed 15 January 2016.
119. This commercial was inducted into the Clio Hall of Fame in 2013.
120. 'Mama Mia', Alka-Seltzer commercial, available from http://www.youtube.com/watch?v=NQhwNtY3N2k, accessed 11 March 2014.
121. Benson & Hedges commercial, available from http://www.youtube.com/watch?v=UEUHV20kH9g, accessed 11 March 2014. More are available at https://archive.org/details/tobacco_rja84e00, accessed 11 March 2014.

122. 7UP commercial, available from http://www.youtube.com/watch?v=m8-eLMuCdfI, accessed 11 March 2014.

123. 'Dodge Fever' commercial, available from https://www.youtube.com/watch?v=tHLsrnBif3o, accessed 11 March 2014.

124. The Clio awards, begun in 1959, are one of the most prominent advertising awards for creative advertising. Tom Dillon, 'What the Computer Has Done for Advertising', special to the *The New York Times*, 22 December 1970, p. 22, BBDO Records.

125. Webber, *Our Kind of People*, p. 153.

126. Ibid., p. 135.

127. Earle Ludgin, quoted in Wainwright, *The Television Copywriter*, p. 105.

128. Price, *Best Thing on TV*, pp. 5-6.

129. Al Goldman, quoted in Webber, *Our Kind of People*, p. 135.

130. 'Stalking the Wild Cranberry', George Gage Productions (1972), available from https://archive.org/details/stalking_the_wild_cranberry_1972, accessed 11 March 2014.

131. Webber, *Our Kind of People*, p. 149.

132. For example, famed Hollywood directors Ridley Scott, Tony Scott, and George Romero began as directors of commercials.

12

The Bear Facts: Commercial Archaeology and the Sugar Bear Campaign

Skip Elsheimer and Devin Orgeron

> There is an implication ... that the job of being an admaker carries with it a unique kind of social responsibility. I happen to believe it is true. For, while everyone [sic] of us on this globe has social responsibilities, and while all business and professional people have special duties to the publics they serve, the obligations of people in advertising are especially significant.[1]
>
> Victor G. Bloede

Victor Bloede's comments, spoken before an audience of like-minded professionals at the International Advertising Association's annual conference in Brussels in 1983, indicate an emerging – perhaps overstated – sense of commitment to the consumer. Representing Benton & Bowles, a firm that held a number of the most sought-after and lucrative advertising accounts in the USA, including the well-known cereal manufacturer Post, Bloede's comments suggest a tidal shift in the game of advertising. But this shift was far from self-motivated and more than a little self-protective.

That same year, the Committee on Children's Television, Inc. sued General Foods Corp. with claims of fraudulent, misleading and deceptive advertising in the marketing of sugared breakfast cereals.[2] Arising from an original class action complaint filed in 1977, the Committee's suit, which details the means by which manufacturers of sugary cereals had employed carefully crafted hard-sell tactics aimed at children during peak hours of television viewing, snapped the industry to attention.[3] Like the tobacco industry before it, the sugar-cereal industry had been quietly aware of its product's potentially controversial, nearly primary ingredient. And the products, since their inception, were advertised in a manner that shaped, and then re-shaped, our collective understanding of sugar's nutritional value as well as its cultural place.

ADVERTISING DEMOGRAPHICS AND MARKETING YOUTH

Introduced in 1949, Sugar Crisp was the first pre-sweetened breakfast cereal – an aspect that, initially at least, made the product unusually convenient for adults and unusually attractive to children. Additionally, the product's early advertisements were the first animated TV commercials aimed specifically at children. It became clear to us, looking at the materials and their cultural surround, that the history of Sugar Bear and the product he pitched is, in many ways, the history of children's cereal advertising more broadly.[4] The campaign also demonstrates very neatly one company's largely successful attempts to sell its product differently across the decades, calibrating its pitch to the tastes and mores of the moment. Sugar Bear, however, was not always this product's pitch-man.

Benton & Bowles hired Disney animator Bill Tylta to create the characters that would populate the earliest print ads for the product.[5] This captivating three-colour full-page ad is no less thematically and graphically focused on children than later ads for the product.[6] But here, the pitch is being made by three bears – one for each of the product's 'virtues'. On the cutting edge in terms of age-specific branding from the start, Sugar Crisp, in this advertisement, moves against the cereal marketing trends of the early 1940s. In the early part of the decade, cereal advertising was aimed more clearly at the primary shopper of the household.[7] Advertising in mainstream, adult-focused magazines, Post appealed to mom's sense of economy and nutritional responsibility. These advertisements used logic, reasoning and hyperbole to appeal directly to the primary shopper's sense of economy and concerns about nutrition.[8] Health appeals are made even more directly in some of these early cereal ads, with very frank discussions of the consumer's 'daily bulk' and the perceived benefits of a diet rich in fibre.

Plain, traditional and rather text-heavy packaging and advertising appeal primarily to the practicality and affordability of whole grains. A full-colour 1941 ad for Post

Post ad (1949), appealing to children graphically, and to adults via the ad's copy

An appeal to the housewife and her husband (1941)

Post ad (1949), appealing to children graphically, and to adults via the ad's copy Post appeals to sturdy American farmers

Toasties, however, indicates a shift in thinking. Combining the logic and persuasiveness of the previous campaigns, here Post banks on its ability to appeal to the idiosyncrasies of young adulthood.[9] Using slang and the unique iconography of the 1940s teenager, Post began to recognise the usefulness of appealing more directly to a different demographic – a category of consumers capable of putting demands on the household's primary buyer). The evolution of Post's advertising indicates the company's desire to reach a younger population.

Cereal, however, was still considered a health food – and a rather dull one at that. A critically important evolutionary moment was the introduction of variety packs: Post called them 'Post-Tens'. A collection of little boxes, Post-Tens created a sense of choice.[10] This domestic democracy, however, became something else entirely when Sugar Crisp was added to this collection of little boxes in 1951, two years after Sugar Crisp was introduced.[11] Both advertisements for Post-Tens are colourful and playful. The inclusion of Sugar Crisp, however, allowed the company to employ a differently tuned visual and textual rhetoric aimed at children. Adult logic is still appealed to, but the bulk of the graphics and the copy are given to a newly discovered and critically important consumer

Films That Sell

Cereal democracy (c. 1950)

1941 print ad for Post Toasties

The game changes (1951)

demographic. Post's clever marketing was designed to create a generation of discerning adolescent and pre-adolescent consumers who would quite deliberately *choose* Sugar Crisp and, if the strategy was successful, demand it from that point forward.

WE WANT OUR MAYPO!: BRAND LOYALTY AND THE ADOLESCENT MARKET

Post's desire from the start was to appeal to youth trends and to capitalise on them. Eventually, the company's advertising campaigns would even serve as a catalyst for these trends, creating a wave of desire and need that stretched well beyond sugar-coated, processed grains. This strategy can be seen even more vividly in the company's groundbreaking television advertising campaigns. Beginning, like the print advertisements, with three bears in the 1950s, Post introduced consumers to the idea of brand-specific characters. In one of the product's earliest television advertisements, a trio of bears – Dandy, Handy and Candy – are introduced, first in a title card that includes their now-familiar hand-drawn likenesses. Then, in a move that would thoroughly revolutionise this and several industries, three live-action bears act out the first part of a sort of 'cereal serial' called 'Camping Out West' (see note for a link to the video; similarly links can be found in the notes for many of the advertisements discussed below).[12]

'Camping Out West' indicates a trend that would come to dominate a generation of advertisements that would capture the interest, attention and, eventually, the dollars of consumers, or their parents: serialisation. Identifiable characters and a series of loosely connected adventures would keep kids watching (and demanding that their parents buy). The cereal itself, in this respect (and in a manner that advertising professionals and scholars have been at pains to discuss since), became a critical *part* of a carefully engineered lifestyle choice, creating a generation of brand(and manufacturer)-loyal young adults (readers growing up in the USA in the 1970s will hear echoes, in our choice of phrasing here, of one of the hallmarks of cereal advertisements in that decade: 'part of a complete, nutritious breakfast').[13]

The future of Post's television advertising, however, would descend in interesting ways from an accidental cereal success story from the mid-1950s. Around this time, the Heublein company had purchased a small Vermont company called Maltex (who produced, among other things, Maypo – a maple-flavoured hot oatmeal product). Believing the brand to be a liability (how, they wondered, does one sell oatmeal in the atomic age?), Heublein came up with a scheme. They'd create an expensive but doomed TV campaign, kill the brand as a result and write off their losses. They hired former Disney animator John Hubley.[14] Perhaps best known for his later work on Mr Magoo, Hubley was fired from Disney for his involvement in the 1941 strikes and was, in the early part of the 1950s, marked out by Disney as a communist and blacklisted. Working independently in New York, Hubley was local, pricey and slightly dangerous – a combination Heublein hoped would bury the unsellable product once and for all. The plan backfired in the most interesting manner. Hubley was given full artistic license (though Heublein suggested, subversively they thought, that he make the spot 'true to life'). Heeding the call, Hubley collected semi-spontaneous audio interactions between himself and his son Mark (who hated oatmeal!), using the choicest bits to accompany an iconically drawn, cowboy-obsessed (and exaggeratedly bratty) Marky 'character' and his animated (and exaggeratedly frustrated) father. The result was an ad that, for a time (and against all odds), made oatmeal desirable.[15] Hubley hit a nerve and two industries paid close attention: the advertising industry had learned a critical lesson about the rhetorical power of animation and the breakfast cereal industry realised that their success hinged on their ability to appeal to a demographic they were only beginning to acknowledge. The cereal wars had begun.

With the assistance of Benton & Bowles, Post fought admirably, using a variety of tactics to sell Sugar Crisp and its other products to generations of sugar-mad TV kids. The company would spend much of the 1950s and early 60s searching for the right advertising formula, hoping to cash in on the kind of success Maypo had won with Marky. The bears, of course, would play an important role in this formula. Post sponsored the widely popular Roy Rogers television programme, a programme (and character) that was already deeply and memorably branded. Spots for Sugar Crisp would weave in and out of the show's narrative and would, at times, interact with and respond directly to the show's key characters. An early 1950s spot (that also capitalises on the surging interest in 3D), moves away from the bears temporarily to focus on Roy and Dale Evans.[16]

Recognising the critical centrality of their own brand, however, Post would soon discover the crossover potential available to them, using the animated bears in clever, highly truncated Roy Rogers scenarios and, when convenient, packaging specially marked boxes with highly sought-after Roy Rogers premiums.[17] The bears and their adventures, the company deduced, were key to their success. The company would begin to exploit this fact more fully, slowly pulling away from their associations with Roy Rogers and other television personalities, animated or otherwise.

As the brand was in the process of making the transition from three bears to one in the 1960s, some Sugar Crisp ad campaigns featured other characters associated (however briefly) with the brand. Although our research into the files of Benton & Bowles reveals little in the way of a deliberate strategy, it seems that Post, at this point in its history, was keen to promote the idea of individualism among its fans (a mechanism that would further allow the company to exploit the illusion of personal choice). Christopher Wheat and The Big Kid are, in this way, examples of the sort of 'kid' Post was attempting to engineer through its carefully crafted marketing strategies.[18] But these characters were merely a transitional segue, easing viewers and consumers into the soon to be unveiled 'Sugar Bear' we have come to know.

The Sugar Bear that would emerge from these experimental, transitional characters would retain characteristics from all of them. He would be strong (because of his choice in breakfast foods), impossibly cool and individualistic (though with a critical sense of community). And 1964 would prove to be a pivotal year in the cereal wars. Lawrence Samuel, in *Brought to You By: Postwar Television Advertising and the American Dream*, indicates that, in 1964, 41 million Americans were under the age of ten – a figure exceeding the entire nation's total population only a century earlier.[19] Toy and cereal manufacturers, he argues, bullishly appealed to this emerging demographic, buying up advertising space left and right. Major changes in animation styles ('limited' or 'streamlined' animation made it possible for networks to turn a profit on thirty-minute animated programmes), coupled with rather loose FCC regulations, saw the rise of this phenomenon we, in retrospect, call 'Saturday Morning'. Programming from 8am to noon was aimed strictly at kids, mostly animated and was punctuated (often and aggressively) by advertisements tailored to their tastes (or, more appropriately, these advertisements effectively 'tailored' those tastes).[20]

THE ANIMATED BIRTH OF SATURDAY MORNING

The Maypo campaign that followed from the 'pilot' referred to above rather subtly relied on the child viewer's inability to differentiate between animated characters designed to entertain them and those designed to sell them products.[21] Additionally, the ads were absurdly popular with adults as well (even if it did result in a culture of 'I want my [fill in the blank]' whiners).[22] Post, guided by the Ed Graham advertising agency and hoping to capitalise on the Saturday Morning market, created their own advertising showcase (of course, they wouldn't have called it this): a half-hour programme called *Linus the Lion Hearted* that featured characters appearing on the boxes of their primary children's cereal products: So Hi (Rice Krinkles); Loveable Truly (Alpha Bits); Linus himself (for the short-lived Heart of Oats, which would become Crispy Critters); and, debuting in 1965, one Dean Martinesque Sugar Bear (for Sugar Crisp). The bear was actually voiced by Gerry Matthews, who was hired to sound like Bing Crosby. When the result was more Dino, they ran with it.[23]

The show's opening, modelled on the look and style of sponsored variety programmes of the era where the show's host would use and/or rave about the sponsoring product, gives some sense of the hard-sell tactics being used.[24] Lasting a mere thirty seconds, in this brief introduction, young viewers would have been exposed to a parade of mascots pitching their products – five in total – to the swinging sounds of the brand's jingle ('Start your day a little bit better … a little bit better with Post'). Linus hands out to the other mascots the product they are associated with: Alpha Bits (mispronounced Alpha Bites), Rice Krinkles (unfortunately pitched by a terribly offensive and thankfully short-lived Chinese caricature), Post Toasties (though the box says Corn Flakes) and Sugar Crisp (introduced by the brand's newest mascot). Linus holds a box of the grotesquely named Crispy Critters. Where, as Samuel indicates, Maypo was delicate in its ability to both entertain *and* pitch, Post here makes no such effort, blurring the distinction between salesmanship and entertainment to an unprecedented degree. And Sugar Bear quickly become the 'star' of the show and the focus of Post's advertising attentions.

On the show, sometimes Sugar Bear would do battle with one Granny Goodwitch (voiced by Ruth Buzzi) in a not-so-subtle attempt to steal her breakfast. More often, he was a relaxed, accidental romantic with an affection for jazz. The show ended production in 1966, but would continue re-running until 1969, when tougher FCC regulations came down, forbidding this sort of direct marketing to children. But in that short time the character of Sugar Bear had been permanently and (from a commercial standpoint) usefully established.

A post-Linus Sugar Crisp advertisement demonstrates the degree to which the Benton & Bowles-led campaign that grew out of the show attempted to make itself indistinguishable from the Saturday Morning cartoons surrounding it (here, for some reason, Sugar Bear is shirtless, a detail that would quickly be rectified).[25] A much more sophisticated update on the 'Camping Out West' spot of more than a decade earlier, this spot initiates a sustained (if highly simplified) narrative logic built around a primary character (Sugar Bear) and an imagined breakfast rivalry that will span across a series of 'villains'. Breakfast, it seems, had become (since the introduction of Sugar Crisp) something so exciting and delicious that these characters would commit crimes to get it.[26] Combining animation and serialisation, Post had arrived at a most perfect strategy. Speaking on behalf of Benton & Bowles around the time when the above-discussed advertisement was produced, Atherton Hobler seems to recognise but downplay this strategy at a 1967 meeting for advertising executives.

> Animation spots had actually evolved from theatrical release cartoons. Since cartoons like Mickey Mouse were so successful in the movie theater, agency executives reasoned that animated characters would prove equally effective in the new home theater: the television set. Thus, these characters with strong brand identification: Post's Sugar Crisp Bears [sic] …[27]

Acknowledging the power of brand identification but stopping short of discussing the increased gains possible when the target audience in question is comprised primarily of children, Hobler's comments speak to the commercial power of animated narratives in campaigns aimed at kids. Success for the company, like success at the box office, is measured in dollars and cents and is reliant on character identification. 'Sugar Bear and his foes want Sugar Crisp badly enough to fight for it,' this logic suggests. 'I, therefore, need Sugar Crisp.'

This identification is so strong, in fact, that Post would never abandon its Sugar Bear character (even as it retired many of its other characters). Rather, Benton & Bowles would continue to update his image through the 1960s and 70s, reflecting the attitudes of the moment and capitalising on the character's impossible hipness and odd cross-generational appeal (that Dino voice, in other words, and the veiled referentiality – substitute Dino's omnipresent drink and oft-feigned need for the same for Sugar Bear's breakfast addictions – served a variety of purposes).

CHANGING WITH THE TIMES: A SUGAR BEAR FOR THE AGES

Post, however, faced obstacles. Though it would take some time before the anti-sugar lobby would force the company (and others) to strike the word 'sugar' from its box (it's now called Golden Crisp, though the product is *still* 50 per cent sugar by volume!), not all parents were convinced and some were concerned that their kid's breakfast choices might be doing more harm than good. One late-1960s spot is unusual as it appeals directly to these parents. Framed like a news exposé and clocking in at a minute (twice the length of most commercial spots), the spot captures an important moment in cereal history: the moment when Sugar Crisp became 'super'.[28] Along with a frustratingly catchy jingle and an aesthetic modelled on the televised news of the 1960s, the ad is fascinating in that, while featuring kids, it purports to be speaking to adults ('wake up the kids', the ad implores). We are also especially interested in the focus here on the vitamins and minerals that make the product 'super' in the late 1960s. This is the 'news' of the spot, meant specifically to appease those aforementioned concerned adults. Fascinatingly, in a bit of mathematics that would seem to be preparing viewers for Sugar Bear's forthcoming stint as a DJ, the commercial's foregrounded and comparatively rather bold text indicates that one bowl of Super Sugar Crisp 'provides 33⅓% of every minimum daily vitamin requirement officially established'.[29] The phrasing here is careful to the point of being awkward. The ad, however, indicates an awareness of adult concern and an attempt to temper that concern (here in the form of spray-on vitamins).

Post's main audience, however, was still obviously adolescent. And the key to this audience's loyalty was through its musical tastes. For a moment in the 1960s and for reasons we are unable to ascertain, this meant The Archies. A 1969 promotion found a flexi-disc featuring an abbreviated selection of The Archies' biggest hits packed in 'specially marked boxes' of Super Sugar Crisp. The ad, somewhat subversively, featured a song that these discs would not carry: the simultaneously addictive and revolting 'Sugar Sugar'.[30]

This premium was hugely successful (and it kept this abysmal song in the charts for weeks). Sugar Bear's DJ and promotional skills would improve, however, as the company learned rather quickly that associating their product with other beloved cultural phenomena through their television advertisements (and making Sugar Bear a spokesperson for those phenomena) was a nearly foolproof strategy.

When Post rolled out its short-lived and poorly planned Super Orange Crisp, they still somehow managed to move boxes by including abbreviated Jackson 5 records.[31] What fascinates us here, more than the sustained use of Sugar Bear as a super-hip disc jockey, is the subtle racialising of the character and the product being sold. What had been an easily identifiable Dino impersonation slowly morphs, around this time, into a slightly hipper soul-brother idiom, here with shades of Cleavon Little's turn as Super Soul in the 1971 Richard Sarafian film *Vanishing Point*.

The point is driven home not so much by the fact that these spots pitch the product with the Jacksons (though this is significant as well). More critical, in our estimation, is the spot's use of flashy, Soul Train-style editing tricks and, on the boxes, the barely glimpsed black power statement 'Right On!' Again, rather subversively, the box is actually emblazoned with the words 'RIGHT ON this Box' (referring, of course, to the record). Typographically, however, the words 'this box' get lost. Post, it seems, was again slowly transforming its mascot and, it seems, reconsidering its target audience.

Again, internal memos from the Benton & Bowles collection stop just short of discussing this move explicitly. But hints of the company's recognition of the importance of African-American consumers, however carefully phrased, indicate a move in the direction of exploiting (they do not use this term) this demographic. Speaking on behalf of Benton & Bowles, Gordon Webber, in a June 1968 speech at the annual ANA/AAAA convention for the Clinic on Integration in Television Advertising, gives some indication as to the firm's desire to couch this and subsequent manoeuvres in terms of *integration* and *equality*:

> So this morning I would like to speak not so much about past failures as about opportunity.
>
> The opportunity we have in the great mass media of television advertising to help 22 million of our fellow Americans to a new level of dignity, self-esteem and economic social equality.
>
> The opportunity, through the integration of television advertising, to change the image of the Negro in the eyes of both the Negro himself and in the eyes of white Americans.
>
> The opportunity for advertisers, by depicting in their commercials a true cross section of American life – white and black alike – the opportunity to enrich and enhance the effectiveness of their advertising.[32]

Their particular work for Sugar Crisp shortly after this speech, however, tells a somewhat different story. In the speech, Webber goes on to discuss the way in which ads might be used to do, as he calls it, 'the Lord's' work. The speech is un-ironically cut from the same rhetorical cloth as some of the more familiar Martin Luther King Jr speeches (King had been murdered in Atlanta just a few months prior). There was, in the late 1960s and early 70s in the USA, simply no avoiding racial politics.

Before adopting an 'inclusive' agenda (albeit, commercially motivated) and populating their advertisements with representatives of many races, Post began to slowly transform its mascot, marking him and his hip self-awareness racially. This is evident in a spot, also from the 1970s, where a more troubling Sugar Bear as pusher/pimp with a heart of gold (a cross between Huggy Bear, from *Starsky and Hutch* and *Super Fly* [1972]) emerges. Here, Sugar Bear is also ecologically minded – the Iron Eyes Cody *Keep America Beautiful* campaign had begun in 1971.[33]

The coding here is fantastically subtle and highly problematic. It is clear that Sugar Bear is an activist. At the very least, he is environmentally aware and his nemesis, Blob (the slob), is a habitual, uncaring polluter. Here, however, is the rub. The spot, to an unprecedented degree, both sexualises Sugar Bear (and his girl, Honey Bear) and plays metaphorically with the language of addiction. Sugar Bear's snack-time singing is familiar and innocent enough (though the 'can't get enough' refrain mutates here). As he munches, however, Honey Bear says, 'Give me some, Sugar', reaches into Sugar Bear's box to grab a handful and, just before she's able to satisfy her craving, she notices Blob's evil-doing.

The coding here is painfully apparent. Honey Bear is tarted up for her walk with Sugar Bear (hair up, short dress and an abundance of make-up) and her addiction (to Sugar Crisp) is in *his* hands. Crime films, TV and cinematic police dramas and black action films from the era would perpetuate the image of the African-American pimp and his whore, and Post seems to be edging dangerously close to this iconography – Honey Bear's 'Give me some, Sugar', in this way, might be read alternatively as 'Give me some sugar' (where the 'sugar' in question is interchangeably his affections or his Sugar Crisp). The idea is euphemistically driven home at the end of the spot, when Honey tells Sugar Bear that he 'deserve[s] a reward'.

The intentions behind this advertisement's sexualised racial stereotyping are difficult to deduce and, needless to say, the Benton & Bowles files offer little explanation. The campaign, however, would eventually come to make race a focal point. Another spot featuring Blob as the villain (here he sounds even more like Marlon Brando doing a JFK impression) is especially frank and especially odd. Blob tries to sic his dog on a mixed-race group of playing children (images of the mid-1960s race riots come immediately to mind) and Sugar Bear comes to the rescue.[34]

The group of children includes an African-American boy, an Asian boy, a white girl and a Mexican girl (as they spin on the carousel, Sugar Bear refers to them as black, white, brown and yellow). Interesting to us are Sugar Bear's attempts to teach Blob about 'brotherhood'. Initially turning his back (and getting his dog, Rover, to do the same) on the mixed group, Blob is unwilling to learn and, quite literally, doesn't get a place at the (breakfast) table as a result. Even Rover, who Sugar Bear wins over, gets a place. Singling out his own racial otherness ('I got fur'), Sugar Bear's lesson on racial harmony is sadly distilled to the search for commonalities amid difference: here, a shared love for Super Sugar Crisp.

The advertisements featuring Blob are especially interesting as they find Post in the midst of a PR crisis. Keen to refine and polish the public image of its children's cereals, Post, during these years, was filling its advertisements with material designed to comfort parents and excite children – goals which might appear to be at cross purposes. While hardly addressing nutrition, the 'lesson on brotherhood' spot is intriguing as it assigns a set of values to the product in question. It is a multi-ethnic advertisement, in its way. But more critically, the ad wants viewers to associate the product itself with tolerance. Gordon Webber's speech, quoted at some length above, is worth returning to again. For all of its protestation, for all of its feigned civil consciousness, Webber's speech is driven by an unsurprising catalyst:

How's our record so far?

Better than a year ago. But still nothing to Jim Crow about ...

There are many reasons, of course, why we should by [sic] trying to improve our record.

First, it's the law of the land. Although laws against bigotry are hard to enforce. Twelve years after the Historic Supreme Court decision on school integration, barely 12 per cent [sic] of the schools in the whole South are integrated, and in the deep South, the figure hardly reaches 2 per cent.

Second, it makes good business sense. The Negroes [sic] national expenditure on goods and services in 1967 was 30 billion dollars – a market no profit-conscious advertiser can ignore.[35]

More than anything, of course, the illusion of integration and racial consciousness is enacted in these advertisements in pursuit of greater economic gain. And, as sugar-coated cereals were being scrutinised from outside (by concerned parents and watchdog groups alike), Post and other companies appear to embrace higher social values in an effort to establish a fan/consumer base whose health and well-being, historically, had been under-protected by these advocacy organisations.

In retrospect, then, Sugar Bear's hipness, his social and ecological responsibility, appear to have been compensatory. It was the product's increasingly dubious nutritional value that was *really* at issue, and the campaign was especially skilled at deflecting criticism in this regard. Two particularly instructive ads from the 1970s underscore the struggle in alarming ways. And both feature our friend Blob.[36]

In the first of these ads, Sugar Bear is glimpsed inexplicably greeting and talking to his breakfast. And it talks back to him! Sugar Bear's toast, milk, juice and cereal bowl point, with disgust and horror, to Blob's breakfast: pickles and soda. Grape soda, to be precise. Sugar Bear and company, in a scenario that resembles the above-explored lesson on racial harmony, attempt to teach blob the importance of nutrition. Sugar Bear's toast is weirdly vocal, saying 'C'mon, we've got lots of good nutrition,' to which Blob responds, 'Phooey on nutrition.' Then Sugar Bear's cereal pipes up, indicating that 'A bowl of Super Sugar Crisp has vitamins your body needs,' to which, rather unoriginally, Blob responds 'Phooey on vit-a-mins.'

Not surprisingly, Blob is as interested in nutrition as he is in racial equality. And this is precisely the point. These seemingly simple little scenarios are building a base of potential consumers by presenting characters with antithetical characteristics. And, more critically, their antithetical behaviour corresponds directly to their distaste for or lack of interest in Super Sugar Crisp, which (as per usual) gives our bear-hero the strength and acumen needed to fend off these foes.

This logic is foregrounded even more aggressively in the next spot, which finds Blob terrorising (once again) a group of school children. Popeye-like, Sugar Bear quickly prepares and ingests a bowl of Super Sugar Crisp, and dispenses with his nemesis ('Pick up the litter and I put it in the basket'). A super-magnified cut to Sugar Bear's spoon is emblazoned with the words 'Super Power'.

Of course, the takeaway of these two ads is what's astonishing. One: that Sugar

Films That Sell

Crisp is healthier than pickles and soda. Okay. Point taken. The other: that Sugar Crisp ('a honey sweet vitamin treat') will give kids super powers so they can kick back against the 'old' people who don't understand – Blob gets the best line: 'I hate kids, they're always havin' fun.' Parents disallowing Sugar Crisp, we are lead to believe, also hate kids … and fun.

Manufacturers of children's products were well aware of this intergenerational tension. Benton & Bowles was not just aware. They were willing to spend money to figure out how to exploit it. In 1966, the firm published the findings of a direct observation study they had sponsored the previous year demonstrating the enormous influence kids had in the supermarket – especially on the cereal aisle – and subtly suggesting ways that influence might be better appealed to.[37] By the late 1970s, however, Sugar Bear's salesmanship would come under more intense scrutiny as concerned and litigious parties began to question these tactics.

Our sense is that steady racialising of Sugar Bear was part of Post's marketing defence strategy (along with several name changes, a packaging and image overhaul, etc.). Few companies in the history of American advertising have so cleverly and consistently managed their audience as Post has. And a present-day scan of the cereal aisle at your local American supermarket reveals something remarkable. With the exception of Grape-Nuts and a few other healthier products, Post (for whom the kids market would come to be primary) is a somewhat scarce brand; unless, sadly, your local American supermarket is in the heart of a predominately black neighbourhood (in which case said market might well be less 'super' and more 'local' or 'discount'). Sugar Bear, it seems, still presides within this demographic and his race has become somewhat less ambiguous.

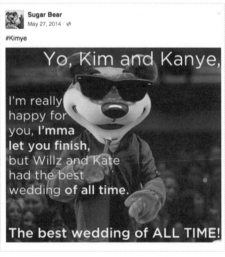

Two strange posts (pun intended) from Sugar Bear's Facebook page: hip-hop and George Foreman references combined with gold teeth; staying on top of the gossip

ACKNOWLEDGMENTS

The authors wish to thank the staff of the John W. Hartman Center for their assistance in making the research for this project both possible and pleasurable. Thanks, too, to our friend, colleague and mentor Dan Streible. The Orphan Film Symposium, where these ideas first took shape, is more than a conference at this point. It has become a way of life. And Dan's vision and his commitment to material like this has, to a degree Dan himself would be too humble to admit, created and nurtured a field of study. We are also grateful to the book's (and the series') editors whose interest in sugar-coated cereal and its history greatly impresses us. Please continue to watch the Orgeron/Elsheimer team as they next tackle the equally complex realm of toilet paper commercials!

NOTES

1. Victor G. Bloede, 'The Advertising Man and his Social Responsibility', 22 November 1983. D'arcy Masius Benton & Bowles Archives. John W. Hartman Center for Sales, Advertising, and Marketing. David M. Rubenstein Rare Book & Manuscript Library. Duke University, Box B&B 6. (Hereafter, DMB&B, Duke.)
2. 'Lawsuit Over Ads For Sugared Cereals is Allowed on Coast', *The New York Times*, 24 December 1983, p. 10.
3. A summary of the 22 December 1983 complaint itself and the resulting opinions is archived at Stanford Law School's SCOCAL (Supreme Court of California Resources) website. See: SCOCAL, 'Committee on Children's Television, Inc. v. General Foods Corp., 35 Cal.3d 197' available at: http://scocal.stanford.edu/opinion/committee-childrens-television-inc-v -general-foods-corp-28335, last visited 23 November 2015.
4. 'Looking at the materials' was made possible by digitising a massive collection of 16mm reels from the DMB&B advertising agency and its predecessor (Benton & Bowles) by Skip Elsheimer, in his capacity as A/V Geeks. Now archived at Duke, this collection included over 10,000 TV commercials spliced together onto more than 400 16mm reels of film. Currently, several thousand of these commercials are viewable online, thanks to the combined efforts of A/V Geeks, Duke and the Internet Archive. Visit http://library.duke.edu/digitalcollections/ adviews_sugar_crisp/. But please, don't stop there! Browse and explore this incredible resource.
5. For a surprisingly detailed history of Sugar Crisp, visit http://www.mrbreakfast.com/cereal_detail.asp?id=351. The website itself is dedicated to historicising, contextualising and celebrating breakfast and the foods associated with it. It's most detailed aspect, however, is its cereal portal. Most interesting to us in researching this material has been the critical importance of the internet and the dedication of enthusiasts, extremists and collectors to tracing, preserving and making this history accessible. Instinctively and practically aware of the advertising industry's secrecy and the processed food industry's unwillingness to reveal its motivations and manoeuvres, consumers and amateur historians have created a widespread alternative pop-historical network. We are as thankful for them as we are thankful to the Hartman Center's more 'official' presentation of the same and related materials.
6. DMB&B (box 80). Though the product is clearly advertised as being suitable for children, the logic of the text, it seems to us, is clearly aimed at the purchasing power of the child's custodian.

Films That Sell

7. DMB&B (box 79).
8. Ibid.
9. Ibid.
10. Ibid.
11. Ibid. (box 80).
12. Video available at: http://library.duke.edu/digitalcollections/adviews_sugar_crisp/ (32).
13. For an excellent and highly accessible history of mid-century advertising and the creation of the American consumer, see Lawrence Samuel, *Brought to You By: Postwar Television Advertising and the American Dream* (Austin: University of Texas Press, 2001). Though not addressed or problematised as such, the notion of the loyal consumer is a thread that moves throughout Lawrence's research. For a contemporary example of this notion, think of Apple's *Think Different* campaign and its offspring, which, in its own manner, created a generation of consumers to whom a computer or gadget packaged with markers of brand loyalty (in the form of stickers) has become *de rigueur*.
14. Hiring Disney animators to sell products was, it appears, a winning mid-century strategy.
15. For more on the revolutionary Maypo campaign, see Samuel, *Brought to You By*, p. 104. The history on the Homestat Farm website (the company that bought Maltex) is even more detailed. For that history and access to some of the campaign's most iconic spots, see: http://www.homestatfarm.com/MemoryLane/TheTaleofMarkyMaypo/tabid/3083/Default.aspx. The video analysed above can be found here (navigate to 'Cowboy'): http://www.homestatfarm.com/MemoryLane/MaypoCommercials/tabid/2992/Default.aspx
16. http://library.duke.edu/digitalcollections/adviews_sugar_crisp/ (50).
17. http://library.duke.edu/digitalcollections/adviews_sugar_crisp/ (54). An ad featuring a Roy Rogers premium can be found here: http://library.duke.edu/digitalcollections/adviews_sugar_crisp/ (65)
18. An exemplary Christopher Wheat ad from 1961: http://library.duke.edu/digitalcollections/adviews_sugar_crisp/ (101) and an exemplary Big Kid ad from 1964, the year Sugar Bear was to be introduced: http://library.duke.edu/digital-collections/adviews_sugar_crisp/ (8). Even before the introduction of Sugar Bear as such, Post would experiment, around the time of the Big Kid and Christopher Wheat ads, with a solitary bear.
19. Samuel, *Brought to You By*, pp. 204–5.
20. Ibid., p. 104.
21. This is most certainly Samuel's assertion. See ibid., where he connects this logic directly to Maypo's marketing strategy. Less developed in Samuel, however, is the critical role played by Post. In a section focused on animated advertising and cereal, Samuel bypasses *Linus the Lionhearted* (thereby bypassing, too, the advertising logic Post's competitors, whom he does explore, were emulating). See ibid., pp. 204–9.
22. The *I Want my MTV* campaign is an excellent case in point. The fact that Maypo also produced a rubber piggybank in the form of Marky Maypo (a situation that caused Hubley some consternation) indicates to an even greater degree the industry's emerging strategy to hook young consumers with more than simply their product.
23. Interestingly, though not surprisingly, Post isn't interested in exploring this aspect of its history on its altogether bizarre website (see: http://www.postfoods.com/about-us/our-history/). In fact, the 'Our Story' section of their Sugar Crisp product (now Golden Crisp) is merely a timeline of the various 'looks' their beloved mascot has adopted over the years

(see: http://www.postfoods.com/our-brands/golden-crisp/our-story/). Mysteriously, they fail to mention the brand's initial campaign, which featured three bears. For reasons we find even more mysterious, Sugar Bear (who is still called Sugar Bear in spite of the brand's attempts to dissociate) has a Facebook presence where his 'habit' is made even more troublingly explicit: https://www.facebook.com/PostSugarBear. Images of Sugar Bear passed out on a park bench or holding his head on Bourbon Street (post-mardi gras) make light of his 'addiction' (the beginnings of which we will explore in these pages). It is, once again, the persistence of fans and enthusiasts that perpetuates this history, in spite of the industry's attempts to bury (or at least veil) it. Also worth pointing to is the relative dearth of sustained critical analyses of advertisements. Ogilvy remains a chestnut resource (see David Ogilvy, *Ogilvy on Advertising* [New York: Vintage, 1985]). But, like the bulk of the more contemporary research being produced, it is geared to advertising professionals. More common still is research aimed at concerned parents and focused on protecting our children in the consumer age. See Juliet Schor, *Born to Buy: The Comercialized Child and the New Consumer Culture* (New York: Scribner, 2005) or Susan Linn, *Consuming Kids: Protecting our Children from the Onslaught of Marketing and Advertising* (New York: Anchor, 2005). Very little in the way of a critical history of advertising or advertising for children is available. In the midst of *Advertising Age* and *Adweek*, *Adbusters* comes closest to the sort of critical voice required, though again, they are less focused on the historical aspects of the industry.

24. https://www.youtube.com/watch?v=7xTkltM6sCw

25. http://library.duke.edu/digitalcollections/adviews_sugar_crisp/ (110).

26. The connection to addiction and criminality is one we shall return to later. For our purposes at this juncture, however, we would simply point to the fact that cereal campaigns had historically used this logic. To some degree, our marauding 1940s bears in 'Camping Out West' initiate this logic.

27. Atherton W. Hobler, 'The First Fifty Years are the Easiest' (1967) (Box 6).

28. http://library.duke.edu/digitalcollections/adviews_sugar_crisp/ (154).

29. 33⅓, of course, is an important number as it is the number of times a 12-inch vinyl record turns per minute (i.e. 33⅓ rpm).

30. http://library.duke.edu/digitalcollections/adviews_sugar_crisp/ (172). We should note, too, that even though Sugar Bear implores kids to 'listen to the smash hit "Sugar Sugar"', none of the three discs produced, as far as we can tell, included that song. One suspects that the missing song would keep kids buying.

31. http://library.duke.edu/digitalcollections/adviews_sugar_crisp/ (215). The ad would appear to be from 1972, based on the reference to Super Orange Crisp, which lasted but a year (and based, more critically, on the relative ages of the Jacksons in the spot itself).

32. Gordon Webber, 'ANA-AAAA Clinic on Integration of Television Advertising' (26 June 1968), pp. 2–3 (box 6).

33. http://library.duke.edu/digitalcollections/adviews_sugar_crisp/ (168).

34. http://library.duke.edu/digitalcollections/adviews_sugar_crisp/ (178).

35. Webber (1968), pp. 4–6 (box 6).

36. http://library.duke.edu/digitalcollections/adviews_sugar_crisp/ (184, 16).

37. William D. Wells and Leonard A. Lo Sciuto, 'Direct Observation of Purchasing Behavior', *Journal of Marketing Research* vol. 3 no. 3 (August 1966), pp. 227–33.

13

Kim Novak and Morgan Stairways: Thinking about the Theory and History of the Tie-in

Patrick Vonderau

Among all the forms advertising has taken on over the course of its long history, product placements arguably are the most contested. Variously understood as merely an expression of cinematic 'realism', or, conversely, as a 'subliminal' manipulation of consumer consciousness,[1] placements have been at the centre of both media policy and aesthetic debates for decades. Despite this prevalent interest in the politics of advertising's aesthetics, however, hardly any research has taken the phenomenon of placing ads into non-advertising content seriously in aesthetic or political terms. This chapter closes the gap by arguing, in deliberate provocation, that product placements are a necessary element of cinema's constituency as a form of art. The argument begins with a succinct articulation of this philosophical claim before delving into the thick of historical examples, in order to finally return to the politics of such advertising practices.[2]

My starting point is *The Transfiguration of the Commonplace* (1981), Arthur C. Danto's famous contribution to an analytical philosophy of art. In this book, Danto recounts an episode which for him marks the end of the history of art and at the same time the moment it developed a consciousness of itself, becoming, as it were, its own philosophy. Visiting the Stable Gallery in New York in 1964, Danto experienced a 'philosophical intoxication' when suddenly faced with replicas of boxes containing kitchen cleaning supplies, or what later became famous as Andy Warhol's *Brillo Boxes*, 'as though the gallery had been pressed into service as a warehouse for surplus scouring pads'.[3] For Danto, this encounter prompted the question of the categorical difference between works of art and everyday objects, an awareness of which Danto identified as an essential component of every kind of aesthetic experience. The fact that *Brillo Boxes*' appearance as an exact replica of the scouring pad's packaging could not explain its aesthetic value is what allowed Danto to make his point. In his view, *Brillo Boxes* marks the moment when the definition of art explicitly became a part of art's essence. Danto experienced this peculiar transformation from a box of scouring pads into art as a quasi-religious 'transfiguration' of wares and thus of objects that, in his view, 'were so sunk in banality that their potentiality for aesthetic contemplation remained beneath scrutiny even after metamorphosis'.[4]

One might argue that for today's aesthetic experience of film, the definition of film as art (or not) has a somewhat analogous meaning. Here, we may relate Danto's argument to a more recent debate invested in thinking about the end of an art form – the end of cinema 'as we know it'. According to authors such as Jon Lewis[5] and Wheeler Winston

Dixon,[6] the end is near because present-day cinema no longer contains anything other than products. In a kind of converse argument, they maintain that we cannot believe in cinema's images as art any more because they seem today mere reflections of the economy that produced them.[7] Obviously, over-branded blockbusters such as *Minority Report* (Steven Spielberg, 2002), or even heavily promotional 'indie' hits have not triggered any 'philosophical intoxication' so far. And yet, if only for the sake of a thought experiment, we may ask ourselves why this, indeed, is the case. Hasn't cinema the potential to realise Warhol's famed motto that 'good business is the best art'? The fact that film is a commodity, that it advertises commodities and that it generates further commodities (such as merchandise) should place it firmly enough within the 'banality' of the everyday so that redefining a perception of it as art is conceivable. Certainly, Danto's Brillo epiphany did not rely primarily on the fact that *Brillo Boxes* reproduced an actual product, or that the boxes were put on sale as a work of art, but that they imitated something seemingly external to all aesthetic experience. Still, for Danto it is the banality of a given *product* that has implications for the definition of an art.[8]

What I am suggesting is that the aesthetic pleasure taken in feature films is related to an awareness of the difference between art and non-art, and that one might understand the presence of commodities in cinema not as an obstacle to, but as *key reference point* for cinematic experience. The casual way and seeming banality by which products make their entrance into any sort of cinematic fiction is, I argue, essential for cinema's aesthetic. In what follows, I am going to describe some facets of such an aesthetic interest or what we may call the 'Brillo dilemma' of film experience.

STRANGERS WHEN THEY MEET: SCEPTICS AND ADVENTURERS

At this point, Kim Novak enters the scene – or to be precise, Kim Novak and Morgan Stairways do. One can gather from the 1960 advertisement that Novak and the Morgan Company's products signify 'perfection'. The ad promotes both a staircase and Richard Quine's melodrama *Strangers When We Meet* (1960), released that very same year; apparently, the star was useful in lending the film's appeal to the stairs. The film came with many such promotions, among them a colour brochure distributed in theatre foyers and extensive photo coverage appearing in magazines such as *Life*, *Reader's Digest* and *Newsweek*. While the film's plot revolved around an extramarital affair that develops between architect Larry Coe (Kirk Douglas) and his neighbour Maggie (Novak) as Coe is building a 'dream house' in Bel Air, these various paratexts dealt mainly with the house itself. This is because production was, in fact, made possible by the actual construction of a house built by a New York architect's office, based on blueprints provided by art directors Ross Bellah and Carl Anderson, and in cooperation with thirty-seven construction companies who shared the $250,000 cost of building it.[9] These companies promoted the film nationwide in their advertise-ments, hoping to benefit, in turn, from CinemaScope and star power endowing their stairs, windows, fences and bricks with the feel of the silver screen. After production was completed, the house was sold while its architectural models continued touring construction trade fairs to promote a new suburban lifestyle that departed from the de-individualised housing developments of the post-war years.

Advertisement for a Morgan Company product (1960)

Such arrangements constituted an organised industrial practice that was and is not only very widespread, but also, in fact, entirely inseparable from Hollywood's history.[10] Various terms have come to describe this practice, among them 'plugging', 'cooperative advertising', 'exploitation', or 'product integration', apart from the more recent 'product placement' or 'branded entertainment'. In what follows, however, I will use the term 'tie-in', which dominated industry discourse during much of the classic era.[11]

Tie-ins are, in economic terms, a barter transaction between manufacturers of films and those of consumer goods or services in which the appearance of a brand in the film and its context is 'tied in' with promotion of the film in the brand's context. This helps the film's manufacturers reduce marketing costs while prolonging its life cycle, using products to remind viewers that the film is still 'out there', waiting to be watched. Product manufacturers, in turn, may link the purchase of mundane objects such as roof tiles, stairs, beverages, or shoes to the experience of romantic love, raising commodities above the realm of economic rationality. Underlying the tie-in is a premise of advertising psychology not to address prospective buyers directly by recommending consumption. Instead, tie-ins put products on display while not showing the intent of selling them.

Historically, we have to distinguish between the phenomenon's first appearance (around 1890),[12] the emergence of an organised industrial practice (in the 1930s) and the increasing public awareness of this practice (since the 1980s). As audiences became aware of this practice and increasingly literate in disclosing its operations, producers and advertisers had to tie-in narrative and commodity worlds in ever more refined and subtle ways. As early as in the 1920s, professional film reviewers showed an awareness of the tie-in, feeling addressed by advertisements while watching fiction.[13] But it was not until the early 1980s that this became a widely discussed aspect of the institution of cinema, when in *E.T. The Extra-Terrestrial* (1981), Steven Spielberg tied the beginning of an unusual friendship with Hershey's Reese's Pieces. In the history of the tie-in, which spans nearly a century, the attempt to tie the purpose of advertising to that of storytelling has subsequently led to formally most diverse results, with endless variety in the ways branded objects are shown, named, or used, and in terms of their inner dramaturgical relationship to other objects and the story's characters.

Now, against a widely shared background of tacit knowledge regarding the difference between art and non-art, tie-ins provoke two different, and mutually exclusive, answers to the question of cinema belonging into the realm of art or not. In order to simplify my argument, I will attribute these two theoretical positions to two model viewers. The first answer is the one provided by a sceptical film spectator; the second could be termed that of an 'aesthetic adventurer', borrowing from Roger Odin who speaks of a 'mode of aesthetic perception' as that of an adventure.[14] Sceptics, we may argue, tend to question cinema's status as art by identifying film with the industry that produces it. This position holds that film is a mere photograph of its institution, and that one cannot believe in its artistic qualities because of a mimetic relationship to economic power.[15] A variation of this argument can be found in current debates concerning the end of cinema: nowadays, theorists maintain, the logic of industrial synergies that holds new media culture together is reproduced in the films themselves.[16] There is a fear that, in the mid-1990s, film lost its place and its identity, 'exploded' into a wide variety of formats, product types and modes of appropriation. For spectators, this arguably entails a loss of the border that in the past shielded the realm of disinterested pleasure from instrumental rationality – a loss of the separation of contemplation and utilitarian thinking, of leisure time and work that had been so significant to the experience of art since the nineteenth century.[17] Thomas Elsaesser, for instance, asserts that, currently, cinema audiences would pay for nothing more than the transubstantiation of experience into goods, in a kind of neo-Marxist reversal of Danto's transfiguration model.[18] Others take a more moderate view, arguing that film is art *despite* the fact that it is an industry (cf. auteurism) or that film is an art *because* it is an industry (as in formalism).[19] Still, proponents of these positions assume a strict separation of the two spheres and thus share a similar concept of experience. Paradoxically, however, the separation of art from external or commercial interests took place at the same time art markets began to emerge and art became a consumer good for the bourgeoisie: art's economic value consolidated itself to the same degree that its aesthetic value became tied to subjective experience.[20]

The adventurer's view is more radical in that it takes Deleuze at his word, according to whom 'money is the obverse of all the images that the cinema shows and sets in place'.[21] What makes cinema distinctive, he claims, is 'not mechanical reproduction but its internalized relation with money'.[22] What if cinema's relationship with money indeed was 'internalised' aesthetically? The adventure would then begin precisely where sceptics would have it end: with the insight into the economic constitution of the filmic world of perception.

Strangers When We Meet (1960): saying goodbye at the house

ON THE AESTHETIC OF THE TIE-IN

Let us take a closer look at the house and the Morgan stairs in *Strangers When We Meet*. In the film's final sequence the wooden building is almost complete and the architect has decided to break up with Maggie for the sake of his wife, though Maggie is the woman he truly loves. Quine laid out the sequence as a long series of pans, tracking shots and colours, accompanied by George Duning's swinging orchestral score. It begins with a bird's-eye view of the house on the Bay Area's sweeping panorama. A distant car approaches, then the camera zooms in on Maggie in a combination of long and medium shots as she stands next to the house, surveying it from the outside; a colour scheme of white, pale blue and light yellow, enriched by the warm red of the rain-soaked wood, gives the scene a morning atmosphere. As if choreographed in a musical, Maggie marvels while gliding from the pool to the windows and the doors and, finally, up the Morgan stairs. Larry's car then moves up the driveway and the slam of its door announces his presence. When Larry reaches the front door, Maggie, as if making a stage appearance, passes through a gate in the fence. Quine brings them out of the long shot to unite the couple in a kiss, while with each approaching shot the wooden planks behind them develop a new intensity of colour, even a tactile quality. This is repeated in the subsequent scenes in front of and inside the house, not least with words: 'I have been peeking in windows – it's beautiful!' says Maggie. 'It is an exciting house, this is really our house.' 'You know what I'd do if we would live here?' Larry answers. 'I'd build a moat around this place. Keep the whole world out.' These words, however, herald their separation.[23]

Following Odin's line of thought, one could say that the appearance of this real, company-branded house would prompt, on the one hand, sceptical viewers (assuming they recognise it as such) to situate the production's actual enunciator outside art – that is, in the sphere of industry – precisely because they are aware of being addressed in a way that runs counter to what is normally associated with the institution of art's aesthetic mode, which raises them above the banal objects and advertising pitches they are forced to hear in everyday life. A critic once summed up the dilemma in a different case: 'Does the character really drive a Ford or did Ford pay for this?'[24] This dilemma becomes apparent as soon as a sceptical spectator finds him or herself confronted with a fictional situation they are prepared to believe, only to have to ask the question of whether it is fictionally true or not. Whether phrased this or another way, the question marks the limits to which one is prepared to accept, in light of film's canonical history, what can and cannot be considered part of a given mode of aesthetic perception, with potential ramifications for the filmic illusion and the reception experience as a whole.

Aesthetic adventurers, on the other hand, will regard a product such as the Morgan stairs not so much as an *opposant* (Greimas) but as a helpful *actant* in their search for aesthetic values and so will not, accordingly, think it a fundamental contradiction to attribute the real enunciator to the institution of an industrial art. In the case of the Brillo boxes, the packaging's designer, expressionist painter James Harvey, is often mentioned for the purpose of emphasising the intrinsic aesthetic value of industrial design and advertising,[25] and one could also speak of the Morgan stairs' intrinsic beauty in a similar vein. Still, somewhat more is at stake than the beauty of the thing itself. While one of the characteristic features of fictional reference is that it fails to provide a complete specification of the world of objects, leaving such reference open or undefined instead, displaying a product necessitates a different, more concrete relationship to an actual object, the point of the tie-in is not to simply duplicate an empirical artefact,[26] but rather to *specify* things that, rather than merely random objects taken from the film's material environment, *like art, have names*. One could argue that all those specific staircases, soft drinks and automobiles to which industry has always tied the art of film constitute a significant portion of its vitality, and this vitality lies precisely in the fact that, in their reproductions, a concept of the material world literally becomes manifest. Brand-name products intervene in the 'transition from a found to a constructed world',[27] and they play an important role when it comes to the representational nature of the filmic world and its aesthetic illusion.

Of course, the particularity of a staircase such as Morgan's also relies on the fact that it addresses the audience through the quality of its own filmic representation. Quine's direction is clearly geared towards an 'attractional display',[28] intending to show the house as being beautifully presented. Tie-ins always address their audience in two ways: both as spectators of a *filmic* world and with a view to their possible future actions as consumers in the *real* one. In our example, this characteristic double temporality of the tie-in nicely relates to that of the melodrama; in a reflexive movement, the scene above shows the house in a future perspective, and it does so for an audience that, when confronted with any product, may feel reminded of something they previously encountered and thought was beautiful, in a kind of desired prolongation of the melodramatic 'too late' and 'if only'.[29]

Apart from their temporality, a second characteristic of tie-ins is the way they confront spectators with the utter randomness of their own occurrence. For what do building materials have to do with romantic affairs? How are refrigerators and secret agents related, like in *Mr & Mrs Smith* (Doug Liman, 2005)? Or mints and teenage pregnancies, like in *Juno* (Jason Reitman, 2007)? While, on the one hand, Morgan staircases and windows, Sub-Zero refrigerators and Ferrero Tic Tacs permit a branded object to stand out in the material world, on the other hand, the question of why *this* object in particular is chosen often remains uncertain. Chance suspends a system of order (or reveals it to be fragile) without introducing another order that would become intelligible as such. Why does Eden Sinclair survive *Doomsday* (Neil Marshall, 2008) in a Bentley rather than a Benz? In *Blue Velvet* (David Lynch, 1986) why do Jeffrey and Sandy drink Heineken rather than Hamm's? In terms of narrative logic, the presence of the car in the action movie and that of the beer at Ben's strange bar seem reasonable, but the appearance of the specific product in each of the two cases can hardly be explained sufficiently in terms of brand presence, 'image transfer', or the proximity of the screen to a given point of sale. Frequently, neither the placement nor the products correspond to the type of experience associated with the given genre at hand, just as Kim Novak does not climb the stairs (a prop that has, after all, long been a core element of melodramatic *mise en scène*) in order to expose the discontinuities inherent in the structures of emotional experience (as often the case in the melodrama), but to identify them as beautiful and useful within a continuity to everyday life. In Quine's film, the house, as a visual metaphor, only partly benefits a melodramatic strategy of indirect subjectivation because it does not, as is often the case, make the protagonists' emotions seem hopeless, instead opening up for them a new and liberating perspective in the end.[30] So once one accepts the fact that the appearance of consumer goods in a given film's narrative does not necessarily conflict with one's quest for aesthetic values, just as the wood is what gives the light its warm, wistful colour at the end of *Strangers When We Meet*, one must also admit that the attempt to wed the world of goods to the narrative world often produces rather absurd results.[31]

Speaking of early melodrama, Ben Singer has described chance as being of a higher form of order that would regularly intervene in the interplay of wish and wish fulfilment and suspend causal and logical series of actions.[32] Singer's early cinema example of a villain hit by lightning at the last minute recalls, for instance, Bill Harding and his team in *Twister* (Jan de Bont, 1996) taking measurements of a tornado raging over their heads with the aid of hastily cut-up Pepsi cans. Chance, in the context of tie-ins, seems to stand for a rather central feature of consumer goods, just as the idea of 'significant form' historically came to stand for art itself. Products intervene unannounced in the interplay of wish and wish fulfilment, which has become

Hollywood's dramatic blueprint, thereby constantly renewing both capitalism's promise that one's every wish can be fulfilled and also the scope of filmic experience. Whether successful or not, product placement consequently has developed a systematic relationship with the types of experience we as spectators have learned to associate with different genres. Mary Ann Doane once aptly remarked that 'the metonymy is the trope of the tie-in'.[33]

The aesthetic of the tie-in is characterised not only by temporality and chance, but – third – also by the fact that products placed within a fiction often expose a surprising capability to act. Random objects suddenly acquire agency by intervening in the storyline, turning into supporting characters – either literally, like Wilson, the famous volleyball in *Cast Away* (Robert Zemeckis, 2000) that becomes Chuck's life-saving companion on a desert island, or figuratively, as in *Strangers When We Meet*, where the house acts as a third main character as described in a production note: 'It comes to life; it grows; and when at last it stands completed on a hill high in Bel Air … our story is over.'[34] The examples are numerous and range from shooting, flying and speaking cars to iPods transformed into robots to lighters, such as the Zippos that, ever since film noir, have lit the way home for so many villains and monsters.[35] If one, like Bruno Latour[36] and others, presumes that objects have social lives, it quickly becomes evident that products are often more than merely adjuncts to the characters in a narrative. Certainly, in feature films the traits of products and characters are usually closely coordinated; what a character can do and actually does often rubs off onto the product. But the reverse can also happen: Rayban sunglasses fit Tom Cruise in *Top Gun* (Tony Scott, 1986) in the same way that Converse sneakers fit Will Smith in *I, Robot* (Alex Proyas, 2004). On an ontological level, trivial things are even one step ahead of the 'human somethings', as Cavell called the screen projections of stars[37] because they are accessible in the real, everyday world and not just on screen, and because they, unlike movie stars, can even be present in the real world at the very moment of filmic experience. In Mr Big, Carrie Bradshaw's great love, *Sex and the City* (Michael Patrick King, 2008) presented to its female audience an undisguised stereotype of female desire that cannot be possessed as such, while at the same time the brand names were what made it possible to extend the film's emotional fantasies into reality: the clothes and accessories worn by every major female character could be bought online (at seenon.com). Indeed, it is no coincidence that feature films have systematically linked heterosexual love to objects since the era of classical Hollywood, objects one can acquire and keep: cinema reminds us of the fleeting nature of romantic feelings and social bonds more generally, by contrasting them with the permanence of goods that seem always available for purchase.[38]

Finally, not only the characters' agency, but also that of the products relies on psychological realism, assuming such realism is understood as a system of motivations that explain qualities, actions and states of affairs. In *Sex and the City* Carrie and her Dior platform sandals similarly follow the idea of 'fearless fashion' – a feature of both the product's personality and that of her character.[39] So, in film, objects even act out their ability to be more than just shoes or sunglasses – also depicted is their 'affordance' for doing something.[40] Can anything more beautiful than a volleyball be imagined for a film called *Cast Away*?[41]

CONCLUSION

One may nevertheless, like the sceptics, perceive the temporality, contingency and agency of the products tied to the film as a disruption of the aesthetic experience in cinema, and the fact that Richard Quine's film has not come to occupy a central place in the canon of the melodrama may support this view. In this chapter, however, I was more interested in showing that the industrial practice of the tie-in is anything but marginal for cinema as an art. Products cannot just be subtracted from the film, at least not without the audience noticing it in an aesthetic sense. Products neither guarantee economic utility, nor are they completely absorbed by such utility.[42] Rather, by entering the filmic universe in an almost casual fashion, trivial objects actually support the process of reality transfer (Bazin's *transfert de réalité*):[43] the names of things provide evidence of the fact that the image participates in the object. This closely connects all the building materials, soaps, mobile phones, sweets, jewels, perfumes and clothes, all identified by name, to cinema as the prototypical medium of modernity, a medium that has made it possible for many present and future theorists to experience the aesthetics of contingency, the delight of chance and the flush of the abundantly rich empiricity of appearance.[44] Seen in this way, the reflection of an industrial art form onto itself is part of what enables the experience of it as art. Critics of the advertising industry, and of the not-so-secret bonds between art and industry, still may console themselves with the fact that the 'international conspiracy' Deleuze wrote about[45] is not just effective in cinema; it is also in cinema where it is particularly good to observe. While the film industry has certainly tried to control its audience ever since film became a mass commodity, the logic of objectification accompanying cinema in the form of practices such as the tie-in does not at all contradict the idea of cinema's autonomy: rather, it allows for it.

NOTES

1. Mary-Lou Galician (ed.), *Handbook of Product Placement in the Mass Media. New Strategies in Marketing Theory, Practice, Trends, and Ethics* (Binghamton, NY: Best Business Books, 2004), p. 9; Kerry Segrave, *Product Placement in Hollywood Films. A History* (Jefferson, NC, and London: McFarland, 2004), pp. 106–8.
2. Several individuals and institutions graciously provided support while I was researching this article, and I would like to thank the Academy of Motion Picture Arts and Sciences (AMPAS) and Barbara Hall, in particular, for unfailingly providing advice during my stay in Los Angeles. An earlier version of this text appeared in the German-language journal *Montage AV* vol. 18 no. 1 (2009), pp. 175–96.
3. Arthur C. Danto, *The Transfiguration of the Commonplace* (Cambridge, MA: Harvard University Press, 1981), p. iv.
4. Ibid.
5. Jon Lewis, *The End of Cinema as We Know It: American Film in the Nineties* (New York: New York University Press, 2001).
6. Wheeler Winston Dixon, *Visions of the Apocalypse. Spectacles of Destruction in American Cinema* (London and New York: Wallflower Press, 2003); 'Twenty-five Reasons Why It's All Over', in Lewis, *The End of Cinema As We Know It*, pp. 356–67.

7. Dixon, 'Twenty-five Reasons Why It's All Over', p. 360.

8. In the art world, connections to the world of commodities remain a matter of controversy, although the debate is not comparable to discussion of the end of cinema – think of Takashi Murakami's Vuitton bags, Jeff Koon's vacuum cleaners, or Baselitz's predilection for Hugo Boss suits, not to mention Matthew Barney's experimental film works or Damien Hirst's Science Ltd.

9. Margaret Herrick Library, Marty Weiser Papers, Folder 484–511 (Strangers When We Meet), AMPAS. The film's production history is extensively documented and an account can be found in my book *Economies of Emotion* (in preparation). This tie-in was thought up by the brilliant Martin B. Weiser (1911–88), who arranged it in 1959 for Richard Quine Productions.

10. Charles Eckert, 'The Carole Lombard in Macy's Window', *Quarterly Review of Film Studies* vol. 3 no. 1 (1978), pp. 1–21.

11. Jay Newell, Charles T. Salmon, and Susan Chang, 'The Hidden History of Product Placement', *Journal of Broadcasting and Electronic Media* vol. 50 no. 4 (2006), pp. 575–94. There is no useful or generally accepted definition even for the term 'product placement'. In addition, the phenomenon's economic, legal and historical aspects, as well as those involving perceptual psychology, are not clearly separated (see Manfred Auer, *Product Placement. Die neue Kunst der geheimen Verführung* [Düsseldorf: Econ 1988]; Florian Asche, *Das Product Placement im Kinospielfilm* [Frankfurt am Main and Berlin: Lang 1996]; Anja Johansson, *Product Placement in Film und Fernsehen* [Berlin: Mensch & Buch Verlag 2001]; Reinhard D. Schultze, *Product Placement im Spielfilm. Grenzen zulässiger Produktabbildung im Rundfunkprogramm* [Munich: C. H. Beck 2001]; Galician, *Handbook of Product Placement in the Mass Media*; and Segrave, *Product Placement in Hollywood Films*). Moreover, the terms in use signify quite different ranges or degrees to which film and advertising are mingled, ranging from cooperative advertising (where there is no reference to a specific product), to systematic product integration, to such films as *The Women* (Diane English, 2008), which was produced by Dove, a cosmetics corporation.

12. According to Charles Musser (in this volume), 'movies were never innocent'. Daniel Morse has shown that the Edison Company was already using its films in the 1910s to promote some of its other products, for example in *The Stenographer's Friend* (1910) and *The Voice of the Violin* (1915). (Daniel Ryan Morse, 'Explorations of the Inhuman: Edison Phonographs in Silent Film' [unpublished manuscript, Temple University, 2008]).

13. In Berlin at that time, Rudolf Arnheim analysed the 'psychology of the [US-style] assembly-line film'. In a remark that was equally sarcastic and apt, he noted that 'The spectator enjoys the car driven by the hero as if he owned it himself' (translation from the German original). (Rudolf Arnheim, *Film als Kunst. Mit einem Vorwort zur Neuausgabe* [Munich: Hanser, 1974], p. 166).

14. Roger Odin, 'Kunst und Ästhetik bei Film und Fernsehen. Elemente zu einem semio-pragmatischen Ansatz', *Montage AV. Zeitschrift für Theorie und Geschichte audiovisueller Kommunikation* vol. 11 no. 2 (2002), pp. 42–57.

15. See Richard Allen, 'Looking at Motion Pictures', in Richard Allen and Murray Smith (eds), *Film Theory and Philosophy* (Oxford: Clarendon Press 1997), pp. 76–94; Noel Carroll, 'Towards an Ontology of the Moving Image', in Cynthia Freeland and Thomas Wartenberg (eds), *Philosophy and Film* (New York: Routledge 1995), pp. 69–85; Noel Carroll, *The Philosophy of Motion Pictures* (Malden, MA: Blackwell, 2008).

16. Casetti, Francesco, 'Theory, Post-Theory, Neo-Theories: Changes in Discourses, Changes in Objects', *Cinémas: Révue d'études cinématographiques* (special issue *La théorie du cinéma, enfin en crise*) vol. 17 no. 2–3 (2007), pp. 33–46.

17. Carroll, *The Philosophy of Motion Pictures*, pp. 152–4.

18. Thomas Elsaesser, 'The Blockbuster: Everything Connects, but Not Everything Goes', in Lewis, *The End of Cinema As We Know It*, p. 10.

19. See David Bordwell, Janet Staiger and Kristin Thompson, *The Classical Hollywood Cinema: Film Style and Mode of Production to 1960* (New York: McGraw-Hill 1985).

20. Carroll, *The Philosophy of Motion Pictures*; see also Thierry Du Duve, *Kant After Duchamp* (Cambridge, MA: MIT Press, 1998).

21. Gilles Deleuze, *Cinema 2: The Time-Image*, translated by Hugh Tomlinson and Robert Galeta (London: Continuum, 1989), p. 75.

22. Ibid.

23. The appearance of the finished house in the sequence at the end of the film had been arranged with the Morgan Company and the other manufacturers just as minutely as Kim Novak's appearance in print advertisements. Thus, the National Oak Flooring Manufacturers Association suggested showing Novak in photographs in a way that would draw the observer's attention to the floor without making Novak look unnatural – 'We would like to have the floor prominent (and Kim Novak, too).' Letter from Holton C. Rush to Marty Weiser, 12 February 1960, Marty Weiser Papers, Folder 497, Margaret Herrick Library, AMPAS.

24. This was in reference to product placement in Faye Weldon's novel *The Bulgari Connection* (2001). 'Fay Weldons Reklame-Roman', *Spiegel Online* www.spiegel.de/kultur/literatur/0,1518,155065,00.html, accessed 24 March 2009.

25. Michael J. Golec, *The Brillo Box Archive: Aesthetics, Design, and Art* (Dartmouth, NH: Brandeis University Press 2008).

26. See Theodor W. Adorno and Max Horkheimer, *Dialektik der Aufklärung. Philosophische Fragmente*, 15th edition (Frankfurt am Main: Suhrkamp, 2004).

27. Gertrud Koch, 'Filmische Welten—Zur Welthaltigkeit filmischer Projektionen', in Joachim Küpper and Christoph Menke (ed.), *Dimensionen ästhetischer Erfahrung* (Frankfurt am Main: Suhrkamp, 2003), p. 172; translation from the German original.

28. Kessler, Frank, 'The Cinema of Attractions as *Dispositif*', in Wanda Strauven (ed.), *The Cinema of Attractions Reloaded* (Amsterdam: Amsterdam University Press, 2006), p. 59.

29. See Stanley Cavell, *Contesting Tears: The Hollywood Melodrama of the Unknown Woman* (Chicago and London: University of Chicago Press 1996), p. 179; Linda Williams, 'Melodrama Revised', in Nick Browne (ed.), *Refiguring American Film Genres: History and Theory* (Berkeley and Los Angeles: University of California Press, 1998), pp. 42–89; and Thomas Elsaesser, 'Tales of Sound and Fury: Observations on the Family Melodrama', in Marcia Landy (ed.), *Imitations of Life: A Reader on Film & Television Melodrama* (Detroit: Wayne State University Press, 1991), pp. 68–91.

30. See Hermann Kappelhoff, *Matrix der Gefühle. Das Kino, das Melodrama und das Theater der Empfindsamkeit* (Berlin: Vorwerk 8, 2004), p. 254.

31. This is particularly extreme in the case of superheroes. In *Superman II* (Richard Lester, 1980) the bad guy hurls the eponymous hero into a parked Marlboro truck; and the hero, in turn, takes revenge by throwing the other man into a neon Coca-Cola billboard. In a similar car chase scene, the hero of *Spider-Man* (Sam Raimi, 2002) runs into a Carlsberg truck after testing his superpowers on a can of Dr Pepper at home.

32. Ben Singer, *Melodrama and Modernity: Early Sensational Cinema and Its Contexts* (New York: Columbia University Press 2001), pp. 136–7.

33. Mary Ann Doane, 'The Economy of Desire: The Commodity Form in/of the Cinema', *Quarterly Review of Film and Video* vol. 11 no. 1 (1989), p. 27. An analysis of tie-ins must take into consideration not only the film and its promotion in the context of its premiere, but also the way in which the placement in question was negotiated between producers, agencies and manufacturers. Documents that could provide evidence are often hard to come by. When they are available, trade journals such as *Variety* and *Hollywood Reporter* contain information that permits identifying the placement as a coordinated strategy of film and product marketing.

34. Letter from Marty Weiser to Richard Stevens, Anderson Corporation, 9 August 1959, Marty Weiser Papers, Folder 488, AMPAS.

35. Just a few examples: the cars in the Bond films; *Wall-E* (Andrew Stanton, 2008), which resulted from cooperation between Apple and Pixar; and for Zippo *Objective Burma* (Raoul Walsh, 1945), *Silent Hill* (Christophe Gans, 2006) and *Die Hard* (John McTiernan, 1998).

36. Bruno Latour, *Reassembling the Social: An Introduction to Actor-Network-Theory* (Oxford: Oxford University Press 2005).

37. Stanley Cavell, *The World Viewed: Reflections on the Ontology of Film* (Cambridge, MA, and London: Harvard University Press, 1979), p. 26.

38. Jane Gaines, 'The Queen Christina Tie-Ups: Convergence of Show Window and Screen', *Quarterly Review of Film and Video* vol. 11 no. 1 (1989), pp. 35–60.

39. See below for further remarks on the concept of 'personality'.

40. See Koch, 'Filmische Welten'; James J. Gibson, *The Ecological Approach to Visual Perception* (Boston: Houghton Mifflin, 1979).

41. There is also an internal conflict between Wilson and the FedEx parcels that were washed ashore with him. The interaction between the two brands would merit a study in its own right (see Michael L. Maynard and Megan Scala, 'Unpaid Advertising: A Case of Wilson the Volleyball in *Cast Away*', *The Journal of Popular Culture* vol. 39 no. 4 [2006], pp. 622–38).

42. This is a general conclusion reached in a number of empirical studies. See Denise DeLorme and Leonard Reid, 'Moviegoers' Experiences and Interpretations of Brands in Films Revisited', *Journal of Advertising* vol. 28 no. 2 (1999), pp. 71–95; Pola Gupta and Kenneth Lord, 'Product Placement in Movies: The Effect of Prominence and Mode on Audience Recall', *Journal of Current Issues and Research in Advertising* vol. 20 no. 1 (1998), pp. 47–59; Isreal Nebenzahl and Eugene Secunda, 'Consumers' Attitudes toward Product Placement in Movies', *International Journal of Advertising* vol. 12 no. 1 (1993), pp. 1–12; Eva Marie Steortz, 'The Cost Efficency and Communication Effects Associated with Brand Name Exposure within Motion Pictures' (MA thesis, West Virginia University, 1987); and Moonhee Yang and David R. Roskos-Ewoldsen, 'The Effectiveness of Brand Placements in the Movies: Levels of Placement, Explicit and Implicit Memory, and Brand-Choice Behaviour', *Journal of Communication* vol. 57 no. 3 (2007), pp. 469–89.

43. André Bazin, 'Ontologie de l'image photographique' [1945], in Bazin, *Qu'est-ce que le cinéma* (Paris: Cerf, 1993), p. 14.

44. See Leo Charney and Vanessa R. Schwartz (eds), *Cinema and the Invention of Modern Life* (Berkeley, Los Angeles and London: University of California Press, 1995).

45. Deleuze, *Cinema 2*, p. 75.

PART III
ARCHIVES
AND SOURCES

•

14

Coming Soon! Lantern Slide Advertising in the Archive

Robert Byrne

Louis Lumière's historic premiere of *La Sortie de l'usine Lumière à Lyon* on 28 December 1895, depicting employees emerging through the gates of his own factory, could reasonably be considered the first screening of a promotional motion picture,[1] but it was not the first instance of using projection apparatus as an advertising medium. This distinction must clearly be afforded to the magic lantern. According to David Robinson *et al.*, lantern slide advertising was 'common in the streets of New York in 1871'[2] and advertising slides were commonly made available to magic lantern performers from the 1870s, with lanternists able to obtain slides free of charge from various manufacturers.[3] With the advent of motion-picture exhibition at the end of the century, magic lantern images naturally complemented moving-picture programmes (and vice versa), featuring song lyrics, announcements, advertisements for local merchants and manufactured products and, eventually, promoting upcoming motion-picture programmes.[4]

Trade ad for motion-picture advertising slides, 1913[6]

Coming Soon! Lantern Slide Advertising in the Archive

223

It is impossible to pinpoint the exact date when lantern slides were first used to advertise motion-picture 'coming attractions', but evidence suggests the practice became commonplace circa 1912, the same era during which film lengths began to regularly exceed two reels and public recognition of individually identified film stars emerged. Not coincidentally, it was also in 1912 that the first American motion-picture trailer was reportedly screened.[5] The earliest examples of motion-picture slide advertisements were not furnished to exhibitors by film studios, but were custom-made by individual showmen or produced by professional slide manufacturers and offered for sale through advertisements in motion-picture trade papers. During the 1920s, film-advertising slide production coalesced into a handful of dedicated manufacturers, and later to studio-affiliated publicity services, though some local producers and individual exhibitors continued making their own slides for decades afterward. While lantern advertising is typically thought of as a silent-era phenomenon (and, indeed, the height of lantern slide advertising coincided with the silent era and early 1930s) the practice continued in the USA into the early 1960s and survived through the mid-80s in other parts of the world.

The history of glass slide motion-picture advertising has yet to be written, an endeavour frustrated in part by lack of access to, and awareness of, numerous institutionally held collections. Advertising, industrial and sponsored films are recognised today as orphans, a categorical designation[7] that has rapidly gained universal recognition, but this increased awareness has not yet expanded to cinema's glass plate brethren. Unlike film prints that circulated from venue to venue, the commercial lifespan of a motion-picture advertising slide lasted only a couple of days, after which it would be discarded, or at best tossed aside and forgotten. Disadvantaged by temporality of purpose and susceptible to breakage, the remaining artefacts of motion-picture slide advertising that survive have done so primarily by chance rather than by design. This benign neglect is echoed today in the collection policies of most modern museums and archives. While there exist major institutions devoted specifically to pre-cinema and magic lantern as an entertainment medium, the formal collection of commercial and motion-picture advertising slides seldom falls within an institution's acquisition mandate or collection strategy. Institutions that hold motion-picture advertising slides generally fall into one of several broad categories: museums devoted to pre-cinema or magic lantern as an entertainment medium (e.g. Museo Nazionale del Cinema di Torino[8]); motion-picture museums and archives whose collections include film-related ephemera such as production artefacts, promotional materials, studio records and advertising slides (e.g. George Eastman House[9]); and historical museums and general research libraries which incidentally include lantern slides within their collections (e.g. Cleveland Public Library,[10] Oakland Museum of California[11]).

What is the current state of archival retention of motion-picture advertising slides, and how might the archival practices of the future respond, particularly with regard to digitisation, cataloguing, metadata and virtual access? The response is based in part on a 2011–12 survey[13] of the archival landscape as regards cinema advertising slides. This broad-based survey garnered responses from twenty-seven collecting institutions located in North America, Europe and the Pacific Rim, and represented a wide range of institutional types, including motion-picture archives, research institutions and public libraries, as well as institutions specialising in magic lantern and pre-cinema visual entertainment.

Coming attraction slide for *The Root of Evil* (1914)[12]

INSTITUTIONS AND THEIR COLLECTIONS

Few organisations that hold motion-picture slides in their collections place great priority on the materials. Film archives and museums possessing motion picture-related ephemera (including lantern slides) typically have acquired the material by way of private donation rather than targeted procurement. These materials have been passively collected and generally reside on the fringes of the institution's collection. Of the institutions surveyed, six out of the twenty-seven stated that they actively seek to acquire advertising slides for their collections, but only half of that number have ever expended funds towards that end. The extensive collections of cinema-related slides at the Irish Film Archive,[14] the Margaret Herrick Library[15] and the Cleveland Public Library all came to those institutions primarily through single large donations. And though these collections are now recognised for their value, their place within the institution's collection has not always been above question. One librarian responding to the survey related a story in which their slide collection was saved only through the guile of a quick-thinking librarian who hid their collection behind a bookcase in order to prevent its deaccession.

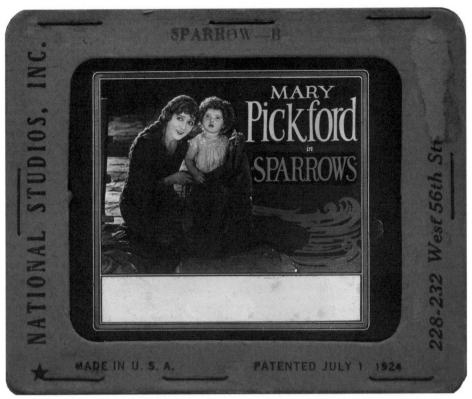

Coming attraction slide for *Sparrows* (1926)[16]

Other institutions that hold motion-picture slides are those specifically devoted to pre-cinema and magic lantern as an entertainment medium. The Museu del Cinema[17] in Gerona, Spain, and the Museo Nazionale del Cinema di Torino, Italy, are primary examples of such organisations. These institutions hold massive collections of slides, though only a handful are related to the cinema. For example, the Museo Nazionale del Cinema di Torino holds more than 80,000 glass slides in their collection, but only eighty are cinema-related, and of those only five are motion-picture advertisements. This is not to imply that these institutions are failing to follow their mission; quite the contrary, it simply demonstrates that the sub-category of motion-picture advertising generally falls beyond the domain of their primary mission. Indeed, among all institutions surveyed, 35 per cent in some way include lantern slides in their collection policy, but that number dwindles to a single institution when the question narrows specifically to cinema-related lantern slides.

ACCESS AND METADATA

Despite their marginal status in most collections, three-quarters of the institutions surveyed have compiled some level of metadata relating to their motion-picture slide

Films That Sell

collections. Five of the institutions, such as the Cleveland Public Library, have a searchable online index and the same number offer to furnish comprehensive lists of their holdings upon request. The extent of the metadata provided in these listings varies substantially. All listings include the film title and usually the actors named in the advertisement, but rarely does the metadata extend to include the advertised film's studio, release date, censorship code or country of origin; and, with the possible exception of noting that a slide is cracked or broken, none of the institutions surveyed record any of the artefact's physical characteristics, such as manufacturer, construction,[18] or dimensions. Like the motion pictures that they advertise, the fabrication processes for commercial advertising slides changed over time and varied by era and manufacturer. Having access to metadata that describes the physical characteristics of a slide can offer important clues regarding a slide's artefactual history. Likewise, different countries and regions standardised on varying physical dimensions and, in the absence of having this information available as searchable metadata, a researcher's only recourse is physical access to the artefact itself. Fortunately, most institutions have reasonably liberal access policies when it comes to their advertising slide collection. Despite the artefacts' obvious fragility, over half of the institutions surveyed allow physical access to their collections, sometimes with exclusion of slides that are cracked, broken, or otherwise damaged. Cinémathèque française[19] takes a unique approach by allowing qualified researchers to physically handle only the slides for which the archive holds duplicate copies.

While physical access to a collection can be important for researchers (at least those with a travel budget), virtual access to a collection via the internet facilitates worldwide access to the collection, making it available to researchers as well as casual browsers. Online access, in combination with complete metadata listings, not only

Coming Soon! Lantern Slide Advertising in the Archive

227

increases the potential audience for a collection, it also provides the means for an institution to protect the material artefacts from the attendant risks of physical handling. Unfortunately, the majority of institutions surveyed have not yet digitised their collections, or have only done so partially or not made them available online. Of the twenty-seven institutions surveyed, three have posted some portion of their collection online and only one, the Cleveland Public Library, has their entire collection openly searchable. Looking to the future, six of the institutions not currently providing online access professed the intent to do so, though none has committed to specific plans or dates.

The argument for, and benefit derived from, facilitating online access to institutional slide collections is not insignificant. When asked to evaluate the public interest in their slide collection, the institutions that provide online visibility typified their frequency of enquiry as 'often' and 'frequent', while institutions that do not facilitate online access characterised their rate of public enquiry as 'seldom' and 'never'. Not only does online access to the collection increase awareness and interest, the technical, logistical and financial barriers to doing so are extraordinarily low. The internet is the perfectly tailored medium for providing access to collections of glass lantern slides and, in addition to the intellectual benefits of providing broad access to the collection, digitising and then properly storing the original (and fragile) slide artefacts provides protection from damage due to handling. Indeed, a comprehensive programme to digitise and make available a collection not only solves the problem of general access, but also melds seamlessly into a comprehensive asset protection strategy.

THE IMPERATIVE FOR VIRTUAL ACCESS

If the study of motion-picture promotional materials can be regarded as a niche concern, then academic consideration of cinema-related lantern slides can at best be described as a niche within a niche. For all practical purposes, the practice of in-cinema advertising is virgin territory as regards academic enquiry, perhaps due in part to the challenges presented in locating and studying the relevant artefacts, specifically lantern slides and trailers. Not only does in-cinema advertising provide fertile ground for new research, such work also is long overdue. Motion-picture advertising trailers and slides are the only promotional materials designed for, and directed exclusively to, an audience already seated for a motion-picture performance. In fact, it is not unreasonable to suggest that in-cinema motion-picture advertisements should be considered part of the programme itself and afforded equivalent status of newsreels, short subjects and singalongs. Unique in the universe of promotional material, slides and trailers were not designed to invite immediate patronage by luring passers-by into the cinema, but instead were intended to convince a current audience to return to the same venue at a later date for a future attraction. These inducements, projected upon the same screen and in the same venue to which they encouraged a return visit, developed and expressed their own language, tropes and coded meanings to memorably convey the promise of a future attraction worth returning for. These conventions survive today in the modern cinemagoing experience. Though rectangular glass slides have given way to digital projection, contemporary pre-show experiences still often include a rotation of static images imploring the audience to purchase a product, silence their mobile phone, visit the snack bar, or take note of an upcoming attraction.

The imperatives of preservation and access to institutionally held advertising slide collections is clear. While a wide variety of institutions maintain such materials within their holdings, the majority of these collections are either ignored or marginalised. In the past, demand for access to these collections has also been low, which would appear to justify the low priority placed on making them accessible. But demand follows awareness, and those collections that have been made digitally available receive considerably greater levels of utilisation. Without question, the academic study of motion-picture promotion is an avenue of enquiry underserved by current scholarship. By individually adopting low-cost initiatives to digitise and make available their collections, museums, archives and collecting institutions would yield the multiple advantages of protecting their collection from damage due to physical handling, increasing the online visibility of their institution, providing significant value to both the public and academic communities and opening a hitherto closed window into a fascinating, but lesser known, facet of motion-picture history.

ACKNOWLEDGMENTS

I would like to thank and acknowledge the individuals and institutions that so generously shared their time, expertise and information regarding their collections by responding to my online survey, and I owe a special debt of gratitude to those who granted my request for follow-up interviews and site visits: Soeluh van den Berg (EYE

Coming Soon! Lantern Slide Advertising in the Archive

229

Filmmuseum), Rob Brooks, Donata Pesenti Campagnoni (Museo Nazionale del Cinema), Rebecca Grant (Irish Film Institute), Ronald Grant and Martin Humpheries (The Cinema Museum), Barbara Hall (Margaret Herrick Library), Nancy Kauffman (George Eastman House), Julie Lofthouse (TIFF Film Reference Library), Laurent Mannoni (Cinémathèque française), Ann Olszewski and Michael Ruffing (Cleveland Public Library) and Tania Strauss (New Zealand Film Archive).

NOTES

1. *La Sortie de l'usine Lumière à Lyon* [also known as *Workers Leaving the Lumière Factory*, *Employees Leaving the Lumière Factory* and *Exiting the Factory*] is a fifty-second film, photographed by Louis Lumière using his recently invented Cinématographe, depicting workers emerging from his factory in Lyon, France. Its initial public screening on 28 December 1895 at the Grand Café on the Boulevard des Capucines in Paris is commonly accepted as the first public exhibition of projected motion pictures.
2. David Robinson, Stephen Herbert and Richard Crangle (eds), *Encyclopaedia of the Magic Lantern* (London: The Magic Lantern Society, 2001), p. 10.
3. Ibid., p. 11.
4. Ernest A. Dench, *Advertising by Motion Pictures* (Cincinnati: Standard Publishing Company, 1916), pp. 173–214.
5. Lisa Kernan, *Coming Attractions: Reading American Movie Trailers* (Austin: University of Texas Press, 2004), p. 27.
6. Available at 25 cents per slide for any film longer than one reel. 'Advertising Space That Doesn't Cost You a Penny!', *The Moving Picture World*, 17 May 1913, p. 755.
7. In this context I refer to the definition of orphan film as that put forward by the Orphan Film Symposia: 'a motion picture abandoned by its owner or caretaker. More generally, the term refers to all manner of films outside of the commercial mainstream: public domain materials, home movies, outtakes, unreleased films, industrial and educational movies, independent documentaries, ethnographic films, newsreels, censored material, underground works, experimental pieces, silent-era productions, stock footage, found footage, medical films, kinescopes, small- and unusual-gauge films, amateur productions, surveillance footage, test reels, government films, advertisements, sponsored films, student works, and sundry other ephemeral pieces of celluloid (or paper or glass or tape or ...).' Orphan Film Symposium, 'What is an Orphan Film?', www.sc.edu/filmsymposium/orphanfilm.html, accessed 14 January 2014.
8. Museo Nazionale del Cinema di Torino, Via Montebello, 20, 10124 Turin, Italy.
9. George Eastman House, 900 East Avenue, Rochester, New York 14607, USA.
10. Cleveland Public Library, 325 Superior Avenue East, Cleveland, Ohio 44114, USA.
11. Oakland Museum of California, 1000 Oak Street, Oakland, California 94607, USA.
12. Slide manufactured by General Film Company, Pittsburgh, Pennsylvania, hand-coloured, dual-pane glass with taped edges, 3¼ x 4 inches. Slide is from author's collection.
13. A voluntary survey organised by the author and conducted January 2011 through July 2012. The survey included an online questionnaire directed to members of the Association of Moving Image Archivists, which was later supplemented by individual email and telephone interviews with representatives of selected collecting institutions. Out of sixty-three

invitations extended, twenty-seven responded and their replies are tallied among the survey results cited in this article.

14. Irish Film Archive, 6 Eustace Street, Temple Bar, Dublin 2, Ireland.
15. Margaret Herrick Library, Fairbanks Center for Motion Picture Study, 33 South La Cienega Blvd, Beverly Hills, California 90211, USA.
16. The notation 'SPARROWS – B' stamped on the frame indicates that more than one slide design was created for *Sparrows*, this one being version B. Slide manufactured by National Studios, Inc., New York City, hand-coloured, single-pane glass with cardboard frame, 3¼ x 4 inches. Courtesy of Rob Brooks Mary Pickford Collection, Toronto International Film Festival Film Reference Library.
17. Museo del Cinema, C/Drain, 1, 17001 Gerona, Spain.
18. Typical variations in slide fabrication include: single-pane or double-pane construction; photographic or hand-etched imagery; hand-colouring, cardboard frame or taped edges; and transparency materials including glass and isinglass.
19. Cinémathèque française, 51 Rue de Bercy, 75012 Paris, France.
20. Slide manufactured by The Slide House, London, England, hand-coloured, dual-pane glass with taped edges, 3¼ x 3¼ inches. Slide from author's collection.
21. Unknown slide manufacturer, India, hand-coloured, dual-pane glass with taped edges, 3¼ x 3¼ inches. Slide from author's collection.

15
The Hidden Film-maker

Dylan Cave

In 2008 the British Film Institute's National Archive (BFI National Archive) received a donation of some thirty-five trailers from the private collection of Rodney Read, a film producer and editor who, during the 1980s, had worked for the UK's National Screen Service (NSS). Read's collection included many trailers on which he had personally worked, ranging from short promotional teasers to major international releases such as *Raiders of the Lost Ark* (1981), *Once Upon a Time in America* (1984), *Terms of Endearment* (1983), *Hope and Glory* (1987) and *The Adventures of Baron Munchausen* (1988). Read was generous with his time and talked through his experiences of working on many of the trailers he was donating.[1] Although anecdotal, his information gave fresh insight into the production process of each title in his collection which, in turn, would enhance our cataloguing.

Read's donation came at a time when the BFI National Archive was undergoing significant changes to the way it operated. It had recently developed its curatorial department, which shifted the emphasis of the archive's work towards a more proactive process, led by a pan-BFI cultural programme. The curators were encouraged to delve deeper into the archive's holdings and to develop areas of specialism. Read's collection and testimonies about each film fit with a new working practice that sought to gain better understanding of the materials held in the archive, especially those items of which little was known. To this end, the BFI was also revising its approach to metadata, developing new databases that could describe and provide effective tools for researching the collection. Many of those significant changes are now in place and we have a database that offers a sophisticated means of describing a complex range of materials. But back in 2008, the information Rodney Read provided about his material gave serious challenge to the way we had been describing our trailer collections. What I want to present in this chapter are the key assumptions about our trailer material that needed revising in light of Read's donation. I also want to illustrate how our new Collections Information Database (CID) now expresses metadata about trailers and promotional film that was previously hidden, and does so in a way that enhances understanding about our collections and enables effective preservation priorities.

The BFI had firmly established cataloguing procedures to describe the high-profile feature films, well-researched nonfiction, or television that dominated the collections. For many years, the BFI's metadata was split across two related but unlinked databases: a vast filmographic database (Summary Information of Film and Television, SIFT) and a technical records database (Tec Rec) of all holdings in the BFI National

Archive. They described much of our collection well, but struggled to express some of its nuances. In particular, describing collections of adverts, logos, promos, interstitials and trailers – the promotional ephemera of the cinema programme – required a level of complexity that our native databases were unable to provide.

In the SIFT/Tec Rec era, procedures for cataloguing trailers rarely involved detail. Much of the BFI National Archive's trailer collection arrived in bulk deliveries either from film laboratory clear-outs, broadcasting collections, or as part of donations from eclectic collectors. In almost all cases there was no contextual information to enhance records; we simply knew the trailer title, the donor and the type of film element held. This had a knock-on effect for preservation strategy. Although conserved to the standard expected of all material held in the archive, detailed preservation work on more ephemeral material, such as trailers, was rarely a priority.

The trailer was closely associated with the work it was promoting. Indeed, in previous years, a trailer for a film was listed in Tec Rec as part of the main element holdings. Until recently, it was still possible to discover trailers sitting among the records for the main feature film holdings, sometimes perhaps mislabelled as Main or End titles. SIFT, our legacy filmographic database, introduced the separation of trailer records from feature film records (which Tec Rec subsequently adopted), but filmographic cataloguing was often rudimentary and the whole trailer collection suffered metadata inconsistencies. Rodney Read's collection exposed the inadequacies of our cataloguing approach and started a re-think in the way we describe and manage our more ephemeral collections.

Rodney Read joined the UK arm of the NSS in the late 1970s. The NSS was an American company set up in the 1920s to handle promotional material, including trailers, for Hollywood. The UK arm was responsible for the British and international publicity of the vast majority of British and US feature films on theatrical release. Read wrote, produced and edited trailers and other promotional short films for UK and so-called 'international' territories (i.e. those outside the 'domestic' US territory). In 1986 Read formed National Screen Productions, a private company that took on NSS's outsourced trailer work. He remained there until 1992, when the company was sold.

One of the main areas raised in discussion with Read concerned the range of creative personnel who make trailers, many of whom are un-credited for the works they produce. Read confirmed that trailers are like most budgeted moving-image works in that they are subject to production meetings and undergo a creative decision-making processes. In many promotional works – in trailers, advertising, pop videos and many sponsored films – there are producers, directors and commissioners, who develop the concept, and writers, editors and designers, who assist in delivering the finished product. Although there is little doubt about the identity of any given trailer, since the film title is very important in the work, there is rarely any reference to the people responsible for the trailer's creation. With a few notable exceptions (Alfred Hitchcock's self-directed trailers for his films, for example), precious little is known about the trailer-makers. Unlike a feature film, they don't get their own credit roll.

And why would they? Few would expect to have to sit through a list of credits for each moving image they are ever exposed to. But, from an archival perspective, this poses a problem for those trying to best describe and clearly identify the promotional works in their collection. As we'll see, a lack of contextual information can lead to misguided assumptions about the relevance of a trailer to a national collection, especially with regard to country of production and national heritage.

The lack of contextual information was one of the main problem areas revealed in discussion with Read. One of his trailers was for *Prick Up Your Ears* (1987), a controversial British film based on the life of playwright Joe Orton and his relationship with his lover Kenneth Halliwell. Directed by Stephen Frears and written by Alan Bennett, the film stars Gary Oldman as Orton, with Alfred Molina and Vanessa Redgrave in supporting roles. When the film was released to British cinemas in April 1987, it was covered by an arts programme on British television, *The Media Show*, episodes of which are also preserved at the BFI National Archive. *The Media Show*'s angle was to report on the entire advertising campaign for the film, concentrating largely on the film's depiction of a gay lifestyle and the significance of the film's release during the height of the AIDS crisis. *The Media Show* reported the way that the trailer was commissioned, designed and produced as part of the promotional campaign – information that is not contained within the *Prick up Your Ears* trailer itself – and revealed the extent to which trailers in general are subject to negotiation, creative discussion and planning.

Read appeared in *The Media Show*'s report and was credited on screen as the producer of the trailer. The programme made clear that Read was working to a brief set by a commissioning party (Andrew Brown, the film's producer, and publicist Zakiya Powell) and, further, that his work was subject to the approval of various other personnel including the art director of the overall campaign, UK distributors Palace Pictures, the British Board of Film Classification (BBFC) and, to a lesser extent, director Stephen Frears. For the archive, the programme confirmed that, in the instance of *Prick Up Your Ears*, the trailer was subject to a creative process quite separate from that of the main feature film. Not simply a miniature version of the film it was promoting, the trailer was a small film in its own right.

In her book, *Coming Attractions*, Lisa Kernan asserts that a trailer should be seen as 'a brief film text that usually displays images from a specific feature film while asserting its excellence'.[2] For Kernan trailers are 'film paratexts',[3] discrete but connected short films. They are works that incorporate, but are separate from, the features they are celebrating. Kernan's assertion resonates with the example of *Prick Up Your Ears*. *The Media Show* report confirms that trailers should be considered beyond their mere relation to the feature film they promote; they are individual creative works. The trailer for *Prick Up Your Ears* has its own creators. It is a 'Rodney Read' production as much as it is related to the Stephen Frears film; but where one party is credited, the other remains anonymous.

Read suggested that the example of *Prick Up Your Ears* was typical of the working practices of the era. Elsewhere, other academic work has implied that many trailers are made separately from the main feature.[4] The producer, writer and editor of the trailer are rarely the same as those for the feature. Expressing trailers as separate works to the features they promote, with their own set of creative personnel, was the first step in creating a clearer metadata description for trailers.

From an archival perspective, the next step was to clarify the precise relationship between feature and trailer, but this too had its challenges. On examining trailers from the vaults, it often emerges that 'trailer' is too singular a definition. Trailers are created in a range of versions to serve across numerous platforms – teaser version, main version, censored version, international version, re-release version, etc. – and sometimes they evolve over the life of a film's promotional campaign. Even physical attributes, such as trailer length, can change if a film gathers awards and critical praise. This can raise problems when identifying the differences between trailers for the same title. Sometimes they are minor: at the BFI National Archive, for example, we hold different versions of the trailer for *Notting Hill* (1998), but they differ by only a small number of frames, depending on whether they show an expletive, merely allude to it, or omit the moment entirely, according to the classification rating of the different edits. In other instances – such as when distinguishing between a trailer, a teaser and an extended promo – the differences are so great, each feels like a separate work.

Another example from the Read collection serves to illuminate. Two copies of the trailer for Martin Donovan's *Apartment Zero* (1988) were passed to us from Read. Although seemingly identical – they are the same physical length, screen duration and consist of the same shots – the films had one significant difference. In the British version two supporting actors – Dora Bryan and Liz Smith – are credited on screen but, as they are little known outside of the UK, their credits were absent from the international release.

Vinzenz Hediger's thoughts on the difficulty of finding the 'original' version of a film are useful here.[5] As part of describing the complexity of identifying single original versions, Hediger draws attention to the vocabulary of the 'original' and how it is used to sell new versions of the same thing.[6] He suggests that, over time, the common understanding of an 'original version' can change – a useful concept for curators to bear in mind when trying to assess the cultural significance of individual trailers against preservation resources. In the case of *Apartment Zero*, as both versions were created at the same time, either element could be seen as representing the original version of the work, albeit in slightly different manifestations.

The issue of multiple versions, and multiple international versions in particular, is pertinent for the BFI National Archive's collecting and preservation approach. Our approach to giving preservation status to trailers has usually followed the credentials we use for features: if a unique trailer element is for a British film, we designate the item with master preservation status, held in the archive under temperature-controlled storage conditions. If, however, the trailer was for a film with no British connection, it would be classified as reference or viewing material. Rodney Read worked on a wide selection of trailers for British and non-British features, exhibited in both the UK and international territories (though less often in the USA). By virtue of his working on them, Read's entire collection of trailers were considered core to our collecting criteria despite some of the trailers being for non-British films. Again, discussion with Read revealed that our basic approach to assigning preservation status for trailers was, on occasion, too simplistic. Another Read trailer, this time for an entirely American production, *In a Shallow Grave* (1988), illustrated this point.

An episode of the 1980s *American Playhouse* television series, *In a Shallow Grave* was initially intended for UK theatrical release. Read's comments on creating the trailer for the film reveal the problems in assuming that the national identity of a trailer necessarily matches the film it is promoting:

The trailer was actually a spin-off … We used to do feature doctoring. It was a first-time director and they'd worked on it for some months but couldn't get a cut together. We were given the movie rushes and asked to re-cut the film. Our cut of the film went back to the States and they then re-cut it again. But it was to give it some narrative form basically. We did that on two or three occasions. It's sometimes easier for people to say, 'We're too much involved in this, we can't get a handle on it, so let someone else have a go.' We re-cut the feature first and then made the trailer.[7]

Here Read's comments show the hidden activity performed by his company in preparing and marketing *In a Shallow Grave* to audiences. Without his contextualisation, we would have assumed that his material on *In a Shallow Grave* was no more than a US trailer for an American film. We would acquire the element as archival viewing material: acquired, for interest, as a reference copy of a low-profile American drama. In fact, the trailer is part of the narrative of the work of Read and his British production company. *In a Shallow Grave* has never been released in the UK, so no other material for this trailer is likely to exist. In another example, the international trailer for American film *Raiders of the Lost Ark* (1980) was designed by Read for UK audiences. However, his cut so impressed producer George Lucas and director Steven Spielberg that, according to Read, he was invited to California and, once there, told that his trailer would now be the one to play across the rest of the world.[8] The *Raiders of the Lost Ark* trailer was not made in the USA but in the UK, by Read at NSS and, like the trailer for *In a Shallow Grave*, it sheds new light on our understanding of British trailer-making. Both are now held as preservation masters in the BFI National Archive collection.

As these examples illustrate, better contextual knowledge about a particular trailer can change preservation strategy. But this level of context is rare. Difficulties over correct preservation policy for trailer works will remain unless an intellectual framework is applied to help archives structure, document and tailor their trailer collections in a way that allows for more detailed information.

Vinzenz Hediger has suggested that we should apply a screening context to trailers. He argues that we should not see trailers in the same way as we view advertising because they are not self-sufficient entities; rather, they are part of an overall film programme.[9] This needs some clarification: today trailers, like advertising, proliferate over the internet as single entities, removed from screening contexts such as cinema pre-show programming or TV advert breaks. But I agree with Hediger that trailers acquire a compounded meaning in the context of the film programme – they not only promote the film they are advertising, but, in the context of the cinema programme, also promote the culture of moviegoing in general. During a visit to the cinema, the trailer feels integral to the programme, warming up audiences as they settle in for their evening's entertainment and noticeable if absent. They are judged and compared by the audience – that film looks good, this one doesn't appeal; they've already shown the best bits, so I won't bother going to see it – and interact with spectators in a dialogue that implicitly supports and celebrates cinema culture as well as performing their own marketing task. Alas, this short moment in the life cycle of a trailer is also its most ephemeral. The precise film programme of a given evening at the cinema can rarely be duplicated once over, only approximated. And when the main feature reaches its audience, one of the trailer's unique attributes – its promise of as-yet-unseen pleasures to come – vanishes. We are left with the trailer simply as text.

Films That Sell

Hediger's screening context has its uses for the archivist, but it is the context of production, rather than reception, that are of most use in describing trailers and ephemeral material. To this end, Thomas Elsaesser's thoughts on the cataloguing of industrial film (in which, I'd argue, we should include trailers) are useful. In addition to the film as text, Elsaesser suggests that we should also consider three As when engaging with industrial film: '"wer war der *Auftraggeber*" (who commissioned the film), "was war das *Anlass*" (what was the occasion for which it was made), and "was war die *Anwendung* oder der *Adressat*" (to what use was it put or to whom was it addressed)'.[10] We can loosely translate this for trailers as being commissioned works (by the feature film producers/distributors), to be shown at a particular moment (in the weeks leading up to and during the screening of the promoted film), for as wide an audience as possible. Creating the framework to capture these complex details has been a priority in developing our cataloguing systems.

The International Federation of Film Archives (FIAF) rules for cataloguing have undergone re-evaluation to recognise the changing needs of archives for dealing with collections with the more sophisticated challenges of describing materials in databases. Complementing the recognised standard advocated by the European Committee for Standardisation (CEN), the proposed changes to FIAF rules acknowledge the need brought about by archives to effectively describe their collections, including the more ephemeral elements. The agreed standard – CEN 15907 – makes room for clearer thinking about the creative process and the way all moving images in archive collections are defined.

At the BFI National Archive, we have benefited greatly from our newly enhanced data management system that provides structural definition and clear differentiation in the way we describe and catalogue all our collections, including the promotional elements. Operational from the end of 2011, the BFI's CID organises information using a hierarchical entity-relationship model similar, though not identical, to the Functional Requirements for Bibliographic Records (FRBR) used in libraries. At the top of the hierarchy, the 'work' level describes the individual artistic creation. Filmographic details and contextual information (including relationships) are detailed here. Beneath the 'work' lies the 'manifestation' level which is a summary of the different guises that the work has existed in. For trailers that may include theatrical release versions, or an extra on a commercial DVD, TV broadcasts, etc., to the relevant manifestations are appended records at the 'item' level, while the physical elements are linked to the database through barcodes attached to the actual prints, negatives, video and digital elements stored within the archive vaults.

In our Read example, the *Prick Up Your Ears* trailer has its own work record. It describes the trailer as a work and details the creative personnel involved – Rodney Read at NSS, neither of whom is credited on screen, and Zenith Productions/Civilhand, who are credited as rights holders. The manifestation of this trailer is a 35mm film that runs to 210 feet and was released by Palace Pictures to UK cinemas in April 1987. This sits beneath the 'work'. Finally, we have the Archive's holdings – the 35mm print donated by Read and a Digibeta viewing copy created from the print for access purposes. Back at the work level, we create a link to the main feature establishing the relationship between *Prick Up Your Ears* and its trailer. In addition, we create a further link to the television broadcast of *The Media Show* in which both trailer and feature are discussed.

Using this system we are hopefully describing our trailers as individual works, designed for their own purpose but related to the main features they promote. CID provides a structure within which we can supply metadata as and when we learn it. From there we are able to apply a more sophisticated understanding of preservation need than that simply based on the nationality of the feature that the trailer advertises. Lisa Kernan asserts, 'Trailers are at once ads and more than ads.'[11] If we agree with her that each work should be seen as individual, Read's examples corroborate the fact that they can sometimes be 'more than' they seem. His collection reveals an industry of trailer and promo production beyond the concern of the individual title and, in fact, part of an international network that we are only beginning to understand.

NOTES

1. The interview with Rodney Read was conducted by Professor Justin Smith (University of Portsmouth) and Dylan Cave, 18 September 2008.
2. Lisa Kernan, *Coming Attractions* (Austin: University of Texas Press, 2004), p. 1.
3. Ibid.
4. See, for example, Sarah Street, 'Another Medium Entirely: Esther Harris, National Screen Service and Film Trailers in Britain, 1940–1960', *Historic Journal of Film, Radio and Television* vol. 29 no. 4 (December 2009), pp. 433–47.
5. Vinzenz Hediger, 'The Original is Always Lost', in Marijke De Valck and Malte Hagener (eds), *Cinephilia* (Amsterdam: Amsterdam University Press, 2005).
6. 'Film students now perceive the latest authenticated version as the true original, as in the case of Francis Ford Coppola and his *Apocalypse Now Redux* (USA: 1979/2001), for instance. Thus the deferred action of the director's cut rewrites, or overwrites, film history, turning previous originals into palimpsests.' Ibid., p. 144.
7. Notes from an interview with Rodney Read by Professor Justin Smith and Dylan Cave, 18 September 2008.
8. Incidentally, the famous gag, where Indiana Jones nonchalantly shoots down a scary opponent with acrobatic sword-welding prowess, was completely out of bounds for Read. However, there is a repeat gag in the sequel *Indiana Jones and the Temple of Doom*, where Indiana casually attempts to shoot two swordsmen but this time finds he has no gun. It's a central piece of the *Temple of Doom* trailer, also cut together by Read.
9. Notes taken from 5th Amsterdam Workshop, 'The Images that Changed your Life: Advertising Films', held at Nederlands Filmmuseum, 19 November 2009.
10. Thomas Elsaesser, 'Archives and Archaeologies', in Vinzenz Hediger and Patrick Vonderau (eds), *Films that Work* (Amsterdam: Amsterdam University Press, 2009), p. 23.
11. Kernan, *Coming Attractions*, p. 8.

16

Robin Hood and the Furry Bowlers: Animators vs Advertisers in Early British Television Commercials

Jez Stewart

In 2010 two large collections were donated to the BFI National Archive from two behemoths of the British animation industry of the twentieth century. The Halas & Batchelor Collection encompassed over 3,500 film and video items relating to the careers of husband and wife team, John Halas and Joy Batchelor, and the company that bore their name from the early 1940s onwards. The Bob Godfrey Collection had around 1,500 film and video items relating to the diverse career of animator, director and occasional actor Bob Godfrey from the early 1950s into the first years of the new millennium.

I knew these film-makers from their independent films, children's television programmes and even their feature films (in the case of Halas & Batchelor). But having worked on the BFI's collection of advertising films since 2003 I also knew them for their commercials. Of the twenty-three commercials on the opening night of commercial television in Great Britain in 1955, three were by Halas & Batchelor and one by Godfrey's company, Biographic. I had seen full-page adverts in the trade press of the time boasting that Halas & Batchelor 'produced over 100 cartoons for the first year of Commercial Television'[1] and that 'Many of the most well known ad films are produced by Halas & Batchelor Cartoon Films.'[2]

Among the many highlights of these two collections I was expecting a rich resource for those interested in Britain's advertising history, and yet I was very wrong. Of the 3,721 film and video items provisionally detailed in the donation of the Halas & Batchelor Collection to the BFI National Archive in 2010,[3] only eleven are listed as containing one or more commercials. While work on the accessioning of the material is ongoing and more material may be found, I have already discovered that one of those eleven is a reel of live-action commercials not produced by Halas & Batchelor themselves, and another contains commercials produced for German companies in the late 1970s and early 80s. For the Bob Godfrey Collection we received no pre-existing lists, but the situation is only slightly better. Outside a couple of dozen cans relating to a popular campaign with a loud-mouthed girl singing the virtues of the Trio chocolate biscuit from the mid-1980s, provisional findings revealed only around thirty other cans encompassing at least three commercial showreels and a range of mute and sound negatives for assorted adverts.

Both companies produced more television commercials than anything else, and yet this part of their histories seems to have been purged. Other sponsored productions for theatrical and non-theatrical screenings were plentiful in the collections, although admittedly often only in the form of combined prints.[4] I believe that some of the roots of this paucity lie in a narrative that played out in the first years of commercial television in Britain, as the animation and advertising industries both flourished in a period of new opportunity, but one which proved ultimately disappointing to many animators. By the end of his career, John Halas pronounced, 'The only excuse for making TV commercials, and by the way I haven't made one for twenty years – thank God – is that it pays for all the other ventures.'[5]

CHALLENGES

Commercial television began in Great Britain[6] on 22 September 1955. In the fourteen months between the Independent Television Act becoming law and opening night, the advertising industry had to take stock and ask itself, 'What will a British television commercial look and sound like?' and 'How will the British public take to television advertising?' There were three precursor models which offered some guidance: American television commercials; cinema advertisements; and, to a lesser extent, commercial radio stations broadcast to Britain from overseas, such as Radio Luxembourg. While most agencies had some experience of each, particularly the larger ones with American links, it was felt that a good, British television commercial would be 'something of its own'.[7]

The Lintas advertising agency produced a twenty-minute film titled *TV Talk* (1954), intended for staff and clients, which highlighted their three main problems. First, television commercials could not be cinema commercials put on the small screen. The difference was not just the obvious technical one of a smaller screen, lack of colour and lower definition; it was more an issue of context: 'Television is the empty chair on the other side of the fireplace in the family living room.' Sitting in that chair was the client's salesman, who had slipped in with the main guest into the potential customer's home, and hence the tone of voice must be very different.

Second was the problem of volume. Where six to eight adverts per year may have met the needs of the client in the cinema, television may require 'fifty-two or 104', which they 'may or may not be able to repeat'.[8] This unprecedented volume would require a rapid expansion of production facilities, and the rate of production would need to be considerably faster.

And, lastly, despite those who described themselves as such, there were no 'experts' in commercial television in Britain as it did not yet exist. However prepared they might be, everyone would have to learn the new medium on the job. They could quiz panels of housewives, mock up living rooms and even create miniature evenings of television programming,[9] but all was speculation and nothing would compare to the real thing in the homes of British public. These were to be the frontier days of commercial TV.

ANIMATION

During this same interim period British animation gathered an unprecedented amount of press attention through the release of the country's first animated feature film

Animal Farm, in December 1954, based on the George Orwell novella. It was produced by Halas & Batchelor Cartoon Films, a company that had been formed under the wing of the advertising agency J. Walter Thompson in 1940, and whose first productions were cinema commercials. British animation companies had always struggled to compete for space on cinema screens with imported American cartoons, often synonymous with the prestige productions of the Walt Disney studio. In 1944 J. Arthur Rank bankrolled Gaumont-British Animation at a studio in rural Berkshire to try to rival Disney with domestically produced entertainment cartoons. Despite investing an estimated £500,000 and hiring David Hand, the director of *Snow White and the Seven Dwarfs* (1937), to oversee almost three years of preparatory training of his animation team, he found little appetite for his films with the British public and could not recover his production costs. The company had folded by 1950.[10]

The few independent animation companies that remained made their living on sponsored films such as cinema commercials, but also longer industrial, educational and propaganda films for non-theatrical venues. Such films could offer considerable freedom of expression to animators, with perhaps the most extreme examples being Len Lye's films for the General Post Office and other sponsors.[11] In the post-war period, large companies such as BP and ICI took advantage of a tax loophole whereby they could pay for such films from their pre-tax profits, so they lavished large sums on prestige films rather than hand the money over to the government.[12] For these films production companies often worked in direct contact with their clients, rather than via an advertising agency, and, as these films had little direct commercial imperative behind them, they again offered much creative freedom.

Such work was available in enough quantity to support a handful of animation units, and demanded a quality which required those units to maintain a resource-heavy production line of animators, tracers and painters – for which they charged their clients accordingly. Commercial television, and the recognised need for a huge increase in advert production, was seen as an opportunity for considerable growth and expansion for those who were prepared to grasp it.

ADVANTAGES

It was believed that animation would have certain advantages for advertising on television. Unlike cinema commercials, which tended to fall into slots of one, two, or five minutes, the high costs of television airtime would mean much shorter spots. Sixty seconds was a rarity, thirty seconds the average, but fifteen- and even seven-second spots were not unusual. Many advertisers were nervous about adopting what might be seen as a 'hard-sell' approach for British audiences.[13] Cartoon imagery offered a simple and more dynamic method of communicating a sales message in a highly compressed form: 'more and more advertisers realise that the cartoon alone can extract the graphic root of the theme for visual exploitation, presenting it with legibility and direct impact'.[14] It was felt that 'the striking power of the cartoon lies in its opportunity to exploit legitimate exaggeration ... the claims can be every bit as bold as the art-work',[15] and that the inherent humour in cartooning would enable advertising copy 'which sells strong in a tone which could be termed "soft-sell"'.[16]

Using celebrities for endorsement was a common advertising strategy, but employing a 'star' spokesperson was expensive, and could prove problematic if their recognition factor began to wane. A carefully crafted, convincing and engaging cartoon character representing a brand could become a kind of celebrity in its own right, and with a reliability and longevity that was above human fallibility.[17] Characters such as Sammy and Susie for Sunblest bread, the Esso Blue Dealer for Esso paraffin products, and the Mother's Pride Mother (again bread) all quickly gained recognition and even affection from British audiences, and could be used as part of a marketing strategy that went far beyond the TV spot and helped shape the brand.[18]

Other benefits included a longer lifespan for animated commercials than their live-action counterparts, with audiences happy to watch them multiple times. Research in the USA gave evidence of higher memorability of advertising copy points and sales pack recognition, perhaps because animated commercials would often stand out when surrounded by live-action counterparts.[19] Such factors were particularly important given the higher production costs of animation, but in the months before September 1955 there was evidence that some advertisers would not baulk at spending big for the right commercial. On 15 June *Commercial Television News* ran a profile of the French Advision studio, who claimed exclusive representation of Ladislas Starevich[20] and Alexandre Alexeieff[21] in Britain. This somewhat contradictory piece describes the need to reduce production times and costs for television, and yet:

> Alexeieff's services were frankly described to me as 'expensive,' and whereas Advision normally allows from three weeks for the making of a one-minute commercial this 'very independent' producer takes roughly the same number of months. ... 'I doubt whether anyone will go away from it thinking it's a bad bargain.'[22]

It is significant that in skimming through the first five years of trade periodicals for commercial television there is an absence of any similar fluff pieces for name directors of live-action commercials, partly because of a seeming antagonism between the more established film industry and the relative newcomer of television. James Garrett, who founded one of Britain's largest advertising production companies, recalled that the film industry regarded working in commercials as 'treachery', and that studios refused to reduce hire rates for the shorter shooting schedules and crews that advertisements needed.[23] In 1959 a 'TV consultant' for an advertising agency suggested that 'quite a lot of the technicians who were employed to work on commercials were third-rate people in the industry, who were not good enough to make the grade at other types of film production'.[24] Although many established film directors would come to direct television commercials, it is noticeable that the earliest examples, such as Lindsay Anderson, Karel Reisz and Clive Donner, were part of a new generation of British film-making at the start of their careers.

QUALITY

The animation industry was more open to television advertising because it needed it more. Companies had very little access to theatrical cinema revenue because so few

British shorts found their way into the cinema programme due to the popularity and easy availability of American cartoons. Advertising agencies and their clients could take their pick from the highest rank of animators, and initially they were granted considerable leeway. A second article on Alexandre Alexeieff from May 1956 is filled with fulsome praise and does not mention the role of the advertising agency once:

> So it is with Alexieff [sic]. His style needs getting used to. It has to be accepted. Once that stage is reached, sitting back and enjoying his methods is itself sheer enjoyment, and the infiltration of his selling abilities is very sure indeed.[25]

The industry also looked across the Atlantic for 'quality', particularly to the celebrated UPA studio. United Productions of America was founded in 1943 (initially under the name Industrial Film and Poster Service) by a group of ex-Disney artists with an ambition to shake up the look and feel of animation, emphasising its graphic nature. Their series of innovative shorts, such as *Gerald McBoing-Boing* (1950), *Rooty Toot Toot* (1951) and even their *Mr Magoo* series (1949–59) gave the name UPA a critical and public recognition not seen for an animation company since Disney in the 1930s. In 1955 the British film magazine *Sight & Sound*, which had a reputation for being rather snooty about such things, took the unprecedented decision to devote a page to drawings from new American television commercials by UPA.[26] Such attention clearly influenced UPA's decision to open a London branch of its studio in the summer of 1956, which was again greeted with a full-page article in *Sight & Sound*.[27] Despite paying their staff 50 per cent more than British studios, and assuredly passing these costs on the advertiser, they had sixteen commercials on television by December 1956.[28]

STYLE

British animation studios wanted to be taken just as seriously, for artistic as well as financial reasons, and worked hard to establish their reputation. By December 1955 John Halas and Joy Batchelor were already publicising their visit to the USA to show their company's British commercials to American sponsors.[29] In March 1957 an International Animated Film Festival was organised at the National Film Theatre in London to highlight the work of seven British companies alongside their foreign competitors, with a commercials showcase being a key part of the programme.

Every opportunity was taken to differentiate their television advertising work from foreign offerings, and emphasise its suitability for British audiences. John Halas was quoted as saying:

> Up to now the American pattern has been accepted by too many agencies, which is understandable considering its success. But the fact that we are in England and not in America and that we possess different traditions has been disregarded.[30]

Another director agreed that 'Too many cartoons are mere reflections of their American counterparts, either Walt Disney or UPA, but what we aim to achieve is a recognisable style of our own directed straight at the British viewer.'[31] Edric Radage, director of his own company the Radage Group, tried to pinpoint the difference in style required:

> [T]he British viewer would not immediately accept the 'extreme stylisation' of what has become known as 'UPA Technique' ... The public have identified the name of Disney with cartooned filming ... It has taken eight or nine years for the American viewer to become accustomed to the UPA style by seeing the various stages of the revolution. We decided to give the British viewer something we knew they could accept.[32]

COST

Ultimately, it was the advertising agencies, informed by their market testing, rather than the animation companies that would decide what quality or style of animation would be acceptable. In July 1956 a company called Telemats was launched in Britain, offering a range of open-ended, 'fully-animated' cartoons 'designed by top Hollywood technicians', which an advertiser could effectively rent and have their brand name tacked onto the end.[33] They promised the advantages of an animated commercial at a fraction of the production costs because they sold the same generic cartoons off-the-peg to a number of clients. A typical example, 'Golfer and Green', ran as follows: 'Little golfer hits golf ball. Camera pans up flag pole. Your animated lettering appears on top of flag-pole (sound effects throughout).'[34] The fifteen-second spots, which could be dragged out or chopped down by five seconds either way, were obviously aimed at smaller advertisers speaking to a local audience, but advertisements for the company quickly disappeared from trade press, suggesting that there was little market for such an approach.

On the 6 November 1959, *Television Mail* profiled the Sketchfilm process which consisted of tracking and panning shots over details of a single still drawing to give an impression of movement. While again the obvious benefit of the technique is economic, the author of the piece describes how it can 'personalise without involvement in personalities, and like animation speak without embarrassment'.[35]

Production time was the other factor that played against animation, and any increase in speed of production was fully embraced. A profile of the Biographic studio in October 1956 highlights a fifteen-second animated commercial that was made for Quaker macaroni over a single weekend to push the product as an alternative during a potato shortage. Biographic was a new production company founded on 1 January 1955, which jumped at the opportunity to take advantage of the arrival of commercial television. Its three directors, Bob Godfrey, Keith Learner and Jeff Hale, had all jumped ship from the much larger Larkins animation studio, which Learner described as being not interested in television.[36] With an average age of twenty,[37] they set up their company in two rooms above a jeweller's shop in Soho and made the best of Bob Godfrey's rather distant contacts at the Lintas advertising agency.[38] Their technical facilities consisted of a 1909 hand-cranked Moy & Bastie camera and a homemade animation rostrum made of two tables screwed together. Their somewhat amateur set-up is further illustrated by Learner's recollection of the Quaker macaroni job, which required a live-action pack and product shot at the end. The macaroni was cooked on a camping stove in the corner of the studio and, as they had no live-action camera and only the vertically mounted camera rostrum, they had to improvise by propping the plate of food up at 45 degrees and filming via a mirror at the same angle. Shot frame-by-frame, the first take resulted in the food seeming to come alive as it slithered off the plate mid-shot. On the second take the food behaved thanks to a sheet of sandpaper stuck to the plate, and the commercial was able to air the following evening.[39]

Such was the maelstrom of early commercial television that even the meagre means of Biographic were enough to attract the biggest clients. When British Animation Group was founded in 1960, they estimated that their burgeoning industry had grown from 120 animation artists in 1954 to some 500, and from a handful of three or four production companies to over twenty.[40] As Bob Godfrey put it much later in his life, 'We didn't know much, but a lot of people knew a damn sight less than we did!'[41] By October 1956 Biographic had already been tipped by some as a British rival to UPA, although this comparison was rightly dismissed as 'a film-land story' by the article that cited it.[42] However, it is clear that speed, imagination and flexibility were equally as important attributes as established reputation when it came to choosing production companies.

THE 'AGENCY TWITCH'

By 1957, there is evidence that animators and advertisers were beginning to feel the strain in their relationship. As part of a series looking at the lessons learnt in the first two years of ITV, John Halas contributed an assessment of the industry which argued that there was too much conformity and adverts were in danger of boring the public.

> After producing two hundred television cartoons, I maintain, more than ever, that the production of a good television commercial is more complex than normal entertainment films for cinemas. Like good poetry, a commercial must be inspired, crisp, meaningful, far beyond its short duration and, primarily, it must be entertaining.[43]

Many advertisers were beginning to come to a very different conclusion, influenced by American advertising. In July 1958 a sales director at Associated Television (ATV) wrote:

> [S]o many commercials still seek to entertain rather than to sell. Hardly a leading agency now believes that what most of them were saying in September 1955 – that the British public would not accept commercials which genuinely set out to put over a sales story without thrills ... In America, advertising is part and parcel of everyday life and recognised and accepted as such by the public.[44]

In October an American TV executive recently appointed to a British agency gave his impression of watching commercial television in his own home: 'I was a little surprised at the number of ... expensive animation jobs with very off-beat soundtracks, or very jingly-jingles – all of which left me wondering half-way through the spot: "What's the product?"'[45] He pinpointed this reluctance to selling as a holdover from cinema advertising: 'When you are talking to an admission paying, captive audience, there is more obligation to be entertaining first and commercial second.'[46]

In November 1957, John Halas was interviewed by the editor of *Commercial Television News* to analyse why British production companies had failed to win any awards at the Cannes Advertising Festival. Under the title 'It's the Agency Men who are at Fault', Halas blames the 'timidity' of agencies as the reason for failure and says, 'There are too many cooks to serve up the pie.' He cites the successes of his company's public relations films, usually produced in a direct relationship with the advertiser rather than via an agency, as evidence there is no lack of talent in the producers.[47]

In the predictable flurry of responses to this provocative set-up it is noticeable that agencies still associated quality with American and Continental production.[48] Such opinions clearly annoyed British animators, with Halas writing, 'I am strongly opposed to the blatant over-charging of some French film units, to the extent of £1,000 for a fifteen-second commercial. No commercial can be worth that much money in a comparatively small market like Great Britain.'[49] But what is more evident is that the two sides, despite calls for cooperation, have very different perspectives, as illustrated in this response from Bob Godfrey:

> Sir, – Most 'furry bowlers'[50] (agency types) suffer from an occupational disease known as 'agency twitch,' which seems to affect everything they touch. As they insist on touching every aspect of production down to the last frame, we stand about as much chance of winning an award at Cannes as we do of launching a Sputnik. Short of the production companies turning themselves into advertising agencies, and thereby exposing themselves to the dreaded twitch, I see no answer to this problem.[51]

CONCLUSION

Many factors dictate what survives in the collections of moving-image archives around the world – strong collections policies, proactive curators, benevolent film-makers and a not inconsiderable dose of plain fate and chance. Data extracted from the BFI National Archive indicates that there are over 1,500 television adverts produced between 1955 and 1965 in the collection, and yet only ninety-six of those are flagged as animated.[52] Estimates have suggested that the actual proportion of animated advertisements was somewhere between a quarter and a third of all productions,[53] a big discrepancy with this 6 per cent. While I was hoping that the acquisition of the Halas & Batchelor and Bob Godfrey collections would help boost this figure, it seems, instead, that research around the work has helped explain some of the reasons for the discrepancy.

In 1990 John Halas and Bob Godfrey took turns interviewing each other as part of a union history project.[54] In the interview, John puts art, animation and commerce at opposite points of a triangle, and says that:

> When TV commercials came in I was very glad to have a source of revenue to pay for the other side. And I must say that even in the late fifties, and the early sixties when commercials boomed, I took the attitude of hoarding of the rich and giving the money for the poor – the poor being experimental films.[55]

Bob Godfrey goes as far as to say that the flood of commercial work that came after 1955 'shattered the dream' of animation as a pure art form which had been building momentum, referring to contemporary developments such as the first animation festival at Annecy and the founding of *Association Internationale du Film d'Animation* (ASIFA) in 1960.[56]

Perhaps it was the occasion and their inner showmanship that enticed these two intelligent, creative men to rather naively dress themselves up as Robin Hoods of the animation industry, dismissing much of the remarkable work that both had achieved in the sponsored field. John Halas, in particular, was the author of a number of books and articles that were part of a movement recognising the importance of commercial art and graphic design in the second half of the twentieth century.[57] And yet it appears that this dismissal of their work has directly affected the survival of such works for advertising researchers today, with their high volume of productions ditched from the company's back catalogue.

To understand this somewhat bitter attitude it is important to note that the prime target for the animators' nostalgic bile is specifically the *television* commercial, as opposed to sponsored work in general. The 'Wild West' of the first months of commercial television proved to be a short-lived playground for animation practitioners, offering growth and some artistic freedoms. As the industry found its feet and the specificities of the television commercial developed, clients, advertising agencies and production companies had to learn a different dynamic than in earlier media. The stakes grew higher and higher; annual independent television advertising revenue rose exponentially from just over £13 million in 1956, its first full year, to almost £83 million by 1965.[58] Sponsors footing this bill demanded results and, as quoted above, agencies found that British audiences were not as offended by direct salesmanship as was first thought. A new breed of television-trained art directors and copywriters did not feel the need to hide their sales punches. With a general move from entertainment to selling, the expertise and authorship moved from the producers to the advertisers, and the voice and, seemingly, the interest of some animation creatives like Bob and John waned.

In 1959 Bob Godfrey wrote a piece for the trade magazine *Audio-Visual Selling* entitled 'Have You Noticed How Dead the Cartoon Industry Is these Days?':

> Three years ago it was a very different ... Money flowed like water and ignorance was rife. In those hectic and halcyon days our company was born ... Now we are respectable – well almost, anyway. The more obvious crooks and phonies have long ago departed and a grey uniformity settles over the survivors – sad, but inevitable. Money is tighter, agencies are getting foxy and more difficult to baffle with science – every Tom, Dick and Harry and tin-pot manufacturer of choc-bars is a budding John Houston [sic] and they descend on the sound studios in droves, raving about tonal values and telling us in great detail just where we went wrong! We bitch and we moan – but we shouldn't. If we had any real talent we would be making features.[59]

It is noticeable that, this time, it was only animators who responded, with Nick Spargo of Nicholas Cartoon Films replying,

> I must agree the cartoon spot of today is somewhat gloomy, but isn't this because we, as producers, expect a cartoon film to be funny? Does it look so gloomy to the agency and the agency's client if it sells the goods?[60]

NOTES

1. Advert for Halas & Batchelor, *Commercial Television News*, 19 October 1956, p. 9.
2. Advert for Halas & Batchelor, *Commercial Television News*, 5 April 1957, p. 7.
3. Various listings of the collection were compiled before the material arrived at the BFI, but all appear to have been generally based on the information written on the can only. As the collection is accessioned it is fully catalogued, revealing minor differentiations with the pre-accession lists.
4. The negatives for many of these longer-form sponsored films for BP, the Central Office of Information and others were kept by the commissioning body and have since been donated to the BFI National Archive.
5. John Halas Interview [BECTU History Project], (1990).
6. Or at least a small part of it, as the opening night was only accessible to those with an appropriately tuned television in the London area. The 'Midlands' signal, covering a large part of England, was switched on in 1956, and other regions of Britain were added piece by piece over the next decade.
7. *TV Talk – Lintas* (Lintas Agency, 1954), http://collections-search.bfi.org.uk/web/Details/ChoiceFilmWorks/150388825
8. The actual volume of commercials per client would have been lower than this estimate, and repeats were common practice, but this concern emphasises how much was unknown at the time.
9. The agency Foote, Cone & Belding did just that in the fifteen-minute *FCB TV Show No. 1* (*c.* 1955), held in the BFI National Archive, which mocked up speculative television programmes to bookend example adverts. http://collections-search.bfi.org.uk/web/Details/ChoiceFilmWorks/150572538
10. Geoffrey Macnab, *J. Arthur Rank and the British Film Industry* (London: Routledge, 1993), pp. 131–6.
11. While the GPO Film Unit under the direction of John Grierson may have seemed to have more creative freedom due to its lack of commercial pressures, Len Lye also made adverts for Imperial Airways, BP and Churchman cigarettes, which were every bit as innovative as his most famous GPO film *A Colour Box* (1935).
12. Keith Learner [author interview], 13 September 2012.
13. Patrick Henry, 'There's Still too Much Soft Selling', *Audio-Visual Selling*, 18 July 1958, p. 6.
14. David Wisely, 'A New Medium Comes of Age', *Television Mail*, 9 October 1959, p. 13.
15. Eric Boden, 'Why a Cartoon Commercial Often Fails', *Audio-Visual Selling*, 3 October 1958, p. 6.
16. Bruce Walker, 'More Animation ... More *Soft*-Sell', *Commercial Television News*, 9 November 1956, p. 6.
17. J. S. Vogt, 'The Choice – Live Action or Cartoon ...', *Audio-Visual Selling*, 7 October 1960, p. 5.
18. Jo Gable, *The Tuppenny Punch and Judy Show: 25 Years of TV Commercials* (London: Michael Joseph, 1980), pp. 141–55.
19. Vogt, 'The Choice', p. 6.
20. Starevich was a Russian stop-motion animator who began animating with dead insects in 1910 and began a celebrated career in puppet films in France after the October Revolution.
21. Also Russian, Alexeieff was an artist, illustrator and animator who worked mainly in France and is most celebrated for the 'pinscreen' films he made with the American Claire Parker in the 1930s.

22. Lynne Reid-Banks, 'Advision Tie-up with French Producers', *Commercial Television News*, 15 June 1955, p. 6.
23. Gable, *The Tuppenny Punch and Judy Show*, p. 30.
24. Godfrey Howards, 'Why Are *so* Many TV Spots *so* Bad?', *Audio-Visual Selling*, 10 July 1959, p. 11.
25. Paul Sheridan, 'Alexieff – the Perfectionist – Gives Individuality to the Product', *Commercial Television News*, 4 May 1956, p. 4.
26. 'TV Spots', *Sight & Sound*, Summer 1955, p. 9.
27. 'UPA in England', *Sight & Sound*, Summer 1956, p. 45.
28. Adam Abraham, *When Magoo Flew: The Rise and Fall of Animation Studio UPA* (Middletown, CT: Wesleyan University Press, 2012), p. 206.
29. 'Mr Halas Shows His Work to America', *Commercial Television News*, 9 December 1955, p. 10.
30. Tony Anderson, 'Behind the Spot – No. 3: Toby Ale', *Commercial Television News*, 1 March 1957, p. 9.
31. Tony Anderson, 'Behind the Spot – No. 1: Steradent', *Commercial Television News*, 18 January 1957, p. 7.
32. Stu Knowles, 'Edric Radage Calls It "Stylised Realism"', *Commercial Television News*, 1 November 1957, p. 6.
33. 'New Technique Slashes Production Costs for the Smaller (15-seconds) Advertiser', *Commercial Television News*, 13 July 1956, p. 4.
34. Telemat advertisement, *Commercial Television News*, 20 July 1956, p. 5.
35. Mike Storm, 'A Cottage or Castle for the Price of a Pencil', *Television Mail*, 6 November 1959, pp. 12–13.
36. Learner (author interview).
37. They are described as having an average age of twenty-two in 1957. Anderson, 'Behind the Spot – No. 1', p. 7.
38. Learner (author interview).
39. Ibid.
40. 'Britain Is Now One of the Largest Centres for Animation', *Audio-Visual Selling*, 3 June 1960, p. 2.
41. Bob Godfrey Interview [BECTU History Project], (1990).
42. 'Biograph Cartoons Are a Commercial Success', *Commercial Television News*, 26 October 1956, p. 3.
43. John Halas, 'The Final Results Are Not Good Enough: There Is far Too Much Conformity', *Commercial Television News*, 20 September, 1957, p. 22.
44. Henry, 'There's Still too Much Soft Selling', p. 6.
45. Stanley Rhodes, 'Why the Reluctance to Identify the Product?', *Audio-Visual Selling*, 3 October 1958, p. 8.
46. Ibid.
47. 'It's the Agency Men Who Are at Fault', *Commercial Television News*, 1 November 1957, p. 4.
48. John Fitzgerald, 'We Have to Look More & More to the Continent for High-Quality Production', *Commercial Television News*, 15 November 1957, p. 5, and Russell B. Insley, 'No, Mr Halas, There Is *Not* Enough Talent in Britain', *Commercial Television News*, 15 November 1957, p. 6.
49. Halas, 'The Final Results Are Not Good Enough', p. 22.
50. The term 'furry bowler' is a Bob Godfrey-ism rather than a common phrase. The bowler hat has an obvious association with the uniform of the London city gent, but the affectation of

adding fur to the mix was just the kind of fashionable embellishment that would be seen in an advertising agency of the period – and would be just thing to outrage and amuse Bob in equal measure.

51. Bob Godfrey, 'Beware Agency Twitch', *Commercial Television News*, 29 November 1957, p. 6.

52. These numbers are based on data exported from an earlier version of the BFI's archive catalogue with some refinements through cataloguing checks, but should not be considered 100 per cent accurate due the difficulties of detailed cataloguing for high volumes of short material.

53. Gable, *The Tuppenny Punch and Judy Show*, p. 141.

54. This oral history project of the Broadcasting Entertainment Cinematograph Technicians Union (BECTU) was conducted over 600 interviews: http://www.bectu.org.uk /advice-resources/history-project

55. John Halas Interview.

56. Ibid.

57. John wrote a long series of articles for *Graphis* and *Novum*, as well as authoring and editing books on the subject.

58. Brian Henry (ed.), *British Television Advertising: The First 30 Years* (London: Century Benham, 1986), p. 512.

59. Bob Godfrey, 'Have You Noticed How Dead the Cartoon Industry Is these Days?', *Audio-Visual Selling*, 24 April 1959, p. 6.

60. Nick Spargo, 'Nick Spargo replies to Bob Godfrey', *Audio-Visual Selling*, 1 May 1959, p. 11.

17

Ahead of Its Showtime: The Packard Humanities Institute Collection at the Academy Film Archive

Cassie Blake

Near the end of 2009, thousands of small boxes flooded the vaults of the Academy Film Archive in Los Angeles. Inside the over 16,000 cardboard containers, hustled upon arrival into hallways and corridors, resided more than 60,000 promotional materials. The archive's holdings had long included theatrical trailers and various promotional films; however, as staff stacked these numbered boxes onto the waiting, empty shelves of a temperature-controlled vault, the newly acquired Packard Humanities Institute Collection singlehandedly transformed the Academy into the world's foremost repository of motion-picture trailers.

Although their history extends nearly the length of cinema itself, theatrical trailers have not always been regarded as essential facets of the cinematic experience. Still, it is difficult to imagine a time when coming attractions did not act as a vital liaison between audiences and features. Notorious for straddling the line between marketing tool and work of art, trailers are multifaceted in their function: at worst, blatant misrepresentations or ruinous messengers of key plot twists; at best, harbingers of excitement leaving wide-eyed anticipation in their wake. Some so well crafted that they are themselves films-in-miniature, to be appreciated in their own right. This chapter surveys the history of the Packard Humanities Institute Collection, its ongoing processing at the Academy Film Archive and its contextual significance as it relates to the critical study of pre-show entertainment.

ORIGIN OF THE COLLECTION

For twenty years, film collector Jeff Joseph curated, owned and operated the largest known collection of theatrical trailers on film: the SabuCat Productions Archive. Joseph admits that conducting archival work was never quite his intention nor his ambition.[1] Similarly, he did not originally intend to specifically amass coming attractions. Despite this lack of intent, he noticed, while purchasing film, that collections always seemed to include trailers and keenly observed that no one else appeared to be deliberately collecting them. After an exchange with one of the major studios in which said studio borrowed a trailer for a fee far higher than any profit he could hope to gain from selling the element outright, he realised the value of licensing public domain previews for their footage. Joseph continued to diligently collect materials that were in the public domain, largely trailers, and, by 1989, he and his wife had formed SabuCat Productions, named after their beloved cat. SabuCat successfully rented public domain materials to studios, television production companies, film-makers and other organisations interested in the footage. It was far more advantageous for those companies to license a trailer from SabuCat for a relatively minor fee than to pay a much higher fee to the rights holders of the feature for similar footage. Notably, not only commercial endeavours benefited from this vast aggregation of materials. UCLA arts librarian and author, Lisa Kernan, also utilised the SabuCat Productions Archive while writing her seminal text *Coming Attractions: Reading American Movie Trailers*[2] and excerpts from the collection (as well as Joseph himself) were featured in the documentary *Coming Attractions: The History of the Movie Trailer*, produced by the Andrew J. Kuehn Jr Foundation.[3] As their trailer collection rapidly expanded, the Josephs realised the archive they began out of their home now needed a dedicated residence of its own. Initially, they rented out various spaces, but their business continued to grow and they eventually purchased a building in the sleepy desert town of Palmdale, California, to accommodate the vault space necessary to house the massive collection.

SabuCat thrived for years, but, nearing the end of a two-decade run, shifts in the trailer-licensing business led Joseph to close shop and seek a buyer for the collection. Joseph knew he wanted to sell the collection as a whole, rather than piecemeal. He successfully struck a deal with David Packard in which Packard agreed to purchase the collection in its entirety before depositing it at the Academy Film Archive, as well as the UCLA Film and Television Archive. The Academy would receive all of the trailers on safety stock, while nitrate materials and many of the non-trailer items, such as newsreels and stock footage, would reside at UCLA.

ARCHIVAL PROCESSING

Processing of the Packard Humanities Institute Collection, formerly the SabuCat Productions Archive, began at the Academy Film Archive in January of 2010. Due to the immense size of the collection, two archivist positions were funded specifically to take on inventorying and cataloguing the items in a systematic and efficient manner. Composed of a wide array of theatrical trailers covering an expanse of time periods and genres, the collection also boasts international and domestic advertisements, production shorts, film excerpts, television spots, public service announcements and the other pre-show mainstay: snipes. Prints in the collection span the 1950s to the early 2000s, existing on 16mm and 35mm film stock (both acetate and polyester), as well as a variety of videotape formats from ¾ inch to Digital Betacam.

Items from the acquisition were originally grouped in boxes containing one or more rolls of film, depending on the length and gauge of the materials enclosed. Boxes are processed sequentially, by order of box number. Collection-specific guidelines were developed for processing items, maximising the level of detail achieved for cataloguing while minimising the amount of time spent inspecting each item. Applying these guidelines, each item is, first, visually inspected over a light box, using split reels and a loupe. Information about condition and content is then recorded in the Academy's database. New title-level records must be created for items without existing records, while duplicates can be entered as item-level records under the same title.

Condition descriptions are entered for each item, ranking the overall state of materials on a scale from *excellent* (used to describe items with no apparent flaws) to *poor* (items exhibiting heavy wear, extreme colour fade, edge damage, or vinegar syndrome). Content notes generally include on-screen credits, copyright dates and any additional information unique to the item; for example, the trailer type (teaser, domestic, etc.) or version (Trailer A, Trailer #2, Trailer 2B), information that is often printed on the item's leader or found in the original SabuCat database. The inclusion of such details in the record is essential to maximising the accessibility of the collection.

After an item has been catalogued, film is wound onto chemically inert 3-inch cores, rehoused in labelled and barcoded archival cans and returned to temperature-controlled vaults. Ancillary items, such as advertisements, snipes and public service announcements, are grouped and spliced together onto compilation reels in order to better utilise the limited amount of space available to the collection and to reduce the number of carriers used to house materials since they are often very short in length. At the date of publication, over 17,000 items have been inventoried and catalogued since full-time processing began; and this number does not take into account that compilations of non-trailer materials sometimes include up to thirty individual items per reel.

Many film titles featured within the collection have multiple, identical copies of trailers, raising the question of whether it is necessary for the Academy Film Archive to house such a large number of duplicate items. Another issue encountered by archivists working on the acquisition is the overall condition of items within the collection. A large number of materials have dirt, oil and scratches. In addition, the majority of the trailers printed on Eastmancolor stock, used primarily from the mid-1950s through the late 70s, are highly prone to extreme colour fade. The Packard Humanities Institute Collection includes a large number of Eastmancolor prints that have suffered the unfortunate fate of fading to a striking shade of red. Other condition defects include perforation damage and edge tears, as many items were either damaged during projection, or stored improperly, without the support of plastic cores in the centre, or the cover of protective leader around the outside of the film rolls.

Theatrical trailers raise numerous analytical questions ranging from modes of production (for example, the domination of National Screen Service) to gender (the glaring absence or overt sexualisation of female voiceover). Part of the significance of a vast acquisition of items historically regarded as ephemeral is the reveal of new ground primed for exploration. As strategic marketers of features, trailers are brief but informative gleams reflecting the cinematic zeitgeist, and a comprehensive collection such as this one lends itself to further study.

SNIPES

Beyond trailers, an essential aspect of the Packard Humanities Institute Collection comes in the form of its physically smallest asset: the snipe. It is worth noting that these brief promotional films have been referred to in different ways over the years, perhaps unsurprisingly, since they take various forms. Depending on their intended function, snipes are commonly referred to as policy trailers, concession advertisements, tags, drive-in intermission shorts and daters. Not all of the Academy's snipe holdings derive from the Packard Humanities Institute Collection. There were a few pre-existing records for 'Theatre Advertisements', but, undoubtedly, the scope and size of the Packard Humanities Institute materials changed the way the archive recognised and processed snipes. While the Academy estimates hundreds of snipes in its moving-image holdings, based on its own database records as well as former SabuCat records, many snipes continue to be found attached at the heads and tails of uninventoried trailers. Consequently, the exact number will remain uncertain until the over 60,000 items of the Packard Humanities Institute project have been processed.

The original database created by SabuCat Productions, Datacat (a version of which is still used by the Academy as a resource), utilised the industry term 'snipe' to identify a wide range of items varying from concession advertisements to contest announce-ments and date cards. As far as titling the materials was concerned, Datacat often employed generic monikers such as 'Intermission' or 'Coming Soon'. From an archival standpoint, the Academy conceded that the blanket term 'snipe' effectively covered a lot of ground, allowing archivists to compile numerous items vastly different in content but similar in length. In practice, an animated intermission announcement produced by National Screen Service could be stored alongside a 'No Smoking' policy trailer, and perhaps ten other similarly sized items in a small film can capable of storing up to 400 feet of film, conserving the archive's supplies and precious vault space. Significantly, the archivists processing the collection recognised how vital it would be to employ as much description as possible per each individual item on these compilations in order to make them identifiable by title; a seemingly small attention to detail that would later become crucial to anyone wishing to access the collection.

The issue that occurs with snipes, however, is that, quite often, there is very little information to go on when it comes to cataloguing individual items. Unlike trailers, which more often than not include copyright information and perhaps a few on-screen credits, theatre snipes of all varieties rarely include such things, unless 'The Management' were to count as a formal credit. National Screen Service and Coca-Cola are popular exceptions to the rule, in that they often include a copyright year on their materials. For other items that do not include such information, archivists may sometimes utilise the edge codes of the film stocks in an effort to gain some descriptive insight. For films without edge code, or any identifying textual information, archivists are left to their own devices to fill in those gaps.

A void remains in what is known about the producers of many of these snipes, in part due to a lack of textual information on the physical items; compounded by the fact that, much like coming attractions, these small pieces of film were often thought of as trivial and records of their production were treated accordingly. One long-standing company known to have produced a sizable amount of these materials is Filmack Studios. Based in Chicago and established in 1919 as the Filmack Trailer Company by former newspaper man Irving Mack, Filmack famously hired Walt Disney in 1920 and Dave Fleischer in the early 1950s.[4] Fleischer, producer of the Popeye cartoons, was responsible for animating one of Filmack's most well-known snipes, 'Let's All Go to the Lobby'.[5] In the year 2000, this snipe was selected for preservation in the US National Film Registry by the Library of Congress after being deemed 'culturally, historically, and aesthetically significant'. Filmack remains in business today and continues to sell their snipes, even acquiring the negatives of fellow policy trailer producers and one-time competitor Pike Productions.[6]

One strategy the archive has employed in the quest for further information and identification has been to reference old film sales catalogues.[7] A 'cool trailer', as snipes promoting a theatre's air conditioning were once described, in the Academy's holdings amusingly warned against the hazards of the TeeVee Jeebies, but, unfortunately, lacked any edge code or visible copyright to help identify it. The Filmack catalogue 'Inspiration' confirmed that various ads for 'cool trailers' began to appear around 1947. The first mention of television in these ads appears in 1951, with an ad warning against the 'TV Wiggles' that occur due to perspiration while watching television at home; perhaps this is a precursor to the TeeVee Jeebies ad appearing in 1955 that matches the archive's snipe exactly. This blending of resources successfully affirmed proper dates and names for items previously lacking this metadata.

Snipes share a similar history and fate with trailers in that they too were fundamentally thought of as dispensable. Of the materials that do survive, the majority are incomplete and commonly suffer from footage loss at heads or tails as a result of being repeatedly spliced onto other items. Frequently, their current state is colour faded, heavily scratched, spliced and edge damaged. Yet, perhaps even more so than trailers, snipes offer a glimpse into the history of the theatregoing experience. These culturally significant snapshots serve to inform us of the antiquated issues of the day such as speaker theft, smoking, seat cutting as an act of vandalism, or worse: vandalism as an act of anti-nationalism!

Snipes inform us of a wide variety of other subjects, such as the bygone era of kiddie matinees, policies against lovers necking, public service announcements recommending church attendance, student discount cards, the 'no masturbation' policies of adult cinemas (there's a snipe for that!) and the miracles of air conditioning by scientific refrigeration. One animated snipe in the archive's holdings cheerfully proclaims, 'Candy is delicious food, eat some every day!' while simultaneously depicting Native Americans in a decidedly offensive fashion. While thoughts on nutrition (and significant issues like the representation of race in animation) have hopefully evolved, these films, or what remain of them, serve as a window into a different time, with different theatres than those known now. These miniature films point to the past perhaps in the same way that snipes produced today will inform future generations of this era's continued love affair with popcorn and Coca-Cola, as well as a torrid obsession with mobile phones.

ACCESS

Since the Academy's procurement of the Packard Humanities Institute Collection, pre-show materials from the acquisition have been featured in numerous Academy screenings and programmes. The appeal of these vintage films makes them equally sought after by outside organisations for projects such as archival screenings or inclusion as special features on new Blu-ray releases. In certain cases, studios no longer have holdings of particular trailers or featurettes and, subsequently, look to the archive to source the items.

The Academy Film Archive encourages the further research of these materials and offers access to its holdings for on-site research and licensing requests. At the time of this writing, the Academy Film Archive is home to an estimated 190,000 inventoried film and video assets; with over 89,000 individual titles. Trailers and snipes from the collection are currently being lent to repertory film houses for no fees, as a lending programme is part of the Academy's mission to encourage the viewing of the medium the way it was originally intended. Further information about the Academy Film Archive's access policies may be found on the Academy's website, Oscars.org

In *Coming Soon: Film Trailers and the Selling of Hollywood Technology*, author Keith M. Johnston posits, 'Only two books, and a handful of academic articles, have considered the trailer as anything other than a loud, over-revelatory nuisance.'[8] Years after the publication of Johnston's extensive work, his sentiment still rings true. The foresight of Jeff Joseph to collect these materials, along with the benevolence of the Packard Humanities Institute to ensure their archival stability, has engendered the exposure of promotional films to future generations of moviegoers. Although the form of the medium has shifted throughout the years and will undoubtedly continue to transform, our fascination with coming attractions remains. It is through the eyes of new audiences that the pre-show lives on.

NOTES

1. Jeff Joseph, personal interview conducted by the author, 12 May 2011.
2. Lisa Kernan, *Coming Attractions: Reading American Movie Trailers* (Austin: University of Texas, 2004).
3. *Coming Attractions: The History of the Movie Trailer*. Dir. Michael J. Shapiro and Jeff Werner. Perf. Robert Osborne. The Andrew J. Kuehn Jr Foundation, 2006.
4. Daniel Eagan, *America's Film Legacy: The Authoritative Guide to the Landmark Movies in the National Film Registry* (New York: Continuum, 2010), pp. 543–4.
5. John Owens, 'Timeless "Let's All Go to the Lobby" Has Deep Local Roots', *Chicago Tribune*, 24 January 2013, n.p., accessed online 11 May 2015.
6. Chad Greene, 'Another Reel in the Storied History of Filmack', *Boxoffice* vol. 144 no. 7 (2008), p. 16.
7. Special thanks to Walter Forsberg and the Donald C. Brown, Jr Collection at Northeast Historic Film for the digitisation and use of Filmack's 'Inspiration' sales catalogues.
8. Keith M. Johnston, *Coming Soon: Film Trailers and the Selling of Hollywood Technology* (Jefferson, NC: McFarland, 2009), p. 179.

18

Parsing the Archive of Rudolf Mayer Film, Vienna, 1937–9

Joachim Schätz

When Kurt Mayer brought the surviving documents from his father's company to the Austrian Film Museum for deposit in March 2011, the materials easily fitted into two bags: one well-filled thick binder, two folders (one bulky, the other slim), an envelope, one duplicating book for delivery notes and a couple of photographs curled by age. Despite this slender volume, those documents, put together with the films that Kurt Mayer had already deposited at the Austrian Film Museum before, form one of the most revealing windows on the lively period of professionalisation in Austrian advertising film that were the 1930s: the archive of Rudolf Mayer Film. The binder proved especially instructive and is the main source of the following observations.

The surviving documents of Rudolf Mayer Film

It contains, in alphabetical order of the client companies, film proposals developed by Rudolf Mayer and his collaborators, as well as occasional business correspondence – papers lost without a trace in the case of most other contemporaneous producers of short films in Austria. They give some clues as to the everyday procedures and networks of advertising film production that neither contemporaneous trade papers and academic studies nor the surviving films provide. To better outline the epistemic value of those papers, I will briefly chart Rudolf Mayer's career and the efforts at professionalising short film production in Austria during the 1930s as known via other sources.

CONTEXT (I): RUDOLF MAYER

Since his youth, Rudolf Mayer (1903–1962) had been working in his father Gustav Mayer's company, Mayer's Filmbüro. Founded in the early 1920s, the company first specialised in actualities and newsreels, but would be one of the most successful producers of advertising films in Vienna from 1934 onwards. When Gustav Mayer died in 1936, Rudolf's younger brother Adi took over the family enterprise, prompting him to start his own company, Rudolf Mayer Film, in October 1937.[1] The new company's output of both advertising films and state-sponsored educational films (*Kulturfilme*) was fairly constant before Rudolf was drafted as a frontline cameraman at the end of 1939. While the family enterprise, renamed Adi Mayer Film, would go on to be one of the most successful and long-living manufacturers of advertising films and TV commercials in post-war Austria, Rudolf Mayer's business would never recover from the forced hiatus during World War II. After the war, he would only produce the occasional commercial and campaign film and specialise (with limited success) in manufacturing special effects in his garage studio.

The written documents in the archive of Rudolf Mayer Film mostly cover the early successful period, from the company's formation in October 1937 to the end of 1939. They also encompass occasional projects dating back to his time at Mayer's Filmbüro, as well as occasional projects taken on by Rudolf for another local producer of advertising films, Hans Ludwig Böhm. The business correspondence in the binder is scarce but informative. The collection of film proposals for the period until the end of 1939, although large, is not complete, as can be measured by the absence of several surviving Rudolf Mayer films. It contains proposals and notes on some seventy proposed films, often in three evolving versions (typescript with handwritten notes). Reflecting the different formats of promotional films produced at the time, the proposals' lengths vary from half a page (usually for *Sprechstreifen*, i.e. film strips containing recorded sound only that were combined with slide presentation) to ten pages (for longer narrative promotional films).

CONTEXT (II): PROFESSIONALISATION OF ADVERTISING IN 1930s AUSTRIA

Before Rudolf Mayer was drafted into service as a cameraman his business seems to have benefited from the National Socialist annexation of Austria, in March 1938.

In the period from March 1938 to the end of 1939, there were hardly any advertising films produced in Vienna by anyone other than Rudolf (fourteen films) and Adi Mayer (nineteen films).[2] The decrease in competition was in no small part due to National Socialist persecution, which led, for instance, to the deportation and eventual death of influential Austrian advertising film producer Robert Reich.

But Rudolf Mayer Film's relatively steady production until the end of 1939 was also shaped by enduring creative and business contacts and rooted in long-running efforts at professionalisation undertaken by the Austrian producers of advertising films and supported by the previous Austro-Fascist government's Ministry of Trade. In the summer of 1935, the established makers of advertising films and other short subjects founded the Verband der Kurzfilmhersteller (Association of Producers of Short Films) to better assert their interests and organise production and distribution.[3] In March 1936, they managed to have the profession of producer of short films changed to a protected profession requiring a licence, thus shielding the market from new competitors. Later in 1936, they also succeeded in having protective measures imposed against foreign film producers making advertising films for domestic companies.[4] The same year, sixty-one advertising sound films were produced in Austria (including state-sponsored promotional films) – a modest number considering the German output of over 650 advertising films in 1935,[5] but still impressive in comparison with the twenty-one films made in Austria in 1932.[6] (Twenty-four – more than a third – of those 1936 films were registered as Mayer's Filmbüro productions in the censorship lists.)

With their steady output and institutional ties, the handful of established producers of advertising and industrial films like Gustav Mayer, Karl Köfinger, or Hans Ludwig Böhm[7] fitted well with the agenda of the Austrian Reklamewissenschaftliche Vereinigung (Association for the Science of Advertising), which prominently included promotional films as a topic in its vocational training course in 1935.[8] Like other Austrian and international advertising trade organisations at the time, the Association for the Science of Advertising stressed a programme of professionalisation that aimed to rid advertising of dubious or ill-informed market participants and thus improve the business's overall reputation.[9] The practice of those established advertising film producers might seem distinctly different from the specific ideas about professionalisation heralded in the trade publications *Kontakt* and *Österreichische Reklame*: it hinged on broad, craftsman-like know-how rather than on creative and scientific specialisation; on tight-knit family enterprises and loose networks of freelancers rather than clear-cut organisational hierarchies and divisions of labour. But, then again, that was mostly the state of affairs in advertising in 1930s Vienna as well, with ambitious small Reklamebüros (advertising companies) fulfilling a variety of functions.[10]

This mode of production in the field of advertising films, markedly distinct from the differentiation of tasks under the supervision of ad agencies that would finally prevail in Austria circa 1960, is partly elucidated by the written documents of the archive of Rudolf Mayer Film. The papers are revealing regarding both advertising films' commissioning and their conception.

MATERIAL (I): COMMISSIONING FILMS

The producers of short films in 1930s Austria were generalists. According to all available evidence and accounts by descendants, this does not just go for their output – which ranged from advertising films and *Kulturfilme* to newsreel segments and film interludes for live performances – but also for the division of labour within the companies. Diverse creative (camera, editing, title cards, directing) and business (contacting possible clients, distributing films) tasks had to be performed by the producer and his staff which often (as in Gustav Mayer's and Karl Köfinger's case) consisted largely of family members.[11] The producers' informal way of keeping contact with both freelance creatives and clients makes it difficult to trace standard modes of procedure – for instance, the way films were commissioned.

Concerning this matter, the papers of the Rudolf Mayer Film archive offer some insight. They reveal, for instance, that differentation of tasks in advertising had evolved to the extent that small advertising offices sometimes worked as intermediaries between clients and film producers and developed film concepts. In a letter, advertising professional Fritz Engelhart informs a perfume manufacturer of his idea for the subject of an advertising film it had commissioned, as well as the film's probable length and production cost. Engelhart claims that he can't be more specific, as he hasn't yet chosen a film company to commission with this film.[12] The existence of a copy of this letter among Rudolf Mayer's company papers suggests otherwise – censorship lists reveal that Engelhart had collaborated with Mayer's Filmbüro for a long time.[13] Another document that points to the intermediary role of advertising agencies is an envelope containing detailed guidelines on a planned advertising film and PR materials from the textile company Ganahl in Feldkirch. It is adressed, not to Rudolf Mayer, but to professional Viennese sales representative Hans Glass, who likely contacted Mayer.[14]

It is impossible to gauge from the surviving materials the ratio of films commissioned via an advertising intermediary versus films commissioned in direct contact between Mayer and clients – an option that, according to practitioners, was still in practice until the 1950s in the small Austrian market.[15] But the documents prove that, by 1937, this mode of doing business already co-existed with a more streamlined divison of labour.

MATERIAL (II): WRITING FILMS

Most of the film proposals in the Rudolf Mayer Film archive are unsigned, except for the stamp of 'Rudolf Mayer, Kurzfilmhersteller [producer of short films], Neubaugasse 25'. Usually, the texts are followed by the blanket statement, 'Non-binding proposal. All rights reserved.' Of course, Rudolf Mayer's company signature doesn't mean that he wrote those texts – ranging from short film descriptions to more fleshed-out screenplays – on his own. First of all, as discussed, both advertising professionals and the clients themselves were active in conceiving of film plots. The aforementioned correspondence with Ganahl highlights the striking level of detail in which a client of middling size would instruct a film producer. A letter titled 'Guidelines for a manuscript' specifies the range of products to be advertised, as well as ideas for the structure of the film (both of which Mayer's subsequent proposal closely adheres to).[16] It also offers this elaborate objective regarding the company's corporate image:

> The film aims to popularize our trademark and company name. Find the enclosed trademark but mind that in the new edition the term 'Montforta' [a former quality description] will take a backseat to the company name 'Ganahl'. So 'Ganahl' is to be advertised first and foremost, and 'Montforta' only in connection, to accustom the viewer to the other name. Yet, this transformation is not to be specifically depicted, but only to be imprinted in passing.[17]

Another letter concerning Ganahl, this time addressed to Mayer's Filmbüro and most likely written either by a company employee or a sales intermediary (the author refers to 'our goods'), contains another set of tasks for the film ('review of products and plea to the consumer, suitable for following a salesman's pitch') and a matching plot outline.[18]

Apart from such detailed writing on the part of the client, Mayer frequently employed freelance authors. While the surviving films' credits are sparse, mentioning little else beyond featured prominent actors and singers and the promoted company,

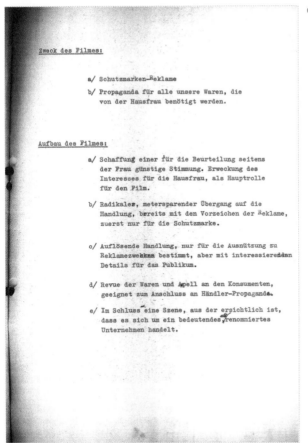

Guidelines for a Ganahl film

the papers allow for a little more insight into Rudolf Mayer's network of collaborators. The authors credited in the proposals include, for instance, journalist Josef Székely and successful *Wienerlied* songwriter Erich Meder, who contributed specially written lyrics for two film proposals.

The use of popular songs, which is also evident in Mayer's surviving advertising films, was fairly typical of 1930s advertising. Mayer productions often announce their singer-stars in the film title (*Franz Schier singt 'Das Lied von Sooß'* [*Franz Schier sings 'The Song of Sooß'*], *Das Bohème-Quartett in: 'Die Vier von der Tegetthoffstraße'* [*The Bohème Quartet in: 'The Four from Tegetthoff Street'*]). But beyond the pervasive popularity of *Schlager* and *Wienerlied* music and their interpreters, building an advertising film around a song had pragmatic advantages made evident by the proposals: songs composed for one proposal could be applied to another if the film wasn't made after all; even songs written specifically for the occasion allowed for flexibility in planning a budget. A proposal for Persil based on new lyrics by Erich Meder, *Wien steht Kopf* (*Vienna on its Head*), is prefaced by an explanation about two possible versions of the film, one significantly shorter than the other.[19] Likewise, a screenplay built around Erich Meder's song 'Qualität bleibt Qualität' ('Quality will be Quality') is introduced by the note that single shots in the film (and the verses they are connected to) could be swapped and cut as desired. The song as a whole, originally written for Abadie cigarettes, would be reused for proposals for the textile shop Sandera and the shoe retailer Delka.[20]

This practice of recycling cannot only be traced across the film proposals and short screenplays in the Rudolf Mayer film archive.[21] It also pertains to the surviving Mayer films which often reapply existing footage, making the best of the broad range of films produced. Here, the film-makers show genuine imagination: with material he very likely had just shot for a *Kulturfilm* about professional raftsmen (*Flößer/Raftsmen*, 1941), Adi Mayer made the advertising short *Nimm das Steuer in die Hand* (*Take the Steering Wheel*) (1941), which promoted insurance by likening life to the navigation of wild waters.

Despite the practical necessities and frugal calculations behind such practices of recycling, there is also a playful, occasionally even baroque streak to some of Rudolf Mayer's screenplays for advertising films. Fully in keeping with his later career as a special effects craftsman who made spaceships fly in the state-sponsored sci-fi oddity *1. April 2000* (1952), the proposal for *Wien steht Kopf* calls for trick photography showing a flooded inner-city Vienna and St Stephen's Cathedral transposed on a nearby mountaintop.[22] The most formally adventurous of those proposals, named *Das Geheimnis der Zehn?* (*The Secret of the Ten?*), commissioned by the Delka chain of shoe stores, was actually filmed. As no copy of the film has been found, it is impossible to say how many of the screenplay's sophisticated superimpositions made it into the actual film.[23] But – to switch from historical analysis to art appreciation for one final moment – the proposal itself has its own special attraction. The 'ten' in the title refers to the number of branch stores Delka ran in Vienna, which Rudi Mayer planned to visualise with a photo-montage of the different shops forming a '10'. This is anticipated by a sketch of the ten, overlapped by a paper clip demonstrating the 'revue of shoes and stockings' to appear out of the zero. The paper clip can be folded, concealing and revealing parts of the sketch behind it. Both functional and somewhat improvised, this image-object might be an emblem for Rudolf Mayer's mode of production. It's movement brought onto paper, a flourish directed at Mayer's clients rather than at the audiences in the cinema.

- 3 -

B i l d .   T o n .

In's Bild kommt groß die Tafel   Sprecher:
D e l k a.   Delka mit seinen 10 Wiener
                                                   Filialen.
Aufzug bleibt stehen.
Tafel zerreißt und es erschei-
nen aus den Rissen, die Ziffer
10 gebildet aus den 10 Filialen
Delka's.

Durch die aus den Filialen
gebildete Ziffer 10,
geht durch die Null eine   Für jeden Bedarf den
Revue von Schuhen und Strümpfen   D e l k a Schuh und auch den
in Großaufnahme.   passenden Strumpf dazu.

Schlußbild.
        D e l k a
    t r ä g t s i c h g u t .

                        E n d e.

Alle Rechte vorbehalten.
Unverbindlicher Vorschlag.

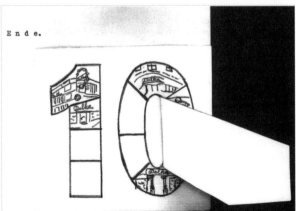

The Secret of the Ten? (*Das Geheimnis der Zehn?*)

DOCUMENTS IN THE ARCHIVE OF RUDOLF MAYER FILM

(owned by Kurt Mayer, deposited in the Archive of the Austrian Film Museum, Vienna)

'Beilage zum Brief an Filmbüro Mayer, Wien'
'Das Geheimnis der Zehn?'
'Freude'
Prucha, Franz, 'Richtlinien für das Manuskript'
'Qualität bleibt Qualität. Ein Werbefilm für "Abadie" von Erich Meder'
'Qualität bleibt Qualität. Sujet für einen Werbefilm'
Reklamebüro Fritz Engelhart, 'Kopie. Titl. Fa. M.E.Mayer. Wien, 2. Sept. 1937'
'Schusterweisheit'
'Wien steht Kopf. Ein Persil-Reklame-Film. Idee von Erich Meder'

NOTES

1. Information on the company's concession obtained in an email from Walter Töttels, MA 63 Zentralgewerberegister Wien, on 6 November 2012.
2. Information obtained researching the German censorship lists at the Bundesarchiv Filmarchiv on 13 November 2012.
3. 'Verband der Kurzfilmhersteller', *Das Kino-Journal* no. 1305 (August 1935), p. 6.
4. 'Zum Schutz der heimischen Kurzfilmindustrie', *Das Kino-Journal* no. 1355 (July 1936), p. 10. Subsequently, in January 1937, a travelling salesman for a company in Zagreb was sentenced to a fine of 800 Schillings for having shot advertising films in Austria without a concession. 'Unbefugte Kurzfilmherstellung', *Das Kino-Journal* no. 1379 (January 1937), p. 4.
5. Ralf Forster, *Ufa und Nordmark. Zwei Firmengeschichten und der deutsche Werbefilm 1919–1945* (Trier: Wissenschaftlicher Verlag Trier, 2005), p. 176.
6. For the numbers, see Emil Guckes, 'Der Tonfilm als Werbemittel in Deutschland' (PhD dissertation, Leopold-Franzens-Universität Innsbruck, 1937), p. 145.
7. Gustav Mayer was a member of the Viennese Industrial Cooperative's film panel; Karl Köfinger was also the sworn official legal expert on the conditions of film copies. 'Werbung durch den Film', *Österreichische Film-Zeitung* vol. 8 no. 42 (1934), p. 5; Karl Köfinger, 'Filmrollen und Filmwirtschaft', *Das Kino-Journal* no. 1387 (March 1937), p. 5.
8. 'Filmvorführung', *Kontakt* vol. 10 no. 6 (1935), p. 22; 'Vortrag: "Wie entsteht ein Werbefilm"', *Kontakt* vol. 10 no. 7/8 (1935), pp. 29–30; 'Verband der Kurzfilmhersteller', *Das Kino-Journal* no. 1305 (August 1935), p. 6.
9. See, for instance, Erwin Paneth, 'Der Aufstieg der Reklame vom Pfuschertum zur Wissenschaft', *Österreichische Reklame* vol. 1 no. 1 (1926), p. 4; Hanns Kropff, 'Die letzten Entwicklungen und die nächsten Aufgaben der Reklame', *Kontakt* vol. 6 no. 1 (1931), pp. 3–9; Charles J. Angermayer, 'Advertising Agency = Anzeigenexpedition +x', *Kontakt* vol. 6 no. 6 (1931), pp. 31–2.
10. This even applies to the consulting jobs of August Lichal, chairman of the *Reklamewissenschaftliche Vereinigung*: 'August Lichal R-W-V', *Kontakt* vol. 6 no. 12 (1931), p. 14. On advertising offices, see also 'Hanns Kropff über aktuelle Rekalmefragen', *Kontakt* vol. 6 no. 12 (1931), p. 34.

11. Interviews conducted by the author, Sema Colpan, and Lydia Nsiah with Rudi Mayer's son Kurt Mayer (6 October 2010) and Adi Mayer's son Peter Mayer (17 July 2011). Josef Navratil, *Das Werk des österreichischen Kulturfilmproduzenten Ing. Karl Köfinger am Beispiel einer Serie von Fremdenverkehrswerbefilmen* (Vienna: Österreichisches Filmarchiv, 1989), pp. 21, 25–6.

12. Reklamebüro Fritz Engelhart, 'Kopie. Titl. Fa. M.E.Mayer. Wien, 2. Sept. 1937', company archive Rudolf Mayer Film, preserved by Kurt Mayer, deposited at the Austrian Film Museum.

13. See 'Der Schlüssel der Gesundheit', 'Das rassige Vollblut', 'Der schneidige Traber' and 'Die lieben Nachbarn', in Thomas Ballhausen and Paolo Caneppele (eds), *Entscheidungen der Wiener Filmzensur 1934–1938* (Vienna: Filmarchiv Austria, 2009), pp. 192, 212, 248.

14. 'Herrn Ing. Hans Glass', company archive Rudolf Mayer Film. On Hans Glass, see Lehmann 1936, vol. 2, 3rd section, 28, 'Schikanederstraße 6'.
http://www.digital.wienbibliothek.at/wbrobv/periodical/pageview/220605

15. Interviews conducted by the author, Sema Colpan, and Lydia Nsiah with Kurt Mayer (6 October 2010), Peter Mayer (17 July 2011) and Harro Pfeiffer, former general manager of the ad agency Eggert (merged with Grey Austria in 2000) in Vienna (27 April 2011). Navratil, *Das Werk des österreichischen Kulturfilmproduzenten Ing. Karl Köfinger*, pp. 10–11.

16. Franz Prucha, 'Richtlinien für das Manuskript', company archive Rudolf Mayer Film.

17. Ibid., translation by J. S.

18. 'Beilage zum Brief an Filmbüro Mayer, Wien', company archive Rudolf Mayer Film. Translation of Fig. 2 by J. S.: 'Purpose of the film: a) Advertising the trademark. b) Advertising for all our wares that are used by housewives. Structure of the film: a) Creating a mood that is beneficial to the evaluation by women. Awakening interest in the housewife, as central character in the film. b) Radical, footage-economic transition to the plot while already signalling towards advertising, first focused only on the trademark. c) Resolution of the plot, providing an opportunity for advertising, now with details of interest to the audience. d) Revue of wares and appeal to the consumer, suitable to follow a salesman's pitch. e) In the end a scene that makes it clear that this is a distinguished, prestigious company.'

19. 'Wien steht Kopf. Ein Persil-Reklame-Film. Idee von Erich Meder', company archive Rudolf Mayer Film.

20. 'Qualität bleibt Qualität. Ein Werbefilm für "Abadie" von Erich Meder', 'Qualität bleibt Qualität. Sujet für einen Werbefilm'. Both: company archive Rudolf Mayer Film.

21. Other proposals that are reused include 'Schusterweisheit' (for shoe businesses BB and Delka) and 'Freude' (used for Delka, coffee brand Imperial and the Aryanised department store Kaufhaus der Wiener, formerly Gerngross). All proposals are part of the company archive Rudolf Mayer Film.

22. 'Wien steht Kopf. Ein Persil-Reklame-Film. Idee von Erich Meder', company archive Rudolf Mayer Film.

23. 'Das Geheimnis der Zehn?', company archive Rudolf Mayer Film. Translation of Fig. 3 by J. S.: 'Image. The plate saying "Delka" appears prominently. The elevator stops. The plate is torn, and from the ruptures, there appears the number ten, formed from the ten Delka branch stores. Through the zero, a revue of shoes and stockings in close-up appears. Final shot. Delka wears well. Sound. Narrator: Delka with its ten branch stores. For every need the Delka shoe/and the matching stocking as well. The End. All rights reserved. Non-binding proposal.'

19

The Film Group's Cinéma Vérité TV Ads

Andy Uhrich

Colonel Sanders hawks his company's new packaging of fast-food fried chicken in a 1968 TV ad called *Sunday Dinner*.[1] In a documentary accusing the Illinois State's Attorney of ordering the assassination of a civil-rights leader, *The Murder of Fred Hampton* (1971), members of the Chicago chapter of the Black Panther Party urge local hospitals to provide health care to African-American neighbourhoods.[2] A rural white family of farmers sits down to a breakfast of Aunt Jemima Pancakes in a commercial made for Quaker Oats.[3] Police violently attack anti-war demonstrators at the 1968 Democratic National Convention in a documentary advocating for a multiracial response to political injustice, *American Revolution II* (1969).[4]

These extreme contrasts between revolutionary politics and pop culture commercialism appear in the television advertisements and radical documentaries made between 1963 and 1972 by the Chicago production company, the Film Group, Inc. If the Film Group is known today, it is for their political documentaries on the Black Panthers and the protest movement. *American Revolution II (ARII)* and *The Murder of Fred Hampton (Hampton)* have been released on DVD in the USA and France. Their seven-part series *The Urban Crisis and the New Militants* (1966–9) was preserved through a grant from the National Film Preservation Foundation. The Library of Congress chose one of that series, *Cicero March* (1966), for the National Film Registry in 2013. Scholars such as Alan Sekula and Jonathan Kahana have mentioned and analysed the Film Group's documentaries.[5] However, their work in television commercials has been overlooked. Possible reasons for this include the general oversight of TV ads by film and television studies (which this book is working to correct), the advertisements' archival absence until the end of the last decade and the Film Group's explicit downplaying of their commercial productions for political reasons.

The recent archival incorporation of these films and TV commercials and their online accessibility by the Chicago Film Archives (CFA) allows for a re-evaluation of the company's mode of documentary production and the close connection between nonfiction film-making and television advertising. Despite recent forays into the topic by Craig Breaden and others, the relationship between documentary film and TV ads has remained obscured by documentarians and underexplored by media scholars.[6] Though many well-known documentary film-makers made television ads and industrials to fund their features, the former are often considered as work-for-hire and outside the social and aesthetic concerns of their true documentaries.[7] While the Film Group assumed this ideological position in interviews with the underground press,[8] the company's radical politics brought them business clients looking to appeal to people of colour and the youth movement. The Film Group is an explicit example of how advertising agencies in the 1960s adopted and adapted the new forms of observational documentaries to sell goods to a radicalising youth market wary of traditional forms of commercial promotion.

ARCHIVING THE FILM GROUP

CFA, a regional audiovisual repository that collects media artefacts from the Midwest USA, now holds these documentaries and TV spots, all shot on 16mm.[9] The work of the Film Group is organised at CFA into two interrelated collections based on the donations by former employees of the production company: the Film Group Collection, 1966–9, and the Chuck Olin Collection, 1965–2001. These two collections were acquired by CFA after 2005. Since 2010, CFA has uploaded many of the Film Group's films to the archive's website including seventy-one of their TV commercials.[10] All of the ads discussed in this chapter are streaming online.

The Film Group's better-known political documentaries depicting civil rights and anti-war movements in Chicago constitute a major part of CFA's identity as an archive devoted to telling forgotten local stories through archival moving images. CFA has received grants to preserve nine of the Film Group's short documentaries. The archive has screened documentaries by the Film Group numerous times over the last decade. Four shorts from the *Urban Crisis* series were exhibited at a commemoration of the fortieth anniversary of the 1968 Democratic Convention and in 2013 a 1970 short on the anti-Vietnam War sentiments in a conservative Chicago neighbourhood was shown on the block where it was originally filmed.

The archive has not ignored the Film Group's ads. All have been processed, catalogued and digitised for access purposes. A number of the ads have been included in thematically organised events produced by CFA including ones on the Christmas holidays and a programme of films on food. However, a number of issues surround the ads, making them more complicated archival objects than the Film Group's political documentaries. [A caveat: the following claims are based on my personal experience as an archivist working for CFA, on a contract basis, on the processing and exhibition of the Film Group's collections. These do not reflect the official viewpoint of the archive nor any of its employees.] First, though they were shot on 16mm film and exist on that gauge, since the commercials were made for television broadcast they are not eligible for preservation funds through the National Film Preservation Foundation, which is the main source of funding for film preservation in the USA. Preservation grants are useful not just for the physical conservation of a film, but in allowing archives to promote their efforts through press releases and restoration premieres that help establish their archival identity through publicity.

Second, there are the questions of the commercials' titles and authors. As the ads do not have even the limited credits of the Film Group's documentaries, it is difficult to determine which member of the Film Group might have worked on a specific commercial, whether the ad has an official title and which ad agency was behind the larger campaign from which the commercial came. The issue of the influence of the ad agency is particularly vexing in regards to the authorship of the commercial. While this is also a factor with industrial films made for a sponsor, the corporate production of TV ads complicates the cinephile ideal of the director as artist that continues to structure how documentary films are discussed.

Third, the Film Group members themselves downplayed the importance of their advertising work. The often-repeated story of the Film Group's move into political documentaries recounts filming a commercial for Kentucky Fried Chicken with the fast-food company's spokesman and living logo, Colonel Sanders. News reports of the violence at the 1968 Democratic Convention compelled the Film Group to leave the filming of the commercial to document the demonstrations that can be seen in the opening sections of *ARII*.[11] The Film Group's assertion that their film-making practice pivoted on this moment of revolutionary conversion denigrates their TV ads as representative of their pre-enlightened and politically regressive period. It also sets up a binary opposition between the two forms of nonfiction film-making (feature versus thirty-second spot, film versus television, politics versus commercialism) instead of highlighting commonalities of formal style, rhetorical argumentation and production method.

A BRIEF HISTORY OF THE FILM GROUP

For the sake of simplicity this chapter uses the singular name Film Group to refer to a production company that went through a number of name changes during its lifetime: Hedman Gray (1963–6), Hedman, Gray & Shea (1966), the Film Group, Inc. (1966–70) and Mike Gray & Associates (starting in 1969). Michael Gray, who later wrote the screenplay for *The China Syndrome* (1979) and a number of nonfiction books exposing the injustices in the war on drugs and in the American justice system's use of the death penalty, was the guiding presence across these changes. Other partners, employees and participants in the Film Group included Lars Hedman, documentary photographer Mike Shea, soundman Jim Dennett, Olin, William Cottle, Brenda Bierbrodt, cinematographer Ron Pitts, Howard Alk and Jones Cullinan, who also worked sound on D. A. Pennebaker's *Dont Look Back* (1967). Olin went on to a long career as a nonfiction film-maker directing educational films and social documentaries. After his time with the Film Group, Alk directed the 1974 music documentary on Janis Joplin, *Janis*, and edited Bob Dylan's film *Renaldo and Clara* (1979).

The Film Group formed to profitably apply the technologies and styles of fly-on-the-wall documentaries to the efficient creation of TV ads. A short article in a 1966 issue of *Business Screen*, a magazine covering industrial and sponsored film-making, announced one of the re-formations of the company. Shea, who directed *And This Is Free ...*, a 1965 documentary on Chicago's famous Maxwell Street public market, is described in the article as 'an advocate of the "direct cinema" technique which applies the candid realism of photo-journalism to motion picture documentary production'. That the unnamed author had to explicitly explain the term 'direct cinema' suggests the novelty of the new form of documentary film-making to corporate film-makers and advertisers. To assure prospective business clients of the company's advertising-friendly nature, the article notes Hedman's ten years of experience in shooting ads and Gray's previous work as a copywriter at an ad agency.[12]

The Film Group produced more than one hundred television commercials for local and national companies including campaigns for Sears, Eli Lilly, Quaker Oats, Hills Bros. coffee, the *Chicago Tribune* and United Airlines. Hired by some of the top ad agencies of the time – McCann Erickson Swift, Rink Wells, Leo Burnett, Edward H. Weiss and J. Walter Thompson – the Film Group was lauded for its ability to shoot on location and capture a sense of hard-hitting verisimilitude. As one advertising executive said of the Film Group, 'You get [them] if you want realism.'[13]

However, radicalised by the state violence enacted against civil-rights advocates and the peace movement, the Film Group eventually became something more akin to a film-making collective instead of a straight-laced production company. They directed a series of political documentaries in collaboration with a number of activist groups such as the Black Panther Party, the Diggers, the Young Patriots and Business Executives Move for Vietnam Peace. These films presented the anti-war demonstrations and racial discrimination in Chicago as a microcosm of the international political unrest of the late 1960s, early 70s. Their seven-part series *The Urban Crisis and the New Militants* was created as a provocative new approach to educational film-making by removing the pedantic voiceover of the narrator to allow high-school students to debate issues of free speech and constitutional rights for themselves. *American Revolution II* explored the question of why more African-Americans were not engaged in the demonstrations against the 1968 Democratic Convention and began a film-making relationship with the Black Panthers that culminated in *The Murder of Fred Hampton*. The latter film originally started as a look at the social programmes of the Panthers, but turned into a citizen's indictment of the Illinois State's Attorney after the killing of two Black Panthers in December 1969.

TV ADS AS NONFICTION FILM-MAKING

The Film Group did not stop producing TV ads during their period of radical documentary-making. During the years that the Film Group was working on their two Black Panther films, *ARII* and *Hampton*, they became a point of intersection between two seemingly oppositional networks: corporate advertising and underground revolutionaries. A 1970 newspaper article on Gray recounts the meeting of these two worlds:

> Panthers, Gray's hip advertising clients, and A[lk]'s underground pals all converged in the [Film Group's] offices and hallways. Panthers leaned over A[lk]'s shoulder at the editing machine, and as their own speeches yelled back at them from the soundtrack, they would murmur 'Right on.' 'Right on' became a catch phrase for Mike Gray, too, even when he conversed with uptight clients; another bit of revolutionary life-style co-opted by the bourgeoisie just as they took over 'psychedelics' and started selling $200 hippie dresses.[14]

In the same article Gray suggests the Film Group's recent political radicalisation has cost the company business from ad agencies: 'Some of our clients don't want to have anything to do with us because of my political beliefs. And my feeling about that is I really don't care to have anything to do with them.'[15] However, their post-1968 political documentaries also brought new corporate clients to the Film Group. In 1970, they made a thirty-minute sponsored documentary called *A Matter of Opportunity* for the American Medical Association (AMA). The AMA hoped to use the film as part of a larger effort to atone for its history of discrimination by recruiting more minority medical workers. An article on the film in the October 1970 issue of *Business Screen* completely ignores the Film Group's expertise in producing commercials to over-emphasise the company's radical ties. That *Business Screen*, a magazine fully representing corporate interests, would so fully promote the Film Group's connections to black power groups and the peace movement highlights the monetary potential sponsors saw in appropriating the image of the revolutionary. The Film Group's five-year experience working for Sears, Aunt Jemima, Blue Cross and Blue Shield and Quaker Oats is left unmentioned in the article. Presumably, highlighting the production company's conservative past would have diminished the revolutionary image of the Film Group, which the AMA were trading on to show their seriousness in reaching across racial and political boundaries, and which *Business Screen* was promoting as a way to make the sponsored film relevant to younger audiences. Instead, the article highlights how the film-makers 'are longhaired, beard and mustached moon-cats who ride monster motorcycles and convince airline stewardess that they's [sic] a rock band'.[16] Though it was 'masochistic' for the AMA to have worked with the Film Group, they did so 'because the AMA, like Gray, is deeply concerned with social problems'.[17] More precisely, Gray was hired due to his 'considerable ... reputation for being able to relate to blacks'.[18] Though the Film Group's support of the anti-war movement and Black Panthers was genuine,[19] the film-makers' credibility as political radicals was a commodity that could be sold to organisations looking to improve their public reputation.

A number of the post-1968 ads from the Film Group's collection suggest other organisations hired them for their political capital, connections to revolutionary movements and documentary ability to capture what passed for reality. The Film Group made a ten-minute film in 1972 on recycling for electrical company Commonwealth Edison called *The Hidden Resource: A Report on Recycling* that evinced a strong anti-consumerist message.[20] The same year, the Film Group directed a commercial for People's Gas titled *Youth Motivation* in conjunction with the ad agency Foote, Cone and Belding. In the thirty-second ad, People's Gas employee Alfred McClinton speaks to a group of high-school students to convince them to remain in school, an odd subject for a company that provides heating and cooking gas to homes. The spot, depicting an African-American man speaking in front of a class of multiracial youths, mirrors scenes in *The Murder of Fred Hampton* where Hampton, as head of the Chicago chapter of the Black Panthers, motivates a group of black and white political radicals. Mr McClinton adopts and modulates the rhetoric of the black revolutionary: 'Nobody's going to give you nothing. If you ain't got it, they're not going to give it to you.' Even the male narrator who comes on at the end of the ad, and can thus be seen as expressing the viewpoint of the corporate sponsor, adopts the discourse of equality by concluding with 'We're all in this together.'[21]

This aspect of the Film Group's production history exemplifies Hazel Warlau-mont's depiction of the advertising industry as co-opting youth and radical culture in the 1960s in her book *Advertising in the 60s: Turncoats, Traditionalists, and Waste*

Makers in America's Turbulent Decade. According to Warlaumont, the 'new advertising' of the 60s was a survival mechanism for advertisers; adopting the look of pop culture allowed them to remain relevant to a younger demographic advocating an anti-consumerist lifestyle. The shift of ad agencies was entirely stylistic, hiding a political and economic allegiance to corporate America beneath the sounds and images of the youth movement. According to Warlaumont, 'Advertisers ... used a number of other techniques to give ads a new look, including unusual camera angles, photographs cropped to create interest, the cinéma vérité style for television commercials to create realism, and psychedelic colours to create emotion.'[22]

Advertisers and the popular press commonly described the ad work of the Film Group as a form of documentary realism. A journalist called them among 'the city's leading practitioners of *cinema verite* – commercial and industrial-film division'.[23] Art directors and copywriters used terms like 'credible', 'natural',[24] 'stark', 'honest', 'unslick' and 'real' to describe the Film Group's commercials.[25]

However, an indexical connection to reality in the Film Group's ads is not immediately apparent when viewed today, especially when compared to their political documentaries. Many of the Film Group's commercials – such as the 1969 spot for Karoll's where Santa Claus breaks into the department store in a bit of corporate espionage,[26] or the Vets' Dog Food ad depicting a dachshund receiving a speeding ticket as it was over-energised by the company's product[27] – reflect an irreverent humour closer to *Rowan and Martin's Laugh-In* (1967–73) than the work of documentary film-makers such as the Maysles brothers and D. A. Pennebaker. However, taking contemporaneous reports seriously shows how thirty- and sixty-second ads can embody documentary approaches.

Many of the Film Group's commercials were shot on location and with non-actors, such as the aforementioned People's Gas and Aunt Jemima ads. If the latter commercial seems entirely constructed now, with a saccharine theme song and a scripted tagline, the Film Group was praised for travelling to the Iowa farm and using a real family.[28] 'With today's lightweight equipment [which was at the source of the new documentary styles], Gray finds no need to shoot anywhere but the actual site.'[29] In a genre where the point of every text is to persuade the audience to purchase a good or service, the Film Group distinguished itself from its competitors through a documentarian's pursuit of the real.

Other television commercials by the Film Group explicitly adopted the visual style of the new forms of documentary film-making originated by Richard Drew, Pennebaker and the Maysles in the early 1960s. In fact, a 1966 ad for A. B. Dick Copier titled *Salesman* is almost a test run for the Maysles brothers' documentary of the same name from three years later. Adopting a fly-on-the-wall approach, the ad follows three salesmen as they ask potential clients about their printing needs. The black-and-white film stock, sync sound, ever-moving handheld camera and use of a telephoto lens to zoom in on the participants' expressions read as a textbook example of direct cinema. The male narrator does not come in for forty seconds and, when he does, the pitch to the viewing audience is restrained, allowing the preceding verisimilitude to make the commercial's argument for the superiority of the brand over its competitors.[30]

CONCLUSION

According to nonfiction film scholar Bill Nichols, 'documentary evidence refers us constantly to the world around us'.[31] The vérité-inclined ads produced by the Film Group from 1963–72 did just that. They revealed to TV viewers the dining room of a farmhouse in Iowa, a classroom where a People's Gas employee was urging teenagers not to drop out of high school and the offices where travelling salesmen peddled copiers. If a documentary's power comes not from the creation of a fictional diegetic world, but the ability to point to something that actually happened, then these commercials were able to sell commodities and services not through a hard sell, but in depicting these goods as operating in a real world outside advertising.

Obviously, truth claims, testimonies and the opinions of real shoppers have long played a central role in advertising. This case study of the Film Group raises the question of how these nonfictional appeals have changed over time, borrowing and adapting new styles from documentary film-making and reportage. Just as the mainstream of documentary film-making moved from the authoritative narrator to the observational styles of cinéma vérité and direct cinema in the early 1960s, factual advertisements adopted these new styles of visual truth-telling to stay relevant to changing political and aesthetic moods. TV ads have genres and these change over time just as those in feature films and television programmes.

The truth claims of an advertisement for Aunt Jemima syrup seems absurd next to those of a film like *The Murder of Fred Hampton* that systematically exposed a structure of state violence directed at black revolutionaries. However, to devalue nonfiction forms of advertising as adulterated forms of the true documentary is to ignore the very real ways the techniques of each have influenced the other; it risks overlooking the economic realities of documentary film production and the influence of corporate sponsors on the genre. Cinéma vérité could be used to sell copiers and syrup as much as it was a revolutionary form of documentary film-making. This fact should not call into question the commitment of the Film Group to the political causes they supported. Instead, it is a call to analyse documentary film from the funding, financial and production side. If working on advertisements allowed the Film Group to pay for their Black Panther films, looking at their commercials today reveals the historic intersection between political idealism, documentary style and pragmatic compromise.

SELECTED FILMOGRAPHY OF THE FILM GROUP AND ITS MEMBERS

Film Group, *Cicero March*, educational film, 1966–9.
Film Group, *Dachshund*, television ad, produced for Vets' Dog Food, 1967.
Film Group, *Farm Family*, television ad, produced for the Quaker Oats Company, 1967.
Film Group, *Salesman*, television ad, produced for A. B. Dick Copier, 1966.
Film Group, *Social Confrontation: The Battle of Michigan Ave*, educational film, 1969.
Film Group, *Sunday Dinner*, television ad, produced for Kentucky Fried Chicken, 1968.
Mike Gray & Associates, *American Revolution II*, documentary feature, 1969.
Mike Gray & Associates, *The Hidden Resource: A Report on Recycling*, sponsored short film, produced for Commonwealth Edison, 1972.

Mike Gray & Associates, *A Matter of Opportunity*, sponsored short film, produced for the American Medical Association, 1970.

Mike Gray & Associates, *The Murder of Fred Hampton*, documentary feature, 1971.

Mike Gray & Associates, *Santa Claus*, television ad, produced for Karoll's Department Stores, 1969.

Mike Gray & Associates, *Youth Motivation*, television ad, produced for People's Gas Company, 1972.

Michael Shea, *And This Is Free ...*, documentary feature, 1965.

NOTES

1. See the 1968 ad the Film Group produced for Kentucky Fried Chicken, *Sunday Dinner*, at http://www.chicagofilmarchives.org/collections/index.php/Detail/Object/Show/object_id/5161

2. *The Murder of Fred Hampton* (1971) can be viewed online at http://mediaburn.org/video/murder-of-fred-hampton-reel-1/

3. *Farm Family* (1967), directed by the Film Group for Quaker Oats Company, http://www.chicagofilmarchives.org/collections/index.php/Detail/Object/Show/object_id/5149, accessed 26 October 2015.

4. The Film Group reworked the opening ten minutes of *American Revolution II* into the educational short *Social Confrontation: The Battle of Michigan Ave.*, which can be viewed online at http://www.chicagofilmarchives.org/collections/index.php/Detail/Object/Show/object_id/2598

5. Alan Sekula, 'The Body and the Archive', *October* vol. 39 (Winter 1986), pp. 3–64; Jonathan Kahana, *Intelligence Work: the Politics of American Documentary* (New York: Columbia University Press, 2008), pp. 159–64.

6. Craig Breaden, 'Carl Sanders and Albert Maysles: Georgia Politics Meet Direct Cinema, 1969–70', *Moving Image* vol. 9 no. 1 (2009), pp. 201–13. Devin Orgeron has worked on Errol Morris's TV ads as part of a larger project on the connections between cinema and TV commercials since the 1990s.

7. For example, Carolyn Faber discussed how another Chicago documentary company, Kartemquin Films, maintains this distinction at the archival level as their sponsored films are stored in different rooms from their better-known documentary features such as *Hoop Dreams* (1994); Carolyn Faber, paper presented at panel on the archival needs of outtakes, Orphans Midwest, Bloomington, Indiana, 28 September 2013.

8. Scott Didlake, 'The Murder of Fred Hampton', *Filmmakers Newsletter*, February 1972, p. 29.

9. The exception was for *The Murder of Fred Hampton*, which the UCLA Film and Television Archive holds as 35mm negatives and prints.

10. The Film Group's TV ads can be found at http://www.chicagofilmarchives.org/collections/index.php/Detail/Object/Show/object_id/2

11. Robert Cross, 'Mike Gray: In a Hurricane, the Eye', *Chicago Tribune*, 12 July 1970, p. 17.

12. 'Hedman, Gray & Shea, Inc. Open Chicago Studio at 430 W. Grant', *Business Screen* vol. 27 no. 3 (1966), p. 61.

13. Cross, 'Mike Gray', p. 16.

14. Ibid., p. 19.

15. Ibid, p. 20.
16. 'Black, Gray, and the AMA', *Business Screen* vol. 31 no. 10 (October 1970), p. 29.
17. Ibid., p 30.
18. Ibid.
19. At the time of his death in the autumn of 2013, Film Group founder Mike Gray was working on a documentary on ex-Black Panther Robert Lee, who was featured forty years earlier in *American Revolution II*.
20. *The Hidden Resource: A Report on Recycling* can be watched at http://www.chicagofilm archives.org/collections/index.php/Detail/Object/Show/object_id/3518
21. *Youth Motivation* can be viewed online at http://www.chicagofilmarchives.org/collections /index.php/Detail/Object/Show/object_id/5283
22. Hazel G. Warlaumont, *Advertising in the 60s: Turncoats, Traditionalists, and Waste Makers in America's Turbulent Decade* (Westport, CT: Praeger, 2001), pp. 175–6. Cf. also Cynthia B. Meyers' chapter in this volume.
23. Cross, 'Mike Gray', p. 16 [spelling and italics in the original].
24. Ibid.
25. Steve Lerner of North Advertising quoted in John J. Fritscher, *Television Today* (Chicago: Claretian Press, 1971), p. 31, http://www.jackfritscher.com/PDF/NonFiction/tvtoday.pdf, accessed 26 October 2015.
26. *Santa Claus* (1969), directed by the Film Group for Karoll's, http://www.chicago filmarchives.org/collections/index.php/Detail/Object/Show/object_id/5259, accessed 26 October 2015.
27. *Dachshund* (1967), directed by the Film Group for Vets' Dog Food, http://www.chicagofilm archives.org/collections/index.php/Detail/Object/Show/object_id/5143, accessed 26 October 2015.
28. Cross, 'Mike Gray', p. 16.
29. Fritscher, *Television Today*, p. 31.
30. *Salesman* (1966), directed by the Film Group for A. B. Dick Copier, http://www.chicagofilm archives.org/collections/index.php/Detail/Object/Show/object_id/5048, accessed 26 October 2015.
31. Bill Nichols, *Representing Reality: Issues and Concepts in Documentary* (Bloomington: Indiana University Press, 1991), p. 115.

20
The Challenge of Archiving Commercials

Catherine Cormon

Recognition of commercials in collection policies of audiovisual archives is a rather recent phenomenon. From being considered an encumbrance in the past, collections of commercials are now turning into assets. Heritage institutions are becoming aware of the sociological, the entertainment and, frequently, the artistic value of this genre.

However, commercials remain a difficult archival object that does not fit comfortably in traditional ways of work in audiovisual archives; this chapter will try to explain why. These observations are based on my experience working as an audiovisual archivist in two different institutions: EYE-Film Institute Netherlands,[1] a large national film archive whose main focus is film as an art form and a cultural experience; and the Heineken Collection Foundation, a very small non-profit organisation dedicated to the preservation of the cultural heritage of a multinational industrial company, in all its forms and on all media. Despite their differences in scale, focus and policies, these two institutes meet with similar difficulties when working with their collection of commercials.

I will try here to describe some of the particularities of commercials that have a bearing on archival work, in order to see what kind of issues have to be taken into account when organising work with this special type of material. In order to do so, I will contrast commercials with feature films, which tend to be the reference point of collection management practices in film archives. This will, of course, require a certain level of generalisation. There is no such thing as a typical commercial: they last from a few seconds to several minutes. For the sake of comparison, I will postulate that an average feature film has a duration of ninety minutes and an average commercial sixty seconds. In the same spirit of simplification, I have rounded up lengths and dimensions to get data in a more manageable shape.

THE CHALLENGE OF VOLUME
The Case of Film-Based Materials

Let us first compare the storage density of 35mm positive prints of average feature films versus commercials:

- Feature film: duration ninety minutes, length 2,500 metres, five cans (height 4cm, diameter 39cm), storage density fifty hours of content per cubic metre.

• Commercials: duration one minute, length 27 metres (excluding leaders), one can (height 4cm, diameter 19cm), storage density twelve hours of content per cubic metre.

Commercials on film base thus need, for the same duration, about four times more storage space than feature films.

In order to minimise storage space, some archives store commercials on aggregate reels (the commercials are spliced one after another on one big reel). This practice, though it offers a gain of space, does not reduce storage volumes to the feature film level: short films will need leader spacing to distinguish them from one another, and negative materials need even longer leaders to keep synchronisation marks intact. Commercials on aggregate reels will still take up approximately 20 per cent more space than their equivalent duration in feature film.

Moreover, aggregating has several major drawbacks. The main one is contamination: when one of the films on the roll decays, it affects all the other films on the roll (or in the can). Since decay is unavoidable (despite being slowed down by proper storage conditions), archives that use aggregate reels or store several rolls per can, in fact, condemn all the films in the can to the shortest life expectancy of the element in the worst condition.

Another drawback of aggregate film reels is the inventory problem they create. The different elements contained in the reel will very likely be needed for projection or reproduction at different times. This will prompt the lifting of individual elements off the reel, which should, of course, be followed by the returning of the lifted elements in their original place. Anybody familiar with archival practice will know that, given the chronic condition of understaffing archives suffer from, the necessary is usually sacrificed to the more indispensable tasks. Experience shows that films lifted off aggregate reels are seldom returned to their original place, while their inventory records are seldom updated to reflect those changes which were expected to be only temporary. This creates confusion in the inventory (since objects are modified over time) and causes the chain of reproduction to become blurred (copies of the same element will differ in their contents depending on their creation date). Thus, storing films in aggregate reels will invariably lead to inventory problems.

The Case of Video Materials

Unlike film, where reel size and duration are linked, a videocassette can contain anything from a few seconds to an hour and a half of content. This makes it impossible to guess the duration of the contents from the size of the cassette. For the sake of demonstration, I decided to consider an object that would represent desirable material for an archive: a master tape of a one-minute commercial on a Beta (BetaSP or DigiBeta) small cassette measuring 17.1 x 11.0 x 3.1cm. Considering the multiplicity of video carriers, this is, of course, rather arbitrary, but this kind of cassette is nevertheless representative of a large period of video production (c. 1986–2000) and forms a good average between the much bigger carriers of early days and the much smaller ones in use in the last years of video on tangible media.[2] On such video carriers, commercials will amount to twenty-nine hours of content per cubic metre. On similar cassettes, feature films would stack up to 547 hours of content per cubic metre. Commercials on videocassettes thus need, for the same duration, up to twenty times more storage space than feature films.

The Case of Digital (File-Based) Material

Trying to quantify the relationship between file size and content duration in digital files is a futile exercise: there are so many file formats (codecs) and so many container formats (wrappers) in use that none of them could be considered as a standard or used to estimate averages with any relevance. Nevertheless, the simple fact that a wrapper is necessary to contain digital data shows that each and every digital moving-image file will need a minimal amount of data space regardless of its duration, therefore again making a multitude of items with short durations take up more space that one single item of a similar total duration.

First Postulate: Advertising is Volume Intensive

Commercials require a great deal more storage space than feature films, up to four times in the case of film base and up to twenty times for video formats.

THE CHALLENGE OF HANDLING TIME
Item Handling

Film viewing in an archive involves a number of steps. An archivist will typically have to retrieve the material from the vault, open the container (can/box), thread the reel on a viewing bench or load the cassette in a video player, view it, rewind it, place it back in its container and return the material to the vault. If the time necessary to view and rewind a film is dependent on its length, all the other actions are not and will take more or less the same time regardless of the duration of the content.

Assuming that handling a feature film (typically on large, twenty-minute reels) would require ten minutes per can, then one would need thirty minutes of handling per hour of content. This means that one has to add about 50 per cent of handling time to the viewing time.

Assuming that handling a commercial would take only five minutes per can or cassette, if we use our average of one minute of content per can or cassette, then one has to count 300 minutes of handling per hour of content. This means that one has to add 500 per cent of handling time to the viewing time.

Metadata Handling

Information about the physical characteristics of a copy is usually recorded per copy; description of a feature film in five reels will usually not take five times as much work time as the description of a commercial on a single reel. Similarly, filmographic information is usually recorded per title and its processing will require some incompressible time, regardless of the film's duration.

We cannot easily decide how much time the basic registration of an item would take: this is, by and large, dependent on each individual cataloguing system in relation to each individual institution policy. Again, I will need to create an average for each type of material. This average is merely an estimation of what seems like a reasonable amount, and its value lays more in its proportionality than in its exactness.

Supposing that the basic registration and description of a feature film of ninety minutes would take ten minutes, this means 6.6 minutes of data input per hour of content. One therefore has to add 10 per cent metadata handling time to the viewing time.

Supposing that the basic registration of a one minute commercial could be performed in three minutes, this means 180 minutes per hour of content. One therefore has to add 300 per cent metadata handling time to the viewing time.

Second Postulate: Advertising is Handling Intensive

Commercials require a great deal more handling time than feature films, up to ten times as much for the material handling and thirty times as much for the metadata.

THE CHALLENGE OF METADATA
Metadata Volume

A catalogue record of a film or a copy will not use a significantly different quantity of bytes whether the film is a feature or a very short commercial. On the other hand, commercials are usually produced in much greater numbers than feature films. It is, of course, a little hazardous to compare the volume of metadata necessary to describe both types of material. Nevertheless, a concrete example may help us to picture the difficulty brought about by advertising collections.

The film collection of EYE-Film Institute Netherlands contains about 40,000 titles, with an average of one hour per title and a total estimated duration of 40,000 hours of unique content (thus not counting multiple copies of the same film). The collections of the Geesink and Toonder studios – two world-famous Dutch animation studios that produced mostly commercials – held in the same institute comprise about 4,000 titles, representing an estimated sixty-two hours of unique content.[3] If we compare those two figures, we see that the Geesink and Toonder collections represent about 10 per cent of the total number of titles held by the institute, while its content represents only 0.16 per cent of the unique content duration of the film collection.

Cataloguing Systems

Most audiovisual archives work with proprietary collection management systems because of the scarcity of collection management systems available on the market that can handle the specific needs of audiovisual archives. One of these basic needs is the necessity of separating the description of the object (the copy) from the description of its content (the film). Commercially available collection management systems are usually built for visual arts, where the object and its content are indistinguishable. In such systems it is very difficult to account for the fact that one single film may exist in the collection as many elements and on many different carriers, each with its own characteristics. The other type of collection management systems commercially available are library systems, where some allowance is made for multiple copies only as long as their description remains fundamentally the same.

Audiovisual archives, however, need to link one filmographic description – containing information valid for all copies of the same film such as title, director, company, year, production country, etc. – to many objects, each with its own particular description (negative, positive, sound mix, 35mm, 16mm, etc.). Only archives with solid IT resources can build proprietary systems to accommodate this specific data structure. Smaller institutes will have to use commercially available systems that do not offer this option and will, therefore, have to perform 'data-gymnastics' to keep track of their holdings. Registration of audiovisual objects in a visual arts or library cataloguing system is extremely complex and requires a lot of tweaking and cheating, since the data model offers no options to record several very different manifestations of the same content. Retrieval of information is even more difficult: search engines and filters are conceived for standard entries and will not retrieve atypical entries.[4]

Visual arts or library cataloguing systems also lack tools to record a very common process of audiovisual archives: reproduction. Visual arts cataloguing systems will usually offer the possibility of recording reproductions (like photos of the object), but these reproductions have no value as collection objects and are not recorded as such. On the contrary, audiovisual archives routinely reproduce their objects to preserve and display them, and these reproductions are considered collection objects. A typical reproduction chain in an audiovisual archive could be something like this: 1) unique positive print; 2) duplication negative; 3) answer print; 4) high resolution digital files; 5) playable digital rendition. All five elements are collection objects in their own right and will need their own catalogue entry with 'genealogical' links to each other to document their relationship. This kind of data structure is seldom supported in visual arts or library cataloguing systems.

Commercials create further difficulties in cataloguing systems, even in dedicated software built by audiovisual archives themselves: their characteristics can be so different from the benchmark feature film for which most systems have been conceived that they will fit only awkwardly. Most traditional film description systems lack the fields that are essential for commercials, like brand, product, campaign, commissioner, or different variations of a given film. Existing fields are also rarely formatted to accept particular demands of advertising. It is often nearly impossible to properly catalogue the same film in its different versions of twenty seconds, thirty seconds, sixty seconds and bumpers.

Furthermore, as we have seen previously, commercials are often stored on aggregate reels, either to save storage space or merely because that is the way they came into the archive (for example, compilation cassettes). Each particular carrier, a roll of film material or a videocassette, may contain many different films. This has to be represented as a many-to-many relationship in the data structure, which is more complex to build and maintain than the common one-to-many data structure.

Third Postulate: Advertising is Metadata Intensive

Advertising collections tend to crowd collection inventory systems, and are mostly ill suited to those systems.

THE CHALLENGE OF DOCUMENTATION

Commercials usually do not contain a visible title to help identification. The same film will be designated by different titles, each one made up by the different entities dealing with the film: the client, the advertising agency, the production company, the laboratory, the distributor, the public and the archive. Censorship records are usually unhelpful, as films are often listed under their brand name.[5] With such variety in titles, it is not uncommon to have several copies of the same film registered under different titles within the same archive, and thereby not identifiable as one work.

Commercials usually do not contain credits either. They are never listed in annual national production summaries or in national filmographies, except when the director is a film-maker famous from a career in another genre (like Oskar Fischinger, Len Lye, or Jean-Luc Godard). There are many renowned film-makers or crew members who specialised in advertising whose names never appear in film history books and whose oeuvre is not identifiable in archive catalogues. The available sources for information on advertising films are few and far between. One can think of the paper archives of film producers, advertising agencies, or commissioning companies, which are very seldom accessible and suffer from a high turnover rate with accompanying archive loss, and catalogues of festivals dedicated to advertising films, which are hard to find and usually contain top-notch films only.

Fourth Postulate: Advertising is a Poorly Documented Genre

Commercials suffer from lack of documentation, which makes them much harder to contextualise than many other types of films.

CONCLUSION

Commercials require more handling time, more storage space and more metadata volume than more traditional genres. They will be more difficult to document and to integrate in cataloguing systems. They will need more resources in general, while delivering less usable content duration than feature films.

Advertising films as collection objects do not fit easily in traditional archival models for audiovisual materials. In order to be able to treat them responsibly and efficiently, archives ought to consider them as special types of material with their own requirements.

In planning projects involving commercials, archives ought to be aware that their established practices may be inadequate to this specific material. They ought to be willing to re-evaluate their policies and procedures and consider what adaptations and changes are necessary to make the projects realistic.

Archives could even consider a possible need for entirely new policies when working with commercials. Though this is certainly difficult, it could open up new possibilities in new areas. It may even eventually enable archives to take better care of the very many new and hybrid products that have appeared, together with the popularity of digital audiovisual formats. These new products have some character-istics in common with commercials (abundant, changeable, undocumented) and it is no coincidence that the borders between commercials and private documents have begun to blur with the appearance of viral campaigns. By looking at the practices of other organisations that have begun to tackle the preservation of these new forms of audiovisual expression, established archives may learn new ways of working that will enable them to take better care of their collections of commercials, as well as the heritage that is in the process of being made today.

NOTES

1. EYE-Film Instituut Nederland was created in 2010 as the merging of Filmmuseum (formerly Nederlands Filmmuseum), Holland Film, Filmbank and the Nederlands Instituut voor Filmeducatie.
2. Video recordings on tangible media such as cassettes and disks have recently been almost entirely replaced by recordings in files stored on hard-drives, whose storage challenges are very different but not simpler.
3. For the Geesink studio collection, see the chapter by Ripmeester in this volume.
4. At the Heineken Collection Foundation, for example, the campaign *Drie Vrienden* (*Three Friends*) (1990s–2000s) for Amstel Beer consists of seven different series (from different countries or with different themes), seventy-two different films kept on forty-six different carriers (videocassettes or DVD). In total, the Foundation holds 482 different copies of films from this campaign, the latter figure being impossible to distill out of the system in any other way than by counting by hand.
5. For example, the same film exists in three different Dutch archives under three different titles: *Flessen* (*Bottles*) at the Nederlands Instituut voor Beeld en Geluid; *Amstel – Bier – Dansende Flessen* (*Amstel – Beer – Dancing Bottles*) at EYE-Film Instituut Nederland; and *Amstel: West-Side Story* at the Heineken Collection Foundation. The censorship record carries the brand name as a title: *Amstel*.

21
The Geesink Collection: Selection Criteria Reconsidered

Leenke Ripmeester

In 2007, a large preservation and digitisation project, called Images for the Future, started in the Netherlands. The project, a consortium of several Dutch archives, had as its main goal the digitisation of a sizable part of their collections for access purposes. This project enabled the Nederlands Filmmuseum (now EYE Filmmuseum) to restore some of their acetate collections which had been lying on the shelves for many years.[1] The Geesink studio's films, containing many puppet animation commercials, were one of the collections to be made available. For the next five years I worked on the Geesink collection as a film archivist, viewing and describing the film prints. An important aspect of my work was deciding which titles should be restored. The selection criteria formulated by the museum's policy were, however, not very helpful, since the collection's commercials had been on the periphery of the film institute's interests. So one of my main concerns was to develop selection criteria that did justice to the genre of advertising and to the studio's history.

Joop Geesink (1913–84) founded Joop Geesink Teekenfilm Productie (JG Cartoon Production) in 1942.[2] Later that year he took on associate business partner Marten Toonder, who later became a well-known Dutch cartoonist. The next year, Geesink met Philips' director for international publicity, Sies Numann. It was he who invited Hungarian film-maker Georg Pàl to the Netherlands to set up an animation

Joop Geesink (1913–84)

department at Philips in 1934. Five years later, however, Pàl moved to the USA, where he continued his career as a famous film director. Numann advised Geesink to try puppet animation as well and, in 1943, Geesink and Toonder produced their first puppet film, *Serenata nocturna*, commissioned by Philips. Then Geesink and Toonder decided to go their separate ways. After World War II, Geesink hired several people who used to work for Pàl: Jószef Misik, Jan Coolen, Frans Hendrix and Koos Schadee. Coolen and Misik introduced an animation technique different from Pàl's prefabricated phases: they developed a so-called 'combination doll' with flexible body parts. Despite the economically difficult times of the late 1940s Geesink managed to attract several clients, such as food company Honig, for which he produced the commercials *Honig werkt* (*Honig Works*, 1947) and *Honig's ideaal* (*Honig's Ideal*, 1948), and coffee milk producer Van Nelle (*The Big Four*, 1946). He received an award for the latter in Brussels.[3] In 1947, Geesink changed the name of his studio to Joop Geesink's Dollywood.

As the economy improved in the 1950s, the number of clients increased. Philips remained Geesink's biggest client and even commissioned longer, ten-minute promotional films such as *Kermesse fantastique* (1951), *Piccolo, Saxo and Company* (1960) and *Philips Cavalcade 75 Years of Music* (1966). Other important (inter)national clients included Campari, Ballantine, Mackeson, Otto Versand, Pril, Pré, Knorr, Peter Stuyvesant, North State, Goebel, Coca-Cola and Heineken. In 1955, Geesink also started producing live-action commercials, for which he used a different studio name: Starfilm. In Germany and Italy – two important markets for the company – he opened his own agencies. Almost 70 per cent of the studio's productions were made for foreign markets, such as the UK, Sweden, the USA and countries in South America, Asia and Africa. Important for Geesink's success was the rise of television commercials in the USA, Germany and the UK. The studio specialised in telling a story in the short time

Kermesse fantastique (1951)

span of twenty or sixty seconds and thereby remained ahead of the competition. However, in the late 1960s the studio got into serious financial problems, due to the failed development of Holland Promenade, a huge amusement park. As a result Joop Geesink had to leave the company, which was taken over by the Toonder studio in 1972. Toonder continued some of the Geesink projects, most notably the character of Loeki the Lion, who featured in bumpers in between commercials on Dutch public television; Loeki became a national icon and was only taken off the air in 2004.

In 1972, a large part of the Geesink collection was handed over to the archive of EYE. Approximately 2,300 prints of 35mm film were stored in the vaults and remained there for thirty-five years. Although the collection was known to be valuable, it didn't have a high priority within the restoration policy of the museum. This can partly be explained by genre. The museum's primary goal was to safeguard their nitrate collection and the Dutch artistic fiction film. The advertising films of the Geesink collection fell outside these objectives. Yet another practical reason why the Geesink collection was not made available was the large amount of short films. Not only would the release and restoration of such a collection require a lot of valuable time, it would also require a logistical tour de force. One would certainly need to have some selection criteria that would enable an archivist to choose which titles should be considered worth the expense of restoration. Selection for restoration is always needed due to limited budget, time and space. With regard to the large amount of possible candidates for restoration, the archivist must be able to argue why a given film should be restored. So when I started working on the Geesink collection, selection criteria were one of my main concerns.

I started with the obvious, straightforward selection criteria as described in the museum's policy. As the national film archive, EYE wants to preserve films that 1) are important parts of the Dutch cinematographic heritage; 2) are part of an oeuvre of an important director; 3) have cinematographic qualities; 4) have artistic qualities; or 5) are representative of Dutch cinema culture. These criteria, however, didn't help me very much, for they did not seem to do justice to the collection. The collection contained primarily films from a genre – commercials – which is seldom considered to be artistic or important for cinematographic heritage. Moreover, the studio did not employ any famous directors and the collection contained many ads made for television and were, therefore, not representative of cinema culture. So, very quickly, as most archivists experience, I had to leave the ideal world of the selection criteria neatly written down in the museum's policy and enter the actual practice of selection which is messy, often somewhat arbitrary, inevitably subjective and without any certainty beforehand whether you have made the right choices.

The biggest problem was a lack of information that could have helped me to make a balanced selection for restoration. The limited amount of research on this type of film has been noted elsewhere in this volume. With regard to production details of the films, there was very little information about titles, production years and crew – director, animator, cast, composer, etc.[4] The museum did have the catalogue of the Geesink studio, but it contained very little information except title, animation technique used, whether the film was shot in black and white or colour and length. Production years and director names were rarely registered. The Philips film catalogue had similar limitations.

This lack of information seems to be partly explained by the genre of advertising itself. In ads, credits often do not appear on screen – although many Geesink films are an exception to this rule – and therefore it is perhaps not deemed necessary by either the production company, the ad agency, or the client, to register this information in their own database. It would cost too much valuable time, I suppose. Registration of credits does sometimes happen but not in a consistent manner. So in the advertising industry credits are often deemed unimportant or irrelevant. This poses a problem for the archivist working with the traditional selection criteria noted above, which are primarily centred on authorship.

With regard to the issue of authorship, the genre of advertising poses yet another problem, due to its presence across various media. For example, during my work on a commercial for Caballero cigarettes which featured a cartoon of a Mexican man smoking, I met Ad Werner, the designer of the character.[5] He claimed to be the author of the commercial because he had originally designed the Mexican figure for billboard advertising. The person listed in our catalogue as the director (Ronald Bijlsma) was merely the animator of something he designed, according to Werner. Similarly, in other commercials one can find characters that have been designed for a company long before the Geesink studio worked with them, such as the figure of Elsie the Cow for Borden dairy products, or the Alka-Seltzer mascot Speedy (a character whose body and hat were an Alka-Seltzer tablet). The presence of advertising across multiple media raises the question of who is the creative force behind a commercial: the client, the ad agency, or the production company? It is unknown, for instance, whether the Geesink studio worked with ad agencies or directly with companies. The little information there is suggests the studio worked both ways.[6] The arrival of television commercials and the growth of the global consumer market from the 1950s probably marked a transition period of professionalisation of the advertising industry, which had profound consequences for the way clients, ad agencies and production companies collaborated. How the relation between these three parties developed historically is unknown.[7]

Not only a lack of information, but also the specificity of the Geesink collection made me reconsider the museum policy's selection criteria. As this policy focused on cinema, one of my main concerns was to establish whether a commercial was made for film or television. This was a task quite difficult in itself, again because of a lack of information. I assumed commercials shot in Technicolor were made for cinema, while I was less sure about commercials in black and white. In the 1950s and 60s films were shot both in colour and in black and white. With regard to television, ads were shot in colour from a certain moment on, but when this transition took place is unknown and will probably have been different for various countries, depending on the moment colour television sets were introduced.[8] The distinction between ads for film and television also led to the more fundamental question of whether a film archive should be interested in preserving television ads at all. Following the museum's official guidelines, I was supposed to disregard all television materials. This, however, would fail to do justice to the collection and to the studio's history. So, other aspects of the collection which fell outside the scope of the official selection criteria were taken into account: campaigns, clients and markets. Selection was aimed at achieving a good representation of the variety and importance of these variables. I therefore developed selection criteria which did justice to the studio's history and the genre of advertising:

important brands and big clients, particular themes that appeared across different commercials, particular modes of address, targeted audiences and so on.

Yet in the end, ironically, I returned to the straightforward selection criteria that seemed so irrelevant at the beginning. After working some time on the collection I knew it was, indeed, quite valuable. The Geesink studio is an important part of Dutch film history because it was a large film studio with over a hundred employees, operating on a global market at a time when there was hardly any money to be found to finance films in Holland. The cinematographic quality of the collection can be found in the professional animation, rich art direction and care with which the films were made more generally. The Geesink films all have similar characteristics, which refer not so much to individual styles of film directors but to the particular signature of the studio's director, Joop Geesink. The collection is, finally, perhaps most valuable because it challenges preconceived notions of Dutch film history, dominated by the tradition of documentary film (Mullens, Ivens, Haanstra, van der Horst, Vrijman, etc.). Geesink, by contrast, approached commercials as a form of entertainment, using Disney as his main example. Geesink commercials appropriate many entertainment genres (the musical, variety, the Western, the film noir, etc.) to tell stories that only in the end reveal themselves as being advertisements. With this approach, Geesink's work is part of a tradition of Dutch entertainment that can be found in the work of animation and commercial pioneers George Debels and George Pàl, as well as Dutch cabaret, television producers Joop van den Ende and John de Mol and contemporary film directors such as Paul Verhoeven, Dick Maas, Johan Nijenhuis and Burny Bos.[9] The Geesink collection is, indeed, an important part of Dutch audiovisual heritage. Yet in order to come to this conclusion I first needed to question the archive's selection criteria and the traditional view on Dutch film history on which these criteria are based. Film materials in the archives continuously challenge both preconceived notions of film history and the selection criteria set up by archivists. The Geesink collection is a case in point.

NOTES

Thanks to Mette Peters.

1. For more information about the project Images for the Future, see http://research.imagesforthe future.org/. In 2012 the project was ended prematurely due to governmental budget cuts.
2. For this short history of the Geesink studio I have used T. de Vries and A. Mul, 'Joop Geesink, poppenfilmproducent', *Animatie* 1 (September 1984), pp. 1–50.
3. The Geesink studio received over eighty prizes for their productions, including the Lion d'Or from the prestigious Cannes Lions International Advertising Festival.
4. One of the few valuable and rich sources of information was de Vries and Mul, 'Joop Geesink, poppenfilmproducent', which also includes an extensive filmography. The article gives a detailed account of the studio's history and is based on interviews with several employees from the studio such as financial director Wim Geesink (Joop's brother) and animator Jan Coolen.
5. This commercial was actually produced by the Toonder studio, which specialised in cartoons and often collaborated closely with the Geesink studio. The Caballero commercial referred to

here is called *Mexican* (1964). The animator that was registered as the director of the commercial is Ronald Bijlsma. The designer of the figure who claims to be the actual director of the commercial is Ad Werner.

6. Anecdotes about Joop Geesink describe him as a person who was always very good at persuading companies to work with him, suggesting he had direct contact with clients without the intervention of an ad agency. See, for example, de Vries and Mul, 'Joop Geesink, poppenfilmproducent', p. 17. Joop Geesink's daughter Louise Geesink remembers her father having good contact with the directors of Campari, Heineken, KLM and other companies. By contrast, she also remembers him working with ad agencies, for American clients in particular (personal correspondence). The name of an ad agency (e.g. Lintas) is even sometimes written on the leader of the film. The promotional film *50 Pairs of Hands* (1961), which the studio made for future clients, also seems to address ad agencies.

7. Some information is hinted at in the article by Karl Cohen. He describes the work of some American animation studios that produced commercials in the 1940s and 50s, including Transfilm Inc. who represented the Geesink studio in the USA, according to de Vries and Mul (p. 22). Cohen describes how film producers had a lot of creative freedom to make commercials in the 1940s. However, the ad agencies increasingly took over the creative control in the 1950s. It was now the ad agency instead of the film producer who designed the story boards and scripts. How Joop Geesink's work methods relate to this development is unknown. K. Cohen, 'The Development of Animated TV Commercials in the 1940s', *Animation Journal* vol. 1 (1992), pp. 44–6.

8. Some people have suggested other possible indications a commercial has been produced for television. One characteristic of television commercials from the 1950s, for example, might be a black-and-white image with low contrast. A freeze frame of ten seconds at the end refers probably to a stipulation from television channels at the time. The length of the commercial might also be an indication for the intended medium, although a lack of precise information about the length of cinema and television commercials makes it difficult to make strict distinctions. Much of this information, however, is based on hearsay and some arbitrary literature rather than reliable documentation. The best indication of the intended medium was a note on the film leader or in the studio's catalogue referring to television.

9. For a more extensive version of this argument, see L. Ripmeester, 'Entertainment uit de Lage Landen: de Geesink Collectie', *Tijdschrift voor Media Geschiedenis* vol. 15 no. 1 (2012), pp. 74–101.

22

The Archivo Nazionale Cinema d'Impresa Collections: An Overview

Arianna Turci

The Archivio Nazionale Cinema d'Impresa (ANCI) – the National Film Archive for Industrial Film – was founded in 2003 in Ivrea, Turin, as a branch department of the Fondazione Centro Sperimentale di Cinematografia (CSC) – the Italian National Film Archive of Rome. The archive was established after an agreement among Piedmont Region, Ivrea Municipality, Telecom Spa Company and CSC. The archive's activities started in late 2006 and today the institute is a member of the International Federation of Film Archives (FIAF). The CSC archive has had industrial and advertisement films collections in its vaults since the 1950s. An Italian law,[1] enacted in 1949, establishes that a copy of every Italian fiction film has to be deposited at CSC. That is why CSC owns and manages most of the Italian film heritage. Because it prioritises fiction films, however, it didn't have a strategy for industrial materials stored by Italian companies. As a result, there had never been any dedicated preservation, collection management, cataloguing and identification policies for these film materials. During the 1990s, a more serious consideration of industrial and advertisement films emerged in Europe, in both academic and film archival fields. As a consequence, CSC decided to set up a dedicated industrial film archive. Moreover, the renewed interest in industrial and commercial films also allowed an updating of Italian fiction film-makers' filmographies, as many of their films of this type of production were unknown until recently. This means that industrial cinema is not just essential to record the history of Italian industry, but even to extend the history of Italian cinema.

At present, the ANCI collection consists of around 65,000 films, mostly on film and a small part on video and in digital formats. ANCI's mission is the identification, cataloguing, storage, preservation and valorisation of industrial and advertising films. The collection consists of films made by a number of important Italian companies: Borsalino,[2] Breda, Innocenti, Edison, Fiat, Olivetti, Martini & Rossi, Birra Peroni, Italgas, Aurora, Venchi-Talmone-Maggiora, Marzotto, Bosca and Recchi. Other collections come either from film studios specialised in producing commercials, such as Film Master and Rectafilm Ltd, or production companies such as Documento Film and Filippo Paolone. Other items have been stored by research organisations, such as Enea (Agenzia nazionale per le nuove tecnologie, l'energia e lo sviluppo economico sostenibile [National Council for New Technology, Energy and the Environment]) and by public institutions such as Aem (Azienda elettrica municipale di Milano [Milan's municipal electric enterprise]), Metropolitana di Milano (Milan's subway company), Ferrovie dello Stato (National Italian Railway and Ministry of Foreign Affairs), which gave the archive the ICE collection (Istituto per il Commercio Estero [agency for overseas trade]).[3]

The archive carries out an intensive restoration and digitising programme for these materials. Between 1930 and 1980, industrial cinema represented an important field of a company's strategy, and its production resulted in a lot of material that records the economic and social history of twentieth-century Italy. The films deal with several aspects of business life: production, such as assembly lines; training films made for employees; or advertising films that hint at the relationship with customers. Industrial films also paid specific attention to corporate welfare programmes for employees: working men's clubs, refectories, welfare work, kindergartens and holiday camps for employees' children. This visual heritage allows us to study the development of industrial production, social relations, the economy and, in more general terms, the world of labour in Italy.

TYPOLOGIES OF ADVERTISING FILMS

Including commercials and so-called *caroselli*, the focus of this brief chapter, the collections contain the following types of advertising films:

COMMERCIAL: Very short film, made to promote an object using a studied language and voice tone, with advanced communication techniques, in order to reach the consumer's attention.

CAROSELLO: Specific Italian advertisement films. The word *carosello* either refers to the TV programme of that name, which lasted ten minutes and consisted of four short, commercial sketches; or to a single sketch within this format.[4] *Carosello* was broadcast by RAI television from 1957–77. At that time, a law prevented RAI, the Italian state television, from producing and showing advertising films. RAI's solution was to advertise new consumer products by creating a short sketch in which, during the last thirty-five seconds, the sponsored product was introduced through a slogan.[5] Italian television viewers in that period were paying a licence fee in order to watch RAI broadcasts. In this context, the only way to justify the introduction of commercials on state television was to offer a little show with celebrity endorsements, in order to promote new products to audiences quickly and successfully.

PROMOTIONAL FILM: Short films lasting between five and fifteen minutes in which a new product is presented in detail, showing all possible uses in different contexts and situations.

TESTIMONIAL FILM: Commercials and *caroselli* featuring a celebrity from the world of music, entertainment, or cinema as a main character to endorse a new product.

PROPAGANDA FILM: Film made in order to promote an idea, to influence people, or to recruit support from the audience. For instance, ANCI holds films made by the animator Luigi Pensuti, commissioned by Benito Mussolini in 1932, to teach the population how to fight tuberculosis. It also has films commissioned by the American Ministry of Defense, made between 1956 and 1960, to legitimate President Eisenhower's politics of intensifying the use of nuclear energy in such fields as medicine and agriculture. The Italian company Enea produced translated versions of these films. It also has films made by the Italian Ministry for Agricultural Policies to promote the consumption of meat.

CITY FILM: Films, usually lasting twenty minutes, that appear to be documentaries but actually promote tourist locations. ANCI boasts several such promotional moving postcards. The majority were realised by the Sicily Region and show cities such as Palermo and Taormina, religious and folk ceremonies, or the beauty of Sicilian landscape.

FILM PROMOTING 'EXOTIC' AREAS: Documentaries showing the life of Italian workers in exotic places, made to persuade spectators to migrate to these areas. Since the 1960s, in their attempts to conquer new markets, Italian companies made trade agreements with foreign companies and relocated Italian labour abroad. The archive has several films, deposited by Fiat and Recchi, that encouraged employees to move to India, Asia, South America, Africa, or the Soviet Union. These films gloss over the discomforts of life in these places and emphasise their exoticism.

INSTRUCTION FILM: Documentary made to instruct audiences about a certain subject, often masking a propaganda or commercial purpose: for example, Fiat's 1970s films on road safety, for which the company used its own cars as examples of efficiency.

DESCRIPTION OF COMMERCIAL COLLECTIONS

The following describes the collections of advertising films in the care of ANCI. The production of commercials and caroselli reached its height between 1957 and 1980, the period of greatest economic development in Italy.[6]

Fiat Collection

ASSETS IN THE COLLECTION: 27,514 reels (12,412 negatives; 15,102 positives). Fiat was founded on 1899 in Turin as a car factory. In a short time it expanded to other sectors and started to produce farm tractors, aeroplanes, lorries and electrical appliances such as refrigerators and washing machines. Fiat began making short advertising films in 1931 with Sotto i tuoi occhi (Under Your Eyes), made to promote the Fiat 522, the first utility car produced by the factory. Advertising film production increased between late 1950s and early 60s, the years of the economic boom and mass motorisation. Being aware of the power of images, Fiat has been making commercials continuously to date. The company also made instructional films; between 1960 and 1969, Fiat realised a series of short films entitled Grammatica della massaia (A Housewife's Grammar) to teach women how to become a modern housewives and make their day more efficient using CGE (General Company for Electricity) appliances, mechanical components of which were produced by Fiat. Fiat also produced several films promoting exotic areas during the 1970s to encourage Italian workers to emigrate.

Edison Collection

ASSETS IN THE COLLECTION: 6,435 reels (2,070 negatives; 4,365 positives). Montedison was created in 1966 through the merger of Montecatini, a chemical factory, and Edison, the first Italian hydropower company. In 2002, this industrial giant became part of an international holding under the name Edison. Its promotional films, mostly made during the 1960s, advertise a wide range of products, such as the insecticide Timor, Candosan bleach, Helion textiles and the plastic material Moplen.[7] Unusual examples include testimonials by Italian actor Gino Bramieri and the musical group Quartetto Cetra. Animated film was the choice for many ads with highly artistic results. The company also produced a number of promotional films to describe the complex chemical processes that led to the discovery of Moplen, a new and revolutionary plastic material. These films show all sorts of products that can be manufactured with Moplen, describe how to use these new objects in daily life and reassure potential consumers about the non-toxicity of their components.

Olivetti Collection

ASSETS IN THE COLLECTION: 1,421 reels (212 negatives; 1,126 positives). Olivetti was founded in Ivrea, Turin, in 1908, and is still active today in spite of a long decline that began in 1990. The production of commercials, caroselli and promos reached its apex between 1960 and 1980, setting an example with ads for its typewriters, calculators, photocopiers and personal computers. Olivetti's commercials stand out because of their innovative 'language' and high levels of visual and conceptual experimentation, thanks to the cooperation of international artists and designers such as Jean-Michel Folon, Hans Von Klier, Giorgio Soavi, Robert Oscar Blechman and Walter Ballmer. Olivetti also made several promotional films that explained innovative and complicated concepts in the company's fields of expertise, first electronics and later computer science, while at the same time making audiences curious about new technologies and, above all, the possibilities offered by new products.

Martini & Rossi Collection

ASSETS IN THE COLLECTION: 897 reels (380 negatives; 517 positives). Martini & Rossi was founded in 1847 in Turin as a distillery. The success of this factory is well known, but the company reached its zenith when it merged with Bacardi in 1993. This brand has produced many advertising films for television and cinema since 1957. The potential of television was immediately understood by Martini: the very first Carosello programme, broadcast on 3 February 1957, contained a Martini commercial.

Over the years, the company has built its advertising strategy on the use of celebrities for testimonials: actors, singers and models. In the 1970s, the brand engaged Italian movie stars actors Paolo Villaggio and Ugo Tognazzi, singer Ornella Vanoni (who created a dedicated jingle for the liqueur China Martini) and Ferruccio Amendola,[8] who became the voice of many Martini commercials. In the 1980s, the company abandoned the use of celebrities and decided to set their commercials in enjoyable contexts, such as swimming pools, Caribbean beaches, the streets of Beverly Hills, or a trendy bar in New York. Since the early 1990s, it has enlisted international stars with captivating faces: in 1995, Charlize Theron was the leading actress of a commercial directed by McCann Erickson, and in the following years the brand enlisted Naomi Campbell, Sharon Stone, Monica Bellucci and George Clooney, among others.

Innocenti Collection

ASSETS IN THE COLLECTION: 226 reels (51 negatives; 80 positives).
Innocenti, a producer of scooters and licensed cars, was founded in Lambrate, Milan, in 1947, and ceased its activities in 1993, when it merged with Fiat Group. Commercials and *caroselli* made between 1961 and 1976 constitute Innocenti's greatest successes: the Mini family, Austin A 40, Regent and scooters. Over a span of forty-five years Innocenti produced several kinds of scooters, the most popular, without doubt, being the Lambretta, a true Italian mass motorisation icon. To sponsor its products, Innocenti used testimonials, mostly by renowned Italian pop musicians and Italian animators like Bruno Bozzetto. In the 1960s, the company also produced films promoting exotic areas to tempt Italian workers to move to South America, as Innocenti built several industrial plants in Venezuela. The films showed, on the one hand, the country's wild beauty and, on the other, the power of mechanisation and the exploitation of natural resources on an industrial scale, all in the service of a better standard of living.

Recta Film Collection

ASSETS IN THE COLLECTION: 206 reels (all positives).
Cesare Taurelli, co-founder with Vittorio Carpignano of Recta Film, a commercial production company that is still active today, composed the *Carosello* series' signature tune. The importance of this collection lies in the fact that it contains different versions of the tune, together with commercials and *caroselli* promoting brands such as Vespa scooters, Findus frozen food, Algida ice-cream, Barilla pasta, Coca-Cola, Colgate toothpaste and De Beers diamonds.

Filmmaster Collection

ASSETS IN THE COLLECTION: 1,537 reels (all negatives).
Filmmaster is an advertising production company founded in Rome in 1976. This film collection contains footage that allows one to follow entire film production chains.

Interesting examples are the audio track with Federico Fellini's voice giving instructions to actors during the shooting of Banca di Roma commercials.[9] Some brands for which Filmmaster produced films include the following: Opel, Ford, Seat and Renault cars, Brooklyn chewing gum, Kraft sliced cheese, Lipton tea, Agip gas stations and Honda motorbikes.

Italgas Collection

ASSETS IN THE COLLECTION: 104 reels (20 negatives; 84 positives).
Italgas, a gas distribution company, began operations in 1837 in Turin; in 1966 control was transferred to Snam, by ENI Group.[10] In the 1970s Italgas started a massive campaign to promote methane gas for domestic use (cooking and heating). The advertisements produced in the 1980s focused on security and energy-saving concepts; those made in the following years highlight the ecological advantages related to the use of gas instead of other energy forms.

Aurora Collection

ASSETS IN THE COLLECTION: 65 reels (all positives).
The Aurora company began operations in 1919 in Turin, and it is still in the business of making pens and fountain pens. Its advertisements, made between 1969 and 1972, were presented inside the advertising programme *Girotondo*,[11] aired in the afternoon and targeted at children to promote school supplies. Other collection advertisements, aimed at adults, fostered the image of the Aurora pen as a status symbol.

Birra Peroni Collection

ASSETS IN THE COLLECTION: 896 reels (225 negatives; 646 positives).
Birra Peroni Company was founded by the Peroni family in Vigevano, Pavia, in 1846. In 1864, the firm moved to Rome, where it is still in operation. In 2003 it was purchased by the South African multinational SABMiller. The collection of films, produced between 1966 and 1986, mainly consists of television and cinema commercials and *caroselli*. The advertisements use endorsements by Italian television and entertainment celebrities. Most commercials have, as a leading character, the legendary Peroni Blonde, the factory's icon, played over the years by different actresses and models like Solvi Stubing, Michelle Gastpar and Anneline Kriel.

Venchi-Talmone-Maggiora Collection

ASSETS IN THE COLLECTION: 27 reels (2 negatives; 25 positives).
Venchi was founded in 1878 by Silviano Venchi in Turin and is still in operation. The factory specialises in the production of chocolate. In 1960 it acquired Talmone, maker

of biscuits and Turin's famous chocolate, the Gianduiotto. In 1974, the new company bought Maggiora, a Piedmontese company specialising in biscuits and candies. Between 1960 and 1975 they made only *caroselli*: in some of them there were testimonials by famous Italians, mostly from Italian television. Other advertising films were created by famous animators like Nino and Toni Pagot and Paul Campani. One of the most interesting series of *caroselli* concerns the renowned candy produced by Venchi, the Nougatine. This candy is represented as a fascinating black lady – probably as a tribute to the Black Venus Josephine Baker – dancing sensually in the middle of the jungle. It is interesting to notice that all *caroselli* of Gianduiotti chocolates were shot in the most touristic and charming districts of Turin, turning them into a kind of short city film.

Marzotto Collection

ASSETS IN THE COLLECTION: 2,100 reels (248 negatives; 1852 positives).
Marzotto was founded as a wool mill in Vicenza, in 1836, by Luigi Marzotto. Today the brand still exists, and it is one of the most famous Italian factories for textiles, yarn and clothing. The company mostly made *caroselli* between 1960 and 1975. In the early 1960s, Marzotto sponsored Italian hand-sewn suit styles by famous tailors Jole Veneziani, Emilio Schuberth and the Fontana sisters. From the mid-1960s, the company signed up several male Italian celebrities to endorse the revival of the ready-made suit. For a long time the perfect Marzotto man was the typical successful person. This association was abandoned in the early 1970s: the new Marzotto man became the perfect father, spending time with his family, while also being an exemplary citizen. This strategy was soon abandoned and Marzotto went back to its first model, a self-confident man who, in the early 1980s, might have been called a 'yuppie'. When the company produced its last *caroselli*, the brand had become a symbol of elegance and refinement. For this reason all *caroselli*, regardless of content, always ended with the slogan, 'A man will always look all right if he dresses in a Marzotto suit.'

Bosca Collection

ASSETS IN THE COLLECTION: 2,527 reels (387 negatives; 2,140 positives).
Bosca was founded in 1831 at Canelli, Asti, by Pietro Bosca. The factory is still in operation and produces liqueurs and wines. In 1985, Bosca bought Cora, a company famous abroad for its bitters. This brand produced a lot of advertising films for television and cinema from 1957–95, enlisting Italian as well as foreign celebrities, such as the English star Terry-Thomas. A long series of *caroselli* were shot by well-known Italian director Luciano Emmer; others were created by renowned animators Nino and Toni Pagot. From the beginning of the 1970s, testimonials for the brand featured several Italian actresses, yet their sensual charm never matched the success of Peroni Blondes.

ACKNOWLEDGMENTS

I sincerely want to thank Sergio Toffetti, director of the Archivio Nazionale Cinema d'Impresa, for supervising the writing of this article; my colleague Stefano Landini for proof-reading this text; and Elena Testa, Valentina Visciglio and Mariangela Michieletto for supplying me with information regarding the collections they manage.

NOTES

1. In 2004, the 1949 law was extended – Law no. 28 section 24 and following – to all written documents related to film, such as scripts and film preparation items. In these laws there is no specific reference to industrial films or advertising films. Largely for this reason, commercial film-related documents are held in other archives, mainly in companies' archives, or other places unknown. It is difficult to have free and easy access to these precious sources, even for cataloguing and identifying advertising films collections.
2. ANCI holds *L'Industria dei cappelli Borsalino* (*Borsalino Hats Factory*), a beautiful example of an early industrial film, made in 1913, by the Italian director Luca Comerio and produced by Milano Film. This film was restored by ANCI in early 2010. Restoration was based on two incomplete prints coming from CSC and Fondazione Luigi Micheletti. The great interest of this title depends not only on the factory's description, but also on the film's plot. It is a fictional narrative inspired by the Robinson Crusoe story. This example allows us to understand that the archive keeps titles, not only for archival purposes, but also for their artistic value.
3. Assets of those collections that will not be studied in depth in this article include the following: Breda, 25 reels (12 negatives; 13 positives); Recchi, 40 reels (all positives); Documento Film, 1,308 reels (594 negatives; 714 positives); Filippo Paolone, 64 reels (4 negatives; 60 positives); Enea, 448 reels (39 negatives; 409 positives); Aem, 476 reels (202 negatives; 274 positives); Milan Subway Company, 180 reels (130 negatives; 50 positives); National Italian Railway, 6,000 reels (1,008 negatives; 4,992 positives); and ICE, 569 reels (22 negatives; 547 positives). A large part of the collections is now available online on the institute's YouTube channel: https://www.youtube.com/user/cinemaimpresatv
4. The *caroselli* promoted only one product per sketch, and the sketches included in a full *Carosello* programme were not related to each other in terms of plot or advertised product. Every *carosello* had to be shot on 35mm film in black and white. Advertising films could fill only 5 per cent of the entire RAI programme schedule.
5. Slogans became so well known that many are still in the collective memory of the Italian people.
6. In several cases companies kept producing advertising films after the 1980s, but did not give these materials to the film archives. Because of the original formats of these films – video or, today, digital – companies assume they can properly store those kinds of materials on their own premises. As a result, archivists lack information that could be essential to the exhaustive study of advertising film collections.
7. Moplen was created in 1950s by the Italian engineer Giulio Natta. For this revolutionary discovery he received the Nobel Prize in Chemistry in 1963.

8. Popular Italian actor whose voice dubbed Robert De Niro, Sylvester Stallone, Dustin Hoffman, Al Pacino, Tomás Milián and Bill Cosby.
9. This valuable item was previewed, with the commercials, at the 2008 Tribeca Film Festival in New York.
10. ENI (Ente Nazionale Idrocarburi – National Hydrocarbons Institute).
11. Over the years several advertising programmes were developed in addition to *Carosello* in Italian television. *Girotondo*, launched in 1964, was one of these programmes.

Select Bibliography

Abraham, Adam, *When Magoo Flew: The Rise and Fall of Animation Studio UPA* (Middletown, CT: Wesleyan University Press, 2012).

Acland, Charles R., *Screen Traffic: Movies, Multiplexes, and Global Culture* (Durham, NC, and London: Duke University Press, 2003).

Acland, Charles R., *Fast Viewing: The Popular Life of Subliminal Influence* (Durham, NC: Duke University Press, 2011).

Acland, Charles R., and Haidee Wasson (eds), *Useful Cinema* (Durham, NC, and London: Duke University Press, 2011).

Adorno, Theodor W., and Max Horkheimer, *Dialektik der Aufklärung. Philosophische Fragmente*, 15th edition (Frankfurt am Main: Suhrkamp, 2004).

Agde, Günter, *Flimmernde Versprechen: Geschichte des deutschen Werbefilms im Kino seit 1897* (Berlin: Das Neue Berlin, 1998).

Agnew, Clark M., and Neil O'Brien, *Television Advertising* (New York: McGraw-Hill, 1958).

Aitken, Ian, *Film and Reform: John Grierson and the Documentary Film Movement* (London: Routledge, 1990).

Allen, Jean, 'The Film Viewer as Consumer', *Quarterly Review of Film Studies* vol. 5 no. 4 (1980), pp. 481–99.

Allen, Robert C. 'The Place of Space in Film Historiography', *Tijdschrift voor Mediageschiedenis* vol. 9 no.2 (2006), pp. 15–27.

Allen, Robert C., and Annette Hill (eds), *The Television Studies Reader* (New York: Routledge, 2004).

Altman, Rick, *Film/Genre* (London: BFI, 1999).

Anderson, Christopher, *Hollywood TV* (Austin: University of Texas Press, 1994).

Araujo, Luis, 'Markets, Market-making and Marketing', *Marketing Theory* vol. 7 no. 3 (2007).

Association of National Advertisers, *The Dollars and Sense of Business Films: A Study of 157 Business Films* (New York: Association of National Advertisers, 1954).

Austin, Bruce A., 'Cinema Screen Advertising: An Old Technology with New Promise for Consumer Marketing', *Journal of Consumer Marketing* vol. 3 no. 1 (1986), pp. 45–56.

Bahloul, Maher, and Carolyn Graham (eds), *Lights! Camera! Action and the Brain: The Use of Film in Education* (Newcastle upon Tyne: Cambridge Scholars, 2012).

Baker, Joseph B., 'Examples of Motion Picture Advertising', *Motography* vol. 5 no. 6 (June 1911), pp. 133–6.

Balázs, Béla 'Visible Man', in Erica Carter and Rodney Livingstone (eds), *Early Film Theory: Visible Man and the Spirit of Film* (London: Berghan, 2010).

Ballhausen, Thomas, and Paolo Caneppele (eds), *Materialien zur österreichischen Filmgeschichte 10* (Vienna: Filmarchiv Austria, 2003).

Ballhausen, Thomas, and Paolo Caneppele (eds), *Entscheidungen der Wiener Filmzensur 1934–1938* (Vienna: Filmarchiv Austria, 2009).

Ballhausen, Thomas, and Paolo Caneppele (eds), *Materialien zur österreichischen Filmgeschichte 11* (Vienna: Filmarchiv Austria, 2009).

Barnouw, Erik, *The Sponsor: Notes on a Modern Potentate* (New York: Oxford University Press, 1978).

Baudrillard, Jean, *The Consumer Society: Myths and Structures*, trans. Chris Turner (London: Sage, 1998).

Baughman, James L., *Same Time, Same Station* (Baltimore, MD: Johns Hopkins University Press, 2007).

Bauma, Pavol, *Ekonomika čs. státního filmu* (Bratislava: Slovenské vydavateľstvo technickej literatury, 1965).

Baxandall, Michael, *Patterns of Intention: On the Historical Explanation of Pictures* (New Haven, CT: Yale University Press, 1985).

Beckman, Karen (ed.), *Animating Film Theory* (Durham, NC: Duke University Press, 2014).

Behrmann, Hermann, *Reklame* (Berlin: Industrieverlag Spaeth und Linde, 1923).

Bellaire, Arthur, *TV Advertising* (New York: Harper, 1959).

Bellotto, Adriano, *La memoria del futuro. Film d'arte, film e video industriali Olivetti: 1949–1992* (Villa Casana: Edizioni Fondazione Adriano Olivetti, Archivio storico del gruppo Olivetti, 1994).

Bellour, Raymond, 'The Double Helix', in Timothy Druckrey (ed.), *Electronic Culture: Technology and Visual Representation* (New York: Aperture, 1996), pp. 173–99.

Bellour, Raymond, 'D'un autre cinéma', *Traffic* no. 34 (2000), pp. 5–21.

Beniger, James, *The Control Revolution* (Cambridge, MA: Harvard University Press, 1986).

Benjamin, Walter, *One Way Street and Other Writings*, trans. Edmund Jephcott and Kingsley Shorter (London: Verso, 1985).

Beusekom, Ansje van, '"Avant-guerre" and the International Avant-Garde: Circulation and Programming of Early Films in the European Avant-garde Programs in the 1920s and 1930s', in Frank Kessler and Nanna Verhoeff (eds), *Networks of Entertainment: Early Film Distribution 1895–1915* (Eastleigh: John Libbey, 2007), pp. 285–94.

Bignell, Jonathan, *An Introduction to Television Studies* (New York: Routledge, 2004).

Bltereyst, Daniel, Richard Maltby and Philippe Meers (eds), *Cinema, Audiences and Modernity: New Perspectives on European Cinema History* (London and New York: Routledge, 2012).

Bird, William, *'Better Living': Advertising, Media, and the New Vocabulary of Business Leadership, 1935–1955* (Evanston, IL: Northwestern University Press, 1999).

Bloom, Ivo, *Jean Desmet and the Early Dutch Film Trade* (Amsterdam: Amsterdam University Press, 2003).

Boddy, William, 'Operation Frontal Lobes versus the Living Room Toy: The Battle over Programme Control in Early Television', *Media, Culture and Society* no. 9 (1987), pp. 347–68.

Boddy, William, *Fifties Television: The Industry and Its Critics* (Urbana: University of Illinois Press, 1990).

Boddy, William, 'Early Cinema and Radio Technology in Turn of the Century Popular Imagination', in André Gaudreault, Catherine Russell and Pierre Véronneau (eds), *The Cinema: A New Technology for the Twentieth Century* (Lausanne: Payot, 2004), pp. 285–94.

Boddy, William, *New Media and Popular Imagination: Launching Radio, Television, and Digital Media in the United States* (Oxford: Oxford University Press, 2004).

Boddy, William, '"Is It TV Yet?" The Dislocated Screens of Television in a Mobile Digital Culture', in James Bennett and Niki Strange (eds), *Television as Digital Culture* (Durham, NC: Duke University Press, 2011), pp. 76–101.

Bordwell, David, Janet Staiger and Kristin Thompson, *The Classical Hollywood Cinema: Film Style and Mode of Production to 1960* (New York: McGraw-Hill, 1985).

Bottomore, S., 'The Panicking Audience?: Early Cinema and the "Train Effect"', *Historical Journal of Film, Radio and Television* vol. 19 no. 2 (1999), pp. 177–216.

Breaden, Craig, 'Carl Sanders and Albert Maysles: Georgia Politics Meet Direct Cinema, 1969–70', *Moving Image* vol. 9 no. 1 (2009), pp. 201–13.

Breard, Sylvester Quinn, 'A History of Motion Pictures in New Orleans, 1896–1908' (MA thesis: Louisiana State University, 1951), published in microfiche in *Historical Journal of Film, Radio and Television* vol. 15 no. 4 (Autumn 1995).

Brignone, Daniela, *Birra Peroni: 1846–1996 centocinquant'anni di birra nella vita italiana* (Milano: Ed. Electa, 1995).

Brodoghkozy, Aniko, *Groove Tube* (Durham, NC: Duke University Press, 2001).

Brown, Les, *Television* (New York: Harcourt Brace Jovanovich, 1971).

Brown, Lyndon O., 'What the Public Expects of Television', in John Gray Peatman (ed.), *Radio and Business 1945: Proceedings of the First Annual Conference on Radio and Business* (New York: City College of New York, 1945), pp. 139, 137.

Buchan, Suzanne (ed.), *Pervasive Animation* (London: Routledge, 2013).

Campbell, Colin, *The Romantic Ethic and the Spirit of Modern Consumerism* (Oxford: Blackwell, 1987).

Campbell, Stanley, *Because of These Things Advertising Pays* (Dallas: Jagger-Chiles-Stovall, 1939).

Casetti, Francesco, 'Theory, Post-Theory, Neo-Theories: Changes in Discourses, Changes in Objects', *Cinémas. Révue d'études cinématographiques* (special issue *La théorie du cinéma, enfin en crise*) vol. 17 no. 2–3 (2007), pp. 33–46.

Casetti, Francesco, 'Filmic Experience', *Screen* vol. 50 no. 1 (2009), pp. 56–66.

Castronovo, V., *FIAT 1899–1999. Un Secolo di Storia Italiana* (Milano: Rizzoli, 1999).

Charney, Leo, and Vanessa R. Schwartz (eds), *Cinema and the Invention of Modern Life* (Berkeley, Los Angeles and London: University of California Press, 1995).

Cogdell, Christina, 'The Futurama Recontextualized: Norman Bel Geddes's Eugenic "World of Tomorrow"', *American Quarterly* vol. 52 no. 2 (June 2000), pp. 193–245.

Cohen, K., 'The Development of Animated TV Commercials in the 1940s', *Animation Journal* vol. 1 (1992), pp. 44–6.

Colomina, Beatriz, 'Enclosed by Images: The Eameses' Multimedia Architecture', *Grey Room* no. 2 (Winter 2001), pp. 5–29.

Cone, Fairfax, *With All Its Faults* (Boston: Little, Brown, 1969).

Cone, Fairfax, *The Blue Streak* (Chicago: Crain Communications, 1973).

Cook, Guy, *The Discourse of Advertising* (London and New York: Routledge, 2001 [1992]).

Cook, Mary Loomis, 'Programs for Women', in Neville O'Neill (ed.), *The Advertising Agency Looks at Radio* (New York: D. Appleton, 1932).

Cowan, Michael, 'Absolute Advertising: Walter Ruttmann and the Weimar Advertising Film', *Cinema Journal* vol. 52 no. 4 (2013), pp. 49–73.

Cowan, Michael, 'Fidelity, Capture and the Sound Advertisement: Julius Pinschewer and Rudi Klemm's *Die Chinesische Nachtigall*', in Sema Colpan, Lydia Nsiah and Joachim Schätz (eds), *Sponsored Films: Strategien und Formen für eine modernisierte Gesellschaft – Zeitgeschichte* vol. 41 no. 2 (2014), pp. 90–102.

Cowan, Michael, *Walter Ruttman and the Cinema of Multiplicity: Avant-garde, Advertising, Modernity* (Amsterdam: Amsterdam University Press, 2014).

Cowan, Michael, 'Taking it to the Street: Screening the Advertising Film in the Weimar Republic', *Screen* vol. 54 no. 4 (2013).

Crafton, Donald, *Before Mickey: The Animated Film 1898–1928* (Chicago: University of Chicago Press, 1982).

Crafton, Donald, *The Talkies: American Cinema's Transition to Sound, 1926–1931* (Berkeley: University of California Press, 1999).

Curti, Merle, 'The Changing Concept of Human Nature in the Literature of American Advertising', *The Business History Review* vol. 41 no. 4 (Winter 1967), pp. 335–57.

Davis, Aeron, *Promotional Cultures: The Rise and Spread of Advertising, Public Relations, Marketing and Branding* (Cambridge: Polity Press, 2013).

de Klerk, Nico, 'The Moment of Screening: What Nonfiction Films Can Do', in Peter Zimmermann and Kay Hoffmann (eds), *Triumph der Bilder: Kultur- und Dokumentarfilme vor 1945 im internationalen Vergleich* (Konstanz: UVK, 2003), pp. 291–305.

de Klerk, Nico, 'The Transport of Audiences', in Richard Abel, Giorgio Bertellini and Rob King (eds), *Early Cinema and the 'National'* (New Barnet: John Libbey, 2008), pp. 101–8.

de Vries, T., and A. Mul, 'Joop Geesink, poppenfilmproducent', *Animatie* vol. 1 (September 1984), pp. 1–50.

Della Femina, Jerry, *From Those Wonderful Folks Who Gave You Pearl Harbor* (New York: Simon & Schuster, 1970).

DeLorme, Denise, and Leonard Reid, 'Moviegoers' Experiences and Interpretations of Brands in Films Revisited', *Journal of Advertising* vol. 28 no. 2 (1999), pp. 71–95.

Dench, Ernest A., *Moving Picture Education* (Cincinnati: Standard Publishing Company, 1917).

Doane, Mary Ann, *The Desire to Desire: The Woman's Film of the 1940s* (Bloomington: Indiana University Press, 1987).

Doane, Mary Ann, 'The Economy of Desire: The Commodity Form in/of the Cinema', *Quarterly Review of Film and Video* vol. 11 no. 1 (1989), pp. 23–33.

Doane, Mary Ann, 'The Indexical and the Concept of Medium Specificity', *Differences: A Journal of Feminist Cultural Studies* vol. 18 no. 1 (2007), pp. 128–52.

Dobrow, Larry, *When Advertising Tried Harder* (New York: Friendly Press, 1984).

Donahue, Suzanne Mary, *American Film Distribution: The Changing Marketplace* (Ann Arbor: UMI Research, 1987).

Dunlap, Orrin E. Jr, *The Future of Television* (New York: Harper and Brothers, 1942).

Dykema, Peter W., *Women and Radio Music* (New York: Radio Institute for the Audible Art, n.d. [1928?]).

Eagan, Daniel, *America's Film Legacy: The Authoritative Guide to the Landmark Movies in the National Film Registry* (New York: Continuum, 2010), pp. 543–4.

Eckert, Charles, 'The Carole Lombard in Macy's Window', *Quarterly Review of Film Studies* vol. 3 no. 1 (1978), pp. 1–21.

Elsaesser, Thomas, 'Dada/Cinema?', in Rudolf E. Kuenzli (ed.), *Dada and Surrealist Film* (New York: Willis Locker & Owens, 1987), pp. 13–27.

Elsaesser, Thomas, *Weimar Cinema and After: Germany's Historical Imaginary* (New York: Routledge, 2000).

Elsaesser, Thomas, *Filmgeschichte und frühes Kino: Archäologie eines Medienwandels* (Munich: Edition Text+Kritik, 2002).

Emmet, B., and J. E. Jeuck, *Catalogues and Counters: A History of Sears, Roebuck and Company* (Chicago: University of Chicago Press, 1950).

Ermanno Olmi, *Il cinema, i film, la televisione, la scuola*, A cura di Adriano Aprà (Venezia: Marsilio, 2003).

Ewen, Stuart, *Captains of Consciousness: Advertising and the Social Roots of the Consumer Culture* (New York and London: McGraw-Hill, 1976).

Ewen, Stuart, and Elizabeth Ewen, *Channels of Desire: Mass Images and the Shaping of American Consciousness* (New York, St Louis and San Francisco: McGraw-Hill, 1982).

Ferrarotti, F., *Un imprenditore di idee: una testimonianza su Adriano Olivetti* (Torino: Ed. di Comunità, 2001).

Fickers, Andreas, and Catherine Johnson, 'Transnational Television History: A Comparative Approach', *Media History* vol. 16 no. 1 (2010), pp. 1–11.

Fielding, R., *A Technological History of Motion Pictures and Television: An Anthology from the Pages of the Journal of the Society of Motion Picture and Television Engineers* (Berkeley: University of California Press, 1967).

Film History, special issues *Small-Gauge and Amateur Film* vol. 15 no. 2 (2003), *Nontheatrical Film* vol. 19 (2007) and *Nontheatrical Film* vol. 25 no. 4 (2013).

Forceville, Charles, *Pictorial Metaphor in Advertising* (London: Routledge, 1996).

Forster, Ralf, *Ufa und Nordmark: Zwei Firmengeschichten und der deutsche Werbefilm 1919–1945* (Trier: Wissenschaftlicher Verlag Trier, 2005).

Fox, Stephen, *The Mirror Makers: A History of American Advertising and Its Creators* (New York: William Morrow, 1984).

Frank, Thomas, *The Conquest of Cool* (Chicago: University of Chicago Press, 1997).

Friedberg, Anne, *Window Shopping: Cinema and the Postmodern* (Berkeley, Los Angeles and London: University of California Press, 1993).

Fritscher, John J., *Television Today* (Chicago: Claretian Press, 1971).

Gable, Jo, *The Tuppenny Punch and Judy Show: 25 Years of TV Commercials* (London: Michael Joseph, 1980).

Gaines, Jane, 'The Queen Christina Tie-Ups: Convergence of Show Window and Screen', *Quarterly Review of Film and Video* vol. 11 no. 1 (1989), pp. 35–60.

Gaines, Jane M., *Contested Culture: The Image, the Voice, and the Law* (Chapel Hill: University of North Carolina Press, 1991).

Galician, Mary-Lou (ed.), *Handbook of Product Placement in the Mass Media: New Strategies in Marketing Theory, Practice, Trends, and Ethics* (Binghamton, NY: Best Business Books, 2004).

Gambrell, Alice, 'In Visible Hands: The Work of Stop Motion', *Animation Practice, Process and Production* no. 1 (2011), pp. 107–29.

Gaudreault, André (ed.), *American Cinema, 1890–1909: Themes and Variations* (New Brunswick, NJ: Rutgers University Press, 2009).

Gaudreault, André, *Film and Attraction: From Kinematography to Cinema*, trans. Timothy Barnard (Urbana and Chicago: University of Illinois Press, 2011 [2008]).

Gaudreault, André, and Philippe Marion, *The Kinematic Turn: Film in the Digital Era and its Ten Problems*, trans. Timothy Barnard (Montreal: Caboose, 2012).

Gauthier, Philippe, 'A "Trick" Question: Are Early Animated Drawings a Film Genre or a Special Effect?', *Animation* no. 6 (2011), pp. 163–75.

Goergen, Jeanpaul, *Walter Ruttmann. Eine Dokumentation* (Berlin: Freunde der deutschen Kinemathek, 1989), pp. 17–56.

Gomery, Douglas, *Shared Pleasures: A History of Movie Presentation in the United States* (Madison: University of Wisconsin Press, 1992).

Gossage, Howard Luck, *Is There Any Hope for Advertising?* (Urbana: University of Illinois Press, 1986).

Grainge, Paul and Catherine Johnson, *Promotional Screen Industries* (New York and London: Routledge, 2015).

Grieveson, Lee, 'The Work of Film in the Age of Fordist Mechanization', *Cinema Journal* vol. 51 no. 3 (Spring 2012), pp. 25–51.

Griffith, Richard, *Films of the World's Fair, 1939* (New York: American Film Center, 1940).

Griffiths, Alison, *Shivers Down Your Spine: Cinema, Museums, and the Immersive View* (New York: Columbia University Press, 2013).

Groskopf, Jeremy W., 'Profit Margins: The American Silent Cinema and the Marginalization of Advertising' (dissertation, Georgia State University, 2013).

Guckes, Emil, 'Der Tonfilm als Werbemittel in Deutschland' (PhD dissertation, Leopold-Franzens-Universität Innsbruck, 1937).

Gunning, Tom, 'Before Documentary: Early Nonfiction Films and the "View Aesthetic"', in Daan Hertogs and Nico de Klerk (eds), *Uncharted Territory: Essays on Early Nonfiction Film* (Amsterdam: Stichting Netherlands Filmmuseum, 1997), pp. 9–24.

Gupta, Pola, and Kenneth Lord, 'Product Placement in Movies: The Effect of Prominence and Mode on Audience Recall', *Journal of Current Issues and Research in Advertising* vol. 20 no. 1 (1998), pp. 47–59.

Gustafson, Robert, 'The Power of the Screen: The Influence of Edith Head's Film Designs on the Retail Fashion Market', *The Velvet Light Trap* no. 19 (1982), pp. 8–15.

Guth, Klement, *Názorná propagace a agitace* (Praha: Státní zdravotnické nakladatelství, 1958).

Häckl, Bohuš, *Propagační prostředky. Jak je vytvářet, posuzovat a používat* (Praha: Vydavatelství obchodu, 1962).

Hahn, Hans, 'Amerikanische Reklamepsychologie', *Industrielle Psychotechnik* vol. 2 no. 2 (1925), pp. 33–42.

Haller, Andrea, 'Das Kinoprogramm: Zur Genese und frühen Praxis einer Aufführungsform', in Heike Klippel (ed.), *'The Art of Programming': Film, Programm und Kontext* (Münster: Lit, 2008), pp. 18–51.

Hansen, Miriam, *Babel and Babylon: Spectatorship in American Silent Film* (Cambridge: Harvard University Press, 1991).

Hansen, Miriam, 'Early Cinema, Late Cinema: Permutations of the Public Sphere', *Screen* vol. 34 no. 3 (1993), pp. 197–210.

Havelka, Jiří, *Čs. filmové hospodářství 1956–1960* (Praha: Čs. filmový ústav, 1974).

Hediger, Vinzenz, *Verführung zum Film: Der amerikanische Kinotrailer seit 1912* (Marburg: Schüren, 2001).

Hediger, Vinzenz, and Patrick Vonderau (eds), *Films that Work: Industrial Film and the Productivity of Media* (Amsterdam: Amsterdam University Press, 2009).

Hendricks, Gordon, *The Kinetoscope: America's First Commercially Successful Motion Picture Exhibitor* (New York: The Beginnings of the American Film, 1966).

Hennion, Antoine and Cecile Méadel, 'Artisans of Desire: The Mediation of Advertising between Product and Consumer', *Sociology Theory* vol. 7 no. 2 (Autumn 1989), pp. 191–209.

Henry, Brian (ed.), *British Television Advertising: The First 30 Years* (London: Century Benham, 1986).

Hetherington, Kevin, *Capitalism's Eye* (London and New York: Routledge, 2007).

Hiršl, Miroslav, *Rozsah a struktura společenské spotřeby obyvatelstva v ČSSR v letech 1945–1970* (Praha: Výzkumný ústav sociálního zabezpečení, 1974).

Hollingworth, Harry, *Advertising and Selling* (London and New York: D. Appleton and Company, 1924).

Hopkins, Claude, *Scientific Advertising* (Lincolnwood, IL: NTC Business Books, reprinted 1966).

Jakes, Frank Henry, 'A Study of Standards Imposed by Four Leading Television Critics With Respect to Live Television Drama' (PhD dissertation, Ohio State University, 1960).

Johnson, Keith F., 'Cinema Advertising', *Journal of Advertising* vol. 10 no. 4 (1981), pp. 11–19.

Johnston, Keith M., *Coming Soon: Film Trailers and the Selling of Hollywood Technology* (Jefferson, NC: McFarland, 2009).

Kalinová, Jana, *Charakter a poslání propagace v socialistickém státě* (Praha: Čs. obchodní komora, 1959).

Kelley, Andrea, '"A Revolution in the Atmosphere": The Dynamics of Site and Screen in 1940s Soundies', *Cinema Journal* vol. 54 no. 2 (Winter 2015), pp. 72–93.

Kerby, Philip, *The Victory of Television* (New York: Harper and Brothers, 1939).

Kernan, Lisa, *Coming Attractions: Reading American Movie Trailers* (Austin: University of Texas Press, 2004).

Kessler, Frank, and Nanna Verhoeff (eds), *Networks of Entertainment: Early Film Distribution 1895–1915* (Eastleigh: John Libbey, 2007).

Kessler, Frank, Sabine Lenk and Martin Loiperdinger (eds), *KINtop: Jahrbuch zur Erforschung des frühen Films* no. 11: Kinematographen-Programme (Frankfurt am Main, Basel: Stroemfeld/Roter Stern, 2002).

Kjellberg, Hans and C.-F. Helgesson, 'On the Nature of Markets and their Practices', *Marketing Theory* vol. 7 no. 2 (2007), pp. 137–62.

Klinger, Barbara, *Beyond the Multiplex: Cinema, New Technology, and the Home* (Berkeley: University of California Press, 2006).

Kouba, Karel, *Plán a trh za socialismu* (Praha: Ekonomický ústav ČSAV, 1967).

Kreimeier, Klaus, Antje Ehmann and Jeanpaul Goergen (eds), *Geschichte des dokumentarischen Films in Deutschland*, vol. 2: Weimarer Republik 1918–1933 (Stuttgart: Reclam, 2005).

Kropff, Hanns F. J., *Wie werde ich Reklame-Chef?* (Vienna/Essen/Leipzig: Barth, 1926).

Kropff, Hanns F. J., and Bruno W. Randolph, *Marktanalyse. Untersuchung des Marktes und Vorbereitung der Reklame* (Munich/Berlin: R. Oldenbourg, 1928), pp. 290–2.

Kuhn, Annette, *An Everyday Magic: Cinema and Cultural Memory* (London, New York: I.B.Tauris, 2002).

Kurtzig, Käthe, 'Die Arten des Werbefilms', *Industrielle Psychotechnik* no. 3 (1926), pp. 311–14.

Kurtzig, Käthe, 'Werbefilm und Volkswirtschaft', *Die Reklame. Zeitschrift des Verbandes Deutscher Reklamefachleute* vol. 20 no. 12 (1927), pp. 417–19.

Kurtzig, Käthe, 'Wo und wie wirkt der Werbefilm?', *Industrielle Psychotechnik* vol. 5 no. 1 (1928), pp. 367–9.

Lamarre, Thomas, *The Anime Machine: A Media Theory of Animation* (Minneapolis: University of Minnesota Press, 2009).

Lasker, Albert, *The Lasker Story* (Chicago: Advertising, 1963).

Lawrence, Mary Wells, *A Big Life in Advertising* (New York: Alfred A. Knopf, 2002).

Leach, William, 'Strategies of Display and the Production of Desire', in Simon J. Bronner (ed.), *Consuming Visions: Accumulation and Display of Goods in America, 1880–1920* (New York: Norton, 1989), pp. 23–36.

Leslie, Esther, *Hollywood Flatlands: Animation, Critical Theory and the Avant-Garde* (London: Verso, 2002).

Levenson, Bob, *Bill Bernbach's Book* (New York: Villard, 1987).

Levin, Miriam R. (ed.), *Cultures of Control* (Amsterdam: Harwood, 2000).

Lewis, Jon, and Eric Smoodin (eds), *Looking Past the Screen: Case Studies in American Film History and Method* (Durham, NC: Duke University Press, 2007).

Linn, Susan, *Consuming Kids: Protecting our Children from the Onslaught of Marketing and Advertising* (New York: Anchor, 2005).

Lois, George, with Bill Pitts, *George, Be Careful* (New York: Saturday Review Press, 1972).

Lukács, Georg, *History and Class Consciousness*, trans. Rodney Livingstone (Cambridge: MIT Press, 1968).

MacCann, Richard Dyer, *The People's Films: A Political History of US Government Motion Pictures* (New York: Hastings House, 1973).

Machlup, Fritz, *The Production and Distribution of Knowledge in the United States* (Princeton, NJ: Princeton University Press, 1962), pp. 207–94.

Macnab, Geoffrey, *J. Arthur Rank and the British Film Industry* (London: Routledge, 1993).

Maltby, Richard, 'New Cinema Histories', in Richard Maltby, Daniel Biltereyst and Philippe Meers (eds), *Explorations in New Cinema History: Approaches and Case Studies* (Malden, MA: Wiley-Blackwell, 2011), pp. 3–40.

Maltby, Richard, Daniel Biltereyst and Philippe Meers (eds), *Explorations in New Cinema History: Approaches and Case Studies* (Malden, MA: Wiley-Blackwell, 2011).

Maltby, Richard, Melvyn Stokes and Robert C. Allen (eds), *Going to the Movies: Hollywood and the Social Experience of the Cinema* (Exeter: University of Exeter Press, 2007).

Marchand, Roland, *Advertising the American Dream: Making Way for Modernity, 1920–1940* (Berkeley, Los Angeles and London: University of California Press, 1985).

Marchand, Roland, 'Corporate Imagery and Popular Education: World's Fairs and Expositions in the United States, 1893–1940', in David Nye and Carl Pederson (eds), *Consumption and American Culture* (Amsterdam: VU University Press, 1991), pp. 18–33.

Marchand, Roland, *Creating the Corporate Soul: The Rise of Public Relations and Corporate Imagery in American Big Business* (Berkeley: University of California Press, 1998).

Marchessault, Janine, 'Multi-Screens and Future Cinema: The Labyrinth Project at Expo '67', in Janine Marchessault and Susan Lord (eds), *Fluid Screens, Expanded Cinema* (Toronto: University of Toronto Press, 2007), pp. 29–51.

Marquis, Alice Goldfarb, *Hope and Ashes: The Birth of Modern Times 1929–1939* (New York: Free Press, 1986).

Marx, Karl, *Das Kapital I*, in Karl Marx and Friedrich Engels, *Werke*, vol. 23, 3rd edition (Berlin: Dietz, 1969).

Mashon, Michael, 'NBC, J. Walter Thompson, and the Evolution of Prime-Time Television Programming and Sponsorship, 1946–58' (PhD dissertation, University of Maryland College Park, 1996).

Mataja, Viktor, *Die Reklame im Geschäftsleben* (Vienna: Verlag des Niederösterreichischen Gewerbevereins, 1910).

Mayer, Martin, *Madison Avenue USA* (Lincolnwood, IL: NTC Business Books, 1992 [1958]).

Maynard, Michael L., and Megan Scala, 'Unpaid Advertising: A Case of Wilson the Volleyball in *Cast Away*', *The Journal of Popular Culture* vol. 39 no. 4 (2006), pp. 622–38.

McDonough, John, and Karen Egolf (eds), *The Advertising Age Encyclopedia of Advertising* (London and New York: Routledge, 2002).

McFall, Liz, *Advertising: A Cultural Economy* (London: Sage, 2004).

McMahan, Harry Wayne, *The Television Commercial: How to Create and Produce Effective TV Advertising*, revised edition (New York: Hastings House, 1957).

Melnick, Ross, *American Showman: Samuel 'Roxy' Rothafel and the Birth of the Entertainment Industry, 1908–1935* (New York: Columbia, 2012).

Mertová, Michaela, Vladimír Opěla, and Eva Urbanová, *Český Animovaný Film (1920–1945) /Czech Animated Film (1920–1945)* (Prague: Národní Filmový Archiv, 2012).

Meyers, Cynthia B., 'Psychedelics and the Advertising Man: The 1960s Countercultural Creative on Madison Avenue', *Columbia Journal of American Studies* vol. 4 no. 1 (2000), pp. 114–27.

Meyers, Cynthia B., 'The Problems with Sponsorship in Broadcasting, 1930s–50s: Perspectives from the Advertising Industry', *Historical Journal of Film, Radio and Television* vol. 31 no. 3 (September 2011), pp. 355–72.

Meyers, Cynthia B., *A Word from Our Sponsor: Admen, Advertising, and the Golden Age of Radio* (New York: Fordham University Press, 2014).

Miller, Toby (ed.), *Television Studies* (London: BFI, 2002).

Mills, C. Wright, *White Collar: The American Middle Classes* (New York: Oxford University Press, 1951).

Montgomery Ward & Co., Department of Magic Lanterns, Stereopticons, Moving Picture Machines, *Catalogue of Magic Lanterns, Stereopticons and Moving Picture Machines* (Chicago: Montgomery Ward & Co., 1898).

Morse, Daniel Ryan, 'Explorations of the Inhuman: Edison Phonographs in Silent Film' (unpublished manuscript, Temple University, 2008).

Münsterberg, Hugo, *The Photoplay: A Psychological Study* (New York: Appleton & Co. 1916).

Murray, Susan, *Hitch Your Antenna to the Stars* (New York: Routledge, 2005).

Musser, Charles, 'American Vitagraph: 1897–1901', *Cinema Journal* vol. 22 no. 3 (Spring 1983), pp. 4–46.

Musser, Charles, *The Emergence of Cinema: The American Screen to 1907* (Berkeley: University of California Press, 1990).

Musser, Charles, *Edison Motion Pictures, 1890–1900: An Annotated Filmography* (Washington, DC, and Friuli, Italy: Smithsonian Institution Press and Le Giornate del Cinema Muto, 1997).

Navratil, Josef, *Das Werk des österreichischen Kulturfilmproduzenten Ing. Karl Köfinger am Beispiel einer Serie von Fremdenverkehrswerbefilmen* (Vienna: Österreichisches Filmarchiv, 1989).

Nebenzahl, Isreal, and Eugene Secunda, 'Consumers' Attitudes toward Product Placement in Movies', *International Journal of Advertising* vol. 12 no. 1 (1993), pp. 1–12.

New York Museum of Science and Industry, *Exhibition Techniques: A Summary of Exhibition Practice, Based on Surveys Conducted at the New York and San Francisco World's Fairs of 1939* (New York: New York Museum of Science and Industry, 1940).

Newell, Jay, Charles T. Salmon and Susan Chang, 'The Hidden History of Product Placement', *Journal of Broadcasting and Electronic Media* vol. 50 no. 4 (2006), pp. 575–94.

Newman, Kathy M., *Radio Active* (Berkeley: University of California Press, 2004).

Newman, Michael Z., and Elana Levine, *Legitimating Television* (New York: Routledge, 2012).

Nichols, Bill, *Representing Reality: Issues and Concepts in Documentary* (Bloomington: Indiana University Press, 1991).

Nsiah, Lydia, '"Es lebe die elementare Gestaltung" – der beseelte Werbefilm', in Karin Fest, Sabrina Rahman and Marie-Noëlle Yazdanpanah (eds), *Mies van der Rohe, Richter, Graeff & Co.: Alltag und Design in der Avantgardezeitschrift G* (Vienna/Berlin: Turia+Kant, 2014), pp. 161–8.

Nsiah, Lydia, '"Wir montieren!" Hans Richters Arbeit an Form und Funktion von Bewegung', in Werner Michael Schwarz and Ingo Zechner (eds), *Die helle und die dunkle Seite der Moderne. Festschrift für Siegfried Mattl zum 60. Geburtstag* (Vienna: Turia+Kant, 2014), pp. 309–17.

Nye, David E., *Electrifying America: Social Meanings of a New Technology, 1880–1940* (Cambridge, MA: MIT Press, 1990).

Ogilvy, David, *Ogilvy on Advertising* (New York: Vintage, 1985).

Orgeron, Devin, Marsha Orgeron and Dan Streible (eds), *Learning with the Lights Off: Educational Film in the United States* (London: Oxford University Press, 2012).

Orosz, Márton, '"The Hidden Network of the Avant-Garde": der farbige Werbefilm als eine zentraleuropäische Erfindung?', in Sascha Bru, Laurence von Nuijs, Benedikt Hjartarson, Peter Nicholls, Tania Orum and Hubert van den Berg (eds), *Regarding the Popular: Modernism, the Avant-Garde and High and Low Culture* (Berlin/Boston: De Gruyter, 2012), pp. 338–60.

Overpeck, Deron, 'Subversion, Desperation and Captivity: Pre-film Advertising in American Film Exhibition Since 1977', *Film History* vol. 22 no. 2 (June 2010), pp. 219–34.

Packard, Vance, *The Hidden Persuaders* (New York: David McKay Co., 1957).

Pauli, Fritz, *Rhythmus und Resonanz als ökonomisches Prinzip in der Reklame* (Berlin: Verlag des Verbandes deutscher Reklamefachleute, 1926).

Pinschewer, Julius, 'Der Film als Werbemittel', *Mitteilungen des Vereins deutscher Reklamefachleute* (1916), pp. 115–18.

Prelinger, Rick, *The Field Guide to Sponsored Films* (San Francisco: National Film Preservation Foundation, 2006).

Presbrey, Frank, *The History and Development of Advertising* (New York: Doubleday, 1929).

Price, Jonathan, *The Best Thing on TV: Commercials* (New York: Penguin, 1978).

Pryluck, C., 'The Itinerant Movie Show and the Development of the Film Industry', in Kathryn Fuller-Seeley (ed.), *Hollywood in the Neighborhood: Historical Case Studies of Local Moviegoing* (Berkeley: University of California Press, 2008), pp. 37–51.

Racine, S., 'Changing (Inter) Faces: A Genre Analysis of Catalogues From Sears, Roebuck to Amazon.com' (PhD dissertation, University of Minnesota, 2002).

Reichert, Ramón (ed.), *Kulturfilm im 'Dritten Reich'* (Vienna: Synema, 2006).

Renoldner, Thomas, 'Animation in Österreich – 1832 bis heute', in Christian Dewald, Sabine Groschup, Mara Mattuschka and Thomas Renoldner (eds), *Die Kunst des Einzelbilds. Animation in Österreich – 1832 bis heute* (Vienna: Filmarchiv Austria, 2010), pp. 41–154.

Richter, Hans, *Filmgegner von heute – Filmfreunde von morgen* (Berlin: Reckendorf, 1929).

Richter, Hans, *Der Kampf um den Film. Für einen gesellschaftlich verantwortlichen Film* (Munich/Vienna: Carl Hanser, 1976).

Riessland, Andreas, 'Der abstrakte Trickfilm in der deutschen Werbung der 20er und 30er Jahre', *Hiyoshi Studien zur Germanistik* no. 35 (2003), pp. 99–120.

Ripmeester, Leenke, 'Entertainment uit de Lage Landen: de Geesink Collectie', *Tijdschrift voor Media Geschiedenis* vol. 15 no. 1 (2012), pp. 74–101.

Robinson, David, Stephen Herbert and Richard Crangle (eds), *Encyclopaedia of the Magic Lantern* (London: The Magic Lantern Society, 2001).

Rodowick, David Norman, *The Virtual Life of Film* (Cambridge: Harvard University Press, 2007).

Roholl, Marja, 'Uncle Sam: An Example for All? The Dutch Orientation towards America in the Social and Cultural Field, 1945–1965', in Hans Loeber (ed.), *Dutch–American Relations 1945–1969: A Partnership. Illusions and Facts* (Assen and Maastricht: Van Gorcum, 1992), pp. 105–52.

Roholl, Marja, '"We'll Go on Trial at the Fair": het Amerikaanse Paviljoen op de EXPO '58 in Brussel', *Groniek* no. 146 (October 1999), pp. 29–40.

Rosen, Philip, *Change Mummified: Cinema, Historicity, Theory* (Minneapolis: University of Minnesota Press, 2001).

Rosenberg, Emily S., *Spreading the American Dream: American Economic and Cultural Expansion 1890–1945* (New York: Hill and Wang, 1982).

Rotzoll, Kim B., 'The Captive Audience: The Troubled Odyssee of Cinema Advertising', in Bruce A. Austin (ed.), *Current Research in Film*, vol. 3 (Norwood, NJ: Ablex, 1987), pp. 72–87.

Rowsome, Frank Jr, *Think Small* (New York: Ballantine, 1970).

Russo, Alexander, *Points on the Dial* (Durham, NC: Duke University Press, 2010).

Rydell, Robert, *World of Fairs: The Century-of-Progress Expositions* (Chicago: University of Chicago Press, 1993).

Sampson, Tony D., *Virality: Contagion Theory in the Age of Networks* (Minneapolis: University of Minnesota Press, 2012).

Samuel, Lawrence, *Brought to You By: Postwar Television Advertising and the American Dream* (Austin: University of Texas Press, 2001).

Schaffer, William, 'Animation 1: The Control Image', in Alan Cholodenko (ed.), *The Illusion of Life II: More Essays on Animation* (Sydney: Power, 2007), pp. 456–85.

Schenk, Irmbert, Margrit Tröhler and Yvonne Zimmermann (eds), *Film – Kino – Zuschauer: Filmrezeption/Film – Cinema – Spectator: Film Reception* (Marburg: Schüren, 2010).

Schor, Juliet, *Born to Buy: The Commercialized Child and the New Consumer Culture* (New York: Scribner, 2005).

Schudson, Michael, *Advertising, the Uneasy Persuasion: Its Dubious Impact on American Society* (New York: Basic Books, 1984).

Schwartz, Frederic, 'Commodity Signs: Peter Behrens, AEG and the Trademark', *Journal of Design History* vol. 9 no. 3 (1996), pp. 153–84.

Schwartz, Tony, *The Responsive Chord* (New York: Doubleday, 1973).

Sconce, Jeffrey, *Haunted Media: Electronic Presence from Telegraphy to Television* (Durham, NC: Duke University Press, 2000).

Scott, Walter Dill, *The Psychology of Advertising* (London: Pitman & Sons, 1932 [1908]).

Sears, Roebuck & Co., *Consumers Guide No. 107* (Chicago: Sears, Roebuck & Co., 1898).

Sears, Roebuck & Co., *Special Catalogue of the Optigraph Motion Picture Machines, Calcium Light Outfits, Films for Moving Pictures* (Chicago: Sears, Roebuck & Co., 1900).

Seeber, Guido, *Der Trickfilm in seinen grundsätzlichen Möglichkeiten. Eine praktische und theoretische Darstellung der photographischen Filmtricks* (Berlin: Lichtbildbühne, 1927).

Segrave, Kerry, *Product Placement in Hollywood Films: A History* (Jefferson, NC, and London: McFarland, 2004).

Sekula, Alan, 'The Body and the Archive', *October* vol. 39 (Winter 1986), pp. 3–64.

Sellmer, Robert, 'Douglas Leigh: The Man Whose Gadgets Lighted up Broadway now Turns to Main Street', *Life*, 1 April 1946, pp. 47–51.

Simmel, Georg, 'The Concept and Tragedy of Culture', in David Frisby and Mike Featherstone (eds), *Simmel on Culture* (London: Sage, 1997).

Slide, Anthony, *Before Video: A History of the Non-Theatrical Film* (New York: Greenwood Press, 1992).

Solberg, Carl, *Conquest of the Skies: A History of Commercial Aviation in America* (Boston and Toronto: Little, Brown and Company, 1979).

Spigel, Lynn, *TV by Design: Modern Art and the Rise of Network Television* (Chicago and London: University of Chicago Press, 2009).

Stacey, Jackie, *Star Gazing: Hollywood Cinema and Female Spectatorship* (London and New York: Routledge, 1994).

Staiger, Janet, 'Announcing Wares, Winning Patrons, Voicing Ideals: Thinking about the History and Theory of Film Advertising', *Cinema Journal* vol. 29 no. 3 (Spring 1990), pp. 3–31.

Staiger, Janet, *Perverse Spectatorship: The Practices of Film Reception* (New York: New York University Press, 2000).

Starr, P., *The Creation of the Media: Political Origins of Modern Communications* (New York: Basic Books, 2004).

Steortz, Eva Marie, 'The Cost Efficiency and Communication Effects Associated with Brand Name Exposure within Motion Pictures' (MA thesis, West Virginia University, 1987).

Sterling, Christopher, and John Kittross, *Stay Tuned* (Belmont, CA: Wadsworth, 1978).

Stokes, Melvyn, and Richard Maltby (eds), *Hollywood Spectatorship: Changing Perception of Cinema Audiences* (London: BFI, 2001).

Strauven, Wanda (ed.), *The Cinema of Attractions Reloaded* (Amsterdam: Amsterdam University Press, 2006).

Street, Sarah, 'Another Medium Entirely: Esther Harris, National Screen Service and Film Trailers in Britain, 1940–1960', *Historic Journal of Film, Radio and Television* vol. 29 no. 4 (December 2009), pp. 433–47.

Streible, Dan, 'Introduction: Nontheatrical Film', *Film History* vol. 19 no. 4 (2007), pp. 339–43.

Strom, Gunnar, 'Desidier Gross and Gasparcolor in a Norwegian Perspective, Part 2', *Animation Journal* vol. 8 no. 2 (2000), pp. 44–55.

Sullivan, Sara, 'Corporate Discourses of Sponsored Films of Steel Production in the United States, 1936–1956', *Velvet Light Trap* no. 72 (Autumn 2013), pp. 33–43.

Susman, Warren, *Culture as History: The Transformation of American Society in the Twentieth Century* (Washington, DC: Smithsonian Institution Press, 2003).

Swett, Pamela E., Jonathan Wiesen and Jonathan R. Zaitlin (eds), *Selling Modernity: Advertising in Twentieth-Century Germany* (Durham, NJ: Duke University Press, 2007).

Tadelis, Steven, 'What's in a Name? Reputation as a Tradeable Asset', *American Economic Review* 89 (June 1999), pp. 548–63.

Thompson, Emily, *The Soundscape of Modernity: Architectural Acoustics and the Culture of Listening in America, 1900–1933* (Cambridge: MIT Press, 2002).

Turner, Fred, *The Democratic Surround: Multimedia and American Liberalism from World War II to the Psychadelic Sixties* (Chicago: University of Chicago Press, 2014).

Turow, Joseph and Matthew P. McAllister (eds), *The Advertising and Consumer Culture Reader* (New York and London: Routledge, 2009).

Uricchio, W., 'There's More to the Camera's Obscura Than Meets the Eye', in Francois Albera, Marta Braun and André Gaudreault (eds), *Arrêt sur image et fragmentation du temps/Stop Motion, Fragmentation of Time* (Lausanne: Cinema Editions Payot, 2002), pp. 103–20.

van der Eng, Pierre, *De Marshall-hulp: Een Perspectief voor Nederland – 1947–1953* (Houten: De Haan/Unieboek, 1987).

Vogel, Harold L., *Entertainment Industry Economics: A Guide for Financial Analysis*, 8th edition (Cambridge: Cambridge University Press, 2011).

Wainwright, Charles Anthony, *The Television Copywriter: How to Create Successful TV Commercials* (New York: Hastings House, 1966).

Waldman, Diane, 'From Midnight Shows to Marriage Vows: Women, Exploitation and Exhibition', *Wide Angle* vol. 6 no. 2 (1984), pp. 42–8.

Walker, S. H., and Paul Sklar, *Business Finds its Voice* (New York: Harper and Brothers, 1938).

Walker Laird, Pamela, *Advertising Progress: American Business and the Rise of Consumer Marketing* (Baltimore and London: Johns Hopkins University Press, 1998).

Waller, Gregory A. (ed.), *Moviegoing in America: A Sourcebook in the History of Film Exhibition* (Malden, MA: Blackwell, 2002).

Ward, Janet, *Weimar Surfaces* (Berkeley: University of California Press, 2001).

Warf, Barney, and Santa Arias (eds), *Spatial Turn: Interdisciplinary Perspectives* (Florence: Routledge, 2008).

Warlaumont, Hazel G., *Advertising in the 60s: Turncoats, Traditionalists, and Waste Makers in America's Turbulent Decade* (Westport, CT: Praeger, 2001).

Wasson, Haidee, *Museum Movies: The Museum of Modern Art and the Birth of Art Cinema* (Berkeley: University of California Press, 2005).

Wasson, Haidee, 'Introduction: In Focus: Screen Technologies', *Cinema Journal* vol. 51 no. 2 (Winter 2012), p. 142.

Wasson, Haidee, 'The Other Small Screen: Moving Images at New York's World Fair, 1939', *Canadian Journal of Film Studies* vol. 21 no. 1 (Spring 2012), pp. 81–103.

Wasson, Haidee, 'Suitcase Cinema', *Cinema Journal* vol. 51 no. 2 (Winter 2012), pp. 148–52.

Wasson, Haidee, 'Moving Images: Portable Histories of Film Exhibition', in John Nerone (ed.), *The International Encyclopedia of Media Studies: Media History and the Foundations of Media Studies* (London: Wiley-Blackwell, 2013), pp. 367–84.

Wasson, Haidee, 'The Protocols of Portability, *Film History* vol. 25 no. 1–2 (2013), pp. 236–47.

Webber, Gordon, *Our Kind of People: The Story of the First 50 Years at Benton & Bowles* (New York: Benton & Bowles, 1979).

Wells, William D., and Leonard A. Lo Sciuto, 'Direct Observation of Purchasing Behavior', *Journal of Marketing Research* vol. 3 no. 3 (August 1966), pp. 227–33.

Wendel, D. H., *150 Years of International Harvester* (Osceola, WI: Crestline, 1993).

Wharton, Chris, *Advertising: Critical Approaches* (London and New York: Routledge, 2015).

Whitted, Gerald W., *New Horizons World Guide: Pan American's Travel Facts about 131 Countries*, 16th revised edition (New York: Pan American Airways, 1969 [1951]).

Williams, Raymond, *Television: Technology and Cultural Form* (Glasgow: Fontana, 1974).

Williams, Raymond, 'Advertising: The Magic System', in Williams, *Problems in Materialism and Culture* (London: Verso, 1980).

Williams, Rosalind H., *Dream Worlds: Mass Consumption in Late Nineteenth-Century France* (Berkeley, Los Angeles and Oxford: University of California Press, 1991 [1982]).

Wiseman, Mark, *Advertisements* (New York: Moore-Robbins, 1949).

Wright, John (ed.), *The Commercial Connection* (New York: Dell, 1979).

Wurtzler, Steven, *Electric Sounds: Technological Change and the Rise of Corporate Mass Media* (New York: Columbia University Press, 2008).

Yang, Moonhee, and David R. Roskos-Ewoldsen, 'The Effectiveness of Brand Placements in the Movies: Levels of Placement, Explicit and Implicit Memory, and Brand-Choice Behaviour', *Journal of Communication* vol. 57 no. 3 (2007), pp. 469–89.

Zimmermann, Patricia R., *Reel Families: A Social History of Amateur Film* (Bloomington: Indiana University Press, 1995).

Zimmermann, Peter, and Kay Hofmann (eds), *Geschichte des dokumentarischen Films in Deutschland*, vol. 3: 'Drittes Reich' 1933–1945 (Stuttgart: Reclam, 2005).

Zimmermann, Yvonne, 'Target Group Oriented Corporate Communication: Geigy Films', in Museum für Gestaltung Zurich (ed.), *Corporate Diversity: Swiss Graphic Design and Advertising by Geigy 1940–1970* (Baden: Lars Müller, 2009), pp. 48–57.

Zimmermann, Yvonne (ed.), *Schaufenster Schweiz: Dokumentarische Gebrauchsfilme 1896–1964* (Zurich: Limmat, 2011).

Zwick, Detlev and Julien Cayla (eds), *Inside Marketing: Practices, Ideologies, Devices* (Oxford and New York: Oxford University Press, 2011).

Index

Page numbers in **bold** indicate detailed analysis; those in *italic* denote illustrations or captions. *n* = endnote. *t* = table/diagram.